The Defenses of Freedom

THE
DEFENSES
OF
FREEDOM

The Public Papers of

ARTHUR J. GOLDBERG

EDITED BY DANIEL PATRICK MOYNIHAN

HARPER & ROW, PUBLISHERS

NEW YORK AND LONDON

The royalties from this collection are to be donated, in equal parts, to the Dag Hammarskjöld Memorial Fund and the Adlai E. Stevenson Memorial Fund.

Contents

Introduction

The appointment of Arthur J. Goldberg in the Summer of 1965 as the Representative of the United States to the United Nations was immediately seen to be an event of international consequence.

The sudden death of Adlai E. Stevenson on July 16 of that year had been a blow to the world order as much as to the American people. The United Nations had lost a spokesman whose very presence had a touch of sovereignty about it: Stevenson not only represented the continuing United States commitment to the UN, in a sense he constituted it.

His death came at a time of deepening crisis for the organization he had helped to found just twenty years earlier. Caught up in bitter conflict over the financing of peace-keeping operations, the 19th General Assembly had been deadlocked and impotent, and in a sense had hardly happened. Here, as in other areas, American disenchantment with the UN potential seemed to grow. To other members the continued absence of Communist China, the world's most populous and now most warlike nation, appeared ever more ominous. As war escalated in Asia the relevance of the United Nations to world peace seemed steadily to recede.

In terms Jefferson had used two centuries earlier (and which Goldberg was to recall) it was necessary to find a successor to Stevenson: no one could replace him. But for that very reason any normal, predictable appointment, because it would constitute such an elevation of the person involved, would inevitably have seemed to diminish the UN. The moment called for grandeur: the person chosen would have to give up something of such unquestioned worth that the very act itself would assert the pre-eminent value reserved for the United Nations.

President Johnson found his man. Stevenson died on Wednesday. On Friday Arthur J. Goldberg was asked would he leave the Supreme Court, where he had only just begun "the richest and most satisfying period" of his career, to re-enter the Cabinet, and to assume the unrelenting responsibilities of his Nation's representative at the UN. He accepted, in his words, "as one simply must."

America's continuing commitment to the United Nations was made manifest in a manner that had seemed unattainable; more than a success, it was a turning point.

In the history of the United States Supreme Court only two men ever have left to undertake a further Presidential appointment. In the autumn of 1942 as war settled on the United States, James F. Byrnes resigned as an Associate Justice to become Director of Economic Stabilization, and in time Secretary of State. Nearly a quarter century later Arthur J. Goldberg departed his brethren on the Court in response to a similar request.

Both the men and the events have striking parallels. Byrnes and Goldberg were born of the people in a now far-off time when the world seemed at peace and only life itself a savage struggle. Each took to the law, and to the great political movements of their day, although developing increasingly divergent views. History determined that they should turn at length to the overriding issues of peace and war, and America's role in world affairs, much as events led Justice John H. Clarke to resign in 1922 to become head of the League of Nations Association, and dictated that John Jay should undertake the fateful negotiations with Britain in 1794 even while serving as Chief Justice.

The prominence of the role Ambassador Goldberg has now assumed in world affairs adds perhaps to the timeliness of this collection of his most significant public papers. Even so, the contents will stand on their own as commentary on the issues of our time by one who has sought to shape them. Certain themes continually appear: the necessity for law, the importance of procedure, the demands of justice, the quest for equality, the interdependence of public and private effort. The outcome of many of the issues touched on in those papers has been influenced by Arthur Goldberg's willingness to state arguments over and again, a discipline more demanding than might be thought by persons to whom the exercise would appear merely inelegant. In choosing selections and passages I have sought to retain this quality of continuity without requiring of the reader, as was sometimes asked of the audience, that they hear the facts again and again until they accepted them.

In his career Arthur Goldberg has been first of all a lawyer, only thereafter an advocate. This has in no way diminished his commitment to the causes he has pleaded, but it has influenced the way he has done so. The restraint and balance of his public pronouncements reflect a mind seeking solutions rather than postures, and fundamentally persuaded that for justice to triumph order must prevail. This temperament is, of course, most fully displayed in his written opinions as a Justice of the Supreme Court, of which twenty-four are included in this collection. The law notes which accompany the opinions are the product of the cheerful diligence of Messrs. Stephen Breyer and Stephen Goldstein, clerks to the Justice during the 1964 term. Mrs. Frances S. Guilbert, whose association with the Ambassador goes back to the earliest documents in this collection, was indispensable, as always.

DANIEL PATRICK MOYNIHAN

Center for Advanced Studies
Wesleyan University
December, 1965

Autobiographical Notes

(The following autobiographical profile is compiled from statements by Arthur J. Goldberg on the occasion of various Senate confirmation hearings, and the acceptance of the position of United States Representative to the United Nations.)

THE CABINET

I was born in Chicago, Illinois, in 1908. I was educated in the public schools of Chicago and received my bachelor's degree and a degree of doctor of laws from Northwestern University. I was admitted to practice in Illinois in 1929, and I am a member of the bar of the state of Illinois as well as the bar of the District of Columbia and of the United States Supreme Court. I married Miss Dorothy Kurgans on July 18, 1931, and I have two children, Barbara and Robert.

I practiced law in the city of Chicago until 1948, with the exception of the war years during which I served as a major in the United States Army in the Office of Strategic Services. In 1948 I moved to Washington where I served as General Counsel of the CIO and of the United Steelworkers of America. Since the merger of the AFL and the CIO I have served as Special Counsel to the AFL-CIO as well as General Counsel to the Industrial Union Department of the AFL-CIO, and the Steelworkers Union. I have been the senior partner in a Washington law firm, Goldberg, Feller and Bredhoff, which has represented various other labor organizations, as well as in the Chicago firm of Goldberg, Devoe, Shadur and Mikva.

Effective January 1, 1961, I have resigned as Special Counsel to the AFL-CIO, as General Counsel to the Steelworkers and the Industrial Union Department, and I have terminated the connection with both law firms. These resignations are firm and final. I have also resigned from the various foundations and boards on which I have served. As of the present moment I have no connection with any law firm and I hold no positions in any organizations except one. Following what I believe to be an illustrious precedent, I have not resigned my position as a member of the Board of Overseers of the Amos Tuck School of Business Administration of Dartmouth College.

I have already stated in public my view with respect to the functions of the Department of Labor and the manner in which I propose to fulfill my responsibilities as Secretary if I should be confirmed in my appointment to that post. My view, briefly, is that our society is not a class society and the Department of Labor should not be a class department. The Department of Labor is charged by statute with the responsibility of promoting the welfare of the wage earners of the United States. As Secretary I will attempt fully to implement that policy, but in so doing I do not believe the department should be regarded as the representative of any special interest group, but as a department representing all sections and interests in our society. It is my firm belief that, although each department of government necessarily must place special emphasis on the sphere of activity with which it is concerned, it must, within that sphere, speak for and promote the welfare of all Americans and not any special group or class. If I am confirmed as Secretary of Labor, I intend to administer the department in accordance with that belief.

Of particular concern to me if I am confirmed will be the improvement of labor-management relations and the growth of the American economy. Both of these areas I believe to be vitally important and of particular concern to the Department of Labor. In both areas I propose to act as the representative in this Administration of the public interest.

The Congress has given to the Secretary of Labor the responsibility of administration and enforcement of various laws. These include not only the Fair Labor Standards Act, the Walsh-Healey Act, the Davis-Bacon Act and others, but also the Labor-Management Reporting and Disclosure Act of 1959. I wish to make perfectly clear that if I am confirmed as Secretary of Labor I shall do everything in my power to enforce these laws vigorously, fairly and without fear or favor, and in the spirit of humanity and common sense which I believe should characterize all law enforcement.

I want to thank the members of the Committee for the opportunity you have given me to express these views and I, of course, am anxious to answer any questions which you may have.

United States Senate Committee on Labor and Public Welfare, January 13, 1961

The Supreme Court

Since I began to practice law in Chicago in 1929 I joined and became a member of the Chicago Bar Association, the Illinois Bar Association, the American Bar Association. . . . I have been a member of many organizations identified with the Jewish faith. . . .

I have been a member of the American Civil Liberties Union in Chicago, I have been a member of the Independent Voters of Illinois—these are the principal organizations—I am a member of the Democratic Party and have been for many years.

. . . No institution in American life, including the Supreme Court of the United States, is immune from criticism by our citizens. Ours is a free society, and no aspect of our society, the executive, the President, the members of the Cabinet, the judiciary, and, I am sure, the legislature—I don't have to tell members of the Congress this—is free from criticism.

It is a healthy and salutary thing that the people of our country, and our press, which is a free press, speak vigorously and openly about any aspect of our national life. I have been the Secretary of Labor now for twenty months. Some of the things I have done have been approved, and some of the things I have done have not been approved. This is the way it ought to be. And if I am confirmed by the Senate, which plays an important role under our Constitution in confirming the President's appointments to the Supreme Court, and many other important functions, I would feel it very important that the press, the public at large, the Congress, and anyone, express themselves freely about our decisions in the Supreme Court.

We are different from totalitarian countries where you get only one point of view, and the hierarchy, whether it is executive, judicial, or legislative, is immune from criticism. I would regard it to be an important function of our democracy, our open society, our free society, that anyone—ordinary citizen, newspaper editor, member of Congress, member of the executive branch—anyone should express himelf openly and candidly about any action taken by any part of our government, whether it is judicial, executive, or legislative. And I would certainly feel that the Supreme Court is not immune from this.

And I would believe that any judge worthy of his name would recognize that because he sits on the Supreme Court this does not exempt him from the criticism, the comment which emanates from a democratic society.

I would not want it otherwise.

I said the other day, and I want to repeat, that a judge is a human being, and all humans are fallible. But I would regard the first function of a judge, whether he sits in a trial court or an appellate court or in our highest tribunal, to make sure as much as any human being can that he puts aside his own prejudices, predilections, viewpoints, prejudices—which we all possess—and knowing that he possesses them, to try to administer justice equally under the law.

We cannot exalt our prejudice into law. If we did that we ought not to serve as a judge. If there is any feeling on this Committee that I as an individual am the type of person who could not recognize my own limitations, put that aside, and when I decide a case on the Supreme Court, try to be as objective as any human being can, then I would say to you, you ought to reject my appointment.

And I would not want to serve under those circumstances.

Throughout my life, everywhere I have appeared, in any forum in which I have spoken, in any area in which I have been engaged—and I have been engaged in many forums and many platforms and many areas—I regard and have regarded communism to be a dangerous international movement, incompatible with our democratic traditions. I have never deviated from that viewpoint from the earliest days of my life.

I have never deviated from that in representing any group that I have represented.

I have written upon this subject, it is an open public matter. I have written a book on the labor movement, *The A.F. of L.-CIO, Labor United.* . . . I have a chapter in that book, chapter 10, devoted to communism and corruption. That book states my philosophy in this area. It is not a new philosophy, it is a philosophy to which I have subscribed through my whole life. I regard the Communist movement to be a perversion of what people have a right to expect from government and from life.

It is completely contrary to our way of life. We believe in freedom and democracy, and the right of people to speak their convictions, and their right to live in a society where they can criticize you or me, where they can take issue with a President of the United States, or a Senator, or a Congressman, or a private citizen.

United States Senate Committee on the Judiciary, September 11 and 13, 1962

THE UNITED NATIONS

With the death of Adlai Stevenson, a great voice of America in the world has been stilled, but the message of Adlai Stevenson to the world must go on. That message is man's ancient supplication: Grant us peace, Thy most precious gift.

What has been prayer throughout the ages is a necessity today.

Adlai Stevenson was the voice of a great and powerful nation, at once

dedicated to peace and implacable in its commitment to freedom. The elo-
quence of his words no more than reflected the richness of his spirit and the
righteousness of his cause. We, and the world, are different because he lived.
Of Adlai Stevenson's departure and my appointment I can only borrow
words uttered on a similar occasion by Thomas Jefferson: I succeed him. No
one could replace him.

I shall not, Mr. President, conceal the pain with which I leave the Court
after three years of service. It has been the richest and most satisfying period
of my career. And I shall have more to say about this in a letter I am sending to the Chief Justice and my brethren on the Court. Throughout my life
I have been deeply committed to the rule of law. The law gives form
and substance to the spirit of liberty and to mankind's sacred stir for justice.

It now comes that the President has asked me to join in the greatest adventure of man's history—the effort to bring the rule of law to govern the
relations between sovereign states.

It is that or doom—and we all know it.

I have accepted, as one simply must.

In my efforts at the United Nations I shall do my best to carry on, in
my own way, the work of my distinguished predecessors. I hope to help
make real and manifest the assertion of the charter that social justice and
better standards of life in larger freedom are indispensable to the achievement
of world peace. I am grateful to the President for judging me capable of the
effort I now commence. I am grateful to the Secretary of State, my friend
and my former colleague in the Cabinet, for welcoming me so warmly to
this post. It is with great humility that I undertake the role of our nation's
advocate of peace in the council of nations. My wife, my son, my daughter
—who is in Chicago and cannot be with us today—my mother-in-law, all
join with me in asking only the prayers of the American people that we shall
succeed.

The White House, July 20, 1965

I appear before this distinguished Committee faced with certain facts of
life which might well give pause to any responsible man asked to assume
the duties for which the President has recommended my name to you.

I am aware as a citizen of the gravity of the constitutional crisis confronting the United Nations. And I share the conviction of the citizens of this
country that that crisis must be resolved, and the work of the United Nations
must go forward.

I am acutely aware of the immense national as well as international stake
in the future of the United Nations, in the growth of its capacity to cope

with the issue of world peace, an issue which transcends every other issue which our country and all mankind have to face.

I am aware of the necessity of the role of the United Nations to carry on the struggle against world poverty and all of its ugliness, and to pursue that ultimate universal goal of human rights which man has aspired to since the beginning of civilization, and social justice for all men everywhere.

I am aware too as a citizen and as a former member of the Cabinet of the depth of the commitment which the United States throughout the years has made to sustain the principles and strengthen the performance of the United Nations. It is a commitment made over and over again these past two decades since the United Nations' creation by Democratic and Republican Administrations. It is a commitment affirmed and reaffirmed by the Congress. And it is a commitment broadly shared and consistently supported by an extraordinary, almost a unique consensus of the American people.

I am aware as well of the special responsibilities which inevitably devolve upon the United States, the most powerful member of the United Nations, but a great and powerful nation which is profoundly dedicated to peace and implacable . . . in its commitment to world freedom. And I know full well that the search for world order, the pursuit of peaceful settlement, and the struggle toward the rule of law in international affairs must be our guiding star, and that it is not an easy path to follow, particularly since our search for a rule of law in the world must be carried forward in a revolutionary setting for many nations of the world in which rapid change is not only likely but in many instances necessary.

But I am sustained and emboldened by the thought that what Adlai Stevenson stood for, worked for, and when need be fought for valiantly, these things are imperishable. And others can and must stand for them and work for them, and when need be fight for them with their own talents and in their own ways however inadequate these talents may be.

And though no one can take Adlai Stevenson's place, I am ready in response to the President's request, with the advice and consent of the Senate, if it so decides, to join the large company of those in which this Committee has always been included and in which the Congress takes a prominent part, of those who in their own way work in the vineyards of world peace to which the President is so profoundly devoted.

If this Committee and the Senate consent to my appointment, I shall devote my full energy to that work and to that end, knowing that in doing so I shall have the help and prayers of the American people reflected not only by the polls of public opinion which show their strong convictions in support of the United Nations, but also in the overwhelming letters from citizens which I have received since my designation by the President was announced.

And I shall also know that I will have, and I would welcome, the counsel and guidance of this Committee and of Congress.

There is a final word that I would like to say, and then I shall be glad to respond to questions.

I need hardly add, I hope, in the light of my public record, that I shall be guided in this new world to which I have been called—this pluralistic world containing peoples of many races with different religious beliefs, and diverse economic and political systems [by the principle that] all nations, large and small, and all peoples are to be treated with dignity, respect, fairness, and equality.

This is the policy of the United States, as I understand it. This is the great concept of the Charter of the United Nations. And this is my own personal faith.

United States Senate Committee on Foreign Relations, July 23, 1965

I

THE PUBLIC PAPERS

I ᔕᕓ

Freedom Under Law

. . . The peace I talk about is not the peace of the grave; it is a peace in freedom, because there are conditions of peace which I do not think are permanent conditions of peace in some countries of the world, that are not conditions of peace in freedom. The only permanent peace for the world, in my judgment, will come when we have a world where conditions of peace exist in free institutions. The other type of peace is, at best, a temporary peace, which submerges grievances and does not solve them.

Overseas Press Club, New York, N.Y., September 15, 1965

PEACE IN FREEDOM

The Necessity for Law

I said when I went to the United Nations, and I say again now, the effort to bring the rule of law to govern the relations between sovereign states is the greatest adventure in history.

This great adventure is beset with greater peril than any in history, for never before has man had the power of ultimate destruction of himself, his environment, and of all future life on earth.

Every edition of our newspapers freshly underlines how difficult it is to smother hostilities, to bank the fires even temporarily, let alone achieve an enduring peace.

A commentator recently said that the United Nations was designed not to establish order but to prevent trouble and preserve peace. I don't wholly agree with that, but I do believe that we can bring about order only if we succeed in our primary mission at the United Nations in preventing trouble and preserving peace.

I have no illusions about the difficulties of this task or the problems that confront the United Nations, but I have entered my position with optimism about the future of the United Nations. During the period when the United Nations was experiencing its constitutional and financial crisis, many observers and many people throughout the world questioned the future of the

3

United Nations. I do not share this pessimism. If we did not have a United Nations in existence today, we would be re-creating a United Nations in order to cope with the same problems with which we are struggling.

As I look back on the history of my own country, and I draw from my experience here as a judge, it was not easy in the development of the United States of America to obtain adherence to the rule of law enunciated in our own Constitution. And all of you who are very familiar with the history of your own countries know of the many instances in every nation's history where adherence to the rule of law has only developed after much difficulty and great frustration. Anyone familiar with history therefore must come to the conclusion that where there is no alternative left to all nations except a painstaking march toward understanding and adherence to international treaties and obligations, then the common sense and the realism of people and nations ultimately will prevail.

I share with Abraham Lincoln the conviction that the common sense of the people of the world will lead to a strengthening rather than a weakening of the United Nations.

And all of us who are devoted to the United Nations as an international peace-keeping agency must concern ourselves with the strengthening of its peace-keeping machinery as much as with the strengthening of judicial machinery.

In the international no less than in the domestic field extension of the rule of law requires development of executive and legislative as well as judicial institutions. Given the great political divisions in the world in the past two decades, I am encouraged that the United Nations has been able to grow as much as it has, and to function effectively in situations not even imagined in 1945.

If the United Nations, in these two decades, has not always been able to fulfill the vision of peace and cooperation so clearly seen in San Francisco almost a generation ago, neither has it failed in its determination to save succeeding generations from the scourge of war. In almost every one of those years, potential sparks that in other times might well have set off major conflicts have been dampened or extinguished by United Nations activity in Suez, in the Congo, in Cyprus, to mention only a few. We have seen unprecedented transfers of political power from European nations to newly independent states—a transfer made far more peacefully because of the existence of the United Nations. We have brought before the conscience of mankind the need to extend the protection of law to the basic rights of all mankind. We have wrought an incalculable gain in economic and technical assistance. Who can measure the degree to which peace has been strengthened and ensured, when, to mention one example, 37 million children are cured of the yaws—a dreadful disease.

And in one generation the United Nations has created more international law than in all previous generations in man's history. It has done so not only by formal agreements but also by wide extension of what might be called the "ground rules" for international cooperation. Its failures cannot obscure that record. If necessity is the mother of progress, I am hopeful, for there is no lack of necessity to strengthen the international peace-keeping machinery. It is imperative.

In recent years we have witnessed a great refinement in techniques of generating civil wars, in methods of infiltrating and subverting authentic revolutionary movements, that almost defy timely detection and defense. The victims of such wars are left to their own resources and the help which they can call on from others.

So far our international peace-keeping machinery has not been adequate to deal with this kind of problem. And until international organizations can do the job, the victims can only turn for help to more powerful friends. I think the United States need yield to no people, and no nation in history, in its devotion to the multilateral idea and the concept of collective security. But we must have collective security, not collective futility. I am hopeful that necessity will open the way to new inches of progress. I am hopeful that we will adopt practical and equitable means by which those willing to share the responsibility for peace can act in concert to maintain and strengthen the indispensable peace-keeping capacity of the United Nations.

There is another vital element to the establishment of the day when we shall bring about a rule of law in this world. Eleanor Roosevelt, who did so much to bring the Declaration of Human Rights to life, once said:

It is not just a question of getting covenants written and accepted. It is a question of actually living and working in our countries for freedom and justice for each human being. And I hope that is what we will dedicate ourselves to in the next ten years, and that each of us will have the feeling that they must do something as individuals. Each of us must do something because this is one of the basic foundation stones if we are ever to achieve what the United Nations was established to achieve—an atmosphere in which peace can grow in the world.

It avails nothing to break down the barriers, to establish the procedure of law, to ensure civil rights in the courts, if in so doing we do not also create an atmosphere in which human dignity has meaning, and human life a value. And so, if as lawyers we stay in the forefront of the fight to bring about respect for law, we must also stay in the forefront of the fight to bring about a world in which there is freedom from want, and freedom from the fears bred of generations of squalor, disease, and cheapness of human existence.

We must continuously remind ourselves that law itself does not make stability. What makes stability is law that solves the legitimate grievances of people.

The late Secretary General, Dag Hammarskjöld, once said that the world is in transition between "institutional systems of coexistence" and "constitutional systems of cooperation," which is a way of saying that we are slowly evolving institutions and legal principles which are essential to assure peace, justice and order.

If we are ever to bridge the gap between "institutionalized systems of coexistence" and "constitutional systems of cooperation" we must find a way to meet the urgent demand of the burgeoning millions of this earth who are impatient to live a better life now. Even as we recite the great accomplishments of these past decades, in and out of the United Nations, we know, too, how vast is the need, how short the time, and how threatening the impatience of those who have not. Millions who for countless generations accepted their condition as the fated lot of man now know that poverty is not ordained by God, nor children born to die of a hundred different diseases. The same science that has destroyed war as a rational alternative in human affairs has also given to us the power to conquer our environment. That enterprise is the heart of a world community.

The Great Society cannot be guaranteed in this land unless it comes about in all lands. To this goal we have pledged our efforts, our good intentions, our vast resources, and our unceasing determination to succeed. President Johnson in speaking at the anniversary ceremonies of the founding of the United Nations in San Francisco said:

We in this country are committing ourselves to great tasks in our own great society. We are committed to narrow the gap between promise and performance, between equality in law and equality in fact, between opportunity for the numerous well-to-do and the still too numerous poor, between education for the successful and education for all of the people.

It is no longer a community or a nation or a continent but a whole generation of mankind for whom our promises must be kept—and kept within the next two decades.

We begin anew with humility and with hope. All of us in our own countries know how elusive is true justice, how imperfect the virtues of mortal men, and how frequent the stops and starts, the detours and the setbacks, along the path to the day when the light of justice may truly light the world. The course of history is strewn with human failure. The history of this generation began with a difference—we dare not fail. It is that or doom—and we all know it.

I have no illusions that peace can be achieved rapidly. But I have every confidence that it is going to be possible to inch forward to it inch by agonizing inch. This we *must* do—for there is simply no alternative in a nuclear age to world peace through the rule of law.

Conference on World Peace through Law, Washington, D.C., September 17, 1965

The Experiment of Cooperation

I have said on several occasions that I consider the role of the United States representative to the United Nations to be a dual one. He, of course, first represents the President of our government at the UN; but second, he also represents the UN to the American people.

I am firmly convinced that I cannot succeed in the first role without succeeding in the second. And in succeeding in the second I must rely heavily on the United Nations Association and all of the organizations associated with it. I know that the people of the UNA are better informed than any other group in this country on the successes and the failures, the adequacies and the weaknesses, of the United Nations. I count on you, then, for measured judgment, as well as for enthusiastic support.

It was a pre-eminent American jurist, Learned Hand, who once reminded us that freedom cannot be preserved in constitutions if it has already vanished from the hearts of its citizens. To keep our many and cherished freedoms alive all citizens, individually and collectively, have the duty to use them vigorously and wisely. One of those freedoms is the freedom to express yourselves in the conduct of our foreign policy. And I can assure you, what you have to say will be heard and respected. For I believe our government can do a better job if we know what our fellow citizens are thinking; and they, in turn, will better be able to formulate opinions if they fully understand the scope and variety of the critical problems that challenge us at every turn.

In short, we—public official and private citizen—must keep a dialogue going in this country—an intelligent dialogue that will constantly examine and probe how our foreign policy is coming along. I do not fear such a dialogue; I welcome it, because it is the expression of a free people determined to remain free, not only on paper as our Constitution specifies, but in our hearts, which as Learned Hand intimated, is freedom's best bastion.

Debate and discussion are keystones of that freedom, and the right to participate in them is limited not only to voices that agree with any given policy or action. I do not subscribe to the notion that the grave problems of today demand unanimity of opinion. And, I can assure you, neither does President Johnson, as he himself has stated, for we are a mature people and we do not fear dissent. I think it only fair to suggest, however, that dissent is all the more powerful when it is responsible and informed, and when its aims are constructive. This is vital under any circumstances; it is a thousand-fold more so when the issue involved is what the President has called that simple little five-letter word—"peace"—a word badly misunderstood but for which, as he said, I have an obsession.

I believe with all my heart that we must succeed in our effort to attain the peace. It is that or doom. This is a simple fact of our times. It is why that little five-letter word "peace" must be the obsession of all people who believe in fulfilling man's sacred stir for justice. It is an obsession I know you in the UNA share with me. I believe most Americans share it, too, because our entire history shows that basically we are a people with a fervent desire to build, not tear down; to create, not destroy.

That is the way we have always chosen since we became one indivisible nation. That is what I am trying to do at the United Nations. That is the only obsession with peace that has any validity or that can serve any useful purpose. It is the only way, too, to a world of law and order to which we are irrevocably committed.

This, of course, was the world Adlai Stevenson envisioned, and he died in pursuit of it. When I took up where he left off, I emphasized that I sought no quick and easy solutions to the problems of our day and time. I promised no dramatic answers. I promised then, as I do now, that our course will adhere to the view, as he put it, "that the most rewarding task of civilized man today is that of reconciling differing points of view."

This, as I see it, is the basic reason for having a United Nations, and had one existed in 1914 the shot fired in Sarajevo might not have been heard around the world, or touched off what history, with its orderly habit for apt labels, called the First World War. Today we mark the end of that war —the war we thought would end all wars. But its end, instead, was a chaotic interlude in which the poisons of hate and rampant nationalism gathered new strength and madness for an onslaught more deadly and vicious than civilization had ever known.

When that Second World War ended with the beginning of the nuclear age, we were resolved that the scourge of war would never again plague mankind, and so we founded the UN to give form to our hopes. Now we are engaged in an effort more massive and more intensive than man has ever known. For in spite of our hopes and determination it is very clear that accident and miscalculation are still possible—and a third, nuclear war would kill as many people in a few hours as were killed in the whole of World War I.

In 1960 an American military research team, we are told, fed all the facts of World War I into the computers. They reached the conclusion that the 1914-1918 war was impossible and that it couldn't happen. There could not have been so many blunders nor so many casualties.

But will there be a computer left to analyze World War III?

In coping with the future we cannot guarantee success; we can only, as Churchill said, try to deserve it. And deserving it means doing all in our power to promote and to keep the peace. It is the only practical road to take and we welcome all who would travel with us. This is the fact above all others that we want to make known to all member nations of the UN. There is nothing new about it, let me emphasize. We have been saying the same thing for the past twenty years, and we will continue saying it just as long as it is necessary. We are a patient people and we are a persistent one in the tasks of peace. We may have our differences with other member states in the UN, and we suspect that we shall go on having differences. But we all have a common stake in the peace; it is the mortar that has bound us together.

The longer it does the greater is the possibility for a change in fixed and even rigid attitudes. It is a hope I would encourage, for the common stake we have in the peace is reflected in the common interests all of us have in building and developing the Charter. And in this development, I would say, I have been impressed by the fact that the attitudes of the UN's internationalism are being shaped, in a sense, in much the same manner as were the attitudes of our own domestic experience.

It was the great Chief Justice John Marshall who set the pace for the development of our domestic attitude with the view that the Constitution gave Congress implied powers that could be used to carry out its express powers. "We must never forget," he wrote, "that it is a Constitution we are expounding."

This, then, is the United States attitude to the Charter and to the UN: We espouse a strong, a vibrant UN, one that is not bound by any standpat philosophy, but that can meet the challenges of the day—a Charter that can be applied to cope with the many crises confronting the UN and the world. But it has taken us nearly 190 years to develop our domestic attitudes, and we have not finished. For interpreting the Constitution is a job that will never be finished. And even as the Constitution is a living, evolving document so is the Charter of the UN. Its age is 20 and it is undergoing daily all manner of testing, as it grows and develops into history's most potent and effective machinery of peace. And I for one am not discouraged if the process is slow. Its very slowness, in fact, can be an asset, for it will help us all define our ultimate goal of peace and law more clearly. In this way, as President Kennedy once said, we will make it "seem more manageable and less remote, we can help all peoples to see it, to draw hope from it, and to move irresistibly toward it." In so doing we will fulfill, too, the audacious long-range goals of International Cooperation Year.

I know there is a natural temptation to look at all the crises and problems of our day—at all the still too prevalent instances of man's inhumanity to man—and scoff at the idea that in 1965 the world knows or very much cares about cooperation. But it does, and the United Nations itself is history's most ambitious experiment in international cooperation.

In assuring its ultimate success, we as Americans must use all the talents of our wonderfully gifted and diverse people. We must use them with boldness and imagination, but above all wisely. It is not beyond the capacity of a nation that was able to expound a Constitution and a free way of life that are "honorable alike in what we give and what we preserve."

United Nations Association of the United States of America, New York, N.Y., November 11, 1965

The Achievement of Peace

Mr. President:

We meet this morning in a mood of accomplishment and gratification. Just twenty-four hours ago, a great milestone in the life of the United Nations was passed. The ceasefire between India and Pakistan, first requested and then demanded by the Security Council, has happily been put into effect by both countries.

I hope, Mr. President, it will not be amiss if I take a moment to pay tribute to the untiring work and the great contribution made by all of the members of the Security Council, permanent and nonpermanent, in bringing about this result. Providence and the rules of the Security Council placed me in the chair, but it was the efforts of my colleagues, patiently pursued, which resulted in the united resolutions which had such a great impact in bringing about this necessary result. I have, Mr. President, in my public and private life had much to do with conflicts of another sort, but I have never experienced such a common dedication to the Charter commitment as I experienced during the past weeks by the members and the nations that they represent. It is, I believe, a happy omen for the future of this great organization that such a grave conflict, the gravest in the history of the organization, can, in its initial step at least, have been contained by this type of common action.

Once again, in rebuttal of the skeptics and the cynics, the United Nations proved to be the decisive peacemaker. Once again the United Nations provided the indispensable and vital element, the only acceptable catalyst to help end the needless bloodshed between the two great countries, two neighbors whose bonds of kinship and friendship so commonly shared by all members of the United Nations must swiftly be restored between themselves. And once again—and not for the first time, I would like to emphasize—the voice of the United Nations has been heeded and respected.

On coming to this parliament from the highest court of the United States, I said that the work of bringing the rule of law to the relations between sovereign states is the greatest adventure in man's history. All of us in this hall are embarked on this adventure together. It is an adventure we dare not fail to conclude successfully. There is no alternative except the excluded one of doom for all mankind.

One of my country's most distinguished jurists, who never reached our highest court, and whose career demonstrates that distinction does not coincide with appointment to the highest office, once said that freedom cannot be preserved in constitutions if it has vanished from the hearts of its citizens. And we are charged with the daily task of keeping burning in the hearts of the peoples of this earth the fires of freedom promised all men by the Charter of this organization twenty years ago—freedom from fear, freedom from want, freedom from indignity, and freedom from war. We are charged, as a beloved participant in the deliberations of the United Nations once said—and you will recognize the words and the person—we are charged with the responsibility of keeping the candle of peace glowing. It sometimes appears to be a fragile candle and its light sometimes appears to be dim, but it has the strength to light the world if we really believe in it.

In this twentieth year of the United Nations, we grope for the full meaning of a world changing rapidly under the headlong impact of science and technology. And we ask ourselves, I am sure every day, every person here and millions throughout the world: Are we headed toward world order or world chaos? And this Assembly should help—this Assembly must help provide the answer.

In my own country we are embarked under the leadership of President Lyndon B. Johnson in a search for a "Great Society." This vision of a just domestic order is based on consent of the governed and due process of law, on individual dignity, on diversity, and on the just satisfaction of political, economic and social aspirations. We in the United States reject reactionary philosophies of all extremes. We seek to build instead on what we regard the most enlightened and progressive philosophy in human history, that the aim of government is the maximum self-fulfillment of its citizens, and that the good life should be within the reach of all rather than a monopoly of the few. Both domestically and in international affairs there can be no island of poverty in seas of affluence.

We espouse equality not only as a principle. We seek equal opportunity for all as an accomplished reality. And we are resolved to enrich the life of our society by developing human, as well as natural, resources. And we are determined not merely to increase material production but to assure such equality to guarantee genuine social and economic justice, to eliminate poverty and also to realize qualitative improvements in the life of our citizens—in more attractive and functional cities, in a more beautiful country-side and through learning and the arts.

And this is not the program of any one group or one class or one political party in our country. Nor is the vision it proclaims exclusively American. It is a vision common to all mankind. It fell to my lot for twenty-five years to represent the great labor movement of our country. And one of the great labor leaders with whom I was long associated, Philip Murray, when I asked, what was the aim of the labor movement, to which he dedicated his life, paused and thought and said that the aim of the labor movement is a society in which each man shall have a rug on the floor, a picture on the wall, and music in the home. And I think that is a good goal for all of mankind.

So what we seek for our own people in a Great Society at home we seek for all mankind. President Johnson I think has said this very well, and I quote him: "We seek no fidelity to an iron faith, but a diversity of belief as varied as man himself. We seek not to extend the power of America but the progress of humanity. We seek not to dominate others but to strengthen the freedom of all people." And the diversity of which our President speaks is the diversity represented in the membership of the United Nations—diversity in its needs, in its philosophies, in its races, and in its institutions—yet united by a common bond of commitment to the obligations of the Charter and dedicated to justice and social progress and the peaceful settlement of conflict.

There is, regretfully, however, a contrasting doctrine of world order. It was put before us earlier this month by the Defense Minister of Communist China in a "manifesto" published in all of Communist China's newspapers and republished broadly throughout the world. The doctrine laid bare by Marshal Lin Piao starts from the premise that "political power grows out of the barrel of a gun." It rests, he said, on a foundation of war and violent revolution. And I quote him again: "The seizure of power by armed force, the settlement of the issues by war is," according to the Marshal and his party and the leaders of his country, "the central task and the highest form of revolution." And again I quote: "War can temper the people and push history forward. . . . War is a great school." The principle of revolutionary war, he says, is not just for China. It, according to him, and I quote him again, "holds good . . . for all . . . countries." The nations of the world are not free according to this theory to develop by their own choice in accordance with their own needs and experience. The nations of the world are not free, according to this theory, to fly their own flag their own way. But, like it or not, the Marshal and the leaders of Communist China say they must accept the Chinese model.

Nor does newly achieved independence provide immunity from this modern imperialism. Quite the contrary. Chinese spokesmen again and again have emphasized that they do not believe that the revolutions which have taken place and led to the national independence of many countries are the acceptable revolution. They do not believe that those countries have the right, as was the great privilege of my country after it made its revolution, to develop its social and economic institutions its own way. The Marshal said, and I quote him again, "The Socialist revolution is the inevitable sequel to the national democratic revolution." In fact, "The more thorough the national democratic revolution the better the conditions for the Socialist revolution." But it should be clear that Marshal Lin is misusing the word "socialist," that he means "communist," with the label buried in Peking.

This incredible manifesto is the antithesis of everything this organization stands for. It is a call to change world order by force and violence in a period when force and violence can lead to the most disastrous consequences for the entire world. It leaves no room for difference of tradition, of culture, or of national aspiration, or for the legitimate right of every people, large and small, to choose their own social and economic order their own way. It leaves no room for genuine self-determination. It seeks to squeeze every nation and every people within the grip of Chinese Communist conformity. It should be read—I know it has been read and pondered by everyone in this Assembly.

The apostles of this philosophy are today attempting to transform the country of South Viet Nam into a proving ground for their theories. This challenge must be met—not in the interests of any single nation—but in the interest of each member of this organization. It must be met in particular in the interests of the smaller nations who cherish their right to choose and follow their own path of national development.

We are helping to meet this threat because we believe it must be met. And our goals in South Viet Nam are plain and simple. We seek only to ensure the independence of South Viet Nam, with freedom from attack and the opportunity for its people to determine their own future. We seek no territory for ourselves, no preferential position, no permanent military presence. We stand ready to withdraw our forces when Communist aggression has ended and South Viet Nam is left alone to determine its own destiny in its own way by principles of self-determination.

And above all we seek a peaceful solution. We have repeatedly stated our willingness to enter into unconditional discussions—and I reaffirm that willingness here today. And we have asked the members of the United Nations, individually and collectively, to use their influence to help bring about such discussions. We have asked the members of the Security Council and the Secretary General to help get negotiations started. And we have offered to join in a massive cooperation program for the economic development of Southeast Asia.

The members of the United Nations, under the Charter, share a common responsibility to demonstrate to those who use violence that violence does not pay. And we can meet that responsibility by using every means to persuade the regimes of Hanoi and Peking to leave their neighbors alone and to begin serious discussions for a resolution of this conflict. And we must also meet that obligation by denying United Nations representation to the regime that denies, in word and in deed, the fundamental restraints on the use of force in our Charter, and hurls insult upon the peaceful efforts of the members of the United Nations to compose this and other disputes.

Most of us, fortunately, have already made our choice between the philosophy of violence and the philosophy of world order which underlies our Charter. Yet our search for world order is gravely threatened by a continuing arms race, a race which adds nothing to the world except insecurity and a drain of valuable resources. Progress has, of course, been made. We have already agreed to cease nuclear testing in the atmosphere, under water, and in outer space. We have established a direct communications link to help prevent war by accident or miscalculation. We have resolved not to place weapons of mass destruction in outer space. Today I reaffirm the commitment of the United States to that agreement.

But the goal of general and complete disarmament to which we are all committed remains elusive. But it is a necessary and indispensable goal. We have to work toward it vigorously and thoughtfully and with good will and not be deterred by what must be momentary setbacks. Most of all we should concentrate on immediate practical steps to reverse the arms spiral.

The first priority, and I repeat, the first priority, in this effort must be given to halting the spread of nuclear weapons. If we do not face this problem squarely now, the opportunity may disappear forever. That is why the United States has tabled in the Eighteen Nation Disarmament Committee the full draft of a treaty binding its signers from taking any action to increase the number of states and other organizations having the power to unleash nuclear weapons. My government has fully committed itself to that underlying policy and urges that this draft become an actual treaty as soon as possible. We hope that other nuclear powers will accept the same commitment as an international agreement. Nuclear proliferation can be stopped, but we must act now. Agreement on this issue clearly is of overriding importance to world peace and security.

We recognize, moreover, that as more and more nations face frankly up to this issue, they must make momentous decisions about their own security, and we understand their concern. As President Johnson has indicated, we believe assurances of support against threats of nuclear blackmail should be available to nations which have foresworn a nuclear capability of their own. Action by the Assembly can be a useful part of such assurances. The United States is prepared to work to this end by this Assembly. Also of great aid in deterring the continuous proliferation of nuclear weapons would be agreement on a comprehensive test ban treaty.

Scientists cannot distinguish between all quakes and underground nuclear tests, but the science of detection is not static and our vigorous research program indicates the possibility of a substantial improvement in seismic detection capabilities. Furthermore, the United States is also now establishing in the state of Montana a large-aperture seismic array, which we hope will hasten major advances in the science of detection.

We stand ready to make the results of our experimental study available to scientists everywhere and to assist in the construction of similar facilities in other countries. The United States will shortly issue invitations to a large number of members of the United Nations to send qualified observers to visit our Montana detection site on October 12 and 13. We want to let each of them see this installation for himself. And we hope that this invitation will be accepted. Let me say clearly that we do not want inspection for the sake of inspection, or for any ulterior motive, and let me also say that we are not inflexible. We do insist on the minimum amount of inspection necessary under the present state of science to give confidence to all that a comprehensive test ban is actually being observed. But we will insist only on a number and type of inspections which are essential to the attainment of this objective.

While pressing ahead, then, on nonproliferation as our first priority, we must also take steps to reduce the dangers stemming from the high level of nuclear capabilities. There is no reason to wait. We are prepared to take practical steps here and now.

First, we should take steps to halt the accumulation of strategic nuclear delivery vehicles. We should continue to explore a freeze on the number and characteristics of strategic nuclear offensive and defensive vehicles. If progress is made in this field, the United States will also be willing to explore the possibility of significant reductions in the number of these carriers of mass destruction.

Second, the United States proposes a verified halt in production of fissionable material for weapons use and the transfer of fissionable materials to peaceful purposes. In connection with such a halt in fissionable material production, we now propose the demonstrated destruction by the United States and the Soviet Union of a substantial number of nuclear weapons from their respective stocks.

The United States is ready to transfer 60,000 kilograms of weapons grade U-235 to nonweapon uses if the Soviet Union would be willing to transfer 40,000 kilograms. If the U.S.S.R. accepts this proposal, each of us would destroy nuclear weapons of our own choice so as to make available for peaceful purposes such amounts of fissionable material. Moreover, the United States government stands ready, if the Soviet Union will do likewise, to add to this transfer associated plutonium obtained from the destroyed weapons in an agreed quantity or ratio and to place the material thus transferred under the International Atomic Energy Agency or equivalent safeguards.

We make these proposals in the interest of rapid and equitable progress in reducing the nuclear threat and as a practical demonstration of our dedication to this end. A more rapid movement toward disarmament would unquestionably decrease anxiety throughout the world. But if we are to progress towards a just world community we must also constantly improve our international machinery for curbing conflict and resolving disputes. The experience in Cyprus, the continuing aggression in Southeast Asia, the shock of violence erupting in Kashmir—all lead to an inescapable conclusion: There is an urgent need to strengthen the United Nations' capacity to keep the peace.

We urge as one such step the continued development of a flexible United Nations call-up system along the lines proposed by our distinguished Secretary General. We hope member states in all regions of the world will earmark and train units for such purpose. We believe also that the military staff, now inadequate, supporting the Secretary General needs to be strengthened. The added experience and burdens of Kashmir and Cyprus have conclusively demonstrated in particular that the military staff available to the Secretary General at Headquarters is overburdened. We must provide him with an enlarged staff whose size is commensurate with the tasks we entrust to him. The peace-keeping capacity of the United Nations is too basic to its purposes and to its very existence to allow it to be frustrated by any one member. For this reason—and in this we are joined by the overwhelming majority of United Nations members—we continue to believe that the General Assembly must retain its residual authority to initiate peace-keeping operations when the Security Council is unable to act. Means must be found to pay for future peace-keeping operations which allocate the burden fairly. In cases where this cannot be done by assessment of every member, we must find other means, including assessment of those willing to be assessed, nonobligatory apportionment, or voluntary contribution.

Less dramatic but equally important is machinery to promote peaceful change and to allow the satisfaction of just claims. Without a strong international institution, able to help in doing this, nations, like individuals, are tempted to take matters into their own hands. We consequently believe it is time to breathe new life into Article 33 of the Charter, a provision of the Charter referred to specifically in the Security Council resolution adopted just the other day in the Kashmir dispute. It has atrophied too long. We must develop workable methods to resolve disputes before they reach the point of potential or actual conflict. If the United Nations is to serve its primary purpose, it must be an instrument for the reconciliation of differences and not merely a forum in which they manifest themselves. Too often has the United Nations had to demonstrate its capacity for quenching fires when it might better have helped prevent them in the first place. For this reason we welcome the initiative of the United Kingdom in introducing an agenda item on the pacific settlement of disputes. The United States will eagerly participate in exploring the many paths it may open.

It is an item, if I may say so, Mr. President, in which I take a personal interest. For the greater part of my adult life has been spent in intimate association with the process of third-party settlement of the differences and disputes which arise between a free labor movement and free employers. I have often seen disagreements become aggravated or prolonged not because they were irreconcilable but simply because the parties involved could not agree upon the go-between. We in our own country have developed machinery such as the Federal Mediation and Conciliation Service that has filled this gap and, in so doing, greatly advanced the pacific settlement of labor disputes in our own country. I know also that machinery which is successful on the national level cannot always be transposed to the international level. Nevertheless, I am firmly convinced that the United Nations might also develop additional mechanisms allowing the parties to a stubborn dispute to use a UN body of mediation or conciliation.

Above all, our basic charge of peace-keeping under the Charter is to join together to assure peace and security. We must continue this quest for collective security and we must renounce collective futility if we are to perform our Charter function. There is an area in which we have been seeking to promote cooperation well before any dispute arises. This is in the peaceful uses of outer space. Over seven years ago the United States inscribed the first item to appear on this Assembly's agenda concerning the peaceful uses of outer space, and introduced a draft resolution sponsored by twenty states which became the first space action this body ever took. That resolution was introduced in the First Committee by the then Majority Leader of the United States Senate, Senator Lyndon B. Johnson of Texas, and as President he continues his interest, his dedication and devotion to that principle. By adopting that resolution this Assembly went on record as recognizing—and I quote from the first preambular paragraph—"it is the common aim that outer space should be used for peaceful purposes only." That principle is one to which we fully subscribed then and to which we fully subscribe now. Since then the General Assembly has laid down valuable ground rules for activities in space and on celestial bodies. In accordance with these rules, our space activities have been, and will continue to be, nonaggressive, peaceful and beneficial in character. But these rules are not enough. Instruments from earth have already reached the moon and photographed Mars. And man will soon follow. Accordingly, we suggest that the United Nations begin work on a comprehensive treaty on the exploration of celestial bodies.

But while we aim for the stars we must also employ maximum resources to promote economic and social well-being here at home. For, while the possibility of creating a just world society may be contingent on success or failure in such fields as disarmament and peace-keeping, our capability of creating it will depend on the efforts we spend not just to prevent disaster but to build healthy economic conditions everywhere. We are near the midpoint of the United Nations Development Decade. Progress has been made which has to be acknowledged, but we all need to do more and do it better. Much more has to be done to increase food production in the developing countries. If current population trends continue, food production will have to triple by the end of the century to provide an adequate diet for all. We thus fully support the proposal for an expanded World Food Program and are prepared to examine further with other developed countries ways of adapting our domestic agricultural abundance to meet the world's food deficit while it exists.

More action is required to limit excessive population growth. We support the program now under way whereby United Nations agencies provide advisory services and training in family planning to any country asking for such assistance, and we must all do more to help accelerate industrial growth in the developing countries, a question to which this Assembly, I am sure, will give special attention. We must also speed up and intensify our efforts to enlarge the export earnings of the developing countries, and to counteract excessive fluctuations in those earnings. The United States will continue to make special efforts in the General Agreement on Tariff and Trade to reduce tariffs on items of special interest to those countries. We shall also participate actively and constructively in the work of the new United Nations trade machinery. It is our hope that in dealing with the hard and difficult problems of trade developed and developing countries will proceed in a spirit of partnership. There must be a free and sustained dialogue and a common search for ways and means by which we can develop mutually beneficial trade patterns.

And, of course, experience shows that we need a much greater investment in the development of that most important resource of all—trained people— and must provide more assistance to the educational efforts of the developing countries. To help get on with these jobs, we support the increased target of $200 million for the United Nations Development Program, on the understanding that the arrangements worked out will be satisfactory to both the developing and the developed countries.

And we are ready to join in practical and concrete ways in a further expansion of multilateral efforts to supply capital for development through regional development banks and international institutions such as the International Bank and the IDA, on the assurance that there will be sound administration, as well as appropriate contributions from others, and we would be prepared to increase the amount of capital flowing through multilateral channels.

I recognize that we are not alone in acknowledging the need for action in these areas. I have singled them out because the United States plans to take or join in specific actions on each of them—not in the vague future but in the months ahead. Faster progress in the Development Decade is a central aim in our foreign policy.

I come now, in conclusion of these thoughts, to the source from which they derived—our determination to enrich the lives of human beings—domestically in our drive to create a Great Society, internationally in our support for fundamental freedoms and human rights for peoples everywhere. The ultimate object of UN activities, the ultimate object of any organized society domestically or internationally, is man the individual. The effect upon his lot, his fate, his well-being—that will remain the final measure of our success—and our failure. And if we talk about the competition between states, that is the only worthwhile competition as to which system, which society, best improves the lot of man and upgrades human dignity.

We are well past the mid-point—indeed in sight of the end—of what history may record as the most exciting and predominantly peaceful revolution in human affairs and this is a movement vitally linked to the dignity of human beings—the movement of self-determination. This movement has seen people in the past few decades assert and gain their right to be free from colonialism, to self-government and independence, their right to be free from control by other peoples. We applaud this historical development and are deeply committed to its success. Of course, among the dependent peoples now remaining in the world—whose aspirations for self-determination command our fullest sympathy—are some very small areas with very limited resources. Whether they will be able to meet the requirements of the Charter that members are not only willing but also "able" to carry out their obligations may require early consideration, as the Secretary General has indicated. But, I repeat, we support the historical development of all peoples being able to gain their self-government or independence when they desire it by principles of self-determination.

And in our concern for the rights and freedom of nations we must not neglect the rights and freedoms of individuals—those who, after all, are the basic unit of any nation. The test of any country's dedication to human rights is, if I may respectfully suggest, not what it says in the General Assembly for all the world to hear but what it does at home for all the world to see.

Our record, like that of other countries, is far from perfect. But with the decision of our Supreme Court of 1954 and the decisions since, in which I hope you will not deem it amiss if I take great personal pride and satisfaction as having participated in some of them, in the passage of the Civil Rights Acts of 1964 and 1965, the American government has put into concrete form and terms its full and complete commitment to the principle of full human rights, of freedom and equality for all of our people.

The UN also has a significant role in promoting, in the words of the Charter, human rights and fundamental freedoms for all. Much has already been done, but the United Nations has not done enough in this area, and we believe much more will be necessary. We are therefore very pleased that the government of Costa Rica has proposed the establishment of a High Commissioner for Human Rights. We think this is an important first step in implementing the Declaration of Human Rights and we shall give this proposal our enthusiastic support.

We can, out of this debate, out of the divergent views expressed here, distill a consensus. As long as we strive for such a consensus and accept the methods of reason and understanding upon which consensus is built, we will strengthen the fabric of this great community of these United Nations, and by its very nature, this must always be a community whose doors are open to those who would turn their backs on chaos, threat, and violence and seek legitimate ends through peaceful means. I said the other day that I am optimistic about the fate of this organization and I am optimistic because if we had not created this great organization twenty years ago we would be creating it out of necessity today.

The road to world order, the road to a rule of law in the world is not an easy one. It will continue to be arduous, and beset by agonizing hurdles, painful decisions, difficult compromises, and, at times, disheartening setbacks. Traveling the road will demand the most from each of us. I pray that we shall be equal to the task.

I hope, also, that twenty years from now, when this Assembly convenes for its plenary session, it can look back on a generation of achievement that we begin today.

President Johnson said: "We seek to establish a harmony between man and society which will allow each of us to enlarge the meaning of his life and all of us to elevate the quality of our civilization."

Out of our diversity, the welcomed diversity of nations and peoples, let us be one in our determination to elevate the quality of all our lives and to build a Great Society of and for all men.

General Assembly of the United Nations, September 23, 1965

HUMAN RIGHTS AND SOCIAL PRESSURES

The Universal Declaration of Human Rights

Monday of this week was the twentieth anniversary of the death of Franklin D. Roosevelt. We remember him as a President great in war and in peace and as a stalwart champion of the cause of freedom and human rights here and everywhere in the world. One of his greatest declarations was contained in a message to Congress on January 6, 1941. "In the future days, which we seek to make secure, we look forward to a world founded upon four essential human freedoms. The first is freedom of speech and expression —everywhere in the world. The second is freedom of every person to worship God in his own way—everywhere in the world. The third is freedom from want—everywhere in the world. The fourth is freedom from fear—anywhere in the world."

Almost twenty-five years have passed since that memorable address. In those years the virulent dictatorships of Hitler and Mussolini were scrubbed from history at the cost of immense individual suffering. The colonial system weathered and cracked at the impact of millions of persons rising from neolithic bondage. Communism, at a time when the world turned toward the new horizons of peace, did not abandon for a moment its intentions of domination. And man's technical capability presented him with the ultimate decision—destruction or survival.

We learned, in those years of triumph and trial, that the Four Freedoms were more than challenging goals; they were and are the essentials if civilization as we know it is to survive.

As Sumner Welles once remarked: "Upon these four freedoms must rest the structure of the future free world . . . we won't get a free world any other way."

And we have learned as well that what Thomas Paine said about freedom at the advent of our own Revolution remains true for as long as freedom remains real. "Those who expect to reap the blessings of freedom," he wrote, "must, like men, undergo the fatigue of supporting it."

If we accept, then, the Four Freedoms as the only basis for a free world, we also accept the responsibility for realizing them here in America, and helping others to attain them elsewhere. This means, as President Kennedy so eloquently stated it, "pay any price, bear any burden, meet any hardship, support any friend, oppose any foe to assure the survival and success of liberty."

Underlying the Four Freedoms is the acknowledgment that intellectual and political freedoms—Freedom of Speech and of Religion—become realities only in a context of economic freedoms—Freedom from Fear and Want.

The true national interest in America is the attainment of individual freedom everywhere in the world—not only intellectually, so that any man might look any other man in the face and speak his piece, but economically, so that want and fear do not become the landlords of any man's private station in life.

In practical terms, it means that no man should be deprived of his fundamental human rights because of race or age or religion. The person who suffers denial of human rights because of prejudice has a right to speak up about it; he must also have the right not to suffer it.

Lord Acton, in the last century, saw this clearly when he said: "The most certain test by which we judge whether a country is really free is the amount of security enjoyed by minorities."

The placing of economic freedoms beside civil freedoms also means preserving the distinction between regulation to limit intellectual freedom and that to limit economic freedom. Ideas, philosophies and opinions require an open market; regulation of them means restricting, sometimes destroying, the freedom required if they are to flourish. This is the danger that the right to assembly, speech and religion guards against. But in the economic field, regulation to limit economic power is designed to produce wider competition, greater opportunity and freer access to the market.

This distinction is now common to us, but it is not so well known to the world, where we are too often pictured as a materialistic nation of the old type. To free man's mind by removing barriers to intellectual intercourse is here paralleled by actions to regulate, by both private and government action, economic life so that the freedoms from want and fear might also be attained.

If America were understood in this light—and I would hope we can develop such an understanding—then the argument of Communists founded on the comparison between their system, pictured as providing full employment and social equality, and ours, pictured as one in which the wealthy owner exploits the workingman and enjoys the perfect freedom to do so, would soon break down.

A way of life that offers intellectual freedom through political guarantees, and also offers economic freedom through wise social and economic legislation, is the highest creation of civilized man. Only from such a system could evolve a concept like that of the Four Freedoms. And if communism steals our rhetoric, abuses our vocabulary, distorts our semantics—they cannot undo the truth of our system.

Both bread and equality, both freedom and security—these are inseparable. We can attain them. Communism cannot. That is the simple message of the Four Freedoms doctrine.

To those who accept it, who believe with Schiller that "man is created free, and is free, even though born in chains," then the vision of the better world, and the better life upon it, is one of universal freedom, in which all men must partake or none may enjoy. If free men are oppressed anywhere, we are. If they hunger, we hunger. If they suffer, we suffer. If they lose their freedom, ours is less.

The community of interest that binds free nations rests upon an identity of purpose—to attain, for individuals, the kind of life in which the Freedoms are living conditions.

And in this regard it becomes ever clearer that the first requisite of a successful foreign policy is to keep our own house in order. As we pursue the work of freedom in the world, we must practice as well as preach respect for human rights at home and make sure that our economy ensures social and economic justice to all our citizens. Our country must be the example to show that this is what political and economic freedom does, this is what it can accomplish, this is the strength it gives to our hands, this is the well-being it provides to our people.

I am hopeful and optimistic about the future of freedom of which Franklin Roosevelt so eloquently spoke almost a quarter of a century ago, that it will gain new strength from new trial, new resolution from new challenge, new conviction from new danger, and new determination from new circumstance. When men know they might be free, they will strive to be free. When men have reason to hope for freedom, they will sacrifice for it. And both the knowledge and the hope are alive in the world, more alive now, perhaps, than ever before. The wind of change blows strongly, promising a new day, a new order, and a new life in the history of the world.

Franklin Roosevelt's quest for universal adherence to the concept of Human Rights and Human Freedoms everywhere in the world culminated shortly after his death in the provisions of the Charter of the United Nations which "reaffirmed faith in fundamental Human Rights and the dignity and worth of the human person." Furthermore, by the Charter all member states pledged themselves to take separate and common action for the recognition of these fundamental values.

The Charter of the UN reflected the consciousness of mankind that the persecution, expulsion and extermination of millions of human beings, including the great body of European Jewry, during World War II exceeded any denial of human rights recorded in the previous history of civilization. This bitter experience awakened world opinion to the importance of extending international protection to the individual.

The United Nations at its meeting in May, 1946, established the Commission on Human Rights charged with the responsibility of submitting to the General Assembly recommendations and reports regarding "An International

Bill of Rights." Mrs. Eleanor Roosevelt, of blessed memory, was elected chairman of the Commission.

The Commission on Human Rights thereupon drafted that great document which properly takes its place in the annals of human liberty known as the Universal Declaration of Human Rights. The Declaration is really in two parts. One deals with economic and social problems, the other with political and civil rights. It plainly reflects its genesis in Roosevelt's Four Freedoms.

The Universal Declaration of Human Rights, though unanimously adopted by the member states of the United Nations almost twenty years ago, lacks means of enforcement. Unimplemented, this great document of human liberty amounts only to a manifesto, a statement of high and lofty ideals, rather than binding law. Yet, the evidence accumulates day by day to confirm the validity of the basic premises of the Declaration that: "[R]ecognition of the inherent dignity and of the equal and inalienable rights of all members of the human family is the foundation of freedom, justice and peace in the world." The time is overdue for the adoption of a binding treaty on Human Rights to implement the Declaration.

Some men of good will believe that world justice through the rule of law can be achieved only with the creation of a full-fledged superstate in which all nations are merged. I do not share this view. My own belief accepts the premise of the late Dean Roscoe Pound that: "[A]ll states need not be merged in a great world state, in which their personality is lost, in order that their conduct may be inquired into and ordered by authority of a world legal order."

Others object to the signing of the proposed treaty guaranteeing international due process on the ground that this "would tend to undermine the sovereignty and independence of states." The simple answer to this states' rights contention is that there is no sovereign right of any state large or small to deny the fundamental Rights of Man—rights which belong to him because as a child of God he is endowed with human dignity.

Moreover, the experience, since the creation in 1953 by the fifteen countries of the Council of Europe of the European Court of Human Rights and the Commission of Human Rights, demonstrates that an international forum and procedure for their enforcement can operate practically and without infringing upon true national sovereignty.

The United States has every reason to be in the forefront of the nations seeking universal adherence to a binding treaty regarding human rights. All such a treaty seeks, in the words of my distinguished colleague, Mr. Justice Brennan is: "International due process of the nature of the national due process familiar to every American: a prompt and speedy trial, legal assistance, including assistance for the indigent; prohibition of any kind of undue coercion or influence; freedom to conduct one's defense; the right to a public trial and written proceedings; the presumption of innocence and the burden upon the state to prove guilt beyond a reasonable doubt; and security against cruel and unusual punishments. These standards of due process, and thus of effective justice, only words now in the Universal Declaration of Human Rights, have their counterparts in our own United States Constitution. The vital difference, however, is that our nation has vitalized them for our people through a national forum and a national procedure for their enforcement."

If we in the United States are faithful to our own Bill of Rights, we need no reservations in a treaty pledging adherence to an International Bill of Rights which mirrors our own. If we are faithful as a people and through our national forums to our constitutional commands, we will not be called upon to answer before an international forum.

There is much talk these days about competition between states. Soviet leaders assert that the Communist system will prevail; that its material and technological advances will overwhelm other systems, like our own. I, together with most Americans, profoundly believe otherwise. We have no doubt of our ability to compete with the Communist world in the very competition of material goods of which they speak.

I wish, however, that there would be more talk about a more important competition—the competition between democratic and Communist governments as to which better safeguards and advances the unalienable rights of man—the rights to life, liberty and the pursuit of happiness. Protection and realization of human rights is the most important aspect of civilization and the most profound area for meaningful competition between societies.

It is because of my faith in the democratic way of life that I urge our country to assume the leadership in this competition by championing the adoption of the Treaty on Human Rights drafted by the United Nations to implement the Declaration of Human Rights. And we should adopt such a treaty without reservations, for none is needed or justified.

With concern for human rights firmly embedded in our national life and in our hearts Americans should be ready and willing to compete—to compete in the market of human values and in the protection and realization of individual liberties. This competition in ideals, rather than in material things, is the real challenge. In this competition no nation, no individual can be neutral. All are deeply committed. We cannot believe in human rights only for ourselves, but we must increasingly seek them for others as well.

It is the profound teaching of the Declaration of Human Rights that the true way to freedom, justice and peace in the world is "recognition of the equal and unalienable rights of all members of the human family."

President Roosevelt expressed the same thought in another way: "We have learned that we cannot live alone, at peace; that our own well-being is dependent on the well-being of other nations, far away. We have learned that we must live as men, and not as ostriches, nor as dogs in the manger. We have learned to be citizens of the world, members of the human community."

American Jewish Committee, New York, N.Y., April 14, 1965

The Coercions of Freedom

This building [the Library of the Hebrew Union College-Jewish Institute of Religion] will be a splendid repository of the learning of the past—a treasure house of the truths of a great religion and the convictions of a people. Within it will be a record of man's success and failure in grappling with his own nature, with reality, and with his own purpose and condition. History is filled with blind waste and magnificent triumph, with angry stupidity and dazzling discovery. In hours of trial a library offers us the opportunity to judge the results of past decisions.

It was Oliver Wendell Holmes, Jr., who said: "Continuity with the past is a necessity, not a duty."

Libraries in particular and educational institutions in general make continuity with the past possible. And we are bound to the past, creatures of time, but free to look to a future we ourselves help to make.

I wonder, then, how it is that modern society fails to resist the impulse to relearn, often in more bitterness, lessons learned so bitterly in the past.

Those who forget the past, said Santayana, are doomed to repeat it. Are we, today, forgetting the past?

I raise this question at this time and in this place because it seems particularly fitting to dedicate a monument to man's collective knowledge when voices are heard urging disengagement from history, withdrawal from the continuity of responsibility that has flowed from father to son in our free nation.

These voices rejecting history are raised because of the genuine struggle of human conscience at a time of truly awesome responsibility. Good people are deeply troubled about man's course toward holocaust. They fear that a race of arms can end in the ravage of civilization.

We all stand in the shadow of the towering giant of nuclear power, the colossal bomb that can obliterate centuries. It is argued by these men of good faith that the sole moral position for a moral people who possess this weapon is unilaterally to divest themselves of it.

This manifestation of pacifism—not new in history—is of course accentuated by the character of the nuclear weapon. But the necessity of continuity with the past requires an answer to evident questions.

Will unilateral abandonment of defensive arms deter aggression? Will the unilateral pledge of our own disengagement actually turn tyranny aside and guarantee universal peace with justice?

In pondering these questions we might turn—for one place—to here, to a library. Contemporary history offers some comparative examples. Many of you will remember the Oxford Oath era in Great Britain prior to the Second World War. Its feeling for peace, its rejection of war, its longing for order in the world's affairs were all emotions that good men could and did share.

This open commitment to disengagement did not stop Nazi aggression. I wondered then, and I do now, whether or not Hitler was encouraged by the policy of disengagement he sensed in the English people. Like every dictator, before and since, he incorrectly judged the stamina and will of a free people.

In this nation, unlike some others, the argument to disarm unilaterally and to divest ourselves of nuclear capability does not enjoy the wide respectability of a movement. I believe that the President spoke for most Americans when he said: "Our arms do not prepare for war—they are efforts to discourage and resist the adventures of others that could end in war."

I am sure that, in the light of the plain postwar record, everyone cognizant of fact and not deluded by propaganda—either of their own making or made for someone else's consumption—recognizes the sincerity and good faith of our efforts to achieve an enforceable ban on nuclear testing and genuine disarmament. I am sure that no one, except the propagandists and their victims, questions the good faith of our President who at this very moment is on a mission of peace—not peace in our time but for all time.

Disengagement, however, takes many forms. There are those respected among us who recognize that unilateral disarmament in the face of the postwar history of totalitarian aggression is an invitation to increased aggression. But they also seek to disengage the nation from the performance of other actions necessary to strengthen our alliances and maintain the free world.

It is this "intellectual disengagement"—this withdrawal of assent to the total demand that freedom makes upon us—that I wish to discuss here.

I am not implying that all intellectuals seek disengagement. On the contrary, the Harvard Manifesto has, in our healthy and free society, brought forth a Princeton Pronouncement. Nevertheless, there is indication of a current of intellectual disengagement in our nation today.

I suggest to the intellectual seeking peace through disengagement that he ponder an activist path toward peace which we can all share. This path leads toward the completion of our own Revolution in other free societies and the making of a world order in which a balance of terror would lose its power. I would suggest to him the historical reminder that peace can only be attained in freedom, and that it is peace in freedom that we all seek and must work to attain.

The President, in the conduct of the foreign policy of his administration, has enunciated several concepts related to the pursuit of peace in freedom.

As a nation endowed by God with great resources and one of history's great examples of just government by law, we are charged with the responsibility to lead the free world. The President has aptly remarked: "This nation was born of revolution and raised in freedom. And we do not intend to leave an open road to despotism."

Second, our whole history and purpose as a people makes it impossible for us to be neutral in our devotion to the cause of peace in freedom.

Third, in terms of the world alliance we lead, the historical encouragement disengagement would give to those intent upon conquest, and the vacuum of responsibility it leaves in a world of growing nuclear mastery, makes it clear that a leader of freedom cannot disengage without leaving not only itself but all others allied with it the quick target of aggressive despotism.

Fourth, we welcome all allies devoted to peace in freedom. In this regard, I think we should all be clear—despite our own intellectual differences—that we respect the right of every nation to seek freedom and equality, order and independence in its own way, flying its own flag, charting its own course.

We support the revolution of peace and hope sweeping the world, and we offer that support, as the President stated, "regardless of which political or economic route they choose to freedom."

Fifth, we recognize the right of every nation not charged with our responsibility or armed with our resources to pursue a policy of non-commitment, whether to us or any other power. Our alliance is one of voluntary commitment to peace in freedom. It is not cemented with force, not held together with the bonds of political domination and fear. We do not force nations to be our allies. And we resist efforts on the part of others to compel, coerce or subvert them to be their allies.

Finally, in this open posture of support for all nations seeking freedom, our sympathies are manifestly with those seeking to end injustice, tyranny and exploitation, anywhere in the world.

The volumes of history that will be contained in this library make it plain why this is so. Even before we were a nation, as a group of rebels seeking freedom we had the support of Lafayette, De Kalb, Kosciusko, Steuben and others. They were brave men who crossed distant seas to help us fight for liberty. After we were a nation we extended the hand of help to Louis

Kossuth, Garibaldi, Mazzini, Carl Schurz, Lamartine and others because they shared the ideals of our own Revolution. Even more recently, I recall with no sense of regret serving as a member of the Committee to Aid America by Aiding the Allies. In those dark hours of 1940 our government welcomed and sheltered thousands of exiles from Europe.

It is clear that the idea of freedom has always been basic to our national policy—and with it sympathy for those fighting for freedom.

We extend our full measure of sympathy and support to the true revolution and not the false one, to the revolution that seeks freedom and does not suppress it.

We know too well from the lessons of history that tyranny often seeks to disguise itself by the assertion of humane goals. For us, means as well as ends are important. And for us, while we recognize any nation's right to achieve a fashion of economic system of its own making, we do not concede the right in moral terms to fashion a political system which denies liberty, human dignity and the rights of man.

I believe that these concepts, which are basic to our President's foreign policy, deserve and command the support of all who believe in a democratic way of life.

Yet, as I read the manifestoes being circulated recently, I find that while there is not disagreement with these principles there is a note of skepticism about our commitment to allow any nation to pursue its own social and economic path to peace and freedom. I believe this skepticism is totally unwarranted. Our words and deeds bear eloquent testimony to our total commitment to the just aspirations of people everywhere. This is what the President, speaking for all Americans, has said on this subject:

"We stand for freedom. That is our conviction for ourselves—that is our only commitment to others. No friend, no neutral and no adversary should think otherwise. We are not against any man—or any nation—or any system —except as it is hostile to freedom. . . .

"Asia, Latin America, Africa and the Middle East . . . theirs is a revolution which we would support regardless of the Cold War, and regardless of which political or economic route they choose to freedom."

The President's actions have been consistent with his words.

In the United Nations we have voted against colonial powers even at the discomfiture of allies.

We have extended material and economic aid to other nations embarked on more sweeping reforms than those of Castro.

The downfall of dictatorships in Argentina, Colombia and Venezuela was followed by American support for the democracies seeking to bring hope and security to their people.

Our quarrel with Castro, as the President stated, "is not over the people's drive for a better life. Our objection is to their domination by foreign and domestic tyrants. Cuban social and economic reform should be encouraged. Questions of economic and trade policy can always be negotiated. But Communist domination in this hemisphere can never be negotiated."

The situation we face is not that of social reform. Let us regard it clearly as the President describes it: ". . . the menace of external Communist intervention and domination in Cuba." The real issue is the survival of freedom in this hemisphere.

I am sure that all men of good will are united in seeking a world in which genuine nonintervention in the struggle of nations to attain peace and freedom is practiced. But the dilemma facing us as a nation is that we who believe in nonintervention are confronted by a force that practices aggression in many forms.

Consider the words of the President: "They send arms, agitators, aid, technicians, and propaganda to every troubled area. But where fighting is required, it is usually done by others—by guerillas striking at night, by assassins striking alone, by subversives and saboteurs and insurrectionists, who in some cases control whole areas inside of independent nations."

The basic dilemma in that kind of situation was described a little more than a century ago by John Stuart Mill:

The doctrine of nonintervention, to be a legitimate principle of morality, must be accepted by all governments. The despots must consent to be bound by it as well as the free states. Unless they do, the profession of it by free countries comes to this miserable issue, that the wrong side may help the wrong, but the right side must not help the right. Intervention to enforce nonintervention is always rightful, almost moral, if not always prudent. Though it be a mistake to give freedom to a people who do not value the boon, it cannot but be right to insist that if they do value it, they shall not be hindered from the pursuit of it by foreign coercion.

Today, in 1961, we must ask:

Will the wrong continue unopposed to aid the wrong while the right declines to aid the right?

I submit these thoughts and questions in the spirit of good intention—not to try to create a pale unanimity of views but to encourage all Americans to consider the full responsibility we carry.

At the signing of the Constitution, Benjamin Franklin remarked that he had been observing the painting of a sun on the chair in which George Washington sat. He said that it gave him happiness to know now that it was a rising and not a setting sun.

I think the world knows now that the light of freedom will rise over the exploited peoples of the world. They know that this nation will commit its power, and its people, to the alliance for genuine social advancement in every nation. They know we stand for freedom and oppose tyranny, wherever it may appear, whatever form it may seek to shield itself from recognition.

It is that knowledge, and our own firm resolution, that will fix the course of history. It is in that spirit I dedicate this new monument to history today.

Hebrew Union College—Jewish Institute of Religion, Cincinnati, Ohio, June 3, 1961

The Achievement of Equality

As the United States representative to the UN, one of my most important responsibilities, I believe, is to convey to the member states the philosophy and the views of the United States government and its people. For this reason, I have told the General Assembly that we in America espouse equality not only as a principle; we seek equal opportunity as an accomplished reality. And what we seek at home we seek for all mankind. But we think the test of any country's dedication to human rights is not just what it says in the General Assembly for all the world *to hear* but what it does at home for all the world *to see*. There can be no public face looking one way at the UN and a private face looking the other way at home.

Not too many years ago we in the United States were looking in different directions when our official government policy espoused total equality for all our citizens, only to have it frustrated in many parts of the country by the accepted practice of too many of our citizens. This is no longer the case.

All Presidents in this generation, the Congress, and the federal judiciary led by the Supreme Court have all taken action in behalf of the people of this country to rid the fabric of our society of its last vestiges of discrimination. The concept of deliberate speed, as our Supreme Court recently said, never contemplated indefinite delay, and today—eleven years after the momentous Supreme Court decision in Brown versus the Board of Education—the time has come to complete all the outstanding promises of emancipation—here and now.

Our laws are now better able to accomplish this and to cope with the challenges put to them because they have been equipped with effective machinery to solve the legitimate grievances of the people. Only laws that do this make for stability in a country and give justifiable reason for hope in the future. However, let me emphasize, we have no reason for complacency, no reason for smug self-satisfaction. We have only reason to work all the harder so that we may achieve the one satisfactory solution to our remaining civil rights problems—their total elimination.

But civil rights without full economic rights, intellectual rights, and political rights is a right to nothing. It has always seemed to me that our democratic way of life, which offers intellectual freedom through political guarantees, and also offers economic freedom through wise social and economic legislation, is the highest creation of civilized man. It is what we seek to perfect here in America. And only when we do will we successfully complete what Adlai Stevenson called our "third revolution." In our first, as he pointed out, we became a nation; in the second we overcame slavery, and now in our third and still ongoing revolution we battle for freedom: freedom for all our people, freedom from discrimination, freedom from ignorance, freedom from poverty, freedom from all that means fear and prejudice, freedom, indeed, to become a truly just and compassionate nation.

With concern for human rights such a traditional part of American life, we cannot stand idly by while human rights are violated anywhere in the world. We share an obligation with the other member states of the UN to search out human freedom and dignity wherever they are oppressed or denied, for we cannot believe in human rights for ourselves without believing in them for everyone else. President Roosevelt, I believe, showed us the way when he said:

"We have learned that we cannot live alone, at peace; that our own well-being is dependent on the well-being of other nations, far away. We have learned that we must live as men, and not as ostriches, nor as dogs in the manger. We have learned to be citizens of the world, members of the human community."

If the first generation of the United Nations was a time for the passing of empires and the coming to nationhood of more than half the world and its peoples—a generation of decolonization and independence—the next generation may well have reason to become known as the human rights generation. But herein lies a delicate and complicated problem of international organization and cooperation. The question is not whether discrimination is to be condemned and abolished, the question is how and when and in what manner. In short, the question before us is one of method.

But before coming to it, we have a prior question that must be asked, because discrimination has many faces and not the least ugly is the one that limits the political or cultural freedom of any man for any reason whatsoever. The question that we must ask, therefore, is this: Has the tide of national freedom of the past generation been matched by a corresponding freedom of the individual?

I am afraid the answer is not the one we would hope for. It is certainly not the answer given by the all too frequently occurring instances of one-party groups concentrating all power in themselves and oppressing or jailing all who disagree with them. For the inescapable fact is that even as the peoples of the world have differing languages and customs, so do they have differing concepts of freedom. And yet there can be only one concept, one meaning to freedom, and we must clearly define it.

We must do the same with the term "discrimination" and all its ramifications. There can be no misunderstanding or confusion about it. Discrimination, regardless of color or gradation of color, is ugly and repugnant, no matter what race or ethnic group is involved. The United Nations recognizes this fact. Indeed, one of the major differences between the United Nations Charter and the League of Nations Covenant is that the Covenant looked the other way but the Charter boldly lays down the objective of "respect for human rights and for fundamental freedoms for all."

Although there have been proud accomplishments—and we need only point to the Universal Declaration of Human Rights—it is my feeling that in the human rights field we must move ahead with ever greater vigor. The peace-keeping and the nation-building machinery of the UN—the heart of its political and economic work—has been developed to a high degree of sophistication. Not so with its human rights machinery, although again I emphasize that much has been done. It is because more is necessary in this area that we are supporting, as I told the General Assembly, a proposal made by the government of Costa Rica calling for the establishment of a High Commissioner for Human Rights. This, I believe, is an important first step in the implementation of the Declaration of Human Rights, one that will enable it to live up both to the noble intent of its name and to the historic purpose of its content—that of improving the lot of man.

The name of the Declaration, I would say, while almost perfectly descriptive of its achievement, also describes its limitation. In twenty years it has received *universal* recognition, but it remains just that, a *declaration*. In these two words thus are reflected both the hope and the tragedy of human rights in our day. We agree all too often on principles, but practice and enforcement have not kept pace with pronouncements.

One of the United Nations' most powerful weapons is its ability to focus the world spotlight of opinion on the darkness of injustice. It is for this reason the United States urged a condemnation of anti-Semitism in the draft Convention on Racial Discrimination currently under consideration. One article rightly condemns apartheid, one of the most malignant, inhuman and vicious forms of racial discrimination. Inasmuch as the Convention covered ethnic as well as racial groups, we believed that calling attention to anti-Semitism as one of history's deadliest and most persistent forms of discrimination was both in order and advisable. I think there should be no misunderstanding over the fact that the UN Committee that turned down our proposal did so because it felt that if it singled out anti-Semitism it should also mention other forms of ethnic discrimination. We do not agree, but we are satisfied that the Convention, in condemning any and all forms of racial and ethnic discrimination, covers anti-Semitism, although, as I say, we would have been better satisfied with a more specific reference. Nonetheless, we believe there will be other opportunities for us to raise the question of anti-Semitism by name in connection with future human rights proposals, and this we shall do wherever it is appropriate, even as we will also denounce every other form of discrimination.

For we have reached the juncture in history, I believe, when we must act and no longer sit in silence while men assault their brothers. The silence can be worse than the offense. I think your distinguished president, Dr. Prinz, expressed it most eloquently when he said: "The most important thing that I learned in my life—is that bigotry and hatred are not the most urgent problem. The most urgent, the most disgraceful, the most sinful, and the most tragic problem is silence."

Too much of the world was silent when the Nazis committed their crimes. We dare not chance a repetition, whether the discrimination be religious, racial or because of national origin. The practices of apartheid in South Africa, as I have said, arouse the deepest shock and revulsion, and we shall not be silent about it. Neither shall we be silent about the situation in Southern Rhodesia, where a black majority does not have the right to self-determination.

I mention these two now because they are among the more dramatic instances of discrimination to come before us at this session of the General Assembly. But there are others—the list, sadly, is far too long—and none can be cloaked in silence, for if we fail to come to grips with any threat to the human rights of the people of the world, if we fail to speak up, we foster a threat that can only grow in the danger it poses to all mankind. I therefore want to reaffirm my own personal belief that the universal realization of human rights is the single most important aspect of our civilization. The ultimate object of all our UN activities, the ultimate object of any organized society, domestically or internationally, is man the individual. The effect upon his lot, his fate, his well-being—that will remain the final measure of our success—and our failure. And if we talk about the competition between states, that is the only worthwhile competition: which system, which society, best improves the lot of man and upgrades human dignity. We have the scientific and technical capability today to eliminate poverty and want wherever it exists in the world. We must match it with the human capability to eliminate all forms of discrimination—for it is only human capability and willingness that, in the last analysis, can give us human rights.

And we as Americans, with our audacious heritage and continuing belief in the freedom of the individual, have within our hands—with the elimination of all discrimination in our own land—the ability to make a lasting contribution not only to the building of our own Great Society here at home but everywhere in the world. In so doing we will enable ourselves and all people to set foot anywhere on the surface of the earth and say, in the words of Benjamin Franklin's prayer: "This is my country."

American Jewish Congress, New York, N.Y., October 31, 1965

The Rule of Law and the Rights of Man

We are gathered today to reflect upon the rule of law and upon human rights in a free society. We meet in a most appropriate setting—in Philadelphia's old City Hall. In this hall the Supreme Court of the United States met in February, 1791, and held some of its early sessions. A few steps to the east is Independence Hall where the Declaration of Independence, the Articles of Confederation, and the Constitution of the United States were signed.

Both this day and this setting give us special cause to consider the rights of men under both democratic and Communist governments. Chairman Khrushchev for the Soviet government has often spoken of competition between his Communist-organized society and those societies, like our own, which are committed to a democratic system. In describing this competition Soviet leaders assert that the Communist system will prevail; its material and technological advances will, so their statements proclaim, in one way or another overwhelm other societies.

Chairman Khrushchev's boasts about the productive ability of his state sound very hollow at a time when he must look to us and to neighboring Canada to augment his wheat and grain supplies. This vividly demonstrates that free agriculture can outproduce collective farming, just as our tremendous outpouring of industrial and consumer goods continually establishes the superiority of our free labor organized in free trade unions over state-regimented labor and of our free business enterprise over the Soviet Union's nationalized economy. It is clear, therefore, that in the very competition of material goods about which Chairman Khrushchev speaks so boldly, our country has responded fully and successfully. I have no doubt of our ability to do so in the future.

There is, however, a more important competition about which Chairman Khrushchev does not speak and about which he is and must be silent. That competition is the competition between democratic and totalitarian governments as to which better safeguards and advances the inalienable rights of man—the rights to life, liberty and the pursuit of happiness. In this, the most fundamental area for comparison between political systems, Communist governments have utterly failed. At best, they boast only of forms, not of realities. In the realization of human rights a free society has an inherent advantage for it is founded on a belief in the dignity of man—of each man. This is a value wholly at variance with the Marxist philosophy, which sets forth as the principle of life, as the basis of its materialistic faith, that men are but the pawns of historical economic forces. When the protection and realization of human rights is recognized, as it must be, as the most important aspect of civilization and as the most profound area for meaningful "competition" between societies, then we can best see the sharp contrast between free democratic governments, on one hand, and Communist-totalitarian dictatorships, on the other. Indeed, the very human rights and liberties which a democratic society most prizes—the rights which reflect its belief in the dignity of man—are precisely the rights and liberties which Communist rulers fear and suppress.

The heart of the democratic faith is in the dependence of government upon the consent of the governed—that people consent to the laws they must live by. In a statement approved by our national Congress in 1774, even before the Declaration of Independence, we recognized that the first grand right of the people is to be "ruled by laws, which they themselves approve, not by edicts of men over whom they have no control." This is what we mean by the "rule of law." We mean not simply a system of enforced rules of life but rather a body of laws responsive to the needs of the general public and dependent upon their consent. The grand right of each man and woman to have an equal voice in the selection of his governors and thus to have an equal voice in the shaping of the laws is a right unique to free democratic societies. A Communist dictatorship, like all dictatorships, cannot in the long run risk exposing itself to the free choice of the people, the governed.

The consent of the governed in a democratic system does not mean, however, that the majority of the moment may abridge or deny the fundamental rights of minorities. It is the particular genius of the men who drafted our Constitution to have recognized that there are basic rights of the individual which the majority cannot take away or abridge. These rights are enshrined in our Bill of Rights. Without them our Constitution would not have been accepted.

Among these fundamental rights is freedom of speech and press. It is the American constitutional conviction that freedom of speech and press is at the core of all liberty. Mr. Justice Cardozo in his felicitous way observed that "Freedom of expression is the matrix, the indispensable condition of nearly every other form of freedom." Implicit in this statement is the recognition of the simple fact that "where men cannot freely convey their thoughts to one another, no other liberty is secure. Where freedom of expression exists, the germ of a free society is already present and a means is at hand for every extension of liberty." The governors of the moment, and the government of today, cannot by our creed be freed from open, public and forceful criticism. It is significant, by way of obvious contrast, that the Soviet Constitution prefaces its formal provision on freedom of speech by providing that it must be exercised "in order to strengthen the socialist system." (Article 125.) In other words, criticism under the Communist system is restricted to that "criticism" which those in authority believe will strengthen their hand. In our society, however, both in our Constitution and in our daily life, the right to speak is not and cannot be restricted by what those in authority deem necessary to strengthen their position. Effective freedom, we have learned, requires that there be freedom to criticize and to blame, however harshly, and not merely freedom to applaud the present system and its governors.

Another fundamental right, cherished in a democracy but long feared by dictators, is the right of free and private association among citizens. A free society has no place for a one-party system with an "approved" list of candidates as in the Soviet Union. Men must be free to associate in groups, including associations explicitly formed for the purpose of electing new governors.

Moreover, as a corollary of the right of free association, each man also must have the right to be left alone if he so chooses. . . . A right to privacy precludes a system of constant governmental surveillance of the private activities of citizens. Free men do not need governmental "Big Brothers" looking after them.

High among the most valued human rights is freedom of religion. We are undeniably a religious people; the vast majority of Americans are members of churches and practice religion in their own way. Our belief in the dignity of man, like the Bill of Rights itself, has roots deep in Judaic-Christian teachings and traditions. History has proved that religious tolerance is a touchstone of freedom. In the Soviet Union, however, religious practices are discouraged and condemned; churches, Catholic and Protestant, and syna- gogues are closed; religious groups are persecuted; and missionaries arrested and convicted. In sharp contrast stands the practice and belief of free demo- cratic societies. In these the state does not espouse an official faith and, instead of repressing religion as a diversion from the state-commanded Com- munist faith, the government protects each man in his right freely to practice his own religion.

Discrimination in the Soviet Union is not confined to religious groups but extends to national groups which are denied the right of self-determination.

In pointing this out I am mindful that as a nation our record in the area of racial discrimination is not perfect. But there is a patent difference between the discrimination in the Soviet Union and the racial discrimination which unhappily still persists in the United States. In the Soviet Union religious and nationality discrimination is practiced by the national government and is the product of governmental action. In the United States governmental policy is directed toward ending rather than extending discrimination. In the Soviet Union, as the current government-sponsored campaign against Jews illustrates, a minority is often utilized as a scapegoat to explain the shortcomings of national life. Instead, with us, our national commitment is to extend liberty and equality to all regardless of race, creed or color—to expose and eliminate, not to cultivate, discrimination.

Finally, a most significant difference between democratic and Communist societies lies in the recognition in democratic societies that a large part of the "substantive" rights of man depends upon his "procedural" rights—his freedom from oppressive procedures. Concerned as we are about ultimate ends, our way of life is equally concerned with methods and means. The rights of life and liberty can be assured only where there is also procedural due process of law. The right to due process embraces the right to trial before an impartial jury, the right to know the charges brought against one, to confront the accusers, to have the effective assistance of counsel, to assert the privilege against self-incrimination and to have protection against state-coerced confessions. Equally important to the liberties of a citizen is an independent judiciary, a judiciary comprised of judges who have not only the constitutional power but the courage to defend the liberty and personal security of the citizen against those wielding the official power of the state. It is not accidental that such important elements of due process are generally lacking in Communist countries. Nor is it accidental that the great writ of habeas corpus is unknown in the Soviet Union. That writ assures that a man will not be confined indefinitely by executive or police authority but will be promptly brought before a judicial magistrate.

Even Chairman Khrushchev has had to concede before the world that the Stalin period was characterized by a reign of secret police terror with utter disregard for due process of law. Although undoubtedly there is more "legality" in the Soviet Union today than under Stalin, Soviet "legality" still falls far short of protecting the freedom and dignity of man.

With concern for human rights firmly embedded in our national life and in our hearts, we stand ready to compete—to compete in the market of human values and in the protection and realization of individual liberties. This competition in ideals, rather than in material things, is the real challenge. In this competition we are not neutral. We are deeply committed. We believe in human rights not only for ourselves but for others as well. Although our nation does not believe in intervening in the internal affairs of other countries, we must be ever alert to cast our weight on the side of freedom and individual rights and to safeguard them against those who would intervene to deny them.

World Freedom Day, Philadelphia, Pa., July 1, 1964

LIBERTY UNDER LAW

The Shared Traditions of Freedom

Both our nations recognize the importance of individual freedoms. We both emphasize their value in the Preambles to our Constitutions. Yet perhaps because we agree with the eighteenth-century writer who said, "Every man by nature has the seeds of tyranny deeply implanted within him," we are not satisfied with declarations. You, in Part III of your Constitution, and we in our Bill of Rights—the first ten amendments to our Constitution—have gone on to guarantee explicitly such human liberties as freedom of expression, of religion, of the press; the right to trial by jury; the right not to testify against oneself; the right not to be tried twice for the same crime.

We all—Indians and Americans—believe in these freedoms because we are all participants in a noble experiment; this experiment is designed to prove that a nation can secure peace and prosperity for its citizens while still allowing them the freedom to say and think what they wish and to direct their own lives. Our experiment is only 188 years old; yours is but 16. Neither has existed for more than a few brief moments in the total span of human history. So far no one can say with certainty that our experiments will succeed. Yet we are both making progress towards the elimination of hunger, poverty and disease; we are also trying to guarantee to each of our citizens the liberty which will assure his dignity as an individual. Oliver Wendell Holmes, a Justice of our Court, pointed out the nature of our experiment and some of the reasons for it when he said:

Persecution for the expression of opinions seems to me perfectly logical. If you have no doubt of your premises or your power and want a certain result with all your heart you naturally express your wishes in law and sweep away all opposition. To allow opposition by speech seems to indicate that you think the speech impotent, as when a man says that he has squared the circle, or that you do not care wholeheartedly for the result, or that you doubt either your power or your premises.

But when men have realized that time has upset many fighting faiths, they may come to believe even more than they believe the very foundations of their own conduct that the ultimate good desired is better reached by free trade in ideas— that the best test of truth is the power of the thought to get itself accepted in the competition of the market, and that truth is the only ground upon which their wishes safely can be carried out. That, at any rate, is the theory of our Constitution.[1]

The vast majority of citizens in both our countries feel that this free trade in ideas—and freedom for the individual—is important because it is necessary if we are to build peaceful and prosperous societies; and, more than that, peace and prosperity are themselves meaningful only when accompanied by freedom.

Today I should like to examine specifically some of the rights protected by our Constitution and to illustrate for you the work of our Court. The rights I shall discuss are some of the more important of those given constitutional protection. First and perhaps most important, for it provides a matrix within which other rights flourish, is freedom of expression. This encompasses freedom to say what one wishes, to associate and organize with those one chooses, and to print what one pleases. The importance of this great liberty was well stated by John Milton when he wrote in behalf of freedom of the press:

I cannot praise a fugitive and cloistered virtue. . . . Give me the liberty to know, to utter, and to argue freely according to conscience, above all liberties. . . . And though all the winds of doctrine were let loose to play upon the earth, so Truth be in the field, we do injuriously, by licensing and prohibiting, to misdoubt her strength. Let her and Falsehood grapple: who ever knew Truth put to the worse in a free and open encounter?

Second, I shall discuss freedom of conscience as it finds expression in religion. Our Constitution, like yours, provides that there shall be complete freedom to worship as one chooses—and there shall be no state religion. Freedom of expression and freedom of religion are both protected by the First Amendment to our Constitution which reads:

Congress shall make no law respecting an establishment of religion, or prohibiting the free exercise thereof; or abridging the freedom of speech, or of the press, or the right of the people peaceably to assemble, and to petition the Government for a redress of grievances.

Our First Amendment guarantees those same rights protected by Articles 19, 25, 26, 27 and 28 of your Constitution.

Third, various guarantees are given to those accused of crimes. The Fifth and Sixth Amendments are similar to Articles 20, 21, and 22 of your Constitution; they provide that an accused shall have a speedy and public trial by jury, that he shall hear the charges against him, that he shall be able to confront and obtain witnesses, and that he shall be represented by counsel.

[1] *Abrams* v. *United States,* 250 U.S. 616, 630 (1919).

He must be indicted by a grand jury, he cannot be put twice in jeopardy for the same crime, and he cannot be compelled to testify against himself. Any prisoner may always apply for a writ of habeas corpus. A judge will then examine the legality of the imprisonment. If it can be shown that the prisoner's trial was illegal because these constitutional rights were violated, he will be freed. Thus the substantive rights of the Fifth and Sixth Amendments are combined with the great procedural writ of habeas corpus to make certain that there will be continued supervision over our system of criminal justice and that the basic rights of defendants will not be violated.

I shall conclude with a short discussion of the right to vote—a right which has been interpreted by our Court to mean that each person must have an equal vote. And I shall try to mention briefly a few of the other rights protected by our Constitution, which have raised difficult legal problems, such as the right to be a citizen and the right to privacy.

Before discussing these rights in greater detail I should point out two characteristics of the American legal system. We in the United States, like you in India, have made the judiciary the final arbiter of the constitutionality of the acts of the executive and legislative branches. This is not the only possible system. One might, for example, have a system—like that in Britain or France—in which the legislature itself carefully debates the constitutionality of each measure but once a law is passed it is unquestionably valid. Our systems, however, provide for a thorough review by judges. Once the Supreme Court of either of our countries holds that a law is unconstitutional it ceases to be a valid law.

We recognize that this institution of judicial review imposes an awesome responsibility upon our courts. Mr. Justice Holmes stated that to hold an Act of Congress unconstitutional "is the gravest and most delicate duty that . . . the Court is called on to perform."[2] Some have criticized this institution as undemocratic; but I do not agree. In fact, judicial review is perhaps one of the highest manifestations of democracy, for it is the means by which the majority imposes restraints upon itself in order to protect the rights of minorities. Just as the sane man develops the quality of self-control so that his strength will not be used to do wrong, so a nation must develop institutions which will control the strength of the majority. Judicial review is such an institution, for it says, in the words of Justice Black, "that no man or organization of men is ever outside the law—outside its protection or outside its limitation. Even the final power of the State is rationally measured . . . and must stop where the law stops it." The limit of the state's power is set by the state itself through its judges and its laws. Moreover, the judges are not really a *final* authority, for constitutional amendment is always possible.

[2] *Blodgett* v. *Holden*, 275 U.S. 142, 148 (1927).

In our country an amendment requires the vote of two-thirds of each House of Congress and must be ratified by three-fourths of the states. In India a two-thirds majority of voting members of each House of Parliament is necessary to pass most amendments and some must be ratified by one half the states. While the amendment process preserves flexibility for the majority, judicial review itself helps us create a government not of men but of laws —through its use, the majority ensures "equal justice under law" to *all* citizens.

A second characteristic of the American system which you must remember is that the first ten Amendments to the American Constitution originally were held to restrict only the federal government. If you recall, the First Amendment said that "*Congress* shall make no law" restricting speech. However, in 1864 the United States ratified the Fourteenth Amendment to the Constitution; it provided in part that no *state* shall deprive any person of "life, liberty or property without due process of law." In recent years the Court has held that the liberty which a *state* cannot take from a person includes most of those liberties which are protected from *federal* interference by the Bill of Rights. Many of our Court's decisions have been determinations of what it is to deprive a person of liberty without due process of law. This has resulted in a gradual extension of the protections of the Bill of Rights so that they protect individuals from action by the states as well as by the federal government.

If, before becoming specific, I may generalize about the trend of our Court's decisions, I should say that the Court has used the authority given it by its power of judicial review, the Bill of Rights, and the Fourteenth Amendment to safeguard primarily *personal* liberty. Our Court has protected the individual's liberty consistently in cases dealing with freedom of speech, of the press, of religion, and numerous other personal rights and freedoms. During a brief period of time at the beginning of this century, however, the Fourteenth Amendment's guarantee that no person shall be deprived of life, liberty, or property without due process of law was used to strike down laws incompatible with a particular *economic* philosophy. The Amendment's Due Process Clause was used "for example, to nullify laws prescribing maximum hours for work in bakeries,"[3] to prevent the setting of minimum wages for women,[4] and to hold unconstitutional a law which fixed the weight of loaves of bread.[5] While holding this view, the Court became a major obstacle to many of the economic reforms believed necessary during the 1920's and particularly during the depression of the 1930's. After a prolonged political crisis during which President Roosevelt threatened to ask

[3] *Lochner* v. *New York*, 198 U.S. 45 (1905).
[4] *Adkins* v. *Children's Hospital*, 261 U.S. 525 (1923).
[5] *Jay Burns Baking Co.* v. *Bryan*, 264 U.S. 504 (1924).

Congress for legislation allowing him to add a sufficient number of judges to the Court to ensure a majority for his economic views, the Court changed the tenor of its opinions and began to sustain the constitutionality of economic reforms.

Since the late 1930's the Court has called a halt to the use of the Due Process Clause as a means of invalidating economic regulatory measures believed by a majority of the Court to be unwise. The Court's current view as to this was stated by Justice Black in *Ferguson* v. *Skrupa*,[6] Justice Black said:

We refuse to sit as a "superlegislature to weigh the wisdom of legislation" and we emphatically refuse to go back to the time when courts used the Due Process Clause "to strike down state laws, regulatory of business and industrial conditions because they may be unwise, improvident or out of harmony with a particular school of thought." Nor are we able to or willing to draw lines by calling a law "prohibitory" or "regulatory." Whether the legislature takes for its textbook Adam Smith, Herbert Spencer, Lord Keynes, or some other is no concern of ours. The Kansas . . . statute [in this case] may be wise or unwise. But relief, if any be needed, lies not with us but with the body constituted to pass laws for the State of Kansas.

It has been said that the Court since the late 1930's has unduly expanded the Fourteenth Amendment's protection of personal rights and unduly contracted the effect of the Amendment in cases involving economic regulation. The Court is charged with having created a "double standard." I do not believe that this charge can be sustained if we refer to the intent of the Amendment's framers. There is every evidence that the Fourteenth Amendment was intended to protect the slaves newly freed by the Civil War and to protect personal rights in general. There is not a scintilla of evidence in the debates and reports that the Amendment was intended to abridge or curtail the police power of the state in any other way. In the *Slaughter-House* cases, speaking of the Civil War amendments, the Court said:

"We repeat, then, in the light of this recapitulation of events, almost too recent to be called history, but which are familiar to us all; and on the most casual examination of the language of these amendments, no one can fail to be impressed with the one pervading purpose found in them all, lying at the foundation of each, and without which none of them would have been even suggested; we mean the freedom of the slave race, the security and firm establishment of that freedom, and the protection of the newly-made freeman and citizen from the oppressions of those who had formerly exercised unlimited dominion over him."[7]

And in *Barbier* v. *Connolly*, the Court said:

But neither the [Fourteenth] Amendment—broad and comprehensive as it is— nor any other amendment was designed to interfere with the power of the State,

[6] 372 U.S. 726, 731-732 (1963).
[7] 83 U.S. (16 Wall.) 36, 71 (1873).

sometimes termed its police power, to prescribe regulations to promote the health, peace, morals, education, and good order of the people, and to legislate so as to increase the industries of the State, develop its resources, and add to its wealth and prosperity.[8]

These statements by Justices who could rightfully say that the history of these amendments "is fresh within the memory of us all" decisively refute the suggestion—implicit in the "double standard" charge—that the Court has now departed from the Constitution. Rather it is my conviction that the Court, in emphasizing the protection of personal freedoms, has returned to the single standard of the framers. Thus I do not find the current tendency of our Court to use both the Bill of Rights and the Fourteenth Amendment primarily to protect personal rights and liberties either surprising or revolutionary.

I think that I can best help you to understand the general trend of our Court's decisions protecting individual liberty by discussing recent problems and cases which have appeared before our Court in the area of each of the liberties I mentioned earlier.

Let me first discuss what is perhaps the most important freedom so long as we have governments which are selected by the people. This is freedom of expression which includes freedom of speech, freedom of the press, and freedom of association.

It is the American constitutional conviction that freedom of speech, of the press, and of association is at the core of all liberty. Justice Cardozo in his felicitous way observed that "Freedom of expression is the matrix, the indispensable condition of nearly every other form of freedom." Implicit in this statement is the recognition of the simple fact that "where men cannot freely convey their thoughts to one another, no other liberty is secure. Where freedom of expression exists, the germ of a free society is already present and a means is at hand for every extension of liberty." Both ancient and modern history teach that the first step of a regime moving toward autocracy is restraint and control of speech and press. This is invariably the beginning of the destruction of all other liberties. Thus our courts and yours are particularly wary of regulation of an expression of opinion; we view with the greatest suspicion any suppression of speech; and the clearest and most overriding state interest in regulation must be shown before an individual can be punished for what he says.

A recent American case illustrates the very heavy burden placed upon the government in showing that restriction of expression is justified.

In *Edwards* v. *South Carolina*, 187, Negro high school and college students

[8] 113 U.S. 27, 31 (1885).

were picketing peacefully in front of the state capitol in order to show their support for Negro rights. They were ordered by the police to move and when they refused to do so they were arrested and convicted of breach of the peace. South Carolina contended that the picketing "breached the peace" because it stirred the white onlookers "to anger, invited public dispute, or brought about a condition of unrest." The Supreme Court reversed the convictions, stating:

The Fourteenth Amendment does not permit a State to make criminal the peaceful expression of unpopular views. "[A] function of free speech under our system of government is to invite dispute. It may indeed best serve its high purpose when it induces a condition of unrest, creates dissatisfaction with conditions as they are, or even stirs people to anger. Speech is often provocative and challenging. It may strike at prejudices and preconceptions and have profound unsettling effects as it presses for acceptance of an idea. That is why freedom of speech . . . is . . . protected against censorship or punishment, unless shown likely to produce a clear and present danger of a serious substantive evil that rises far above public inconvenience, annoyance, or unrest. . . . ."[9]

Our Court has held that freedom of expression includes the right to associate with others and organize groups in order to make ideas effective. Several years ago the Court was faced with an Arkansas law which required all schoolteachers to list the names of all organizations to which they belonged. Arkansas is a Southern state in which lingers hostility to the National Association for the Advancement of Colored People, an organization instrumental in the fight for the rights of Negroes. To reveal that they were NAACP members would have exposed many of the teachers to much unpleasantness, perhaps rudeness by neighbors, perhaps even the loss of their jobs. The Court held that to require teachers to list the names of the organizations to which they belonged was unconstitutional because it interfered with their freedom of association, which is part of the freedom of expression guaranteed by the First Amendment. It would have discouraged them from belonging to the NAACP. Their right to organize and work for a set of political beliefs would have been hindered.[10] Might the listing requirement have been justified by a legitimate state interest? Perhaps the state was not really interested in discovering who belonged to the NAACP, but only wished to know which organizations its teachers belonged to so that it could discover if they were devoting enough time to their teaching duties. But even had this been the state's motive, in the opinion of the Court's majority it did not justify the danger the requirement posed to the teachers' freedom of association. If such an elaborate scheme of reasoning

[9] 372 U.S. 229, 237 (1963).
[10] 364 U.S. 479 (1960).

could be used to find a legitimate state interest, then many incursions on liberty could be justified.

Another freedom of association case decided last year [1963] presented the Court with a difficult problem of categorization: whether speech and association are protected "expression" or unprotected "solicitation."

The legislature of Virginia, drawing by analogy on the old common-law crime of barratry, made it a crime to solicit legal business for a lawyer who would be paid by an organization which had no direct pecuniary interest in the case. This law seriously handicapped the work of the NAACP in desegregating schools and other facilities in Virginia. The NAACP would send representatives into an area where schools were segregated. They would try to convince the Negroes living there to bring suits to desegregate the schools. If the resident Negroes agreed, lawyers would be supplied by and paid by the NAACP. Under the Virginia statute this activity would become illegal. The Supreme Court held that the Virginia statute was unconstitutional.[11] It saw the particular solicitation of legal business as part of a larger scheme of political expression. The NAACP was involved in a large-scale attempt to achieve equality of treatment for Negroes. Litigation was one of their weapons in this battle—essentially a political battle—and as such it was due some of the First Amendment's protection. Even dissenting members of the Court agreed that "Freedom of expression embraces more than the right of an individual to speak his mind. It includes also his right to advocate and his right to join with his fellows in an effort to make that advocacy effective. And just as it includes the right jointly to petition the legislature for redress of grievances, so it must include the right to join together for purposes of obtaining judicial redress."[12]

In these circumstances Virginia could not show an interest sufficiently important to justify forbidding the NAACP from supplying its lawyers to those who wished to begin suits. Their interest, that which justified the common law's prohibition of barratry, in forbidding the stirring up of litigation was not deemed sufficient. The Court was able to make effective the First Amendment protection of freedom of expression because it could weigh the importance of the provision to the state against the deprivation of liberty which it produced. The balance was struck in light of the strong policy of the Bill of Rights in favor of freedom of expression.

These recent cases show that the Court does much more than prevent *arbitrary* restraints on liberty. It protects freedom of expression by throwing the burden upon the state to show a legitimate reason for regulation. As our Court stated in *Thomas* v. *Collins,* "Any attempt to restrict those lib-

[11] *NAACP* v. *Button,* 371 U.S. 415 (1963).
[12] 371 U.S., at 452 (Harlan, J., dissenting).

erties must be justified by clear public interest, threatened not doubtfully or remotely but by clear and present danger. . . . Whatever occasion would restrain orderly discussion and persuasion . . . must have clear support in public danger, actual or impending."[13] And doubts are "resolved in favor of freedom of expression rather than against it."

I might give one more example, which involves freedom of the press. The Supreme Court just this year held, in the case of *New York Times* v. *Sullivan*,[14] that a newspaper cannot be sued for libel of a public official unless it is shown that the paper deliberately, with malice, published false and harmful information about the plaintiff. The *New York Times* published an advertisement asking for money to aid Martin Luther King, a Southern Negro leader. Certain statements in the ad were false; for example, the advertisement stated that King had been arrested on minor charges seven times, when actually he had been arrested only four times. Mr. Sullivan, a police commissioner of Montgomery, Alabama, claimed that he had been libeled by the advertisement because it implied that he had not done his job well. He won a $500,000 verdict. Newspapers could hardly publish if they were continually threatened with this sort of verdict for having made minor mistakes. The First Amendment is particularly concerned to protect that expression which criticizes the government. Thus, the Court held that a public official cannot recover a libel judgment in the absence of a malicious intent by the publisher. Although this will subject public officials to the risk of some harm resulting from false statements, it also will protect newspapers in their right to criticize freely.

In a concurring opinion I argued that the Court should have gone a step further. In my view the First and Fourteenth Amendments to the Constitution afford to the citizen and to the press an absolute, unconditional privilege to criticize official conduct despite the harm which may flow from excesses and abuses. I think that our Constitution allows every citizen to speak his mind and every newspaper to express its view on matters of public concern; no one may be barred from speaking or publishing because those in control of government think that what is said or written is unwise, unfair, false or malicious.

The ideal held before us for freedom of expression was well put by John Stuart Mill, when he stated:

If all mankind minus one were of one opinion, and only one person were of the contrary opinion, mankind would be no more justified in silencing that one person, than he, if he had the power, would be justified in silencing mankind. . . . We can never be sure that the opinion we are endeavoring to stifle is a false

---

[13] 323 U.S. 516, 530 (1945).
[14] 376 U.S. 254 (1964).

opinion; and if we were sure, stifling it would be an evil still. . . . Truth gains more even by the errors of one who . . . thinks for himself, than by the true opinions of those who only hold them because they do not suffer themselves to think. . . . In this age, the mere example of nonconformity, the mere refusal to bend the knee to custom, is itself a service.

The First Amendment to our Bill of Rights also provides for freedom of religion. Like Articles 25 and 26 of the Indian Constitution, it forbids interference with the free exercise of religion. And it goes on like Articles 27 and 28 of your Constitution to forbid the establishment of religion. Church and state are separate. The state cannot help the church, just as it cannot hinder it. The importance of this separation was well expressed by Gandhi when he wrote:

Any creed or dogma which coerces others into following one uniform practice is a religion only in name, for a religion worth the name does not admit of any coercion.

Two cases recently before our Court required us to investigate the concept of an "establishment of religion." One of them, *Engel* v. *Vitale*,[15] involved a prayer written by the New York State school authorities. Each day all the students in New York would begin class by reciting the few simple lines: "Almighty God, we acknowledge our dependence upon thee, and we beg thy blessings upon us, our parents, our teachers, and our Country." In the other case, *Arlington School District* v. *Schempp*,[16] class was begun with a reading of the Lord's Prayer, a Christian prayer, or reading from the Bible. The question presented was whether it was a violation of the constitutional principle of separation of church and state to allow these prayers in public schools.

The Court, in these and previous cases, recognized that our nation is a religious one. In *Schempp* Mr. Justice Clark, speaking for the Court, said, "The fact that the Founding Fathers believed devotedly that there was a God and that the unalienable rights of man were rooted in Him is clearly evidenced in their writings, from the Mayflower Compact to the Constitution itself."[17] Mr. Justice Black, also speaking for the Court, in *Engel* observed: "The history of man is inseparable from the history of religion. And . . . since the beginning of that history many people have devoutly believed that 'More things are wrought by prayer than this world dreams of.' "[18] Mr. Justice Douglas in *Zorach* v. *Clauson* recognized that "We are a religious people whose institutions presuppose a Supreme Being."[19] And

[15] 370 U.S. 421 (1962).
[16] 374 U.S. 203 (1963).
[17] 374 U.S., at 213.
[18] 370 U.S., at 434.
[19] 343 U.S. 306, 313 (1952).

in *Schempp* I observed that "Neither government nor this Court can or should ignore the significance of the fact that a vast portion of our people believe in and worship God and that many of our legal, political and personal values derive historically from religious teachings."[20]

It has long been held that parents have the right to send their children to private schools, including religious schools, where instructions may be given in religion and religious services may be held. Nonetheless, in *Engel* and *Schempp* the Court held that prayers and devotional readings from the Bible may not take place in public schools. The religious nature of the services in *Engel* and *Schempp*, the fact that they involved impressionable young children whose school attendance is required by statute, and the fact that the prestige, power and influence of the staff and authority of a government school are involved all combine to make these services a violation of the constitutional separation of church and state. We held that these practices violated the First Amendment.

The religious wars of the seventeenth century, the Inquisition, the burning at the stake of Michael Servetus in Geneva, seem far removed from these relatively inoffensive readings of prayers in schools. This is surely a good sign. Perhaps it indicates that mankind is beginning to realize the futility and senselessness of persecution because of religion. We can afford to be concerned about prayers in schools because most persons are allowed to practice their religion in perfect freedom.

However, I should like to suggest that the separation of church and state serves another important function in the United States and in India. The populations of our countries are made up of many diverse groups; we attempt to weld these groups into one homogenous unified nation. Keeping religion separate from the state helps prevent members of a minority religion from feeling separate and not a part of the state. Justice Frankfurter pointed out that when the state school becomes involved in religious services:

The children belonging to . . . nonparticipating sects will thus have inculcated in them a feeling of separatism when the school should be the training ground for habits of community, or they will have religious instruction in a faith which is not that of their parents. . . . These are consequences not amenable to statistics. But they are precisely the consequences against which the Constitution was directed when it prohibited the Government common to all from becoming embroiled, however innocently, in the destructive religious conflicts of which the history of even this country records some dark pages.[21]

Thus our separation of church and state has a positive and a negative aspect. It not only is an attempt to prevent religious persecution; it not only

[20] 374 U.S., at 306.
[21] *Illinois ex rel. McCollum* v. *Board of Education*, 333 U.S. 203, 227-228 (1948).

removes legal disabilities from members of minority religions, but it also attempts to promote national unity by creating harmony out of separate and individual consciences.

In turning to a discussion of the guarantees afforded criminal defendants, I think we should remind ourselves that, concerned as we are about ultimate ends, our way of life is equally concerned with method and means. The history of man's struggle to be free is in large degree a struggle to be free of oppressive procedures—the right to be free from test oaths and legislative attainder; the right to trial by jury; the right to confront the accuser face to face; the right to know the charge and to have a fair opportunity to defend.

Rather than discuss all of the rights of an accused, I should like to illustrate the work of our judiciary in this area by showing you how the right of a poor criminal defendant to have a lawyer supplied by the state has been developed and protected. One of the first cases on this subject to appear before our Court arose in 1932. The Scottsboro boys, a group of young Negroes, were accused of raping a white girl. Although the judge made a general appeal to the lawyers of Gadsden, Alabama, to defend young Powell and his friends, perhaps because of the hostility of the community, no one helped them. They were tried and convicted in one day. But the Supreme Court in *Powell* v. *Alabama*[22] reversed the conviction, holding that under the circumstances, since Powell was accused of a capital crime, and since feeling was so strongly aroused in the community, not to give Powell a lawyer violated the Fourteenth Amendment, for it deprived him of his life without "due process of law."

The Court gradually extended the requirement that an accused be furnished a lawyer, but the most important case in the area was decided only a year ago. Mr. Gideon, a poor man, a part-time gambler, who lives in Florida, was convicted of robbing a poolhall. Though he asked for a lawyer at his trial, he was not given one, for he could not afford a lawyer's fee and Florida did not supply lawyers free in all criminal cases. From prison Gideon wrote to the Supreme Court asking that he be released. The Court appointed a special counsel to argue the "right to counsel" issue before it. The Court's decision, overruling cases which held to the contrary, was that both state and federal government must give a defendant a lawyer in *any* criminal case if the defendant cannot afford to pay for one himself.[23] Not to do so is to deprive a person of his liberty without due process of law and to violate the Sixth Amendment's guarantee of a right to counsel. This guarantee now applies in all state as well as federal criminal cases. Mr. Gideon's case was

[22] 287 U.S. 45 (1932).
[23] *Gideon* v. *Wainwright*, 372 U.S. 335 (1963).

sent back to Florida. He was ordered retried; this time he was to be represented by a lawyer. At the new trial, it turned out that the state's primary
witness against Mr. Gideon was a very suspicious character who himself
might have committed the robbery. Gideon's court-appointed lawyer did
some investigating and at the trial was able to cast enough doubt on the
witness's testimony so that Gideon was acquitted. Today, Gideon is both
free and famous. Lest you think Mr. Gideon did not appreciate the Court's
decision, I should add that one day a thank-you note from Mr. Gideon
appeared in the mail of our Supreme Court.

The final case involving right to counsel which I wish to mention is one
decided this past term, *Escobedo* v. *Illinois*.[24] Danny Escobedo was arrested
for the murder of his brother. He was brought to the police station, questioned intensively, and he and his lawyer were refused permission to see
each other. At no time during the questioning was Escobedo warned that
what he said might be used against him, nor was he told that he had a right
to keep silent. He finally made several very damaging statements which
were taken down by a police attorney. He was then allowed to see his
lawyer. These statements were used against him at the trial and helped the
state to convict him.

The Supreme Court held that this conviction was unconstitutionally obtained because, on all the facts, Escobedo had been deprived of his right to
counsel.

Our Court has also recently decided cases involving the right of a defendant not to testify against himself—a right protected by Article 20 (3)
of your Constitution and the Fifth Amendment to ours. The privilege
against self-incrimination, as Erwin N. Griswold puts it, "registers an important advance in the development of our liberty—'one of the great land-
marks in man's struggle to make himself civilized.'" It reflects many of our
fundamental values and most noble aspirations: our unwillingness to subject
those suspected of crime to the cruel trilemma of self-accusation, perjury
or contempt; our preference for an accusatorial rather than an inquisitorial
system of criminal justice; our fear that self-incriminating statements will be
elicited by inhumane treatment and abuses; our sense of fair play which
dictates "a fair state-individual balance by requiring the government to
leave the individual alone until good cause is shown for disturbing him and
by requiring the government in its contest with the individual to shoulder
the entire load."[25]

Last term in *Malloy* v. *Hogan*,[26] our Court held that the Fifth Amendment's provision that no person can be compelled to testify against himself

[24] 378 U.S. 478 (1964).
[25] 8 Wigmore, Evidence 317 (McNaughton rev. 1961).
[26] 378 U.S. 478 (1964).

was one of the fundamental liberties which the Fourteenth Amendment protects against encroachment by the states. Mr. Malloy thus did not have to answer questions about his past gambling activities though he had been ordered to do so by Connecticut authorities. State governments no longer can compel a man to testify against himself in any way.

In *Murphy* v. *Waterfront Commission*[27] the Court eliminated a practice which had become all too prevalent. The federal or state government often granted a person immunity from prosecution and then forced him to testify. The sovereign which did not grant immunity would then prosecute him for a violation of one of its laws. The Court in *Murphy* held that this practice was unconstitutional, for a state may force a witness to answer a possibly incriminating question only if the witness is guaranteed immunity from any prosecution—state or federal—arising from his answers.

Before leaving the subject of protecting the rights of criminal defendants, I should like to add that such cases do not present only questions of liberty. It is important to remember that rich or well-connected defendants have little problem finding lawyers or in securing all the constitutional protections to which they are entitled. The indigent, the itinerant worker, the illiterate, the confused and poor will often not have good legal advice. Thus the extension of liberty by protecting the rights of criminal defendants is often a question of equality—of making certain that rich and poor are treated alike.

A giant step in the direction of such equality was taken in *Gideon* when it was held lawyers must be supplied free to poor defendants. But the Court has done more. In 1956 the Court struck down an Illinois law which conditioned appeal of a criminal conviction on the purchase of a transcript of the trial. This in effect denied an appeal to defendants who could not afford to buy the transcript. In holding this procedure unconstitutional, the Court said: "There can be no equal justice where the kind of a trial a man gets depends on the amount of money he has. Destitute defendants must be afforded as adequate appellate review as defendants who have money enough to buy transcripts."[28]

These general pronouncements have since been applied to a number of other state rules which limited the right to appeal.[29] And the Court has invalidated a number of state rules which permitted the trial judge and the public defender to decide, in effect, whether an indigent would be permitted to appeal.[30] Moreover, in *Douglas* v. *California*[31] the Court held that a defendant must also be provided a lawyer for his first automatic appeal.

[27] 378 U.S. 1 (1964).
[28] *Griffin* v. *Illinois*, 351 U.S. 12, 19 (1956).
[29] *Eskridge* v. *Washington*, 357 U.S. 214 (1958); *Burns* v. *Ohio*, 360 U.S. 252 (1959).
[30] *Draper* v. *Washington*, 372 U.S. 487 (1963); *Lane* v. *Brown*, 372 U.S. 477 (1963).
[31] 372 U.S. 353 (1963).

Since *Hardy* v. *United States*,[32] defendants in federal courts must be furnished free of charge with a transcript of proceedings to make appeal easier.

The problem of discrimination against the poor defendant in a criminal case is still very far from solution. The institution of bail is most unfair to the poor; the rich man can be released pending trial by posting a bond; the poor man who cannot afford the bond must languish in jail. Many minor infractions carry penalties which are put in the alternative: pay a fine or go to prison. The rich criminal pays his fine but the poor man is placed behind bars. A final injustice is the fact that an accused must pay the costs of his defense even if he is acquitted. Thus the man who is not rich enough to bear the cost easily and yet is not so poor that the state supplies him with a lawyer can be ruined financially, for he must bear the costs of trial though the result proves him innocent. And must not something be done to aid the victim of a crime? We should confront the problem of the victim directly; his burden is surely not alleviated by denying necessary services to the accused. Great Britain is experimenting with a system of government compensation for victims of crime. Society is in part responsible for the crimes which are committed, and society should assume at least some of the responsibility for repairing the injuries produced.

Though these problems are serious, some progress is being made toward their solution. The recent report of our Attorney General's Committee on Poverty and the Administration of Federal Criminal Justice was a milestone which promises to have continued influence. It has already led to the development of a public defender system for the federal courts. Moreover, a special section of our Department of Justice will be given the responsibility of seeing that trials and procedures in prosecutions by the government are fair to the accused. Projects are under way to re-examine the institution of bail. In the District of Columbia the entire problem of bail is being rethought; just a short time ago the first experiment was conducted in releasing an accused on his own recognizance pending trial.

Our nation is gradually becoming aware that the rights of criminal defendants must be safeguarded adequately not only to protect the innocent from false accusation but also to allow the poor equal justice. Our progress so far has been slow, but its rate increases rapidly as awareness of the problem grows.

I should now like to address myself briefly to another area where the concepts of equality and liberty overlap: the guarantee of the right to vote. The right to vote is, of course, the key political right in a representative democracy. A student of our Constitution, noting the framers' emphasis on

[32] 375 U.S. 277 (1964).

representative government and their commitment to political equality, would naturally conclude that the Constitution, whose source is the people, safeguards the right to vote so that the ballot of one citizen would have no more weight or influence than that of another in selecting legislative representatives. He would surely have to agree with what the Court recently said in *Gray v. Sanders:* "The conception of political equality from the Declaration of Independence, to Lincoln's Gettysburg Address, to the Fifteenth, Seventeenth and Nineteenth Amendments can mean only one thing—one person, one vote."[33] This concept of political equality basic to a democracy was urged by Madison in the *Federalist Papers* when he said, "Who are to be the electors of the federal representatives? Not the rich more than the poor; not the learned more than the ignorant; not the haughty heirs of distinguished names more than the humble sons of obscure and unpropitious fortune. The electors are to be the great body of the people of the United States. . . ." Yet it is only since the case of *Baker v. Carr,*[34] decided in 1962, that the Court has been willing to investigate the voting systems of the states to see if they were so unfair as to deprive citizens of their constitutional right to "equal protection of the laws." Once the Court expressed willingness to hear this type of claim, a host of lawsuits revealed that many states provided for the election of representatives to state legislatures in very unfair ways. Some electoral districts were far larger than others, so that in some states voters in one district (usually farm areas) had 35 to 40 times the voting power of voters in the cities. Just last term in *Reynolds v. Sims*[35] and several other cases, our Court held that the seats in both houses of state legislatures "must be apportioned on a population basis." In other words, all electoral districts for state legislatures and all Congressional districts within a state must contain approximately the same number of voters. The vote of each citizen must be counted equally.

These recent decisions fit within the Court's traditional protection of voting rights. We have held that states cannot prevent persons from voting because of their race; nor can political parties prevent citizens from voting in a party primary on racial grounds. We have now simply held that states cannot deprive any group of their right to vote by making the votes of some worth less than the votes of others. People who live in cities and suburbs will have the same proportionate voice as those who live on farms.

Before concluding I should like to mention very briefly a few of the other liberties which our Court has been called upon to protect.

[33] 372 U.S. 368, 381 (1963).
[34] 369 U.S. 186 (1962).
[35] 377 U.S. 533 (1964).

Several cases before us have involved the rights of citizenship. In *Kennedy* v. *Mendoza-Martinez*[36] we held that Congress could not deprive a man of citizenship because he deliberately stayed outside the country to avoid being drafted into the army. The Court stated that deprivation of citizenship is a severe punishment; therefore it cannot be inflicted without all of the safeguards of a criminal trial, including indictment, notice, confrontation, jury trial, assistance of counsel, and compulsory process for obtaining witnesses. *Schneider* v. *Rusk*,[37] which appeared before us just a few weeks ago [May 18, 1964], decided that naturalized citizens cannot be treated differently than native-born citizens. Thus a statute which deprived a naturalized citizen of his citizenship if he continuously resides for three years in his country of origin was found unconstitutional because no restriction on the length of foreign residence applied to native-born citizens. The only difference between the two classes of citizens which exists is that qualification, written into our Constitution, which states that only a native-born citizen can become President of the United States.

Our Court has also had many cases involving what Mr. Justice Brandeis considered the supreme right, "The right to be let alone—the most comprehensive of rights and the right most valued by civilized men." This right is in part guaranteed by our Fourth Amendment's prohibition of all "unreasonable searches and seizures." Our Court has been primarily concerned with devising a method by means of which this prohibition can be enforced. The state and local governments are notoriously unwilling to punish policemen who have caught criminals by making illegal searches. A private right of action is usually worthless, for a convicted criminal will have the greatest difficulty in proving and collecting damages from the policeman who arrested him. Against this it has been argued that if we do not allow illegally seized evidence to be admitted at a trial, then the criminal goes free solely because the policeman erred. Our Court has chosen the last-mentioned course in spite of its disadvantages. In *Mapp* v. *Ohio*[38] we held that illegally obtained evidence could not be admitted in state or federal trials. Although some guilty persons will escape punishment because of the policeman's error, this seems the only practical way to discourage police departments from conducting illegal searches.

Indian Law Institute, New Delhi, September, 1964

---

[36] 372 U.S. 144 (1962).
[37] 377 U.S. 163 (1964).
[38] 367 U.S. 643 (1961).

2 🙠

Human Needs and Social Justice

Wealth is a pleasure, but it is also an obligation. And the people of our most fortunate nation have a clear and undeniable obligation for the humane and decent treatment of the less affluent among us, the lame and the blind, the children of those who have suffered misfortune, the adult worker who cannot find a job through no fault of his own, the youth who sits on the doorsteps of the city slums without prospect of either education or work, the person denied full access to opportunity because of his race or color or religious belief.

American Public Welfare Association, Chicago, Ill., November 29, 1961

THE MORAL BASIS OF SOCIAL ACTION

To Pray for Light

My own interpretation of Social Action—a subject which I understand you have been discussing—is a very simple one: it is to act, to bring the force of ethical ideals and religious insights strongly to bear upon important social problems.

I can think of no great issue of the day—from hard-core unemployment to foreign aid—that does not involve ethical imperatives and moral judgments, whether or not they are recognized as such. Religion has been a driving force in Western society throughout its entire formation; when religion ceases to inform and inspire, when the social action of religion fails to have an impact upon the people and the state, then the road to the concentration camp, to the suppression of right, to the confinement of the individual is made broad and wide.

Our synagogues and churches today are too often silent, too often afraid to offend, too often the victims of the conformity of thought and the tyranny of community thinking they should deplore and expunge from society. This is certainly not the lesson of the prophetic tradition of the Old Testament. The prophets were in the thick of it; their voices rose above the people. Nor is it the lesson of the New Testament, which proclaimed a faith that society, the world itself, could be changed. Neither the Jew nor the Christian can stand in the light of his tradition and declare that his faith exists in a vacuum of theology and introspection.

I believe that the cherished constitutional doctrine of the separation of church and state was drawn, here in America, because of a belief in the independence and effectiveness of churches, not out of fear of them. A free church has no obligation but to its own conscience. The National Council of Churches, the Catholic Bishops, this Union and the other organized Jewish religious groups often do speak out. Pope John XXIII's Encyclical is the most recent major statement from a religious leader that deals in modern social and economic problems. We should have more, and not less, of this from the churches. And we should have specifics, not only guiding generalities.

The obligation to speak carries with it, also, the obligation to speak in favor as well as against. The church, the temple, the meetinghouse, the synagogue have been sounding boards of dissent. Castigation of material values and denunciation of the stultifying American preoccupation with things is a common and tolerated expression of religion. But how about the reverse of that—advocacy and endorsement? The compulsion to denounce and attack is a strong one, as one who has sat through his share of sermons knows, but I have not heard from the pulpit in equally clear tones support for controversial proposals in matters of public policy which should command the attention of the synagogues. Castigation has its place, but we must also set our feet on the right path and lift our vision to the greater horizon.

One of the great rabbis of Reform Judaism, Stephen Wise, understood and accentuated the positive as well as the negative. He is remembered not only for his high moral statements in regard to a just and fair society but also for his support, endorsement and leadership in the fight for a minimum wage, for legislation to aid the migrant worker, for housing acts to eradicate slums. Rabbi Wise joined more committees than you can think of—and so should you, whether you are religious or lay leaders, if you really believe in religious and moral principles as guides to human action. Your fellows in the congregation will respect the right of any individual to do so.

Nor should the disagreement or disapproval of a minority discourage the leaders of a congregation from speaking out on specific matters of public policy, on particular pieces of legislation and particular bills. In American life it is understood that no one man speaks monolithically for an entire group, and those who speak out make that clear themselves.

I welcome the Washington Center for Religious Action. I hope it will join with other similar centers, such as the National Catholic Welfare Council and the National Council of Churches, in expressing the ethical principle in relation to specific proposals. In the age of the specialist we often make the rabbi and the priest and the minister the specialist in that limited area, confined to a certain time each week, in which we meet a religious obligation as we would a luncheon date or a club session. But we tell him to keep his nose out of our business, out of our private affairs, out of our community life—except when we need him for a benediction—and out of our government.

Well, he who accepts that shirks his vocation. The men in our Congress and in our government welcome the advice and opinion of men of faith. They listen to their voices with respect. And consider the experience of those communities faced with the often difficult challenge of achieving full equality for all in their educational systems. In those places where religious leadership has come forward and exerted the moral initiative, we have seen an extraordinary influence for good.

Show me a community in which religious leaders are willing to lead, and I will show you a community that is willing to face its problems. Show me a nation in which religious leadership stands to be counted on every important social and economic issue, and I will show you a nation that will hold its head high before all of history.

There is a growing debate in this nation about our system of providing welfare for the needy; there is a question whether our unemployment insurance system is adequate to our needs; there is the problem of persistent long-term unemployment and the stress it places on family life and individual dignity; there is the mounting problem of unemployment among our youth, especially in urban areas; there is the question of equality and the denial of equality in economic life; there is the question of trade policies and their effect upon people here, and upon the long-range good of the country; there is the question of housing and urban development.

All of these embrace moral issues. All of them reflect the purpose of our society—a purpose that is defined morally or not at all. All of them find expression in individual policies of government and proposals in the Congress. All of them merit and deserve from religion a genuine response.

I must turn to another layman to find the keynote of my feelings about the purpose of Social Action, in the face of issues I have raised and in the momentous world decisions that confront us. In 1949 William Faulkner brought honor to himself and to the United States when he was awarded the Nobel Prize for literature. In his acceptance speech he stated a conviction that I share, and that motivates men of good will the world over. "I decline," he said, "to accept the end of man. It is easy enough to say that man is immortal simply because he will endure. . . . I refuse to accept this. I believe that man will not merely endure; he will prevail."

The triumph of man is uniquely in the keeping of religion—the informing of his spirit, the firing of his conscience, the awakening of his soul to the fact that in observing the spirit of the Lord he is exercising the only true freedom. But these need not be slogans on banners nor messages on wreaths laid at the feet of monuments to past and meaningless events. They need not be so incarcerated into history as to be beyond the reach of living men. In one of the great passages of Homer, Ajax, surrounded by darkness and facing his foes, prays for light "that we may see our fate, and die at least, if such thy will, in the open light of day." He does not pray for victory; he does not pray to live; he prays for light, that he may stand to the full height of a man and face his fate.

Today we also seek light. We seek it not to avoid our problems but to face them as true men. We do not seek religion to remove our trials, to tranquilize our problems—but for light, for illumination, for the true meaning of moral and ethical imperatives. Over 63 per cent of our population are members of churches. Over 114 million persons of all faiths, testifying to a greater Power, and practicing religion in their own way. Perhaps a great number of them do not realize the stakes in the world, unless they read of the recent suppressions and persecutions of Jewish leaders in the Soviet Union, unless they hear of the closing of Catholic churches behind the Iron Curtain, unless they read of the arrest and conviction of Protestant missionaries.

Religious tolerance has become a touchstone of freedom. Where tolerance is found, there also free men dwell. Religious intolerance has become a touchstone of totalitarianism, as Hitler and Stalin demonstrated, and as Khrushchev is demonstrating now. The history of all churches, through all ages, has demonstrated that religion must recognize its obligations as well as its rights to preach and practice moral values, or fail in its mission. This is the light that illuminates a real democratic political system. Social Action for the churches and synagogues is necessary for society—and for the churches and synagogues themselves if they are to maintain their vitality as living forces in a society whose fate will be decided by the pressing social problems of a modern age. Socially minded churches and synagogues are guarantees that religion will be an ally, not an enemy, of democracy.

Social Action in these terms means more than bulletins and rallies and letters one to another. It means helping this nation go forward here at home —realizing the just society, defending the rights of all citizens to full citizenship, commending and supporting good legislation, speaking out on important matters, leading in the fields of equality of opportunity for all, and an economic chance for every man. And it means helping this nation to realize its objective abroad—peace in freedom for all who seek it.

I believe that the fate of free religion in the world is part and parcel of the fate of our own nation. The survival and success of our political ideals is crucial to the survival and success of the free religions that flourish within our borders. Not only Judaism and democracy, not only Christianity and democracy, but religion itself and democracy have a mutual interest in this troubled world. When communism comes—whether to a Buddhist or a Moslem or a Hindu or a Christian or any other nation—religion goes.

The President has described the path to freedom as a lonely one. We have no illusions about the difficulty of the road, or the perils that lie along it. But we will make that journey in good spirit. While preserving the separation of church and state in our country, we proudly assert the right of all religious groups, all churches and synagogues to preach what is good and what is more important—if a layman may say so—practice what is good.

General Assembly of the Union of American Hebrew Congregations, Washington, D.C.,
November 15, 1961

The General Welfare

I would like to put a proposition to you this morning. It is this: "First, one may not take as the ultimate criteria in economic life the interests of individuals or organized groups, nor unregulated competition, nor excessive power on the part of the wealthy, nor the vain honor of the nation or its desire for domination, nor anything of this sort. Rather, it is necessary that economic undertakings be governed by justice and charity as the principal laws of social life. The second point [is that it is] basic . . . that both within individual countries and among nations there be established a juridical order, with appropriate public and private institutions, inspired by social justice, so that those who are involved in economic activities are enabled to carry out their tasks in conformity with the common good."

I am sure that this audience will recognize that I am not quoting from the President's Council of Economic Advisors but from Pope John's Encyclical "Mater et Magistra." I believe the Holy Father's statement is sound. I believe it is good ethics and good morality and good economics. And I believe that our forefathers, drawn from many religious faiths, echoed the same essential point of view when they wrote into the Constitution, as one of the fundamental purposes of a government, the promotion of the general welfare. I am convinced that the common good, or the public interest, or, in the words of our great founding document, "the general welfare" is indeed a true and honest measure of individual responsibility.

In the United States today this is not only a principle established by the founders of the nation and determined by democratic philosophy of self-government—it is also an imperative dictated by world circumstances. We have been stressing the national interest. The President has been stressing it; I have been stressing it; the entire Administration has been stressing—and we have been doing so because the world situation demands it. But nothing we have said indicates in any way that we do not want to or cannot advance standards in America the way we have always done. An important part of our foreign policy, indeed the bedrock of our ability to construct and implement a foreign policy, is what we do here at home.

Here at home the impact of automation upon employment and business practice; the need for a stable price level; the need to maintain a balance of payments that will not threaten our gold reserve; the need for greater economic growth to put unused capacity and idle men and women back to work; the need to eliminate the vestiges of poverty—all these needs converge at the point of national policy.

The dimensions of the task are very, very great. We seek to maintain a growing economy with a stable price level, and to set about lifting the depressed elements of our population to a level more commensurate with the dignity of human life. At the same time we must discharge our responsibilities to the world community. We seek to ensure the freedom of the collective bargaining relationship and encourage the pursuit of wage and price policies that contribute to national goals and purposes. These are complex and heavy tasks. Those who accept them do not endear themselves to all of the segments of our society all of the time; nor do they receive the plaudits of every group every time. But in this world there is no escaping the responsibility, and I can assure you that the President has no intention of escaping it.

Free men will reserve to themselves their precious right to agree or disagree, to consent or dissent. But free men will also, I believe, understand the nature of the responsibilities they face. They will recognize the desirability and the necessity of exercising responsibility, of acting in the best interest of the nation even though other interests may be involved.

I have not related these remarks to any specific issues that have occupied the national attention over the past few years, and I have not done so with purpose. Issues involve many facts, many claims and counterclaims, many particular circumstances and considerations; they must be dealt with practically and pragmatically. But we must also give attention to the ideals behind the actions, to the motivation that all of us acknowledge, to the overriding purposes we set for ourselves and our country.

As every man of religious conviction knows in his heart, these rest in man's spirit.

Communion Breakfast, Local #3, International Brotherhood of Electrical Workers,
New York, N.Y., May 6, 1962

The Moral Issue of Unemployment

You have asked me to speak on economic conditions. In doing so I would like to accept your own frame of reference. You view man as a moral being, capable of decision and commitment and thus responsible action. Economic life, the sum of individual choices, thus has moral roots. Economic issues are, in the last analysis, moral issues.

This is true not only in regard to businesses with obvious ethical implications but to every business, every labor union, and every individual job. The businessman, the labor leader, and the individual working person who believe ethics have no place in the business world are saying that our society has no place in man's history. A morally inert people is a doomed people.

With that conviction as a preface, I would like to describe some of the moral aspects of hard-core unemployment.

Yesterday afternoon, the Department of Labor released the latest figures on area labor market trends. They reveal that of the nation's 150 major labor markets, a record number of 101 continue to experience substantial unemployment. The number of smaller communities with this persistent problem grew between March and April from 184 to 199.

These areas are spread all over the country. The question is: What causes them? Hard-core unemployment, with its killing impact on the life of a small community, is the waste product of progress. A new product shoulders an old one out of the market. A new technique makes obsolete older ones. A natural resource is no longer a prime source. An industry gives way to new competition. Progress continues. Improvements are made. But in the wake—human distress. We all benefit from progress, and we should all bear its cost. A society that looks to its industrial complex to provide a rising standard of living must also return its fair share of energy and resources to provide for those whom progress harms. That is a moral commitment that a free society must make.

In the past we have resorted to different devices to fulfill this obligation. Management and labor have bargained privately and collectively. From this have come a number of benefits in the welfare and pension area that protect the individual. Government has instituted programs, like the unemployment insurance system, to tide a working family over periods of transition.

The situation we face now is this: Collective bargaining, by its nature, cannot contribute permanent solutions to hard-core unemployment. Government programs, for their part, cannot and should not carry the whole load. Some new form of creative partnership linking private and public policy is needed.

The President's Advisory Committee on Labor-Management Policy will be breaking some ground in this field. But it is not, in itself, the instrument through which the partnership is achieved. Labor and management must do much more than they have done to provide resources for retraining and training. They must do more to understand the problem they face in common. They must do more to achieve a spirit of understanding, on the industry level and the plant level.

Government has a great role to play. The precedent of the Area Redevelopment Bill is a good one. It indicates how the resources of the people as a whole can be brought to bear upon the problems we face in several particular areas.

And certainly the states and local governments can and must do more about hard-core unemployment. In those places where the people of a community, and their state government, have responded to the obligation, they have developed a plan and a program. That in itself is a beginning. Perhaps they need more capital. Perhaps they need more knowledge. Perhaps they need more facilities. Whatever their need, they have met the first one—and that is to respond, to accept the obligation, and to discharge it as far as they are able.

Here, then, are three powers that society has at its disposal to discharge its obligation rising from hard-core unemployment. Each can make a significant contribution. And the contribution of each is necessary. What force can bring them together into a working relationship? In this nation we have traditionally relied upon the moral force of the people themselves. The President and his administration have been calling national attention to the problem of unemployment in the hope that public opinion will make itself felt—upon businessmen, upon labor leaders, upon local officials, and upon national officials.

It is here that an organization such as yours can render a valuable service. Public opinion often speaks through your councils. You give voice to popular assent regarding moral obligation. You know the profound personal distress inherent in long-term unemployment. You realize, too, that powers exist to alleviate it. The force to create the partnership of those powers is the kind that you wield.

Immense changes come rapidly in the modern world. History accelerates. Old patterns of life and forms of activity break. And there is nothing to guarantee that change will not harm many individuals outside of our determination that it shall not. In a world where poverty is the common condition of most of mankind, our willingness to bend every resource for the benefit of a person adversely affected by change is a concrete demonstration of our moral commitment to better each individual life.

In doing what is economically sound we also do what is morally right. That is the kind of action upon which we should stand, and the kind that a free society, in performing, shows its enduring merit and value.

General Board of Christian Social Concerns of the Methodist Church, Washington, D.C.,
April 26, 1961

The Future Belongs to Faith

Oliver Wendell Holmes, Jr., wrote to William James: "The great act of faith is when man decides that he is not God."

Today man has seized the power that many an ancient god was never granted; Zeus' thunderbolt is a toy when measured against a nuclear bomb. But man is still not God—and the great danger in the world is that he will not become godlike and walk in charity and humility and forgiveness.

Someone once described history as a race between education and catastrophe; I think it is rather a problem of moral enlightenment. Moral behavior is a product of belief. What happens, we might ask, in a society that begins by rejecting religion, refusing belief, turning its face away from the spiritual? Its behavior will be entirely pragmatic and self-centered, its goals material, and its word reliable only as long as it suits its purpose. We presently confront such a society.

We must ask ourselves further, then: Are we disadvantaged by our own convictions and our own honor? Is the moral nation endangered by its own sense of responsibility to the truth?

I am firmly convinced the opposite is true. As I view man's comparatively brief history, especially that of civilization, I am struck by the fact that we are going away from the barbaric, the brutal, the nonmoral, and going toward higher spiritual discovery and understanding.

The future belongs to faith, but it still takes courage and will to realize it.

Washington Cathedral, Washington, D.C., October 9, 1961

The Liberal Spirit

Today we are challenged on a far broader scale than the liberal thinkers and doers of the last century, and the century before that. Their concern was individual right in a new land. Ours is individual dignity among all peoples of the world.

Our sense of morality and our sense of practicality tell us that we cannot long survive—and are not worthy to survive—as an island of affluence and smug contentment surrounded by rising currents of hunger, disease and privation. The whole family of man is discovering that the cord of birth is not an unbreakable chain to poverty. This explosion of aspiration, blasting loose the centuries-old crust of economic exploitation and class division, finds its charge in the idealism of our own Revolution and in the success that freedom enjoys in this land. We have long thought that words like "liberty of thought and action" and "freedom from want" were peculiarly American in origin—as though we had a copyright on them. We now are awakening to the fact that they are the common property of all humanity.

It is against this background that the challenges to the liberal spirit are and must be measured. And only in this scale can the urgent measures being advanced for domestic economic growth and social equality be fully understood.

I am going to discuss some of those domestic measures today, but I would first like to emphasize that the liberal spirit of which I speak is not a political nor a partisan attitude. It is rather that attitude described by the Spanish philosopher Salvador de Madariaga: "To define what is desirable; to define what is possible at any time within the scheme of what is desirable; to carry out what is possible in the spirit of what is desirable."

I am fond of that quotation, and I have mentioned it at times before. Each time I do, someone writes to me recommending a complementary quote. Earlier this week I received a letter from here in New York suggesting a line from Genesis: "A ladder was set up on the earth, and the top of it reached to heaven."

It is this attitude of idealism based upon the possible that is characteristic of the liberal. . . .

I recently completed a three-day, five-state trip through areas where unemployment is substantial. The impact from a trip like that is the shock of recognition when the neat statistic on the Washington memorandum becomes the bewildered and discouraged human being waiting for a relief check or a food package. Some people have questioned my choice of language in describing this situation. They object to the word "recession" and they say that all of my economic brushes are black. With 5½ million persons wanting to work but unable to find work, with the incomes of those families cut off so that the mortgage payment and the doctor bill and the tuition fee suddenly go begging, with over half of our major industrial areas classified as depressed, with industrial production declining again for the sixth straight month, with payrolls and personal income falling off, with long-term unemployment growing at a rapid rate—I can only reply that to ignore the gravity, and the truth, of this recession is to do the worst kind of disservice to the American people.

Let us remember that the gravity of the present unemployment problem is due not only to business cutting back but to a long-term trend throughout the manufacturing industries, a trend especially severe during a recession but latent in good times as well. The poor recovery from the 1958-1959 recession, coupled with this long-term trend in manufacturing, is sufficient reason, I believe, to express deep concern about the economy getting back onto the track as soon as possible. And ample reason to call a spade a spade.

Now, this recession will end. There is no question of that, and we are going to help it end. The President is sending to the Congress several programs designed to get us moving again: to bring long-needed, in many cases desperately needed, aid to depressed areas; to increase the minimum wage; to provide additional unemployment insurance benefits to those who have exhausted their present ones. In addition, he has taken several administrative actions, from the pilot food stamp plans to releasing veterans' insurance dividends early, to relieve human distress and increase the tempo of the economy.

These are first measures, not total programs. I have said, and I will say again, that the forward progress of the economy rests primarily with private industry in the United States and its ability to provide good jobs at good wages. This Administration, working now to revive economic life, will move forward with broad policies to create a climate of business opportunity that will fuel a higher rate of economic growth.

Concern for human welfare, for a just society, and concern for business advancement are not incompatible—they are complementary. We face the task of creating more than a million new jobs each year to provide for the merely normal increase in our labor force, without reference to national and international obligations. Another million jobs a year will be needed to provide employment alternatives to working people displaced by improvements leading to needed higher productivity. We know the size of the job before us and we know the responsibility rests upon a flourishing enterprise system that encourages new business and expansion of old business. But we also know that one cannot trust to blind economic forces to provide for the serious human problems that economic change sometimes brings. That is the work of men's minds and men's hearts. Judge Brandeis wrote that the Founding Fathers considered "the final end of the State is to make men free to develop their faculties" and thought that in their government "the deliberate forces should prevail over the arbitrary." In government's response to the question of economic growth, the freeing of men to develop their faculties is an end met not only by encouraging business but also by providing for the welfare of distressed persons whom economic change has deprived of opportunity.

This is an approach to governing, a reading of responsibility, in which all men of good heart can and should share. Brandeis, in the same paragraph I mentioned, said that "the greatest menace to freedom is an inert people." I think you will agree with me that inertia is not one of the marks of a liberal disposition. We need that energy, that conviction, that willingness to think and work for a better national life.

New problems require new programs. New times necessitate new ideas. Under the bust of Mark Twain in the Hall of Fame are written these words: "Loyalty to petrified opinion never yet broke a chain or freed a human soul."

Liberal Party Testimonial Luncheon, New York, N.Y., February 18, 1961

EQUAL JUSTICE UNDER LAW

The Advance toward Equality

I am honored to have this welcomed opportunity to speak to the students and faculty of Howard University at this beginning of another school year. I know that you share with me great anticipations about the future—the future of opportunity, the future of equality, the future of our nation. That anticipation stood in the shadow of forlorn hope for many years, but now I believe we are in the act of breaking through in our search for full equality and in the effort to achieve one class of citizenship for all of our people.

The question of genuine, practical equality has been put to law—and the law has responded affirmatively. The great landmark, of course, was the school desegregation decision of the Supreme Court, followed by other decisions outlawing segregation in our national life.

But beyond this referral to law, this necessary clarification of right in a society governed by law, the question of equality has been submitted to the American conscience by Negro citizens themselves—by the simple act of asserting their citizenship.

The clear identification of right and the actual exercise of that right are bringing us closer to the day when right is realized without difficulty. I am fully aware that many well-meaning people say that they wish the Negro wouldn't press so hard. Well, let me put to them a simple proposition. Can anybody be condemned for asserting a constitutional right in a democracy, so long as it is done in a legal way without violence? I think not.

I salute the courage of the little child who walks to school under her legal and constitutional right to do so, often in a hostile environment. And I salute the courage of the parents who allow the children they love to be exposed to possible abuse and violence because they know that for the child's ultimate good this action must be taken. Incidentally, I read a story the other day about the mother of a little white girl who came to pick her daughter up after the first day of desegregation in the second grade of one of our Southern schools. "How did everything go in school?" the mother asked. The answer came promptly. "There was a little Negro girl sitting next to me all day." Cautiously the mother then asked: "What happened?" And her daughter replied: "We were both so scared, we held hands all day."

I cannot see where the exercise of right is anything but a good thing for America, both soon and late. I believe the advance toward equality will succeed because it is taking place within law, and within the protection of human right. Long ago in this country, at a time when the purpose of economies and the reason for social organizations were being called into question all over the world, the American labor movement faced the decision whether to seek its goals within the framework of political freedom and economic free enterprise or whether to strike out for new social forms and economic arrangements. It has become a great force for good in our nation because it chose for law and freedom and took its place as a free institution in an existing free order. Today the Negro citizens of our nation seek equality within law, and that is why we will succeed in realizing equality.

I would be remiss, and I am sure that you will forgive me if I do so, if I did not mention the contribution of the Kennedy Administration to the new climate of opportunity. In the eight short months of the Kennedy Administration we have seen truly outstanding advances toward our goal of equality.

First, the very election of President John F. Kennedy was a symbol of the revolution which is taking place in American life. No more can it be said that a man's religion is an unfortunate handicap to his right to seek high office. President Kennedy's election has been accompanied by appointments on all levels in the executive branch in which religious or racial attributes have been disregarded. This is the way it is and the way it will be in this Administration.

Second, this Administration stands completely behind the decisions of the United States Supreme Court declaring segregation unconstitutional. We support these not only because they are decisions of the Supreme Court, and as such must be obeyed by law-abiding citizens, but because they are decisions which are morally right.

Third, this Administration has issued clear and strong executive orders which spell out how discrimination is to be eliminated with respect to work in and for the government. Under the chairmanship of our distinguished Vice-President, Lyndon Johnson, and with myself as vice-chairman, the Equal Opportunity Committee will enforce the President's executive order. This order means exactly what it says. It speaks for the President and for the Vice-President. Its enforcement will be fair, reasonable, but firm. And every department and agency of the government has pledged itself in its employment and procurement policies to implement the executive order.

I believe that these achievements are something for all Americans to be proud of. Of course, we still have a long road to go before we can achieve our goals.

The administrative actions I have listed, and all of the efforts to eliminate second-class citizenship, are taking place against a background of gradually improving economic position. In the twenty years from 1939 to 1959 wage and salary incomes for Negro workers rose some 400 per cent, while that of white workers was going up by 300 per cent. Today, however, the Negro suffers an unemployment rate about twice as high as that experienced by the white worker. This is because of the large proportion of Negro workers in the unskilled and semiskilled ranks—the first to be laid off during a recession and the last to be rehired. The plain economic fact is that there will be a permanent employment depression in the kinds of jobs that unskilled workers have held in America. My concern over that, I might say, is balanced by my confidence in our economic future when I stand before an audience such as this one.

From this audience, I feel sure, will come the leaders of the future—and we can hopefully predict that there will be no bar to their participating fully in American life. We have made a start toward breaking down those bars. . . . Today in Washington and throughout the federal service any job, every job, is open to a Negro, or a Catholic, or a Jew, if he can qualify. No longer is a man's or a woman's position in the federal service predestined at birth regardless of their abilities. And we in this Administration do not believe that *any* person's ultimate position in life, economically or socially, should be determined by the chance of birth.

I believe it is clear that this Administration is determined to provide affirmative leadership to implement its constitutional duty and to fulfill the moral imperative to eliminate discrimination in government employment and in work on government contracts. This we are fully determined to do at all reasonable speed. But government cannot do the job alone.

The community itself must face its responsibilities. The denial of opportunity in employment, promotion and upgrading is far too prevalent in commerce and industry and must be corrected by the managers of our industrial life. And in the years ahead, as our employment patterns change from predominantly blue-collar to predominantly white-collar, executive and professional employment, it will be more and more important to insist that opportunity in such employment not be foreclosed because of prejudice.

I think businessmen have a particularly important contribution to make in this area. They can help, as community leaders, to establish a climate of understanding in those communities where discrimination is the established pattern, by practicing nondiscrimination in their hiring and promotion policies. While there have been some businessmen who have done an outstanding job, in this respect, too often businessmen are too timid in playing their full part.

Likewise labor unions, which have proclaimed laudatory objectives in this field and are to be commended for what has been accomplished so far, have much yet to do. The time is past when it is tolerable for trade unions to restrict apprenticeship or to deny membership to anyone because of race, religion or color. The very nature of trade unionism, its moral origins, demands that trade unions truly be their brother's keeper. A trade union cannot justify discriminatory practices and policies on the ground that it is no different from other members of the community. Trade unionism as a way of life imposes the highest requirements of moral behavior, and particularly in the area of economic opportunity.

Recently the President set up a task force on employee-management relations in the federal service. I serve as chairman of this group. One of our first actions was to state categorically that we would not deal with any employee organization that practices discrimination.

I have this past week directed that a full and complete study be made of apprenticeship programs in this country to determine the prevalence of discriminatory practices. I intend to see to it that no support or recognition is given by the Labor Department to those programs which practice discrimination.

In addition to trade unions, other private groups must do much more than they are doing now to eliminate discrimination. It may well be that in some cases there is no legal requirement which demands compliance by such groups. There is, therefore, a great ethical obligation upon them to set a shining example to the rest of the community.

Just as organizations and groups such as this one can do much to combat prejudice, so can individuals in their daily lives. I am convinced that greater efforts can and should be made in this area. Too many of us consider it sufficient to announce that we are without prejudice while failing to realize that we, above all, must demonstrate in our daily existence a leadership which no government can or should exercise or impose.

Now, it is obvious that the treatment we accord our minority groups is being watched with great interest by the rising, uncommitted nations of the world. And I would hope that while it is, of course, an important consideration, no American would believe that the only reason for fighting discrimination at home is because it affects our popularity and moral strength abroad. Our concern over the problems of prejudice should come from within ourselves, from a sense of inner morality. We know perfectly well that in a world where totalitarianism trumpets its phony equality, America has little to be ashamed of. In the struggle against political slavery, America is a devoted champion. We do not seek and we oppose the substitution of one kind of colonialism for another. We abominate the kind of discrimination which the Soviet Union is flagrantly guilty of against all religious creeds and faiths. Totalitarianism practices the very evils it claims to be against. We admit our weaknesses, but we honestly seek to overcome them, in a spirit of toleration.

If we accept respect for human dignity as the only basis for a free world, we also must accept the responsibility for realizing this ideal here in America, and helping others to attain it elsewhere. This means, as the President so eloquently stated it, we must "Pay any price, bear any burden, meet any hardship, support any friend, oppose any foe to assure the survival and success of liberty."

I am hopeful and optimistic about the future of equality and human dignity. It will gain new strength from new trial, new resolution from new challenge, new conviction from new danger, and new determination from new circumstances. When men know they might be free and equal, they will strive to be free and equal. When men have reason to hope for freedom and equality, they will sacrifice for it. And both the knowledge and the hope are alive on this earth, more alive now, perhaps, than ever before. The wind of change blows strongly, promising a new day, a new order, and a new life in the history of the world.

For our own country, we are determined to go forward as a people and a nation aware of our strength, resolved to meet our responsibilities, and determined that in our day freedom will be well and honorably served.

Howard University, Washington, D.C., September 18, 1961

Equal Justice Under Law

The twin themes of the American Revolution were liberty and equality.[1] The United Colonies sought both "to be Free and Independent States . . . Absolved from all Allegiance to the British Crown"[2] and to vindicate the egalitarian principle that no man, including the king, had any natural

[1] See Robert Harris, *The Quest for Equality* (1960), p. 14.
[2] The Declaration of Independence, July 4, 1776.

dominion over another man. Just as in Article 18 of your Constitution, the American Constitution clearly renounced monarchial titles and trappings.[3] Revolutionary thinkers considered the people, and not the king, to be sovereign. They advised their sons to "Remember that you are as good as any man—and that you are no better."[4] Thomas Jefferson proclaimed the revolutionary creed in the Declaration of Independence:

> We hold these truths to be self-evident, that all men are created equal, and that they are endowed by their Creator with certain unalienable Rights, that among these are Life, Liberty, and the pursuit of Happiness.

Since the realization of equality was a primary goal of our new nation, it seems strange that the Constitution prior to the adoption of the Fourteenth Amendment in 1868 did not expressly mention equality. This should be contrasted with the explicit declaration in the Preamble to your Constitution setting forth as one of the Constitution's purposes "to secure to all [India's] citizens . . . Equality of status and opportunity." There are in my view several reasons for this omission. Although not expressly mentioned, the idea of equality pervades the document. Section 4 of Article IV guarantees to every state "a Republican Form of Government." Thus, the ancient inequality of king and subject, of lord and vassal, is rejected and the political equality of all men asserted. More generally, Articles I, II, and III by their terms and necessary effect assume and construct a republican form of government for the nation. Section 2 of Article I mandates that representatives in the national House be chosen "by the People of the several states." This embodies the concept that the legislature should fairly and equally represent the electorate. Benjamin Franklin, one of our Founding Fathers, deemed this necessary since "the *all* of one man is as dear to him as the *all* of another . . . the poor man has an *equal* right but the *more* need to have representatives in the legislature than the rich one."[5]

There is another reason why the framers did not find it necessary to mention equality. They naturally assumed it was encompassed within the concept of liberty whose blessings they heralded in the preamble to the Constitution and later specifically guaranteed in the Due Process Clause of the Fifth Amendment. In treating equality as a component of liberty—and liberty as a synonym for equality—the framers of the Constitution were drawing upon the history and traditions of Western freedom. In the fortieth clause of Magna Charta, King John had promised the barons: "To no one

---

[3] United States Constitution, Art. I, § 9 ("No title of Nobility shall be granted by the United States . . . ."), § 10 ("No State shall . . . grant any Title of Nobility").

[4] Louis Hartz, *The Liberal Tradition in America* (1955), p. 56, quoting *Roots of American Civilization* (C. Nettels ed. 1938), p. 315.

[5] Harris, *op. cit.*, note 1, p. 14, quoting the Writings of Benjamin Franklin (A. H. Smythe ed. 1910), Vol. 10, pp. 59–60, 130–131.

will we sell, to no one will we refuse or delay, right or justice." This became in Anglo-American tradition a guarantee to all of equal justice under law. It was natural, therefore, in 1954 for the Supreme Court in *Bolling* v. *Sharpe*[6] to recognize the merging of the concepts of liberty and equality. In that case the Court held that federal laws segregating students in the public schools of the nation's capital, which is part of no state, constituted a deprivation of liberty, just as the Court had concurrently held that state public school segregation laws violated the Equal Protection Clause of the Fourteenth Amendment.[7] The concept of liberty, embodied in the Fifth Amendment, was once again assumed to embrace the American ideal of equality. This was reaffirmed just this past term when the Court reviewed legislation that deprived naturalized, but not native-born, citizens of their citizenship if they stayed out of the country for certain periods of time.[8] In holding this legislation unconstitutional, the Court held that the Due Process Clause of the Fifth Amendment prohibited the federal government from discriminating between native-born and naturalized citizens. There is no doubt that protection of freedom of expression and particularly freedom of religion also tends to ensure equality of treatment of persons holding beliefs and tenets not shared by the then current majority. Moreover, vigilance in the protection of the liberties involved in the administration of criminal justice tends to have a favorable effect on the elimination of inequality in that realm.

A further reason for the omission of equality language was that many of the new states in their constitutions had specifically guaranteed equality before the law.[9] This being so, the framers may have believed it unnecessary to guarantee equality of treatment by the federal government. They may have assumed, as indeed they did in originally omitting a bill of rights, that denial would emanate primarily from state action and that the state constitutions were adequate to guard against this risk.

Finally, the omission of "equality" language was in part undoubtedly attributable to the political difficulty of achieving union without floundering on the hard reality of slavery.

Before the American Revolution slavery existed to some extent in each of the original states of the Union, but by the time of the adoption of the Constitution in 1789, a majority of the states had but few slaves.[10] In several states acts for the abolition of slavery had been passed.[11] However, the slave states formed a powerful group and the most the pragmatic framers could

[6] 347 U.S. 497 (1954).
[7] *Brown* v. *Board of Education,* 347 U.S. 438 (1954).
[8] *Schneider* v. *Rusk,* 377 U.S. 163 (1964).
[9] See Z. Chafee, *Documents on Fundamental Human Rights* (1st Pamphlet, 1951), pp. 181–237 (State Constitutions before 1791).
[10] Stroud, *Slavery* (1827), p. 158.
[11] *Ibid.*

achieve was to empower Congress to prohibit the importation of slaves after 1808.[12] Such a prohibition was passed by Congress on March 2, 1807, to take effect on January 1, 1808, the first permissible date under the Constitution. It is interesting to note that as early as 1794 Congress passed legislation preventing American citizens from engaging in the slave trade for the supply of foreign countries. A contemporary writer characterized this act as evidencing the fact that at least a majority of the people of the United States abhorred the slave trade.[13]

The Constitution considered the institution of slavery at two other points, and again pragmatic accommodations had to be made. In determining the population of each state for purposes of the number of its representatives in the House of Representatives and apportioning direct taxes it was provided that there shall be added "to the whole number of free persons . . . three fifths of all other persons."[14] Thus a free man, including presumably a free Negro, was to be counted as a whole person with a slave being counted as three fifths of a person.

Finally, it was considered necessary specifically to guarantee that member states would be obligated to deliver up fugitive slaves.[15]

In sum, then, the Constitution of the new nation, while heralding liberty, in effect declared all men to be free and equal—except black men, who were to be neither free nor equal. This inconsistency—this "American dilemma" —reflected a fundamental departure from the American creed, a departure which it took a civil war to set right.

Prior to the Civil War, at least up until the *Dred Scott* decision which I shall discuss shortly, the Supreme Court was not closely involved with the pressing issue of slavery and the rights of Negroes. This was basically because the Constitution left these questions to state control.

There were, however, some important decisions of the Court in the early nineteenth century. For example, in 1835 in a suit by former slaves to be declared free, the Court liberally construed a statute of a slave state providing that a master could free his slaves by his last will and testament.[16] In so doing, the Court was influenced by the nature of such an act—the "giving of liberty."

In 1841 the issue arose of the power of a state to abolish slavery and to forbid the importation of slaves into its territory. It was argued that, since slaves were property and thus articles of commerce, such state action unconstitutionally encroached upon the exclusive power of the Federal Con-

[12] United States Constitution, Art. I, § 9.
[13] Stroud, *op. cit.*, p. 159.
[14] United States Constitution, Art. I, § 2.
[15] United States Constitution, Art. 4, § 2.
[16] *Fenwick* v. *Chapman*, 9 Peters 461.

gress to regulate commerce among the states. In holding that state abolition was constitutional, the Court unequivocally stated that slaves were not property, not articles of commerce; that "the Constitution treats slaves as persons."[17]

At the same time, however, the Court decided cases in which it followed the constitutional mandate of the fugitive slave clause. It held in 1842 that this clause meant that the owner of a slave had the same right to seize and repossess him in another state as the local laws of his own state conferred upon him. Therefore, a state law that penalized such seizure was unconstitutional.[18]

All these cases were a prelude to the famous case of *Dred Scott* v. *Sandford*,[19] decided by the Supreme Court in 1857. Dred Scott was a slave who had been taken by his master from the slave state of Missouri to reside in the free state of Illinois, for two years, then to reside for two years in a free territory of the United States which had not yet become a state and then finally returned to Missouri. After his return with his master to Missouri, Scott sued his "master" in a federal court for assault. The defense was that the assault was justified by the master-slave relationship. Thus the issue of whether Scott was a slave or a free man was joined. Under both the law of the free state of Illinois and the United States free territory, Scott had become free when brought in by his master. A majority of the Supreme Court, over the vigorous dissent of two justices, first held that the lower federal court had no jurisdiction over the suit as Scott was not a citizen and thus could not bring a suit in a federal court. This decision was based on a determination that no Negro, whether free or slave, and whether or not even descended from Negroes who were free at the time of the adoption of the Constitution, could be a citizen within the American Constitution's meaning of that word. The Court then went on to hold that whether or not residence in the free state of Illinois made Dred Scott free on his return to Missouri was a question of Missouri law, and that, under Missouri law, he was not free.

Lastly, the Court held that residence in the United States free territory did not make Dred Scott free even though an act of Congress was interpreted to mean that it did. Here there was no doubt that Missouri law could not affect a constitutional federal statute. However, the Court held the statute to be unconstitutional. Freeing a slave was held to be the taking of the master's property without due process of law.

The verdict of history and legal scholarship is clear in its conclusion that the *Dred Scott* decision was wrong. As Justice Curtis showed in his dissent-

[17] *Groves* v. *Slaughter*, 15 Peters 449, 506–507.
[18] *Prigg* v. *Penna.*, 16 Peter 539 (1842).
[19] 19 How. 393.

ing opinion in the case, Negroes had been considered citizens in most of the nonslave states, and as such had the right to sue in the federal courts. As I have pointed out earlier, the Constitution made no distinction at all between free Negroes and whites. Also, the majority holding flew straight in the face of earlier Supreme Court cases that had allowed suits by Negroes in the federal courts.

Although, therefore, this holding of lack of jurisdiction was clearly wrong, the jurisdictional point could and should have ended the case. The further points in the opinion were not only also wrong but were unnecessary dictum.

Finally, the holding that Congress could not enact legislation freeing slaves, because this would be the taking of the master's property without due process of law, is refuted merely by its statement. As had previously been determined, a slave was a person and not property. It must be the ultimate of ironies that the Due Process Clause—the protector of liberty—could be so subverted as to be a weapon to prevent attempts to achieve the most basic liberty of man, freedom from enslavement.

The popular judgment of its day was in accord with the verdict of history that the decision was wrong, both legally and morally. It took, however, a bloody civil war to overrule it. A war that was to begin four short years after the decision.

During the course of the Civil War, on September 22, 1862, President Abraham Lincoln issued the famous Emancipation Proclamation. This Proclamation provided that on January 1, 1863, "all persons held as slaves within any state, or designated part of a state, the people whereof shall then be in rebellion against the United States, shall be then, thenceforward and forever free." On a narrow basis the Proclamation was an act of war on the part of President Lincoln, as Commander in Chief of the forces, by which slaves were to be taken from people at war with the United States, just as other assets might be taken, to subtract from their resources and add to those of the United States. However, on broader grounds the Proclamation was based on the moral imperative felt by Lincoln and the North in general. In issuing it, Lincoln, so his biographies tell us, felt strongly that he was executing divine will.[20] This moral imperative is evidenced by the fact that shortly after issuance of the Proclamation, Lincoln proposed a constitutional amendment that would free all slaves, whether in rebellious or loyal states.

Following the Civil War, the Thirteenth Amendment to the Constitution was adopted in 1865. This amendment states clearly and unequivocally that "neither slavery nor involuntary servitude . . . shall exist within the United States, or any place subject to their jurisdiction."

[20] See Charnwood, *Abraham Lincoln* (1916), c. X.

However, after the adoption of the Thirteenth Amendment, a number of former slave states passed so-called Black Codes, which were designed to restore the substance of slavery in different forms by placing serious disabilities upon Negroes with respect to contract, ownership of property, access to courts, and the like. As a result Congress passed the Civil Rights Act of 1866. This act heralded the coming of the Fourteenth Amendment and was of great importance in shaping the Congressional attitude on the idea of equality.

After making all persons born in the United States and subject to its jurisdiction, excluding Indians not taxed, citizens of the United States, the act went on to provide that

. . . such citizens, of every race and color, without regard to any previous condition of slavery or involuntary servitude, except as a punishment for crime . . . shall have the same right in every state or territory in the United States, to make and enforce contracts, to sue, be parties, and give evidence, to inherit, purchase, lease, sell, hold, and convey real and personal property, and to full and equal benefit of all laws and proceedings for the security of person and property, as is enjoyed by white citizens, and shall be subject to like pains, and penalties, and to none other, any law, statute, ordinance, regulation, or custom, to the contrary notwithstanding.

The Fourteenth Amendment, proposed by Congress in 1866 and formally adopted in 1868, was in part designed to provide a firm constitutional basis for the Civil Rights Act of 1866 and to place that legislation beyond the power of Congressional repeal.

Section 1 of the Fourteenth Amendment provides:

Section 1. All persons born or naturalized in the United States and subject to the jurisdiction thereof, are citizens of the United States and of the state wherein they reside. No state shall make or enforce any law which shall abridge the privileges or immunities of citizens of the United States; nor shall any state deprive any person of life, liberty, or property, without due process of law; nor deny to any person within its jurisdiction the equal protection of the laws.

To finally secure the rights of the newly freed slaves, the Fifteenth Amendment was proposed by Congress in 1869 and formally adopted in 1870. This amendment provides:

Section 1. The right of citizens of the United States to vote shall not be denied or abridged by the United States or by any state on account of race, color, or previous condition of servitude.

The adoption of these three amendments to the Constitution expressly guaranteed freedom and equality to all—regardless of "race, color, or previous condition of servitude." These amendments cleared the way for our "new kind of society—fresh, equal, just, open, free, and forever respectful of conscience."

The Fourteenth Amendment in particular provides, in part, that no state shall "deny to any person within its jurisdiction the equal protection of the laws." This has come to be known as the Equal Protection Clause. It is in light of the American commitment to equality and the history of that commitment that I read this equal protection clause "as . . . revelation of [one of] the great purposes which were intended to be achieved by the Constitution as a continuing instrument of government."[21]

This great purpose was followed by some of the early cases interpreting the Civil War Amendments. In 1873 the Supreme Court observed:

No one can fail to be impressed with the one pervading purpose found in . . . all [these amendments], lying at the foundation of each, and without which none of them would have been even suggested; we mean the freedom of the slave race, the security and firm establishment of that freedom, and the protection of the newly-made freeman and citizen from the oppressions of those who had formerly exercised unlimited dominion over him.[22]

A few years later, in 1880, the Court had occasion to observe that these amendments were written and adopted "to raise the colored race from that condition of inferiority and servitude in which most of them had previously stood, into perfect equality of civil rights with all other persons within the jurisdiction of the states."[23] In that same year the Court in *Strauder* v. *West Virginia*,[24] stated that the recently adopted Fourteenth Amendment must "be construed liberally to carry out the purposes of its framers." In this *Strauder* case the Court held that it was a violation of the equal protection clause to exclude Negroes from juries. In so holding the Court stated:

The very fact that colored people are singled out and expressly denied by a statute the right to participate in the administration of the law, as jurors, because of their color, though they are citizens and may be in other respects fully qualified, is practically a brand upon them, affixed by the law; an assertion of their inferiority, and a stimulant to that race prejudice which is an impediment to securing to individuals of the race that equal justice which the law aims to secure to all others.[25]

It should be noted that two years before this the Court had used the constitutional prohibition against a state burdening interstate commerce to strike down a state law requiring segregation in interstate transportation.[26]

However, in *Plessy* v. *Ferguson*,[27] decided in 1896, and the cases that followed it, the Supreme Court too often negated the great purpose of the

[21] *United States* v. *Classic*, 313 U.S. 299, 316 (1941) (per Chief Justice Stone).
[22] *Slaughter-House Cases*, 16 Wall. 36, 71.
[23] *Ex parte Virginia*, 100 U.S. 339, 344–345.
[24] 100 U.S. 303, 307.
[25] *Id.*, at 308.
[26] *Hall* v. *DeCuir*, 95 U.S. 485 (1877).
[27] 163 U.S. 537.

equal protection clause. In *Plessy*, the Court held that a state law requiring separate cars and other facilities for white and Negro passengers in intra-state railroads did not violate the Thirteenth or Fourteenth Amendment. The Court stated, in clear opposition to the language of *Strauder*, that state-enforced separation of the races was not a state pronouncement that it considered one of the races inferior. Thus, segregation did not violate the equal protection clause so long as the separate facilities provided for whites and Negroes were themselves equal. In upholding this doctrine of "separate but equal" facilities in railroad accommodations, the Court laid the legal foundation for a variety of other state required or permitted segregated facilities, including public education, public recreation facilities, and numerous other forms of public accommodations.

It was just at this point in history that a number of states began to enact countless laws mandating unequal treatment in public places and facilities.[28] These were based primarily on the legal keystone of the "separate but equal" doctrine. It was not until three quarters of a century later that this doctrine was repudiated and the keystone of the segregated society removed.

Even before this final repudiation, however, the "separate but equal" doctrine was subjected to a process of erosion. In 1917 the Court held invalid, as a violation of due process of law, a zoning ordinance, the object of which was to require the compulsory separation of the races in residential areas. Later, the barring of Negroes from participating in primary elections—intermediate steps in the electoral process by which party candidates are nominated—was held invalid even where the primary was conducted by the political party's own discriminatory rules and without state required discrimination.[29]

In neither of these cases were separate but equal residences or political parties held to satisfy the requirement of equal protection.

Lack of sympathy with segregation was also expressed in cases which continued the doctrine that segregation in interstate facilities constituted a burden on interstate commerce.

In the field of education itself, one of the archetypes of "separate but equal" facilities, the doctrine also withered away.

In 1938 the Court held that a Negro had to be admitted to an all-white law school where this was the only law school in the state. The payment of tuition for Negroes to go to out-of-state law schools was not sufficient, as the state had the duty to provide equal opportunities within its own borders.[30]

In 1950 two cases found that alleged separate but equal facilities were not

[28] See C. V. Woodward, *The Strange Career of Jim Crow* (1955), pp. 15–26.
[29] *Smith* v. *Allwright*, 321 U.S. 649 (1944).
[30] *Missouri ex rel. Gaines* v. *Canada*, 305 U.S. 337 (1938).

truly equal. The question in one was whether a newly established law school for Negroes offered the student "privileges, advantages, and opportunities substantially equal to those offered to white students." In holding that it did not, the Court pointed out that the white law school was superior in terms of number of faculty members, variety of courses, opportunity for specialization, size of student body, scope of library, and availability of student activities. As a barometer of its views, however, it also stated that the white law school was superior in intangibles—reputation of faculty, position and influence of alumni, traditions, prestige, and opportunities to engage in exchange of views and contacts with members of the dominant white society.[31]

In the other case the Court held that it was a denial of equal protection to admit a Negro student to a previously all-white university to study for a doctorate degree, to permit him to use the same classrooms, library and cafeteria as the white students, but—under state law requirements of segregated education—to assign him a classroom seat in a special row and special tables for library and cafeteria use. The Court held that such intraschool segregation set the Negro student apart from the other students and thus impaired and inhibited his ability to study, to engage in discussions and exchange views with other students, and, in general, to learn his profession.[32]

The groundwork had now been laid for the monumental decision in the 1954 case of *Brown* v. *Board of Education*.[33] This case was really a combination of three cases in which Negro school children sought to be admitted to segregated public schools to which they had been denied admission solely because of their race. In two of the cases the lower courts denied the Negroes actions to compel admission to the all-white schools on the grounds that the segregated school systems involved were valid since they provided separate but equal facilities. In the third case the lower court held that the alleged "separate but equal" schools involved were not truly equal and thus required the admission of the Negro children to the previously all-white school. In the Supreme Court, the plaintiffs made a frontal assault on the "separate but equal" doctrine by arguing that separate facilities by their nature were not, and could not, be equal. The Chief Justice delivered the opinion of a unanimous Court. The Court noted that the appearance of the "separate but equal" doctrine in the 1896 case, *Plessy* v. *Ferguson*, was not in accord with the earlier cases construing the Fourteenth Amendment.

The Court then went on to state:

To separate [Negro children] from others of similar age and qualifications solely because of their race generates a feeling of inferiority as to their status in the community that may affect their hearts and minds in a way unlikely ever to be undone.

[31] *Sweatt* v. *Painter*, 339 U.S. 629 (1950).
[32] *McLaurin* v. *Oklahoma State Regents*, 339 U.S. 637 (1950).
[33] 347 U.S. 483 (1954).

In conclusion, the Court decisively held that "separate . . . facilities are inherently unequal."

Thus the Court repudiated the aberration of *Plessy* v. *Ferguson* and returned to the principles enunciated in the early cases. Since *Brown* v. *Board of Education*, the Court has firmly and consistently sought to give real meaning to the equal protection clause "as . . . revelation" of a great constitutional purpose. Today, as the framers of the Civil War amendments intended and as was correctly stated in the *Plessy* dissenting opinion, "Our Constitution is color-blind, and neither knows nor tolerates classes among citizens."

Brown v. *Board of Education* naturally has been a much-discussed case. It is significant that the consensus of virtually all commentators, regardless of their otherwise differing analyses, is that the "separate but equal" formula of *Plessy* was not in accord with the precedents before 1896 and that *Brown* and the decisions that followed it were not an abrupt departure in constitutional law or a novel interpretation of the guarantee of equal protection of the laws.

Brown v. *Board of Education* was decided by a unanimous Court. Four years later in *Cooper* v. *Aaron*[34] the Court, in an unprecedented opinion, signed by all of its members, reaffirmed the *Brown* decision. The Court stated:

> The basic decision in *Brown* was unanimously reached by this Court only after the case had been briefed and twice argued and the issues had been given the most serious consideration. Since the first *Brown* opinion three new Justices have come to the Court. They are at one with the Justices still on the Court who participated in that basic decision as to its correctness, and that decision is now unanimously reaffirmed.

Since *Cooper* v. *Aaron*, two new Justices—Mr. Justice White and myself—have come to the Court. The subsequent decisions of the Court dealing with state-sanctioned racial discrimination in schools and other public facilities have established that the new Justices join in upholding the correctness and logic of the *Brown* decision.

Since that decision the Court has consistently invalidated all forms of state-sanctioned segregation. Previously the Court had held that state courts cannot enforce, either by direct injunction or by the award of damages, a restrictive covenant by which area residents agree not to sell their houses to members of certain racial or religious groups.[35] The Court has also held that a restaurant owner operating in facilities leased from the state cannot refuse to serve people because of their race.[36] No law compelling segregation, be it state

[34] 358 U.S. 1 (1958).
[35] *Shelley* v. *Kraemer*, 334 U.S. 1 (1948).
[36] *Burton* v. *Wilmington Parking Authority*, 365 U.S. 715 (1961).

statute or municipal ordinance, can be given any effect. Moreover, the Court has held that a private restaurant cannot discriminate where a local ordinance requires segregation, even though the restaurant manager insists that he would have discriminated against Negroes even if this ordinance were not in existence.[37] The Court has also held discrimination invalid where there is no local ordinance but the mayor and superintendent of police have made public statement against desegregated service.[38] And just this past term the Court held discrimination invalid where a person acted as both a police official and a representative of a private amusement park in enforcing segregation in the park.[39]

In all of the above cases, there was some element of state involvement. The Court has, since 1883, insisted on such state action as a basis for invoking the Fourteenth Amendment.

I am struck by the similarity between this and your own Constitution. The sweeping Equal Protection Clause of Article 14—which incidentally is very similar to that of our Fourteenth Amendment—and the equally sweeping provision of Article 15 (1) prohibiting "discrimination against any citizen on grounds only of religion, race, caste, sex, [or] place of birth" apply only as prohibitions against the state. Moreover, the equal employment opportunities provision of Article 16 relates only to "any employment or office under the state."

It is only Article 15 (2)'s more restricted prohibition of denial of access to "shops, public restaurants, hotels and places of public entertainment" that applies to so-called private discrimination.

Whether so-called private discrimination practiced by places serving the public is without the additional elements of state involvement noted in the previous cases, violative of the Fourteenth Amendment is a most complex question. The latest case in this area is *Bell* v. *Maryland*,[40] decided last term. In that case a group of Negroes were criminally prosecuted for refusing to leave a restaurant when so requested by the manager, after they had been refused service because of their race. There was no state or local law requiring segregation nor was any public official otherwise involved except the police officers who made the arrest and the state judicial machine which tried and convicted the petitioners. A majority of the Court did not, however, reach the broad question involved, because subsequent to the conviction of the petitioners the state involved had passed a law requiring equality in public accommodations. Thus the case was remanded to the state court for recon-

[37] *Peterson* v. *Greenville*, 373 U.S. 244 (1963).
[38] *Lombard* v. *Louisiana*, 373 U.S. 267 (1963).
[39] *Griffin* v. *Maryland*, 378 U.S. 130 (1964).
[40] 378 U.S. 226 (1964).

sideration in light of the fact that now the activity involved was not only no longer criminal but was in fact the exercise of the state-provided right to equal treatment in public accommodations. Three Justices dissented and stated their view that the discrimination in public accommodations here did not violate the Fourteenth Amendment. Three Justices, myself included, expressed the view that such discrimination *does* violate the Fourteenth Amendment.

Just two months ago the United States Congress passed, and the President signed into law, the Civil Rights Act of 1964. In addition to providing additional aids to the enforcement of equal protection in voting rights, public education, and programs assisted by the federal government, the Act provides in Title II:

All persons shall be entitled to the full and equal enjoyment of the goods, services, facilities, privileges, advantages, and accommodations of any place of public accommodation, as defined in this section, without discrimination or segregation on the ground of race, color, religion or national origin.

With certain qualifications not severely restrictive of its scope, the "public accommodations" are then defined to include hotels, restaurants, theaters, and other places of amusement and sport exhibitions. Violation of this provision can be enjoined in actions brought by private complainants or by the Attorney General on behalf of the government. It is striking how close this provision is to Article 15 (2) of your Constitution.

It should be noted that a recent survey showed that 24 states have laws prohibiting discrimination in public accommodations.

A lower federal court has held this section of the Civil Rights Act to be constitutional and an appeal from that decision is currently pending before the Supreme Court. An early hearing on this case is contemplated.

Title VII of the act provides, with certain qualifications and restrictions, for nondiscrimination in employment. It outlaws discriminatory conduct on the part of employees, employment agencies, or labor unions.

State and municipal legislation prohibiting discrimination in employment has become increasingly widespread in recent years. Over the past two decades 25 states have enacted laws designed to ensure equal employment opportunities for members of racial, religious, and ethnic minorities in all types of employment. Also, numerous local governments, including seven major cities, have adopted ordinances aimed at combating employment discrimination.[41]

It should be noted that the Civil Rights Act and the state and local provisions in this area apply to private as well as governmental employment. In

[41] Jack Greenberg, *Race Relations and American Law* (1959), p. 379.

this regard they go beyond the provisions of your Constitution which, in Article 16, provide only for equal employment in government service.

By presidential executive orders dating back to 1941, discrimination based on race, creed, color or national origin has been prohibited in employment by the federal government and by private firms who contract with the government. Committees to enforce this prohibition have been set up by every President since Franklin Delano Roosevelt. In an executive order promulgated by President Kennedy in 1961, the President's Committee on Equal Employment Opportunity was explicitly given the authority to cancel contracts or to bar from future contracts any employer who engaged in discriminatory employment practices.

The American governments, both state and federal, have also been increasingly more active in attempts to ensure equality in residential accommodations. I have already adverted to Supreme Court decisions that struck down racial zoning ordinances and state enforcement of private covenants prohibiting the sale of houses to certain racial, religious, or ethnic groups.

By the end of 1962 some 19 states and 55 communities had also taken steps to equalize housing opportunities. In November, 1962, President Kennedy signed the Executive Order on Equal Opportunity in Housing which directed agencies of the federal government to act to prevent discrimination in the sale or rental of "residential property and related facilities" owned by the federal government, or aided or assisted by it after the date of the order.

As shown by this history of equal protection concerning discrimination based on race, the basic issue is one of human dignity. This was pointed out by our House of Representatives in its committee report concerning the Civil Rights Act:

The primary purpose of [the Civil Rights Act], then, is to solve this problem, the deprivation of personal dignity that surely accompanies denials of equal access to public establishments. Discrimination is not simply dollars and cents, hamburgers and movies; it is the humiliation, frustration, and embarrassment that a person must surely feel when he is told that he is unacceptable as a member of the public because of his race or color. It is equally the inability to explain to a child that regardless of education, civility, courtesy, and morality he will be denied the right to enjoy equal treatment, even though he be a citizen of the United States and may well be called upon to lay down his life to assure this nation continues.[42]

The Supreme Court has also been aware that the issue is one of human dignity. This was graphically pointed out by a case this past term. The case did not involve the right to an effective vote, or to unsegregated schools or to public accommodations, but the simple right of being addressed in a re-

---

[42] U.S. Code Congressional and Administrative News, 88th Cong., 2d Sess. 1742 (1964).

spectful manner. In certain areas of the country it has been customary for Negro witnesses to be addressed by their first names and white witnesses by their last names, prefixed by Mr., Miss, Mrs., etc. In this case, a Negro girl was held in criminal contempt for politely but firmly refusing to answer questions asked of her by the state prosecutor until he addressed her as "Miss Hamilton" rather than as "Mary." On appeal the Supreme Court unanimously reversed the conviction of criminal contempt in a *per curiam* opinion. The Court thus made clear that the Constitution tolerates no state-involved manifestation, no matter how slight, of a racial caste system.[43]

The object of the Indian Constitution, as set forth in its Preamble, is to "*secure* to all its citizens" "Justice," "Liberty" and "Equality" and to *promote* among them "Fraternity." It then states that such securing and promotion will assure the "dignity of the individual and the unity of the nation."

We, in the United States, share these ideals. Government, both federal and state, is striving continuously to secure justice, liberty and equality. In my opinion we are now well on our way to securing liberty, although, of course, we must always remain vigilant in its defense.

We have not yet fully achieved equality, either for nations or for people within nations. We still have a long way to go in this area. Little nations in the world are no longer satisfied to be treated just as free nations—they want an equal voice in the determination of whether or not this civilization is going to continue. I am optimistic that we will achieve equality—throughout the world and in your nation as well as mine. Both India and the United States have made this achievement a guiding principle of governmental action. In my opinion we in the United States are now on our way to securing equality and justice for all our citizens.

As your Constitution so beautifully points out, however, the goal to which we are all striving is the ideal of fraternity, and when that is reached your Constitution states that we will have assured the dignity of the individual and the unity of the nation. I might add that we would also have assured the unity of the world. Again, though, as your Constitution points out, government, be it the executive, legislative or judicial branch, cannot "secure" fraternity, but can only "promote" it. Fraternity is promoted by securing justice, liberty and equality. When government thus makes the atmosphere conducive to fraternity, it is then up to the people to accept each other as brothers. As Gandhi so eloquently stated in pleading for abolition of the caste of untouchables:

We must not throw a few miserable schools at them: we must not adopt the air of superiority towards them. We must treat them as our blood brothers as they are in fact. We must return to them an inheritance of which we have robbed them.

[43] *Hamilton v. Alabama*, 376 U.S. 650 (1964).

And this must not be the act of a few English-knowing reformers merely, but it must be a conscious voluntary effort on the part of the masses.[44]

This universal brotherhood of man is an age-old aspiration of the human race. It is a condition under which men will deal with other men on a basis of not what they are merely compelled to do by law but on the basis of mutual respect for each other's origins and personalities.

This goal of fraternity, the brotherhood of man—the dream of Gandhi, Lincoln and Kennedy—is the goal to which we all must strive, both for our respective nations and for the world community.

Indian Law Institute, New Delhi, September, 1964

POVERTY AND THE LAW

The Guarantee of Equal Justice

Our Court recently observed that "[p]roviding equal justice for the poor and rich, weak and powerful alike . . . is the central aim of our entire judicial system." Judge Learned Hand expressed the same thought another way: "If we are to keep our democracy, there must be one commandment: Thou shalt not ration justice."

"Equal justice" obviously does not mean that government—state or federal —must equalize all economic inequalities among citizens. Nor does it mean that the government cannot impose burdens or exactions which by reason of economic circumstances fall more heavily upon some than others. It does mean, however, that in so far as possible the legal rights of the poor man and his ability to enforce those rights should be the same as those of his richer neighbor. The wealth or poverty of a man standing before the bar of justice should be irrelevant.

To seek to minimize differences in the law between rich and poor is, of course, to work for the achievement of a worthy ideal. But "equal justice" is more than a noble sentiment; it is a concept supported by extremely practical considerations closely related to the law's function of ensuring a peaceful, orderly and harmonious society. We often think of law as a stabilizing influence—if not the most important factor promoting stability—in our society. We must not forget that the law promotes such stability and order not simply because it is law promulgated by authority but, rather, because in large measure it satisfies the reasonable expectations of those who live under it. When people's just expectations are satisfied, the law is accepted and respected, and a peaceful, orderly and harmonious society is possible. When these expectations are not fulfilled, confidence in the law is diminished, people are alienated from the law and society, and instability, unrest and

[44] Quoted in W. O. Douglas, *We the Judges* (1956), p. 426.

even violence can replace order. And one of the most reasonable expectations of any person is to have his legitimate grievances redressed.

The law, in working for a stable and harmonious society, cannot remain static, but must constitute a flexible, living and dynamic force in society. In particular, it must remain capable of satisfying reasonable demands for equal justice for poor and rich alike. It must do so because the principle of equal justice is ethically sound and because such a principle is the only practically sound method for creating a unified and harmonious society.

The continuing task of achieving equal justice for the rich and the poor is not an easy one. It requires a considerable re-evaluation of policies and programs. It likewise requires considerable reorientation of the attitudes of legislators, judges, lawyers, teachers, bar associations, and the public at large. And it requires continuous efforts to make certain that the law does not discriminate either substantively or procedurally against the poor.

Practical distinctions between the rich man and the poor man are found throughout the area of criminal law. The rich man may be summoned to the police station; the poor man is more often arrested. The rich inebriant may be escorted home by the policeman; the poor drunk is almost always tossed into jail. The rich accused is released on bail; the poor defendant cannot raise bail and remains in prison. The rich defendant can afford the best legal advice, he can summon psychiatrists and other expert witnesses, he can afford a thorough investigation of the facts of his case, and can raise every possible defense; the poor defendant, until the recent *Gideon* decision, often had to defend himself, and even today in many jurisdictions he is denied many other important tools of advocacy. After conviction, when a fine is imposed, the rich man pays it and goes free, but the poor man who cannot afford to pay a fine must go to jail. The rich man who can be guaranteed a job may qualify for probation or parole; the poor man lacking a job more often goes to or remains in prison.

In pointing up these discriminations I do not mean to imply that any or all of them are of constitutional dimensions. Nor do I mean to indicate that our legal system, which I believe superior to any other in existence, is riddled with class distinction. Rather, since our goal is equal justice and since we abjure class distinctions, I direct attention to existing inequalities in order to emphasize the need for their elimination wherever possible.

Happily, our national conscience is awakening to needed and overdue reforms in this area. On August 20, 1964, the President signed the Criminal Justice Act, a statute which has profound implications for the administration of justice in this country. The act provides that when defendants in the federal jurisdiction are unable to afford counsel of their own, the court must appoint counsel for them as early in the proceedings as possible, which generally means when the defendant is first brought before the United States Commissioner. It also allows compensation for assigned counsel in criminal cases. Moreover, it makes provision for the appointment and compensation of expert witnesses. This act presents a challenge to both the bar and the federal judiciary; if administered in a spirit which reflects complete acceptance of the principles that it embodies, the promise of fair procedures for the poor which it makes can be fulfilled in practice. I would hope that the state legislatures will emulate the good example of the Congress by enacting similar legislation.

Moreover, a beginning has been made in some parts of the country toward removing the gross inequities of the bail system. The bail system as it presently operates in most jurisdictions is one of the most outrageous examples of discrimination between people with and without means. After arrest the accused who is indigent is often confined to jail because he cannot raise bail, while the accused who can afford bail is free to return to his family and job. Studies in Philadelphia, New York, and in the federal court system indicate that substantial numbers of persons cannot make bail when it is set as low as $500, and that well over 50 per cent of the accused cannot make bail that is set at $1,000 or more. The result of this inequity is hardship to the accused and his family, substantial and unnecessary expense to the government, and more importantly, an adverse effect on the actual trial itself.

The present bail system means that the poor defendant is not as freely available as the more affluent one during the critical period between arrest and trial to help his attorney with the investigation and preparation of his defense. It often also colors the trial proceedings. According to a study, published in the *New York University Law Review* for June, 1964, 73 per cent of those studied who were not released on bail were convicted, while only 53 per cent of those studied who were released on bail were subsequently convicted. The study attempted to hold constant other factors that might account for the increased number of acquittals of those released on bond, and concluded that there exists a strong causal relation between the isolated factor of detention in prison pending trial and an unfavorable disposition of an accused's case.

Recent studies have indicated that, if carefully screened defendants are released pending trial on their own recognizance and treated with dignity, they will appear at trial. I applaud the projects that are under way to reform the bail system in New York, in the District of Columbia, and in other jurisdictions. Moreover, the first National Bail Conference in May, 1964, co-sponsored by the Department of Justice and the Vera Foundation, was a milestone in stimulating interest in and study of the subject—the first step in reform. I hope that the proposals for reform that have arisen from these studies and the Conference will be put into practice throughout the nation.

While certain long-needed procedural reforms in the criminal law designed to bring equal justice to the poor are under way, we have scarcely begun to embark upon the important substantive problems in this area. Any judge, criminologist, sociologist or prison warden can testify to the close connection between crime and poverty. The great bulk of our prison population comes from the ranks of the economically underprivileged. A root cause of crime is economic distress and its concomitants—broken families, ignorance, illiteracy and discrimination. This is not to say that if we solve the problem of poverty we shall solve the problem of crime, for crime also involves individual maladjustment and numerous other factors which we do not yet fully understand. It is to say that winning the war on poverty is an indispensable element of winning the war on crime. Our rightful concern with the problem of protecting society from the incidence of a rising crime rate necessitates that we treat not only the symptoms but the causes of this disease. The distinguished and recently retired director of the Federal Bureau of Prisons, James V. Bennett, in his final report, Annual Report 1964, had this to say on the subject:

There is a hue and cry in the land about violence in the streets and a resurgence of the argument that we must return to harsher methods in which the rights of the individual are subordinated to the lust for retribution and the passion to punish the transgressor. But I am confident that reason will prevail and that our nation will instead try harder to cure the social ills out of which crime and delinquency fester. These efforts will take a good deal of time, energy and money, but they are more likely to bring results. A rich and enlightened nation should at least test their efficacy before returning to primitive and long-discredited punitive techniques.

We also need to do much more in the area of rehabilitation of the criminal. One of the important keys to rehabilitation of a convict is finding him a decent job, and the obstacle to doing so is not only his criminal record but often also his lack of education, skill, training, motivation, and the other factors that contributed to the start of his criminal career. Wardens of prisons are the first to testify that our jails today are simply not staffed and equipped to rectify these disabilities. The need, as Mr. Bennett has pointed out, is "fewer . . . prisons and penitentiaries and more . . . clinics, treatment centers, halfway houses, camps and domiciliary facilities."

We also need more enlightened methods of reclaiming offenders. California has developed a system whereby men and women who have served a prison sentence may apply to their local courts a reasonable time after their release from prison for a certificate of rehabilitation. If the court finds that the applicant is rehabilitated, it grants the certificate, the receipt of which by the Governor automatically constitutes an application for a pardon. And full pardons are usually granted to those who are certified as rehabilitated. The rehabilitated are thus given a strong incentive not to return to a life of crime. Psychologists and sociologists tell us that people continuously treated as criminal types are often confirmed in their identity as criminals. The California example, which allows a man to discard his criminal identity, is worthy of widespread emulation.

I am also glad to note that Congress is considering the difficult subject of developing better methods to rehabilitate narcotics addicts. I hope that similar consideration will be given to the treatment of chronic alcoholics. Both narcotics addiction and alcoholism are closely connected with criminal behavior.

Judges and lawyers are also becoming increasingly aware of the inadequacies, both substantively and procedurally, of our criminal codes in dealing with offenders who are emotionally and mentally ill. A continuing dialogue between judges, law teachers, lawyers and psychiatrists is to be welcomed as an essential element in achieving much-needed reform of our law in this area.

Our consideration of the problem of poverty and crime should also include thought of the plight of the criminal's victim, who often is himself quite poor. A year and a half ago I pointed out in a lecture at New York University that New Zealand had designed a system of governmental compensation for victims of crime which was worthy of our study. Since that time Great Britain has adopted a similar system under which a public board examines individual cases of victims of violent crimes and, where appropriate, compensates them from public funds. Reports indicate that Britain's scheme is likewise working satisfactorily. I believe that we should give serious consideration to compensating victims of violent crimes because, in a real sense, the law has failed in protecting them.

The time is also long overdue for an objective study in depth, by our most eminent citizens and qualified authorities, of the causes of crime itself. I therefore welcome the announcement by the President that he will appoint a commission charged with probing the causes of crime and developing proposals for resolving the overwhelming problems with which crime presents us. I trust that such a commission in the discharge of its duties will bear in mind these wise words expressed by Sir Winston Churchill more than a half century ago:

A calm, dispassionate recognition of the rights of the accused, and even of the convicted criminal, against the State; a constant heart-searching by all charged with the duty of punishment; a desire and eagerness to rehabilitate in the world of industry those who have paid their due in the hard coinage of punishment; tireless efforts towards the discovery of curative and regenerative processes; unfailing faith that there is a treasure, if you can find it, in the heart of any man—these are the symbols which, in the treatment of crime and criminal, mark and measure the stored up strength of a nation, and are sign and proof of the living virtue within it.

The legal problems of the poor are not limited to problems in the area of the criminal law. Our civil law also needs thorough re-examination with the aim of embodying in its practices our goal of equal justice. I am pleased to note that some of this re-examination is currently taking place, and I welcome recent developments in this area as well.

The recent Conference on Law and Poverty sponsored by the Department of Justice and the Office of Economic Opportunity, the conference of last year sponsored by the Department of Health, Education, and Welfare, and numerous articles and symposia have begun to focus upon the legal problems of the poor. In particular, proposals have been made to provide the poor with the tools necessary for them to enforce those rights which the law grants them. Surely the rights of a poor man under the civil law are ephemeral unless he knows of them and can enforce them in practice. With this fact in mind, established legal aid bureaus have made great contributions to aiding the poor, and new groups in New Haven, Boston, New York, the District of Columbia, Oakland, and other cities and rural areas have developed, or are in the process of developing, neighborhood legal service systems to supply legal assistance to the poor.

As was the case when the now-accepted legal aid bureaus were first founded, the establishment of neighborhood legal service systems has raised certain issues under the canons of ethics of the bar, and perhaps calls for modification of certain of the bar's rules. Above and beyond the issue of the canon of ethics, however, are the questions: Will the organized bar respond voluntarily and creatively to the challenges of new forces, new conditions and new needs? Will it set the example for other professions, or take an obstructionist and restrictive role? The response should be an awakening by the bar to its responsibilities in a time of social change, in a time when we increasingly appreciate the role which the law and the legal profession can play in assuring the dignity of the individual.

These programs to bring legal representation to the poor are, of course, of great importance and must be strengthened and expanded. Supplying legal representation, however, is unfortunately far from sufficient to allow the poor man to assert his legal rights. Congested dockets and the consequent delay in civil litigation often prevent the poor man from having his day in court. A man with a justifiable tort claim arising out of an accident may incur great medical expense, and he may be unable to work because of his injury. In a country which experiences about 11½ million automobile accidents each year, there are many in this category. Because the victim of an accident must find the means to pay for his living expenses and medical bills, he often must settle whether or not the terms of the settlement are just, for he cannot hold out while his litigation is in progress. Thus justice delayed too often becomes justice denied. Of paramount importance in achieving our goal of equal justice in civil litigation is a frontal attack on this problem of litigation delay.

A further substantial obstacle to the assertion of legal rights is the high cost of litigation which affects all but weighs most heavily upon the poor and those of modest means. It is this high cost which in part prompted Judge Learned Hand's observation: "After now some dozen years of experience I must say that as a litigant I should dread a lawsuit beyond almost anything else short of sickness and death."

Our country has rejected the British system which taxes major costs of litigation, including counsel fees, to the losing party. We believe that the average man might be deterred from suing in court through fear of having to pay the other party's costs if the suit is lost. Our general view that each party must bear his own major costs of litigation, however, should be re-examined in some areas in light of the fact that high litigation costs can still deter a man from suing on a modest claim, for his own costs may eat up much of the amount recovered even if he wins his suit. Congress has recognized and dealt with this problem in the Fair Labor Standards Act, by providing that when an employee is successful in proving that his employer has not complied with minimum wage standards, he recovers attorneys' fees as well as double damages. Similarly, the successful plaintiff in a private anti-trust action recovers attorneys' fees as well as treble damages, again without being liable for attorneys' fees if he loses. These exceptions to the general American rule have been made in favor of successful plaintiffs in areas where Congress has determined it necessary to do so in order to encourage plaintiffs to assert their legal rights. Study is clearly merited as to whether or not similar rules should be enacted in other areas where similar policy considerations apply, such as, for example, housing and consumer litigation.

We must do more, however, than ensure that the poor as well as the rich have facilities for asserting their legal rights. Pursuit of the ideal of equal justice requires re-examination of certain areas of substantive law as well as areas involving the assertion of rights. Such re-examination is vitally necessary in many areas such as the law of landlord and tenant, laws governing consumers, family law, and law governing the administration of welfare rights and the relationship between the individual and governmental agencies in general.

The need for study into these and similar problems brings me to the question of the crucial role the law schools must play in the area of poverty and the law. We in this country are fortunate in having a widespread and undoubtedly the best institutional system of legal education in the world. But as the recognized needs of our society change, so must the curriculum and role of the law school change. A glance through a typical law school catalogue finds it heavily weighted with courses which train a lawyer for a business practice. It is perhaps symptomatic of this emphasis that courses on the law of debtor-creditor relations are often entitled "Creditors' Rights." In my day in law school it was symptomatic of the state of the law of labor relations that cases on this subject were listed in the digest under the heading "Master and Servant." The time is overdue for the law schools to devote more attention throughout their curriculum to the legal problems of the poor— problems now almost exclusively confined to the single course of criminal law.

Attention to the problems of the poor on the part of the law schools requires not only that law students are made aware of these problems but also that they become involved in them. Such involvement would be to the mutual benefit of both the student and our legal order. My Brother Brennan has recently spoken about the value to him of having participated in the Harvard Legal Aid program while in law school. Justice Brennan wondered whether this experience should not be made available to a greater percentage of the student body. I think it should be made available to all. Involvement of third-year students in legal service seems to me to be a way of giving greater meaning to the third year of law school attendance—a year which, as presently constituted, has been variously termed "the wasted year in legal education," "the awkward year," "the year the faculty lost the pennant." At the same time, such involvement would make a substantial contribution to the problems of poverty and the law.

I do not mean by this that the problems of the poor should be turned over to law students. Of course, as the medical and dental experience has shown, there must be active faculty and bar participation and supervision. Nor do I mean that the third year should consist completely of all students working in legal aid societies and neighboring law offices although these, of course, would be obvious places for serving what I would term a law internship. There are numerous other places in which the annual crop of approximately 11,000 third-year law students could learn skills, gain insights into the workings of our society, and at the same time contribute to the development of that society. To name just a few: Law students could work as law clerks to trial court judges, many of whom do not now have this aid. They could work in the offices of prosecutors as well as those of public defenders. They could work in public agencies, particularly the ones dealing with the poor, such as welfare and public assistance agencies. Law students could participate in bureaus which, like the Scandinavian Ombudsman, investigate complaints of citizens. And they could also constitute a pool from which private lawyers performing their duty to represent indigents could draw for assistance.

Service in these and other areas could be combined so that the third year would provide the student with a variety of grass-roots experiences. Such a plan would, of course, need the active support of the bar as well as the law schools. While recognizing that there may be difficulties inherent in the proposal, I believe it deserves the consideration of both law schools and the bar.

The current discussions of the legal problems of the poor remind us once again that law is a powerful force. Law can provide a man with the promise of its equal protection and the guarantee of equal justice. It is perhaps well also to remember in treating of poverty and the law that law alone cannot make a man fully free. The rights conferred by law and enforceable by court order are not sufficient in and of themselves to bring opportunity and dignity to all. It will take the resources of all segments of our society to make the larger promise—the promise of equal opportunity and human dignity—the promise of America—a reality.

National Conference on Law and Poverty, Washington, D.C., June 25, 1965

THE QUEST FOR FULL EMPLOYMENT

The Many Who Are Poor

In his Inaugural Address President Kennedy stated his belief that "if a free society cannot help the many who are poor, it cannot save the few who are rich." He was talking then about foreign affairs, but the principle is equally true of our domestic affairs. It is the same spirit evidenced in another Inaugural Address, that of Franklin D. Roosevelt in 1937, when he said: "The test of our progress is not whether we add more to the abundance of those who have much; it is whether we provide enough for those who have too little."

The admonition of Presidents Kennedy and Roosevelt is of particular application to us today, members of the most affluent society in man's history, enjoying an unprecedented amount of personal wealth, comfort and security.

Per capita income, after taxes, in the United States today is close to $2,000 —a king's treasure to many millions in the world who seek to maintain life on per capita incomes like those of fourteen countries in Asia of under $100, eleven countries of South America of under $200, and seven countries of Africa of under $200.

The median income of *all* families in our country is over $5,600; half of our families have higher incomes than that.

Sixty-two per cent of Americans own their own homes.

Seventy-six per cent of our families own automobiles.

The amount of life insurance per family is $10,200.

We spent $22 billion on recreation last year, and the trend is upward.

We provide education for 45 million children in grammar and high schools and for over 3 million college students.

The checklist of our abundance is endless.

Most Americans are thankful for these material blessings but, more than that, they are thankful for the blessings of a free society, for a government of laws and not men, and for the inherent rights to religion and speech that are guaranteed to our people.

That wealth in itself brings a special charge to the conscience. The end of economic life is, after all, not the mere accumulation of material goods and the satisfaction of material appetites. The end of economic life is governed by the principle of justice—to make available to all persons, without distinction, the means to live a life of real dignity.

Wealth is a pleasure, but it is also an obligation. And the people of our most fortunate nation have a clear and undeniable obligation for the humane and decent treatment of the less affluent among us, the lame and the blind, the children of those who have suffered misfortune, the adult worker who cannot find a job through no fault of his own, the youth who sits on the doorsteps of the city slums without prospect of either education or work, the person denied full access to opportunity because of his race or color or religious belief.

There is no one who can seriously and in good conscience question that obligation or fail to support the discharging of it.

Today it is sharper in focus, especially in the press, than ever before. There is a great deal of discussion about our welfare programs, much of it for the wrong reasons but nevertheless welcome. I look upon this discussion, first, as a good thing for a free society and, secondly, as a great new opportunity for the American people to discover again the value, integrity and success of our welfare programs, and the dedication of the persons who spend their lives in this humanitarian field.

The charges that have been made against our welfare programs bespeak a great ignorance of them.

It is said that public assistance is a way of life for chiselers and loafers who would rather have a handout than a job.

Of the little over 7 million persons who receive public assistance, over 5½ million are children, or aged, or blind or permanently disabled. Fraud, as recent experiments in cutting back welfare programs have clearly shown, is minimal.

It is charged that providing assistance to dependent children is a cause of illegitimacy. This is probably the worst view of human nature in modern times. The facts are that a small percentage, one in every eight illegitimate children in this nation, receives Aid to Dependent Children assistance. There are a few, I suppose, who would willfully bring a child into the world in order to receive an extra $12 dollars a month for it, but to generalize from those and castigate the truly underprivileged and direct punitive action against the helpless children themselves is a tyranny of false righteousness that shames our ethical concept of man.

It is said, too, that the act of assistance to the needy in itself disables them, makes them dependent, ties them permanently to the public purse.

Yet those who receive public assistance continue to do so for a limited period of time. I know from my own experience, growing up here in a crowded neighborhood in Chicago, struggling through the depression along with everybody else, and spending many years in the labor movement through recessions and bad times in certain industries, that men want work. They want jobs, not handouts. They want to hold their heads up and receive fair payment for honest work if they can find it. That is the America I have known, and the one we all know.

These charges, I say bluntly, are not well founded. There are some, certainly, who will attempt to abuse any system designed to provide assistance to those in need. But they are an insignificant number.

Is there any American who refuses to recognize the special obligation we have to the handicapped, to the permanently injured, and to the blind?

Is there any who would refuse aid to the aged who are ill and in need?

Is there any citizen who would visit upon a child a rebuke because of a fault in the mother?

And can any American, in his conscience, question the obligation of his society—that gives us sustenance and well-being and opportunity—to provide help to those who cannot find work because the economy is not providing enough jobs for all?

As we take common counsel over these questions and explore into the real purpose of economic life, there is room for all legitimate differences of opinion that are based on fact. And I would hope that from this discussion comes a new awareness of improvements we can make to reach the goal of freedom from want.

For example, a part of the financial burden for public assistance is due to the fact that men and women without work for long periods of time exhaust every resource. It might be well to increase the assistance, but it would also be well to look into the adequacy of the unemployment insurance system, designed originally to provide better protection than it now does. The original intention of the law was to provide about half of the lost weekly wage, yet today the unemployment insurance benefit as a percentage of earnings has fallen from 43.2 per cent in 1940 to 37.6 per cent last year [1960].

We in this Administration are determined to meet our obligations and develop improvements in our welfare program. But, more important in many ways, we are equally determined to strike at the cause of economic disadvantage by helping to create better job opportunity, by providing training and retraining to those workers who remain without work for long periods because of the lack of qualification, by meeting the special needs of young people who need a fair chance, and by establishing a permanent unemployment insurance program that meets our needs and does not have to be bolstered up during every recession.

We would want to create in America a rate of economic growth that results in good and useful jobs for all the people, not only during periods of expansion and national effort but all of the time, to every generation.

We are determined to do our rightful share in helping to bring down the remaining barriers to full employment opportunity. The median money income of nonwhite families is $3,233—half making less than that—and, while this is vastly better than much of the world's, it is also evidence that by our own standards the nonwhite worker has not enjoyed the opportunity he should. He suffers twice the unemployment rate that the white worker does. He makes up a large percentage of the unskilled.

There is another aspect to this, and let us be frank about it. It is said, and it is true, that there are many nonwhites on relief and receiving welfare payments. The pertinent question is not—how many?—but why? They are in that position for several reasons, and one of them is that years of discrimination have blunted their opportunity for jobs. Let's be frank about that as well. Certainly, the nonwhites who are drawing welfare payments did not conspire among themselves to create the system for their own dubious advantage in the small wealth it provides them. It is rather, a case of our own failure to live up to the plain constitutional commitment to provide open opportunity for all.

The New Frontier is that place where all Americans may stand together for the same purposes, freedom and opportunity for all, that Americans have stood together before on other frontiers.

In realizing the opportunities that are before us, we have the good counsel of the past to guide us. Sumner Welles once said: "It will take much wisdom, much cooperative effort, and much surrender of private, shortsighted, and sectional self-interest to make these things all come true, but the goal is freedom from want—individual security and national prosperity—and is everlastingly worth striving for."

In this striving we welcome the support of this organization. I was pleased to see among the Federal Legislative Objectives of this Association your support for legislation to provide medical care for the aged under the sound and tested concept of the prepaid Social Security system. That legislation enjoys a high priority in the list of Administration objectives in the next session. Having your voice in our favor is important and most welcome.

And here, again, there is a direct relationship with relief and welfare. The interest of the legislation is a broad one, including all of our aged in many different economic categories, but within it is the special interest of those most familiar to the welfare worker, the aged who are in great need, who are ill, and who must find help somewhere. I believe it is far better to provide that assistance to our aged on the basis of Social Security than to offer it on a degrading and often embarrassing means-test basis.

There are other high-priority items equally deserving of the support of all Americans. The discussion about welfare programs has brought new light to an already known fact—that our technology is moving faster, as it must, than the ability of our total labor force to adjust to new jobs and new skills. The phenomenon of long-term unemployment concurrent with the highest monthly employment levels of our history is due in great part to this fact. The unemployed are totally without skill; they are those whose skill is out-moded or unwanted; they are those without any education or with an education unsuitable to qualify them for new jobs.

I have traveled a good deal in the past year and have talked with many hundreds of people around the country—in mining towns and industrial centers and steel and auto cities and in smaller one-industry communities hit hard by change. I have seen this everywhere—jobs available to those who can qualify, and men standing idle because they cannot qualify.

The Manpower Development and Training Act, and its companion measure the Youth Employment Opportunities Act, do not spring out of a void. They arise from a compelling need. They arise because of the dilemma of people stranded by circumstance while the current of progress sweeps by.

Such unemployment can be a staging area for the welfare rolls. I believe that all Americans would rather make an investment in new skills for these people, and return them to a productive and meaningful life, than assign them to public assistance. That is what we intend to do—give them a new lease on economic life, for their own welfare and that of the entire nation.

We have never in our history responded to human problems by policies of denial, and we cannot realize the opportunities before us now by policies of rebuke in place of sympathy, especially in our welfare programs, and generally throughout our economic life.

Is welfare a burden to us? No, it is the credential of a society free to do what is right, which is the only real freedom in a world so often filled with wrong.

Without man's humanity to man, without charity, we are, in the words of St. Paul, "sounding brass, or a tinkling cymbal." This mighty nation of diverse peoples who have conquered a continent, brought nature to man's service, produced the greatest abundance of wealth ever known, mounted twice in my lifetime the force and power to destroy aggressors, and reaches now to the limits of space must look to its validity in that ideal. "Though I have all faith, so that I could remove mountains, and have not charity, I am nothing."

American Public Welfare Association, Chicago, Ill., November 29, 1961

The Irons of Poverty

It has been said that "he who has not the spirit of his age has all the misery of it." The tragic fact is that hundreds of thousands of our young people do not have the spirit of our age, but they do have the misery of it. We live in that long-awaited time of history when man has awakened to the possibility of breaking the irons of poverty and disease with the swift stroke of industrial technology. We plot courses to the stars. We have engineered and operate an economy of incredible abundance. In the sciences, in art, in commerce it is the time for the adventuring mind and the will to achieve. Yet in the slum areas of our large cities, in our poor rural communities, are a million young people who are as effectively isolated from this spirit of achievement as though they existed in some other world.

Their image is often obscured and lost sight of in the general statistics of employment and unemployment. The very need to act specifically on their behalf has not been granted the general attention and approbation it deserves because of this fact.

Our unemployed young people today are isolated, not only from opportunity but also from the economic trends that mean improvement in the lot of others. . . . The unemployment figures for January [1962] showed that the rate had dropped below 6 per cent for the first time in 16 months and that unemployment, at 4.6 million, was 700,000 less than a year ago.

But the number of persons out of work for four months or more had not changed from a year ago and still numbered 1¼ million. A great number of them are young people. Of the 1 million young people out of work and also out of school, fully half can be found in the undiminishing ranks of the long-term jobless.

Nothing short of a major national effort is going to dislodge them from that tragic rut.

This Administration is going to do its share in that effort. We are going to discharge our responsibility. We are going to recognize opportunity when we see it.

Now, you know and I know—and let me say that knowledge has been deepened in the year just passed—that when you set out to do something, to act, to break the inertia that often surrounds opinion, all sorts of forces are set into motion. There arise, on the one hand, those whose answer to every problem is to do nothing. There arise, on the other hand, those who want to do everything at once. One side considers change with fear and the other with scorn.

I want to say quite candidly that neither emotion is beneficial to progress. When a clear and present need exists, as it clearly and presently exists in regard to youth opportunity, a free society and its government respond. At the same time, the nature of that response is necessarily conditioned by lack of precedent, by the attitude in legislatures, by the apportionment of funds throughout a great number of programs, and by the way one particular program is enforced and supplemented by others.

In the light of the human need so apparent our proposals in the youth field may seem to some to be modest and moderate. They are, when viewed in that single light. But that is to take the narrowest view of them. I would like to suggest two other views, each with a truth as compelling as that of need.

First, the Youth Employment Opportunities Act and the Manpower Development and Training Act do not stand alone. They are not single monoliths erected against the failure of economic life to include opportunity for all. They are, rather, members in an arsenal of weapons.

I have heard it said that public policy sometimes seems to go in different directions. That is because some are unable to widen their view to see that public policy, certainly in the last year, is expressed by a variety of specifically designed programs all going in the same direction, toward a better society. The effects of the programs are cumulative and singular, as any comparison of the national economy today with that of a year ago will show, not to mention our position in the world.

The programs for youth will succeed not only in themselves but as parts to the broad stimulation of the economy toward a higher growth rate, the widening of employment opportunity for minority workers, the encouragement of business toward greater production and job creation, the opening of wider trade with a resurgent Europe, and the assistance of newer nations to obtain firmer economic and social footholds in the soil of freedom.

All of these things have an effect upon the future of our young people, upon the opportunity available to them now, and upon the resources at our disposal to aid them.

To charge our youth programs with being too moderate is to leave out of account the extremely viable and progressive context in which they exist.

I commend to the nation's attention another, more immediate consideration. The President has said: "Let us begin. . . ." And one must begin at the beginning. If our programs do not anticipate the kind of effort immediately that might be developed with experience, it is obviously because they are a beginning.

I rate as a significant part of this beginning the establishment of the President's Committee on Youth Employment. This Committee, in conjunction with others like the National Committee on the Employment of Youth, is doing much to arouse the public attention that is a necessary prelude to informed action.

And let me say that the problem itself seems complex enough, and difficult enough, and charged with human need enough, to command one consensus of opinion above all—let us make a beginning.

While legislation of the type we have proposed asserts the concern of the federal government and reflects the determination of government to fulfill its obligations, it also demonstrates that total solutions cannot always be afforded by the action of the federal government. The unemployed youth are not to be found walking the halls of Congress or seated in the councils of the executive branch. They walk the streets and gather on the corners and live in the homes of communities. The responsibility of local and state governments is manifest. To recognize that this is a national problem is not to absolve local obligation but to underscore it.

Our programs look forward, as well, to the support and sponsorship of labor unions, trade associations, educational groups, chambers of commerce and civic clubs. We are not seeking artificial opportunity, which would be in the nature of a restraining order from delinquency and despair. We are seeking to create genuine work opportunity, and this must rise from our communities themselves and from ourselves as citizens and employers and educators.

Let us remember that we are not dealing exclusively with the lack of opportunity for those young persons who are presently unable to find work. We must think, as well, in terms of the many millions who will be entering our labor force in the years immediately ahead—26 million young men and women will be flooding into the labor force, a full 7 million more than during the 1950's.

We must not only devise ways and means to unlock the cage of prejudice and ignorance in which unemployed and out-of-school youth are now isolated; we must build a better economic and social world.

There are many walls in the world—some shutting hope in, others shutting opportunity out. Some of these walls are of our own making and others are inherited from the past. None is more detrimental to a free society, more dangerous to the welfare of that society, or more harmful to the individual than those erected out of ignorance and prejudice. What society in its right mind believes it can long tolerate the denial of opportunity to its young people or endure the generation-long effects that follow from crowded slum conditions in which young people drift aimlessly and turn with hostility against authority?

Yet who builds these walls? We do. We build them by tolerating them. We build them by failing to act. We build them by accepting discriminatory practices. We build them with hiring policies and uneven educational expenditures, and by thinking that it is somebody else's problem.

No wooden horse ever rolled into Troy was more dangerous or explosive than what we are harboring among our unemployed youth. For the first time, I believe that this year has seen a national awakening to this fact and the beginning of a national determination to do something about it. It is a privilege to be a part of this beginning.

You are familiar with the concept of mutual benefit that underlies our legislation. Both the giver and the receiver of assistance are rewarded in the exchange of useful service for the opportunity to serve and learn. I believe that the concept extends far beyond the employer-employee relationship. It is equally appropriate for the entire effort in the youth field.

In the giving of time and labor and money, our society ultimately receives that greatest of awards—a younger generation capable of understanding and defending the ideals of freedom. And when we consider that all we have to give is opportunity, the price for that kind of future is ridiculously small.

You have been here for many hours today, and heard, I am sure, many, many words both knowledgeable and wise. I would add to them only this: We in Washington are absolutely committed to action. We have recommended legislation that represents the beginning of that action. We believe it merits the support of every citizen. We will not have it said of this generation of Americans that we permitted the future to escape us because we were not concerned with the loss of opportunity for our youth.

National Social Welfare Assembly, New York, N.Y., February 5, 1962

The Manpower Challenge

This nation today faces the challenge of achieving and maintaining full employment and an adequate and rising standard of living for all of our people. At the same time we must meet the political and economic threat to the free world and the obligations we have to aid underdeveloped nations.

To meet these challenges it is imperative that we devote increasing amounts of our energy toward educating and training our youngsters that they might be better equipped to cope with our rapidly changing social, political and economic environment. Because they represent a critical resource in our economy and society, it might be useful to review what the expectations are for our youth during this present decade.

First, because of the dramatic growth in our population since World War II, a growth that we fully anticipate will continue, workers under 25 will account for nearly half of the increase in the nation's labor force during the 1960's. This growth will occur notwithstanding the trend toward increased school enrollment and longer school attendance among those of high school and college age.

Along with the increased competition for jobs that will stem from the entry into the labor force of large numbers of youths, there will be a marked change in the kinds of jobs available, reflecting the increased pace of automation, with more and more industries demanding higher and higher proportions of skilled and professional personnel. During our lifetime we are witnessing a revolution in the composition of our work force connected with the dramatic advances we have made in technology and in the industrial structure of our economy. The number of white-collar jobs, which has already increased by over 25 per cent over the past decade, will probably go up by another 30 per cent between 1960 and 1970. White-collar jobs will constitute close to one half of all jobs by that date, in contrast to only a little over 20 per cent of all jobs in 1910.

During this decade alone the employment of professional and technical workers is expected to increase by about 40 per cent, and clerical and sales, managers and proprietors by a quarter. It is obvious that increased schooling will be necessary to fill these jobs even if the educational requirements for these occupations are not raised over the decade. On the other hand, while all other occupations will show growth, the number of laborers is expected actually to decline, reducing the opportunity for employment of youngsters who have failed to complete their basic schooling.

The ability of youth to take advantage of job opportunities in the occupations that are expanding and the ability of the nation to fill its job needs depends to an overwhelming extent on one factor—education and training. With technological change and the development of complex industrial techniques has come the demand for a better educated labor force.

Even today three of every four professional and technical workers have at least some college education; half of the clerical and sales workers have a high school diploma and about one third of the proprietors and managers have either a high school diploma or at least some college education.

Yet, despite the urgent and growing need for education to meet the skill requirements demanded by automation and technological growth, studies by the Office of Education show that of children enrolled in the 5th grade in 1952-53:

10 per cent dropped out by the 9th grade;

40 per cent dropped out before being graduated from high school;

70 per cent did not enter college.

The effects of this lack of educational preparation on the work careers of youths is clearly shown by studies in October of recent years on the job experience of young persons from 16 to 24 years of age, comparing those who were graduated from high school in the previous June with those who dropped out of elementary or high school prior to graduation.

Of the 1¾ million young men and women who were graduated from high school in June, 1961, almost half were enrolled in college the following October. Of those who were graduated but did not go on to college, most were in the civilian labor force. Their unemployment rate was 18 per cent. In sharp contrast, the unemployment rate of young persons of the same ages (16 to 24 years) who quit elementary or high school between January and mid-October, 1961, was 27 per cent. Among white males the 1961 school dropouts had an unemployment rate almost twice that of June graduates, 30 versus 16 per cent.

Moreover, there was a distinct difference in the skill levels of the jobs obtained by graduates and by dropouts. The kinds of jobs obtained by school dropouts were, in general, much less desirable. Thus, 28 per cent of the employed men who dropped out of school in 1961 were working as farm laborers, as against only 12 per cent of the employed men who graduated. Another 17 per cent of the dropouts were working as nonfarm laborers. Altogether, 45 per cent of the dropouts were laborers, primarily farm workers, while 35 per cent of the graduates were laborers, primarily in nonfarm industries. It is hardly necessary to point out that the future of farming as an occupation is a very precarious one and that job opportunities in farming are continuing to decline.

About the same proportion of men dropouts as graduates (one third) were working in semiskilled jobs (e.g., operatives), but only 5 per cent of the dropouts were craftsmen compared with 10 per cent for graduates. The difference in the caliber of jobs between dropouts and graduates was even more striking among women—only about one out of six of the employed women dropouts of 1961 were clerical workers compared with almost two thirds of the women graduates.

In addition to more unemployment and lower grade jobs there also tended to be more unemployment among dropouts than among graduates. Among men, about 30 per cent of nongraduates who last attended school in 1961 or 1960 worked fewer than 35 hours a week; the corresponding proportion for 1961 male graduates was less than 20 per cent. Eighteen per cent of the women graduates worked less than 35 hours a week compared with about 30 per cent of the nongraduates, due primarily to the fact that the latter were more highly concentrated in such unskilled jobs as household work, where part-time employment is more common.

In addition, education also bears an important relationship to earnings. In 1958 the median annual earnings of male high school graduates were around $4,500—$1,300 more on the average than earnings of workers who had quit school after the elementary grades, whose earnings averaged $3,200. In the same year college graduates were earning $6,600 on the average, or $2,000 more than high school graduates. The advantage of better education is also portrayed in the advancement of earnings. Between 1949 and 1958, among men 45 to 54 (the age group when highest incomes are normally attained) incomes of college graduates rose by about two thirds, those of high school graduates by about one half; and those of men who had not completed elementary schooling by one quarter.

The effect of dropouts therefore represents a problem of serious dimensions. We are at a point in our history where not only our economic and social well-being but our very survival as a great nation may depend on our ability to increase our rate of economic growth. Among other things, this requires greater technological advances, more automation in its broadest sense, more research and development, and more skilled and educated manpower to carry out these advances.

During this decade there will be a total of 26 million youngsters entering the labor market for the first time to embark on a work career. If we continue as we have in the past, 7½ million of these youngsters will not have finished high school.

It should be of some interest, and some concern, that while unemployment among school dropouts ranges up to 30 per cent, there is still a demand for skilled workers which cannot be filled. We know from our research that many dropouts have the intelligence to benefit from continued schooling, and that a good share of the dropouts could make the grade as skilled, highly trained blue-collar workers, or in clerical and sales work, if they had stayed in high school until graduation. We owe it to them, and to ourselves, to seek ways in which adequate education and training can be provided to give these youngsters a chance to earn a decent living and at the same time provide the nation with the skilled work force it needs to survive and prosper.

Conference on Social Ethics and Automation, Georgetown University,
Washington, D.C., July 12, 1962

The Continuing Task of Training

. . . Our country today is thinking about its manpower problems in many ways for the first time. We are seeking better ways to measure our potential and our needs. We are opening new approaches to the whole question of career and skill development. Perhaps for the first time in our history we are setting out to make opportunity a matter of design and not chance.

These are, then, momentous times for the educator, the vocational specialist, the government official, and everyone interested in a competent society able to compete in a challenging world.

Americans have always been proud of their technical know-how, their productivity, and their managerial skills. Our people have always recognized the value of formal education and good occupational training. The generally high quality of our public education facilities reflects this fact. The typical American family exerts itself to the utmost to provide the benefits of the best possible education for its children.

Furthermore, our country has faced major manpower challenges in the past: the settlement of vast uninhabited areas on the frontier, the absorption of millions of immigrants, and massive wartime demands. In the long run such challenges have been met successfully.

Why, then, all this recent interest in manpower development and training, an interest reflected in continuous public discussion, countless recent publications, and new government legislation? The reason for this interest is, I think, that Americans have come face to face with a dramatic new manpower situation—a situation requiring adjustments for which our existing structure of training institutions and practices is not adequate. This new situation is due to the fact that the normal tempo of change in the basic manpower needs and composition of our country has been accelerated beyond anything we have witnessed in the past. Furthermore, this upsurge in the rate of change of our manpower requirements is not a temporary or accidental condition. It reflects fundamental social and economic forces that are likely to be with us for a long time.

One of the most important of these forces is, of course, the progressively faster pace of technological change. If George Washington could see America as it was in 1899, a hundred years after his death, it would not have taken him very long to catch up with the changes of technology that had occurred. In fact, he would have seen millions of persons still living quite similarly to the way that many people had lived in his own lifetime. But if he could see America as it is today, it would seem like an entirely different world.

Over a relatively few years the advance of technology has created whole new industries—missiles, electronics, business machines, plastics, new forms of research—to mention a few.

New technology has substituted brand-new skills for older skills of traditional importance. We can cite data such as the fact that professional and technical employment rose 50 per cent in the decade of the fifties—more than three times the rate of increase in total employment—but the dry figures do not even begin to convey the drastic impact of the change.

New technology has been squeezing the unskilled worker out of the labor market and putting a premium on ever more advanced training.

Even more dramatically, new technology has shown a rising tendency to substitute machines for workers of all types. This process has been popularized as "automation," but giving it a name is of little help to the many thousands of displaced workers who must adjust to other industries and occupations in seeking their livelihood. The effects of this process on miners, manufacturing workers, farm workers and others are too well known to require comment.

The pace of technological change gives every promise of continuing to increase. We should note also that tax allowances to stimulate more rapid replacement of existing industrial equipment and facilities, currently under consideration by the government, will further accelerate technological change.

A second condition underlying the rising pace of change in labor requirements consists of shifts that have been occurring in the demand for the products of various industries. Such shifts are not new in our history; changes such as the substitution of petroleum products for coal for many purposes are familiar to us all. What is new, I believe, is a more rapid pace of such changes in recent years. We are all familiar, for example, with the dislocations that occurred in some areas recently when emphasis was shifted from the manufacture of aircraft to the manufacture of missiles and other space-related products. On a much broader scale, we may cite the surging growth of service industries. In 1949, employment in the service industries exceeded employment in the goods-producing industries for the first time. Last year [1961] the employment figures were 34.4 million in service industries compared with 25.2 million in goods-producing industries. Serious manpower adjustments are required to handle such dramatic shifts.

In recent years, too, a third trend has become visible—marked shifts in the *location* of job opportunities. Such shifts also are not new in our country. We have seen them in the advance of the frontier, the flow of people from farms to cities, and the partial migration of some industries such as textiles. But recent shifts have been sharper, over shorter periods of time. The distribution of prime defense contracts, involving billions of dollars, provides one illustration of this trend. The type of products required for the defense arsenal changed under the impact of new technology over the past decade or so, with much less emphasis on items like tanks and much more emphasis given to missiles and electronics. As a result, the share of military prime contracts going to the East North Central States fell from 27 to 12 per cent while the share going to the Pacific and Mountain States almost doubled to 33 per cent.

Another illustration can be drawn from comparisons of the rate of employment growth among different states. Between 1947 and 1960 nonfarm employment in Florida more than doubled. In California and Texas it increased by 59 and 46 per cent, respectively. In contrast, employment actually declined in West Virginia and Rhode Island.

Such shifts in the location of job opportunities must be understood in terms of the difficult personal adjustments required of individual workers. We are also increasingly aware of the fact that such shifts have often led to some areas becoming pockets of persistent unemployment and low income. Such areas require special attention to be returned to productive economic activity.

In considering our manpower requirements we must not overlook foreign trade relationships. Foreign trade, of course, has always influenced our labor needs. However, as our planet contracts in size, as so dramatically underscored by the Telstar satellite, the influence of other world economies upon us has become sharper. This interrelationship is also strengthened by the needs of our national foreign policy. We must be prepared, I believe, to recognize that significant and flexible adjustments of our manpower requirements will have to be made in line with the development of closer trade relationships abroad.

All of these forces have contributed and will continue to contribute to the sharp acceleration of the rate of change on the manpower scene. Over relatively short spans of time whole new industries and occupations must be manned and large groups of workers shifted to new industries, occupations, and areas. The swift currents of manpower needs require rapid and sensitive adjustments of our labor force to prevent personal and social dislocations. This is why such intensive emphasis is being placed on the whole field of manpower development and training.

In the face of the manpower changes I have touched upon, experience has shown that the existing structure of institutions and practices for developing and utilizing our human resources cannot adequately cope with the many new problems. Excellent as they often are, existing institutions and practices cannot keep up with the new forces which continuously upset the equilibrium between manpower supply and demand.

Look at today's labor market from the point of view of the individual worker. He usually receives a reasonably good education which facilitates his entry into the labor force at 18, 20, or 22 years of age. At this point he starts on his career with almost 40 years of work ahead of him. Under today's conditions, by the time 10 years have elapsed, his industry or occupation may have completely changed as to labor needs or job content. His job may have disappeared due to new processes or loss of demand for the products of his industry. His job opportunities may be shifting to other locations hundreds or thousands of miles away. The individual worker cannot be expected to adequately predict the bewildering fluctuations of labor needs, to foresee shifts in the location and type of job opportunities, to plan and finance his retraining or relocation, and to absorb the heavy costs of subsistence while retraining or seeking employment. New institutional arrangements must be developed to assist the individual as he faces today's complex job market.

Too many workers have found themselves shut out from the mainstream of economic life by the lack of suitable job opportunities. There are about one million long-term unemployed (persons who have been unemployed for at least 15 weeks) in our vastly rich country. Some 600,000 of these have been out of work 6 months or longer.

Under the pressure of technological innovation, we are coming to realize that there is also a need for innovation in the development and allocation of our manpower. We are beginning to see the pressing need to work out imaginative new ways to facilitate manpower adjustments without undue strains on the individual or the economy. This is a new challenge faced by the American economic system—a challenge to adapt our institutional framework to meet the complex new problems involved in full utilization of human resources.

I believe that, as always in American history, our economy and our government will prove responsive to the new challenge. We are privileged to witness and participate in the development of a new framework of concepts, institutions, and approaches to meet the needs of our people. Moreover, these new arrangements will be of a lasting nature, just as the various forms of social insurance and labor-management relation innovations of recent decades have become a basic part of the fabric of American life.

Underlying our new approaches to manpower development is a growing acceptance of the fact that the federal government must play an important role. Many forward-looking state governments have pioneered with new training programs for the unemployed and underemployed and with payment of unemployment compensation to unemployed workers enrolled in training courses. Many forward-looking industrial and labor leaders also have shown leadership in this field. But the task of manpower development and utilization is beyond the resources of individual states or private organizations. It is national in scope. It is related to national policies in such fields as defense and foreign trade. Its courses transcend the limits of particular areas or industries. And it requires a massive attack to keep pace with the massive changes that are occurring.

What approaches have been followed by the federal government?

1. The United States Employment Service, working with the state employment security agencies, has been strengthened. The employment security system is providing more comprehensive information on job opportunities and labor market conditions. It is seeking to identify in advance those industries and occupations which are going to be affected by technological or other changes and to facilitate the adjustments needed by workers and employers. The employment security system is extending its services to individual workers to assist them in adjusting to the demands of the labor market.

2. A pioneering step was taken with enactment of the Area Redevelopment Act of 1961. This law provides federal assistance to areas of substantial and persistent unemployment or very low income which have been left behind by rapid economic developments. The act includes the payment of training costs and living allowances for unemployed people in these areas, to equip them with skills needed to find suitable employment.

3. A still broader approach was taken in the Manpower Development and Training Act of 1962. This act provides for a program of basic research into manpower problems and into future manpower needs and resources. It is hoped that this will provide a basis for effective long-range planning to meet the manpower challenge.

The Manpower Development and Training Act also establishes a federally financed program for training unemployed and underemployed workers in occupations where there is a reasonable expectation of employment. This involves careful surveys to identify industries and occupations in which labor demand is present and permits the orderly transition of jobless people to productive employment. You are all familiar with this law and the role played by the Department of Health, Education, and Welfare and the state vocational education agencies.

Significantly, the MDTA adds additional innovations to the approach taken in the Area Redevelopment Act—it is not limited to redevelopment areas, it provides special programs for youth, and transportation and subsistence allowances are provided for trainees.

4. To facilitate adjustments caused by the easing of foreign trade restrictions, the Trade Expansion Act of 1962, currently under consideration by the Congress, provides for retraining assistance to adversely affected workers.

It is interesting to note that the proposed bill goes one step further than the Manpower Development and Training Act by authorizing allowances to help unemployed workers relocate to areas of labor need.

5. The Youth Employment Opportunities Act is another law under consideration which will help to round out our new approaches to manpower development.

All of these laws or proposed bills add up to a new institutional framework for handling our new manpower development problems. It is my belief that as this framework is improved through the day-to-day experience of experts like yourselves, it will provide the sensitive, flexible adjustments called for by the accelerating pace of change in our manpower requirements. In many respects we have a long way to go to meet all of our manpower needs, but I am confident that our government and society will prove responsive to the new conditions that face us.

At the same time we must accept the fact that the new approaches I have outlined are not a final answer to all manpower problems. They will not be of immediate benefits to more than a fraction of the 4½ million unemployed. They are not a substitute for measures to increase the rate of general economic growth. But they do represent a bold new departure in the area of manpower development and training. In this new departure, this group will play a key role.

Leadership Development Conference for Manpower Development and Training, Washington, D.C., July 31, 1962

3 🙠🙡

The Instruments of Freedom

Freedom means an ability to choose. But to be able to choose, a man must not only be outside prison, and not subject to the dictates of other men; he must also be able to make an informed, rational and intelligent choice. He must understand himself, his desires and his capabilities; he must have a stake in the community and an active interest in its affairs. He must understand the society in which he lives and the world around him.

City College of Chicago, Chicago, Ill., June 2, 1965

FREEDOM OF EXPRESSION

Freedom and Responsibility of the Press

A constitution which commands freedom for the press should inspire responsibility by the press. The framers of our Bill of Rights contemplated both a free and a responsible press. They vested in the courts the duty of assuring the constitutional freedom of expression and in the press itself the prime responsibility for making sure that its freedom is employed in the service and not in the destruction of liberty.

Every editor, I am sure, has found occasion to recall Thomas Jefferson's classic statement: "The basis of our government being the opinion of the people, the very first object should be to keep the right; and were it left to me to decide whether we should have a government without newspapers, or newspapers without a government, I should should not hesitate to prefer the latter."

Fortunately, in our free land we are not compelled to make this choice. I would paraphrase Jefferson to say: We cannot have a free government without a free press and we cannot have a free press without a free government.

Both ancient and modern history teach that the first step of a regime moving toward autocracy is restraint and control of speech and press. This is invariably the beginning of the destruction of all other liberties.

The first and primary responsibility of the press is therefore as protector and promoter of all the rights and liberties of Americans. The entire Bill of Rights is in the press's charge—not only the Free Speech Clause of the First Amendment. A newspaper which fails to exercise its right of free expression in protest against the invasion by any branch of government—the executive, the legislative, or the judicial—of freedom of thought, of conscience, of assembly, and of the person defaults in its most elementary duty and responsibility. The press must be the protector of all the amendments not only against their invasion by government but against their infringement by the press itself.

Our Bill of Rights assures the press freedom to report and comment; yet at the same time it guarantees to all a certain modicum of privacy. It requires that all trials be "public" and that the press have access to them; yet at the same time it guarantees to those accused of crime a trial by "an impartial jury" and with "due process of law." It is often urged that these rights are incompatible; that there can be no right of privacy unless the freedom of the press is curtailed; that there can be no "impartial jury" or "due process of law" unless the press is under the control of the courts. I, for one, cannot agree that these rights are incompatible or divisible; that one must be sacrificed if the other is to survive.

Under the principles of the Bill of Rights the prime responsibility for assuring that the press does not unduly invade the rights of privacy and fair trial rests not with the government, as it does in many parts of the world, but with the press itself. The press must measure up to this responsibility.

The press has a particularly acute responsibility in the area of crime reporting, especially in the pretrial phase. Of course, here, as elsewhere, the press must report the news. Suppression of this news, like suppression of any other news, is not to be tolerated. The rights of accused persons, however, must also be respected. The public—from whom the jurors will be selected—must be informed but not prejudiced. It must be informed so that it can prevent abuses both by governments and by criminal elements in our society. All too often, however, we must resort to jurors who are not informed in order to be certain that we are getting jurors who are not prejudiced by what they have read in the newspapers. It is sad that in this highly literate and educated country the only acceptable jurors are frequently those who can take an oath that they have read no newspapers and magazines for the past year. It is regrettable that experienced defense attorneys on occasion are compelled to say, and judges to rule, that a juror who has read newspaper accounts of the crime and arrest is bound to have prejudged the case against the defendant.

Some of the fault lies simply in the labels chosen by the press to describe those accused of crime. Weeks before, and even on the eve of trial the accused is all too often referred to as the "killer," the "robber," or the "hoodlum." All the good that courts do in reiterating our constitutional presumption of innocence can be easily erased by the press's constant reference to the "accused" as the "criminal."

Take, for example, the case of the fifteen-year-old New York youth named Peter, to whom Edward R. Murrow devoted a program some years ago. Peter had been charged with the brutal murder of an elderly man in Central Park. Newspaper headlines referred to the boy as a "young hoodlum" and a "vicious killer." Little mention was made of the boy's clean record, to his unequivocal denial of the charge, or to the paucity of evidence against him. As it turned out, the only evidence against the boy was the testimony of a thirteen-year-old girl with whom he had been in the park on the night of the killing. In court the girl admitted that her testimony was given because of her ambition to be a star witness in a big trial. In court it was also revealed that the dying man had made a statement identifying his assailants as two big boys. Peter was quickly acquitted. He was fortunate where others have not been. But, even so, the damage to his name and to that of his family is immeasurable, and doubly tragic because irresponsible press comment compounded his difficulties. The remedy in cases like this is not to curtail the press's freedom; it is to encourage responsibility.

Some of the fault lies in lack of knowledge and a failure of communication between the bar and the press. The bar, when it is critical of the press, must remember that few newspapermen have had legal training and that what may be elementary to the lawyer is fraught with jargon and complexity for the layman. The bar must be willing to inform the press and the press must be willing to listen. Northwestern University Law School has for the past few years conducted an annual course in crime news analysis and reporting which brings together members of the press and the bar in an effort to educate for professional responsibility and self-restraint. Programs such as this one hold much promise.

It would be most helpful in this area if this organization were to revive and refurbish its existing code of ethics by adding specific standards of crime reporting which, while preserving complete freedom for the press, will also adequately safeguard the rights of an accused. I am sure the bar will be glad to cooperate in a joint effort to articulate these standards.

Freedom of the press is not an end in itself. It is the means of guaranteeing that ideas deserving a public hearing will have a public hearing. The press which has the constitutional freedom to print the news therefore has the correlative moral obligation to supply the public need for accurate and comprehensive news coverage. Today, in the nuclear age, every citizen is importantly involved in public policy and newspapers must supply the public need for the source materials which are necessary to fashion policy. Increasingly in this country we are of one mind with Pericles when he said in the memorable funeral oration: "We alone regard a man who takes no interest in public affairs, not as a harmless but as a useless character." If we are not to be a nation of "useless characters," the press must supply us with the facts—the news not only of national but of international affairs. In a complex world our future as a nation depends upon a mentally alert society —a citizenry with experience, thought and feeling about their own and other lands and peoples beyond the range of private observation. It is a responsibility of an uncensored press to assist in keeping the people mentally alert. My colleague, Mr. Justice Douglas, has accurately described the state of men denied access to a free press: "Those who doubt the thesis that man needs full freedom of expression to realize his own capacities and become a cultured citizen of the world need only visit the totalitarian states and see how man has shriveled under the impact of censorship, how poorly he has fared under the diet of one creed. The horizons of the citizen in the conformity state are so limited he cannot react intelligently to the world around him."

It is our great strength as a nation that in our nonconformity state the horizons of our citizens are as wide as our free education and our free press will extend them. News coverage should be extensive; it should also be truthful. The Constitution precludes the imposition of liability on a newspaper for false statements in the public area that are not malicious. This constitutional standard is not fashioned to encourage or excuse deviations from accuracy but so that First Amendment freedoms will not be chilled by harsh penalties for mere misstatements. A newspaper's creed, however, must always be that stated by that great journalist, my fellow townsman, Melville E. Stone, upon the founding of the Chicago *Daily News:* "I had a view that the relation of a newspaper to a community was not very different from that of an individual. And so, in our dispensing the news, we were not unlike the witness in court, bound to 'tell the truth, the whole truth, and nothing but the truth.'" E. W. Scripps, cofounder of the Scripps-Howard newspaper chain, said the same thing in different words: "We shall tell no lies about persons or policies for love, malice or money."

If reporting the news objectively, truthfully and adequately is the first function and responsibility of a newspaper, then stating its opinion about the news is a close second. Bryce in *The American Commonwealth* said that "Newspapers are influential in three ways—as narrators, as advocates and as weathercocks." A newspaper which is only a narrator and not an advocate misconceives its responsibility to the public. The public need cannot be served by reporting the news alone; it requires vigorous and informed comment. The editorial page of every newspaper should be the proud badge of a great profession. Ideally it should reflect a variety of vigorous opinion. I emphasize variety as well as vigor because in many one-newspaper towns the publisher and the editor have the plain responsibility of providing columns and other materials presenting views which do not merely echo the editorials. The newspaper in the one-newspaper town must, on its editorial pages, serve the role of several newspapers with different opinions.

The one thing which is excluded, however, for any newspaper worthy of the name is editorial neutrality. Here again I quote Melville Stone: "The paper while independent in all things must be neutral to none." The very classless nature of American society imposes a particular responsibility upon the press. Social conflict here is of a sophisticated kind and not as overt as in other less fortunate lands. The press, however, would render a great disservice to ignore our conflicts or to fail to place them in proper perspective. The Commission on Freedom of the Press in its 1947 report astutely stated the problem: "Free expression is destined not to repress social conflict but to liberate it. But its intention is that the level of social conflict shall be lifted from the plane of violence to the plane of discussion." A responsible press should not be a cowardly press.

The press must be an example for all citizens that we have staked our all as a nation on the proposition that "there is no cure for bad arguments either in refusing to argue or repression of the free critic of the patient attempt to reach the elements of reasonableness in the mass mind."

A century and a half ago that perceptive visitor to our shores, Alexis de Tocqueville, anticipated one of America's present dilemmas: "The more equal the conditions of men become and the less strong men individually are, the more easily they give way to the current of the multitude and the more difficult it is for them to adhere by themselves to an opinion which the multitude discard. A newspaper represents an association; it may be said to address each of its readers in the name of all the others and to exert its influence over them in proportion to their individual weakness. The power of the newspaper press must therefore increase as the social conditions of men become more equal."

. . . The social conditions of men in America have become more equal since de Tocqueville wrote these words. The power of the press has increased, as he predicted. And so have its responsibilities. Our Constitution has made the press free; you have it in your charge to make it responsible. It is for you to demonstrate that press freedom and responsibility are viable and indivisible concepts.

American Society of Newspaper Editors, Washington, D.C., April 16, 1964

THE ARTS AS A COMMUNITY RESPONSIBILITY

The State of the Performing Arts

The financial crisis of the Metropolitan Opera, which raised the prospect that the 1961-62 season might not take place, may prove to have been an event of larger significance in the history of American culture. In an age when we must accustom ourselves to a welter of untoward and unwelcome events, there are yet some things that are unthinkable. It was unthinkable that the Metropolitan Opera season should not take place. Yet suddenly that very prospect faced us. Few events could have produced so instant a national awareness that an artistic calamity of the first order was in the offing. The insistent, repeated warnings of artists, critics, and benefactors as to the financial crisis of the performing arts in America were confirmed in the most dramatic possible way.

It is worth emphasizing that this situation was confirmed rather than discovered. The problem has been well known to and thoroughly expounded by any number of persons in responsible positions in cultural affairs. . . . It is not necessary to review the full range of information which is available on the financial condition of the performing arts nor to recapitulate the many valuable proposals that have been put forth to improve that situation. One central fact, however, is worth emphasizing. The problem of the performing arts in America today are not the problems of decline. They are the problems of growth: a growth so rapid, so tumultuous, so eventful as to be almost universally described as an explosion. . . .

Resources such as these for the consumption of artistic creation do not of themselves ensure creativity, but one could hardly hope for a climate more receptive to the creative artist. An era of unequaled achievement may well be upon us. Recently the *Times Literary Supplement* observed from England: "If neither a Bach nor a Michelangelo has as yet appeared in Detroit, a splendid mass of evidence has been assembled to point the way. Not only is the talent visible in ever-increasing quantity but the facilities for using it exist as nowhere else."

The American artistic scene today is alive and vibrant. At the same time some of the foremost institutions of American culture are in grave difficulty. The Metropolitan Opera is not alone. Other opera companies and a number of our leading symphonies share in a substantially similar financial plight. The artists, moreover, are generally underpaid. The details may differ, but the general condition is the same. The problem, of course, is money. The individual benefactors and patrons just aren't there, as they once were. Just as importantly, as we become more and more a cultural democracy, it becomes less and less appropriate for our major cultural institutions to depend on the generosity of a very few of the very wealthy. That is a time that has passed, and the fact is evident.

The question before the nation, then, is how to restore the financial viability of these institutions and to promote the welfare of the artists upon whom these institutions in the final analysis do and must depend. It is, to repeat, unthinkable that they should disappear at the very moment when they have achieved an unprecedented significance to the American people as a whole. They are a heritage of the past. They are equally as earnest for the future: they stand as our expectation of the quality of the American creative artists whose works they will perform.

The answer to this question is evident enough. We must come to accept the arts as a new community responsibility. The arts must assume their place alongside the already accepted responsibilities for health, education and welfare. Part of this new responsibility must fall to the federal government, for precisely the reasons that the nation has given it a role in similar undertakings.

The issue of federal support for the arts immediately raises problems. Many persons oppose federal support on grounds that it will inevitably lead to political interference. This is by no means an argument to be dismissed, and the persons who make it are to be honored for their concern for the freedom of artistic expression. In an age in which a third of the globe languishes under the pathetic banalities of "socialist realism," let no one suppose that political control of the arts cannot be achieved.

The overwhelming evidence, however, is that the free American society has shown a deep respect for the artistic integrity of the artist. Every attempt to interfere with that freedom has been met with vigorous opposition, not least from the artistic community. Artists are as susceptible to pressure as the next person, but for every artist who capitulates there is another to take his place from the unruly band which Russell Lynes has described as "the uncaptured, the disrespectful, and the uncomfortable searchers after truth."

The answer to the danger of political interference, then, is not to deny that it exists, but rather to be prepared to resist it. A vigorous, thriving artistic community, close to and supported by a large portion of the public, need not fear attempts at interference. Let our writers, and composers, and performers give as good as they get. Indeed, when have they done otherwise? The situation is no different from that of academic freedom in our colleges and universities: it is by defending their rights that our faculties strengthen them. This is ever the condition of freedom.

This is not an area in which we are without experience or precedent. For many years the arts have received support from public funds in many different forms. Much experience supports the general proposition that public support is most successful when it represents only a portion of the total funds involved. The principle of matching grants has clearly proved its validity and should be the basic principle of any federal participation in support of the arts. The variations of this arrangement are many, and perhaps as a general rule it may be said that the more levels of government, institutions and individuals involved the more likely it is that the artists themselves will retain control over their work.

The principle of diversity of support for the arts should accompany the principle of community responsibility. Our objective should be the establishment of a six-point partnership that will provide a stable, continuing basis of financial support for an artistic community that will at once be responsible to the needs and wishes of the public and at the same time free to pursue its own creative interests.

First. The principal source of financial support for the arts must come, in the future as in the present, from the public. Art is consumed in many forms, by a vast and widely diverse audience. The essence of a democratic culture is that the artistic community should have a large audience, drawn from all areas of the society, which returns value for value in a direct and equal relationship. While, if anything, greater provision should be made for special children's concerts and below-cost performances for special groups, the general musical and theatrical public must expect to provide a greater portion of the costs of the performing arts through devices such as season subscriptions and special associations for the support of particular activities.

Second. The patrons and benefactors of the arts have a continuing and vital role to play. It is inevitable that in an age of aesthetic creativity the interests and tastes of many of the best artists will run ahead of, or even counter to, the general standards of the time. Here the support of the enlightened patron can have the most profound and fruitful consequences. Similarly, there are many artistic forms of the past, of which opera is but one, which are simply too expensive to be supported entirely by ticket sales or general purchases. In such instances the support of art patrons makes it possible to preserve for the present and future many of the most profound creative achievements of the past.

Third. Private corporations must increasingly expand their support of community activities to include support for the arts. One of the hallmarks of American free enterprise is the remarkable extent to which business has voluntarily contributed to educational, charitable and health activities in localities throughout the nation. In line with the wider recognition of community responsibility for the arts, business corporations would do well to consider allocating, as a matter of course, a portion of their total contributions to these activities. . . .

Fourth. The American labor movement has a responsibility for support of the arts similar to that of American business. This has been recognized to some degree, as in the contributions several unions have made to support children's and other special concerts, but on the whole the community contributions of American trade unions have been directed for activities similar to those which have attracted business support. A parallel adjustment is in order.

Fifth. Local governments, and to a lesser extent state governments, are already providing a considerable measure of support for the arts, in line with the clearly manifested interest of the American people in expanding the artistic resources available to the general public. The support of art museums is already a general practice. Everyone accepts the fact that it is appropriate for a state or local government to provide housing and custodial support to such museums. The question naturally arises why this support should not be provided for our operas and symphonies as well. Of course, the main source of public support for the arts should continue to arise from the spontaneous, direct desire of local and state governments to provide for the needs of their own communities. This is an ancient tradition in the arts, one on which we might draw more extensively. For example, the practice of universities of making provisions for artists-in-residence might profitably be adopted by municipalities—one recalls that Bach for the last quarter century of his life was the municipal cantor of Leipzig.

Sixth. The federal government has from its beginning provided a measure of support for the arts, and there can be little question that this support must now be increased. This can and should be done in a variety of ways. The federal government may be a direct consumer of the arts, by commissioning sculpture and painting and awarding music scholarships. One of the most important, and perhaps the most proper role of the federal government is to help state and local governments and private nonprofit groups to build and maintain the physical plants required by the arts. Theaters, concert halls, galleries are the precondition of many of the arts. Public support at all levels of government in the area of helping to provide and maintain art facilities poses the minimum danger of government interference with the arts themselves. A splendid example of such cooperation is the Lincoln Center for the Performing Arts, where city, state and federal funds are all being combined to provide a magnificent cultural center in New York.

The concentration of public support upon providing physical facilities for the arts should not preclude programs of direct federal subsidy for theatrical and musical performances and similar activities. However, federal subsidies of this kind should be granted on a matching basis, with much the larger proportion of funds provided by private sources or by other levels of government.

The government has a larger responsibility toward the arts than simply to help support them. President Kennedy observed not long ago that the federal government "cannot order that culture exists, but the government can and should provide the climate of freedom, deeper and wider education, and the intellectual curiosity in which culture flourishes." Our concern with the condition of the arts in America must ultimately and principally take the form of concern for the position of the artists. Our principal interest is that the American artist should remain a free man. Without freedom there is no art or life worth having. That there are more comfortable conditions than freedom has no bearing on this central fact. However, we may also legitimately concern ourselves with the status of the artist in our society. An artist may be well fed and free at the same time. That an artist is honored and recognized need not mean he is any the less independent. America has a long way to go before our musicians, performers, and creative artists are accorded the dignity and honor to which their contribution to American life entitles them.[1]

Metropolitan Opera Arbitration Award, December 14, 1961

EDUCATION FOR FREEDOM AND EQUALITY

A Universal Provision for Learning

H. G. Wells once wrote that "Human history becomes more and more a race between education and catastrophe." This is particularly true in our nation, which is a democracy and must rely upon decisions made not by an elite ruling clique but by the majority of its citizens. This is particularly true also of our times, in which both technology and politics have become increasingly complex and difficult to understand and control. Education is necessary if we are to have a prosperous society, where the benefits of technology are made available to all; it is necessary if we are to have a peaceful society, internally harmonious and cooperative in its relations with

[1] On September 29, 1965, President Johnson signed Public Law 89–209 creating the National Foundation on the Arts and the Humanities.

other nations; it is necessary if we are to have a free society, for, as Thomas Jefferson pointed out, freedom and ignorance are mutually incompatible.

Freedom means an ability to choose. But to be able to choose a man must not only be outside prison, and not subject to the dictates of other men; he must also be able to make an informed, rational and intelligent choice. He must understand himself, and his desires and his capabilities; he must have a stake in the community and an active interest in its affairs. He must understand the society in which he lives and the world around him. In fact, education for freedom is education which accords with the suggestion of the President's Commission on National Goals: that we must work for "individual self-fulfillment," that we must develop "manpower with new and ever-improving skills," and that we, as a democratic nation "must have an informed and responsible electorate."

Education for freedom must be education which develops the individual. It must teach him to think critically, to integrate facts and principles into meaningful patterns, to apply the knowledge that he acquires in one area to problems in other areas. It must develop a set of personal and social principles and ethical standards. Above all, it must develop a man's creative abilities and his personal talents. As Justice Oliver Wendell Holmes stated, "Life is action, the use of one's powers. As to use them to their height is our job and duty, so it is the one end that justifies itself. . . . With all humility, I think 'Whatsoever thy hand findeth to do, do it with thy might.' " I believe that there is no greater tragedy than the tragedy of wasted talent. Today there are almost one million young people under twenty-one both out of work and out of school. They comprise, through no fault of their own, a disgraceful national waste. Their talents, as well as the talents of those young men and women who are presently working or studying, must be developed through education, so that what now constitutes a tragic national waste will become an invaluable national, as well as personal, asset.

Developing the minds and the abilities of our youth has, perhaps, become a more difficult task as knowledge multiplies at a furious rate, and the more comprehensive training is required to fulfill the increasingly complex technological needs of our society. If twelve years was once sufficient to transmit our cultural, intellectual and scientific heritage to succeeding generations, it is certainly no longer so. The particular virtue of the junior college system is its realization of the need for widespread education after high school. I believe that education ought to be expanded broadly at all levels, and, in particular, I think that fourteen years of compulsory education for all would be desirable.

I stress the word "all" to show that I sharply disagree with that school of thought which holds that higher education is only for the intellectual.

Rather, in my view, the pursuit of excellence in education is as important to the common laborer in his sphere as it is to the Ph.D. in his. It is not true that some are not qualified for education. In fact, everyone is *capable* of being educated. Clearly people have different needs and different abilities. But, it is the duty of a democratic society to build an educational system, public and private, which fits the abilities and fulfills the needs of each particular individual. We must take special care to see that no one is held back because his family is poor or because his early family life did not adequately equip him for school and education. But, beyond this, I believe that the day must soon come when our educational system develops, and does not let go to waste, the minds and the abilities of every one of our youth. For this to occur, some education beyond high school will be necessary for everyone. It should at least be available to all, and perhaps even compulsory. As James Russell Lowell said, "But it was in making education not only common to all, but in some sense compulsory on all, that the destiny of the free republics of America was practically settled." The fulfillment of this destiny now requires that the education which all have in common be broadened and deepened; it must not only be made available to all in theory, but each person must in fact receive this education.

Education for freedom is education that enables each man and woman to take his place in our nation's working force. When he finishes school there must be a job available for him and he must be capable of performing that job. The educational demands placed upon young people today as they go out looking for jobs are much greater than ever before.

There is a revolutionary change taking place in the nature of the work force. The need for unskilled workers is rapidly disappearing. The kinds of jobs available reflect the increased pace of automation, with more and more industries demanding higher and higher proportions of skilled and professional personnel. The number of white-collar jobs, which has already increased by over 25 per cent over the past decade, will probably go up by another 30 per cent during the 1960's. White-collar jobs will constitute close to one half of all jobs by 1970, in contrast to only a little over 20 per cent of all jobs in 1910. The National Science Foundation has estimated that by 1970 all industry would require more than 1,300,000 technicians. This figure, contrasted with 775,000 employed in 1960, gives some sugges-tion of the education and training job ahead. On the other hand, job oppor-tunities for unskilled young people will become rarer. Take the telephone industry, for example, where between 1950 and 1960 the number of tele-phone operators 18 to 24 years old dropped from 130,000 to 81,000, while the number of telephones in use grew by 31 million. Automation alone made it possible for the industry to reduce the number of inexperienced young women employed as operators by 40 per cent during a period when the volume of traffic increased by 60 per cent. And in banking, to take another example, once banks install a magnetic ink system they stop hiring high school graduates as machine bookkeepers. Two large New York banks reported that in 1960 they hired 144 machine bookkeepers; in 1961, 115; in 1962, 5; and in 1963, none. The Secretary of Labor has pointed out that "[t]he machine now has a high school education in the sense that it can do most jobs that a high school graduate can do, so machines will get the jobs because they work for less than a living wage. A person needs 14 years of education to compete with machines."

I agree fully with Secretary Wirtz that fourteen years of education is no longer a luxury but a necessity. The ability of youth to take advantage of job opportunities in the occupations that are expanding and the ability of the nation to fill its job needs depends to an overwhelming extent on one factor—education and training. With technological change and the development of complex industrial techniques has come the demand for a better educated labor force. A high school diploma is no longer sufficient to qualify for the jobs that are most available in industry. Even today, 3 out of every 4 professional and technical workers have some college education. Within a few years the young person who has only a twelfth-grade education may be as handicapped on the job market as the high school dropout is today.

Yet, in order to be free a man must have a job; he must have economic security; he must have freedom from want. Years of experience in this country as well as throughout the rest of the world have taught us that where there is poverty, and where there is unemployment, there is no freedom of any sort. Aristotle said that "Education is the best provision for old age." In fact, it is the best provision for any age. Today, it is more important than ever that young men and women receive the adequate education necessary for them to take their place as productive members of society.

Education for freedom means education that prepares men and women to take an active part in the governing of this democracy. Each citizen has an affirmative responsibility to determine for himself whether the actions of the government of the day are right or wrong and to cast his vote in accordance with his beliefs. But this determination must be informed and intelligent— it must be an educated judgment. The complexities of today's political problems require education for their understanding. The far-reaching importance of political decisions—concerning, for example, the use of atomic weapons or full employment—the effects of which are immediately and directly felt by every single citizen, requires that each of us attempt to make judgments as to the correctness of these decisions. The necessity that political control remain in the hands of the people requires that the educated judgment of each of us be exercised. As Jefferson pointed out, the diffusion of knowledge among the people is the only sure foundation that can be devised for the preservation of freedom. Where the people are enlightened, "tyranny and oppression of both mind and body will vanish like evil spirits at the dawn of day." We have always trusted to the vote of the people to preserve our country from tyranny. In today's complex world that vote, if it is to be effective, must be an informed and an educated vote. I quite agree with the sentiments of President Garfield that "next in importance to freedom and justice is popular education, without which neither freedom nor justice can be permanently maintained."

Education for freedom must also be education in freedom. Freedom of instruction, the toleration and sounding of a variety of viewpoints, an open climate of discourse and inquiry—all these must be present in the college and university if democracy is to be present in society. Moreover, and in my view equally important, education in freedom requires an education of the heart and spirit as well as the mind. I believe that a university, to be true to its faith, should not only fuel the minds of its students but should also fire their bellies. It should give them a sense of commitment, a willingness, even more an eagerness, to "plunge . . . deep in the stream of life . . . to share its passion, its battles, its despair, its triumphs." In other words, education in freedom not only requires an atmosphere in which free discussion takes place, but it also requires interest and commitment on the part of students in problems that are worth talking about.

I am one who welcomes the concern among students about the great problems which confront our nation. I fear intellectual disengagement more than I do involvement, although I hasten to add that involvement to be effective must be informed and responsible and not merely emotional. But, more importantly, involvement and concern must continue after graduation. For, whatever the case may be with students, by and large college graduates all too often seem disengaged from the problems which confront us.

A college graduate in a world of science and automation will find a job and at good pay—he is isolated from and largely indifferent to the plight of the 5 among his 100 fellows who, lacking education or training, cannot for years on end find work. A college graduate will work in the cities and live in the suburbs—shutting his eyes and closing his mind to the slums which breed delinquency and crime. A student in a Northern college or university will live and mix with all races and creeds and vigorously endorse resolutions and often participate in demonstrations for civil rights, only later to withdraw in his social life and neighborhood from the benefits and burdens of the open society which presumably is our democratic goal. The educated man will unthinkingly applaud flagrant violation of law by officials under the excuse of necessity, never reflecting that if those sworn to enforce the law do not uphold it, respect for law by all is undermined. The better paid, educated man can ensure his child's education in private schools—the neglected state of public education need not concern him; he can hire a lawyer to defend his son who gets into trouble—the concept of equal justice under law for rich and poor alike is for the courts, not for him. I could multiply the examples which illustrate the growing isolationism of our educated class from the body of our citizenry.

For me the real enemy of a free society is not an opposition to essential reform but rather a general inertia and general unawareness or lack of concern, a general disengagement of the individual from social responsibility. . . . Thus I believe that education in freedom must be education that produces commitments and interests which will last over a lifetime. It is education in an atmosphere conducive to free discussion and debate. In educating for freedom, it develops the minds and abilities of our youth, it fits them for a useful role in society, and it prepares them to play an active part in the affairs of our democracy.

Education for freedom must also be education for equality. We have learned over the past few years that freedom and equality are not opposed to one another. Rather, they complement each other and advance together, hand in hand. The man who is discriminated against because of his color, or his religion, or because he is poor, is a man who is not free. And it is of particular importance that everyone be afforded the equal opportunity that only education can give.

Yet it is plain that, in spite of remarkable advances, even an equal opportunity for education is a goal which we are far from achieving. In 1960 there were 1,079,000 high school graduates who did not go on to college; and 42 per cent indicated that finances played a role in their decision not to go. Of these nearly half flatly said that they could not afford to consider college at all. Thus, some 217,000 high school graduates who would have liked to have continued their education were prevented from doing so by financial inability. Of the number of young people who did go on to higher education, 22 per cent dropped out by the end of the first year. Of these, 28 per cent gave lack of money as the prime reason for dropping out. The relation between family income and college attendance is clear. In 1960, for example, 78 per cent of all high school graduates whose families had incomes of $12,000 or more per year went on to college. By contrast, only 33 per cent of students whose families earned less than $3,000 per year went on to higher education.

And many of the students who simply cannot afford college are among the most academically qualified. According to the findings of the Office of Education's Project Talent, 30 per cent of the high school seniors in the 80 to 90 academic percentile of their class and 43 per cent of those in the 70 to 80 percentile fail to enter college. Of the top 50 per cent of the boys graduated from high school—the top 50 per cent with respect to aptitude—37.9 per cent of those from families with incomes of less than $3,000 did not enroll in college, while the figure for those from families with incomes of $12,000 is only 10.5 per cent.

These figures make clear that except for the student of rare ability—the student who is in the top 2 per cent of his class—whether or not a young man or woman goes on to college is determined by his level of income. As the Commissioner of Education has stated, "In the light of our needs as a nation, this situation represents serious loss. In the light of our traditions, it is shameful."

The reason, of course, that family income seems to dictate whether or not a child will have a college education is that college education is becoming increasingly more expensive. The average cost for a year's study at a state university is $1,700, and it is $3,350 at some of our private universities. A year's study at a public junior college costs an average of only $750. Junior colleges have in this way provided the opportunity for thousands of students to profit from the collegiate experience who could not have done so if they had had to travel miles from home and pay dormitory, tuition and board costs.

The junior college exercises its democratizing influence in numerous other ways. I am pleased that the Chicago City College has seen fit to open nine different campuses, serving widely separated sections of the city. Proximity seems to be a major factor in motivating students to attend college, particularly when they are from low-income families and must work while attending school. Most of the students at colleges such as Chicago City live within a mile of the campus where they study.

A college such as this one also provides opportunity for students who, without it, could not get a fair chance. Foreigners with English language difficulties or students from families with little education often do not do well on tests and in interviews but can derive considerable benefit from college work. There are numerous instances of "late bloomers" whose high school record is no key to inherent ability. I suppose that one of the most famous of these is Winston Churchill, who often pointed out the fact that he would not have been able to gain admittance to college had he been forced to pass entrance examinations.

With their open admissions policy, its low costs, and its proximity to the homes of its students, city colleges are able to have a student body which is truly diverse, consisting of all types of students from differing backgrounds, with different interests and differing opinions. This in turn goes far in providing equal opportunity for education and also in providing education in the type of equality which is a necessary part of democracy.

Education for equality must do more than merely provide equal opportunity for education and provide an environment in which students from various backgrounds can meet. It must also, somehow, so impress students with the values of mixing with all types of people that they do not later, after leaving college, withdraw into the confines of a narrow group. It never ceases to amaze me how men who as students lived and mixed with all people—people of different races, different religions, different political views, and different economic backgrounds—soon after leaving college begin to restrict their social contacts to those of similar race, similar religion, similar political position, and similar wealth. They join exclusive clubs, they live in restricted neighborhoods, they limit their social contacts primarily to persons who share their general outlook and beliefs. Education for equality must be education that both emotionally and intellectually convinces the student of the value of drawing his acquaintances from and maintaining contact with all sorts of different people from the entire spectrum that life in all its richness provides; and it must convince him of the value of maintaining this practice not only during his student days but throughout his entire life.

Many centuries ago Epictetus pointed out that "only the educated are free." Today we not only realize the need for education so that each of us may be freed from the bonds of ignorance, but we recognize that a free and democratic society can survive only if each and every one of its citizens is educated. We must, therefore, each assume the burden of working for more universal provision for learning, so that its light shines not only in the life of each of us but in the life of our nation as well.

City College of Chicago, Chicago, Ill., June 2, 1965

The Courts

Reflections of the Newest Justice

When a peripatetic Secretary of Labor becomes a sitting Associate Justice of the Supreme Court some do and many would like to inquire about his reactions to the change. I propose tonight to attempt to satisfy this natural curiosity.

One is "elevated" to the Court and consequently, in socially conscious Washington, eats higher on the hog, but the Secretary, though outranked at the table, is driven to dinner in a government Cadillac, whereas the Justice steers and parks his own car. Who gains by the exchange depends on a value judgment—whether a good chef is to be preferred to a competent chauffeur.

The Secretary's phone never stops ringing; the Justice's phone never rings —even his best friends won't call him.

The Secretary continually worries about what the President and an unpredictable Congress will do to his carefully formulated legislative proposals; the President, the Congress and the Secretary wonder what the Justice will do to theirs.

The Secretary's infrequent and sporadic vacations are inevitably interrupted by unanticipated strikes; the Justice's publicized long recess by an apparently endless flow of petitions for certiorari, difficult stay applications, and the certitude that if he vacations too obviously he will be "time charted" by Professor Hart and the editors of the *Harvard Law Review* in the forthcoming November issue.

The Secretary numbers among his several thousand employees doorkeepers to guard his privacy; the newest Justice is, himself, the doorkeeper to protect the Court's.

Both Secretary and Justice need the support that only prayers can give in resolving the grave problems of office. The Secretary can ask freely for yours; the Justice hardly is in a position to do so.

But enough of differences in status, what about functions? The Secretary is expected to mediate labor disputes; the Justice, presumably freed from this role, early in his first term becomes increasingly aware, to quote Professor Black, that "The real problems of law involve not faithful obedience to beauteous maxims but the mediation of competing claims each with a measure of soundness!"

There are, of course, many profound differences in the respective mediatory roles. The Secretary deals with conflicts between labor and management. These can be very difficult, as my successor in the Cabinet is, at this very moment, experiencing. But the Justice's mediation is infinitely more complex. It involves conflicts between state and nation, state and state, the individual and all branches of government both state and national, and individual and individual.

The Secretary can persuade the contending parties to settle their differences—he cannot compel them to; the Justice must decide the controversy, not merely recommend settlement terms. He cannot escape the inexorable duty of judgment—but a Court's decision cannot merely rest upon "it is so ordered," it must also persuade. . . .

The Secretary, as a mediator, inevitably is driven to seeking peace—for him a settlement without any strike, or at least without a prolonged strike, is the goal. He can *hope* that the settlement will prove to be fair and equitable to the public as well as to the involved parties, but this can be no more than a hope, since sanctions are lacking and strong-willed parties are involved.

The quest of the Justice in resolving conflicts is justice under law. The Judge seeks the right settlement—not the expedient one. The Secretary's objective is peace—peace almost at any price. The judicial process assumes peace; it rests upon unreserved acceptance of and compliance with the decisions of the Court of last resort. Democratic government cannot endure if the law is defied by those in or out of authority. Ever since Chief Justice Marshall, one hundred and sixty years ago, in *Marbury* v. *Madison*, declared that "It is emphatically the province and duty of the judicial department to say what the law is," it has been a permanent and indispensable feature of our constitutional system that, unless changed by the orderly processes of the Constitution, the decisions of the ultimate Court must be respected and obeyed.

Decisions in a democracy are not immune from criticism; they may be changed by legislation or constitutional amendment or even reconsidered by the Court itself but, until and unless so changed, to defy them or obstruct them is to deny the law itself.

No judge or lawyer worthy of the name can attach any constitutional importance to current revivals of the old and discredited doctrine of interposition or nullification. . . .

It is too late in our history to revive the wholly academic contention that the Fourteenth Amendment is unconstitutional. The Court throughout the years, and as recently as last term, has applied the Amendment in many cases. It is clear beyond peradventure from an unbroken line of the Court's decisions that the process by which that Amendment was ratified does not present a justiciable issue.

Another pervasive difference between judging and labor mediation is that the labor mediator lacks guidelines for settlement of disputes and that no one has been authorized to provide them. Judges, on the contrary, have as their decisional touchstone the Constitution, provided by the people themselves.

I remember all too well the rather tentative attempt of the Administration during my tenure as Secretary to suggest guidelines for wage settlements in the Economic Report of the Council of Economic Advisers. Both labor and management joined not only in rejecting them but in challenging the very right of government to enunciate guidelines, even as suggested goals rather than commands. I had to fall back on government's right of free speech to defend the suggestions.

For judges the Constitution provides the guidelines. The greatest political document known to man is a brief paper consisting of a preamble and seven short articles containing in all about six thousand words. Yet in it we seek and find the answers to the complex problems of liberty and order in a nuclear age. Although judges often may wish for more precise guidance in groping for decisional light, all surely recognize that the genius of the Constitution rests, in considerable measure, in the flexibility of the document, in the purposeful generality of its eloquent phrases, and in the nobility of its stated ideals. This has enabled it to endure to this age and, the people willing, will preserve it for ages to come.

One can inquire as to who is the rightful definer of the public interest in labor disputes; no one can legitimately question the source of the Constitution. The Constitution of the United States is an act of the people. Its very first words are "We the people of the United States." It was drafted by a convention, submitted by Congress, and ratified not by state legislatures but by special conventions. Under our Constitution the sovereign people are the real sovereignty. This does not gainsay that important powers are reserved by the Constitution to the states, just as others are delegated to the United States. Both nation and state are vital in our constitutional structure and no judge upholding the Constitution would deny to the states their legitimate rights nor fail to recognize the vital necessity of preserving the states as strong and vigorous government units. . . .

State and federal judges may legitimately differ as to whether particular decisions of our Court correctly apply constitutional principles of federalism and a continuing dialogue in this difficult area is to be welcomed. There is no place, however, for differences between state and federal judges in the basic proposition that the Constitution is the "supreme Law of the Land" and is of binding effect on the states, "anything in the Constitution or Laws of any State to the Contrary notwithstanding." All of us, federal and state judges, members of Congress and state legislatures, federal and state executive officers are solemnly committed by oath "to support this Constitution."

This oath to support and defend the Constitution is more than a solemn obligation; it is the irrevocable bond of a brotherhood dedicated to the fulfillment of the great promise of our democracy.

The 9th Secretary of Labor of the United States served in an office replete with the excitement of the moment; the 94th Justice serves in one filled with the excitement of the ages. The Secretary left his post having tried, to the best of his ability, to fulfill the statutory mandate of advancing the interests of the wage earners and the industry of the country; the Justice enters upon his judicial office conscious that he has been called upon to do his part in the "sacred stir toward justice" and with the trembling hope "that the flame will burn bright while the torch is in [his] keeping." . . .

American Bar Association, Chicago, Ill., August 12, 1963

The Judicial Task

It was said by the very distinguished man who occupied the seat that I occupy, that when a judge puts on his robe, he becomes a different man. Like all sweeping generalizations, that is only partially true. Of course, when he puts on his robes he is the same man that he always was during his lifetime. He is the product of his experience, his background, his predilections, his basic, deeply felt points of view. It would be idle and wrong, and mischievous, I think, for any judge, sitting in any court, to deny this; and it is not helpful, in my opinion, in the course of a democratic constitutional tradition for it to be otherwise. Indeed, psychologists would tell us that, even if we wanted to, it could not be so. But yet there is truth in Justice Frankfurter's observation, because when you do put on that robe you change. You are bound to change. You are assuming functions which are quite different from the functions you have performed throughout all the rest of your life.

I, as the judge said in the introduction, had a long career at the bar. I was admitted on a Black October day in 1929, when the stock market crashed. I spent the years of my early practice in the depths of the great depression, the early part of it in the general practice of the law and the latter part of it in the field of a newly developing area of the law, labor law.

No one who lived through that experience, the experience of a great war, the experience of the postwar world, who has served very proudly in the Cabinet of a new Administration, could not be affected by that experience. And yet, as I have said, when you put on that robe, walk in through the marble palace which is our courtroom, to sit in the conference room, bare of all adornments except the picture of the great Chief Justice John Marshall, and you are handed by the marshal the genealogy of your seat on the bench, and you realize with great awe and with great humility that you are sitting in the seat which was occupied by Oliver Wendell Holmes and by Benjamin Nathan Cardozo and by Felix Frankfurter, and, to go very far back, by Joseph Story, then a profound change is bound to take place in your life, in your thoughts, in your attitude, and in your views.

It has been also said, and here there is no gainsaying the fact, that judging is a very lonely business; and it is a very lonely business. You are catapulted, by the way our democratic country works, from affairs of the world, from being a very busy, energetic Secretary of Labor, occupied every moment with important—or so they seem to you—incidents of the day, of great domestic disputes, of great economic problems, to the bench, and, as I said the other day in Chicago, much to my regret since then, your phone, which has been ringing every minute, suddenly doesn't ring at all. . . . Having said that, I received, upon returning from Chicago, where I made that statement at a Bar Association meeting, about eight hundred telephone calls, which swamped the inadequate facilities of our Court.

But it is a lonely business only in a certain sense. It is lonely in the sense that you must deal, by yourself, basically, and for yourself, basically, with the great problems which confront you as a judge. It is not lonely in the sense that you commune with very great spirits, with those masters of the law who preceded you, who teach in our law schools, and who practice at the bar, who are the great fraternity that makes up a relationship, one to another, of the legal system of the United States. . . .

I propose to talk about two things: First, I would like to tell you about how our Court works. Secondly, I would like to make some observations about the changing notion of the substantive doctrine that we deal with.

I have found great misunderstanding about the way the Court works, partly due to our own fault and partly due to the fault of the public at large. There have been, and I am sure you have read, some of you who have had constitutional law, some descriptions of the way our Court functions as an institution. It has been one of the traditions of the Court that judges on occasion talk about it. I think it ought to be more talked about, because I found the public at large just doesn't understand it. . . .

Our Court sits as a Court, a single Court. We do not sit in divisions, and everything we do we do as a Court of nine men. We are, therefore, unlike some courts of review in the United States. Many courts of review, for very good reasons, sit in panels or divisions, so as to dispatch their judicial business promptly and effectively. There is no criticism to be implied from my comments about the way we operate. We operate as a unit, nine of us sit together in every case that comes before us, not only in every case, in every motion that comes before us, except applications to individual Justices for stays when the Court is not sitting. That is a tradition of our court. Some say . . . it is a constitutional requirement. Since that has not been argued before us, in a case or controversy, and since we only pass on cases and controversies, I can't tell you whether that is correct as a matter of constitutional law. I have learned to inhibit my own opinions about constitutional law until a case is argued before me.

We sit as a group, and that imposes great burdens on the Court, because we have a great and increasing volume of business before the Court. The public believes, because they do not know, that the Court disposes by written opinions of about 130 or 140 cases a year. That is correct. Those are the cases in which we write opinions. But we also dispose, for all practical purposes, of another, the past term, another 2,200 cases, by order which is not accompanied by a written opinion. In the last term of Court that we concluded, we disposed of 2,350 cases. Those dispositions were made—again I want to emphasize—by the whole Court.

I know lawyers who are the victims of our actions in disposing of these cases by the denial of petition for certiorari, or by summary affirmance or dismissal of appeal, wonder sometimes whether the Court can dispose of 2,350 cases, and we have even been time-charted by the editors of the *Harvard Law Review*, who have demonstrated that if we were to dispose of 2,350 cases our average time for disposition is about one minute and a half per case. Well, I have not, since I left the Department of Labor, used much mathematics in deciding issues, but I would merely like to say that our procedure is such that we do collectively consider and dispose of all cases.

The way that's done is this. Lawyers ought to know this. Every case that we have is listed on a conference list when we go into conference. There are a number of cases where, by common consent, we note the name of the case and we agree that it does not present any issue worthy of adjudication. But, as a safeguard against too summary a disposition of such cases, any Justice—any Justice—can note for conference that he would like that particular case discussed at greater length. And if any single Justice so notes, that case is discussed. So we do, however, dispose of a large number of the 2,300 by common agreement that there is no issue worthy of review. You know that if four of the nine Justices agree that a case ought to be reviewed on certiorari, that case is reviewed . . . we have the rule of four. And you can readily assume that the rule of four itself is not too inflexible a rule. If as few as three, or sometimes two, of the Justices feel strongly that an issue that is in a case is important enough for the Court to take, other colleagues not initially so disposed, because of their respect for convictions strongly held by this minority of the Court, will vote to grant certiorari, and a case will be heard.

When a case is heard, it is argued before our Court. And our normal system is to allow an hour on each side for argument, except in cases where we feel that we don't need that much argument, in which we allow a half hour on each side. It is my equally happy experience now to sit on the bench and hear cases argued. And, if I may, I would like to give a word of advice to you as future practitioners before our Court. And perhaps what I say is true of any court, I don't know. I can only talk about the Court on which I sit. What our Court wants to know, and I presume what any Court wants to know, when a case is to be presented to us, is the essential, underlying, fundamental nature of your case, what it is about, and why your client should prevail—the essential . . . constitutional equity of your case. . . . And if, as future advocates, you want a tip from me, spend more time on your facts than on your law in arguing before our Court. I said that advisedly, not that we are not a court of law—we are deeply committed to the principles, the basic law, what it is—but . . . what you can bring to bear is that infinite detailed knowledge of your case, and your conviction as an advocate of having a case, that your client is entitled to win.

Do not orate before our Court, but that does not mean that you should not speak strongly, convincingly and thoroughly about what your case is about. The days of the great orators, of the old-fashioned courtroom, I think are pretty well vanishing. I think it is correct that when Daniel Webster addressed the Court he addressed it for several days. You've got to be a great orator, I suppose, if you are going to talk for several days. But when you have half an hour . . . which is often the case, then that requires an economy of voice, and of content, which did not discipline great advocates like Daniel Webster.

After a case is argued before us—once you get through certiorari, a case is argued—we would then go to conference. We hear arguments four days a week; we have conferences on Friday. We go to conference right that week and vote on the cases that are argued that week, which again emphasizes the important role of oral argument on our Court. The first vote takes place right after we have heard you, while the case is fresh in mind, and at conference we vote and discuss and vote, every Justice participates, and immediately after conference the writing of opinions is assigned by the Chief Justice if he's in the majority, by the senior Justice who is in majority if the Chief is in dissent.

Our process then is to go into what I earlier described as the lonely process, if you have been assigned the task of composing the Court's opinion; not your own, when you're in the majority. You don't have the liberty that you have when you're in dissent. . . . The writing of the majority opinion, the Court's position, is a long process. One time last term, in writing an opinion for the Court, I circulated ten printings of the opinion before it was settled by the Court as the opinion of the Court. Dissenters, of course, have the luxury of dissent, a very heady business for judges, I might say, because in a sense when you dissent you are free from responsibility. You may assail and attack, and, indeed, dissenting judges have been known to do that. You may point out the great errors and shortcomings of the majority in terms that sometimes are too sweeping. Remember, however, when you read a dissent, and, for that matter, some concurring opinions, remember that you must not take your authoritative construction of what the majority says from a dissent. That's a dangerous business to do, because there is no restraint about what a dissenter may say. There is a restraint upon the majority Justice. He must keep the votes of his colleagues in order to hand down an opinion of the Court.

I would like to say a word now about the nature of the Court's business.

Throughout the history of the Court, the nature of its business constantly changes and, again, laymen wonder why. Should not the course of constitutional adjudication be a straight, steady and consistent course? What kind of law do you have if the nature of the Court's business changes, and, indeed, if decisions change, as they do?

Well, there are two explanations, I think, which we can advance for this. The nature of the Court's business changes because the times change. Conditions change. We live in a world far removed from the world of the framers of the Constitution, a world in which physical sciences have advanced, the economic structure has changed, of the country, indeed of the world, and a world which in many ways could not have been visualized at the time the Constitution was adopted. And, therefore, we handle many, many cases which are new cases, new in the sense that the issues involved, the direct issues involved, have never been decided before. It is a constant source of interest to me, as a new Justice, to see how many cases come before us with respect to which there is no controlling precedent.

But the Court changes too. We must be frank about that. And I think frankness, instead of making the public feel that there is no stability in our institutions, frankness will make the public better understand the reasons which compel a constitutional court to change its decisions, to acknowledge error, and to rectify error where error has occurred. If you look at the history of our Court you will find that sometimes rectification of an error means, instead of adopting new principles, going back to very old principles. Indeed, my impression is that in those cases where our court acknowledges error, makes changes, those changes have tended to go back instead of embarking upon new areas of constitutional theory.

This term we handed down a unanimous decision in a case involving a Kansas statute for debt adjustment in which the legislature of Kansas adopted a law to prohibit people other than lawyers from carrying out what is called "debt adjustment," getting debtors in, taking their assets privately, not in bankruptcy, apportioning among creditors. Presumably the Kansas legislature did this because they found great abuses in this process, people were taken advantage of, generally people with very few assets found themselves paying enormous sums of money to so-called "debt adjustors," and the creditors didn't get the benefit. The Kansas court, the state court, held that statute unconstitutional, as violating the due process clause of the Fourteenth Amendment, on the ground that it was an unreasonable regulation of a private business. Our Court unanimously reversed and in the reversal said that the time is long past when our Court, or any Court dealing with the constitutionality of state legislation, ought to act as a superlegislature, ought to substitute its judgment of what is wise and sound for the judgment of the legislators on economic and social legislation, and that, therefore, the statute was valid.

Well, I don't have to tell you who have studied this problem the history of substantive due process in the law. And this case illustrates that what is a new decision was a restoration of some old doctrine which had prevailed in the Court and which had been changed in another age. So, to put it in terms that I used to use when I was in the Cabinet and made political speeches, which I am no longer allowed to make, very often the way to the New Frontier is to return to the old frontier.

Whenever the Supreme Court hands down a decision which changes a prior decision, overruling it, or whenever we deal with an issue of great emotional impact to the public, there is revived in America the whole question of what about the function of this Court. What about judicial review? Isn't it bad, isn't it undemocratic, doesn't it mean that the country is run by the Supreme Court instead of the elected representatives in Congress, or by the Executive?

I'd like to give you an impression, as a new Justice, about that. Every lawyer, of course, bred in the American tradition, is very involved in the whole concept of judicial review. We are bound to be. This is the stuff of the law, as far as American lawyers are concerned. Everything is implicit in that.

Well, it is a great mistake particularly in the modern world—so it seems to me as a new Justice—to confuse judicial review with judicial supremacy. I am more impressed as I have sat on the bench this last year, with what judges do not do in relation to the affairs of life, than what judges can do.

Why do I say that? Well, in this world in which the life of the universe trembles—and indeed it does—our Court cannot make war nor can it make peace. That power, which is the overriding power, is vested elsewhere, under our constitutional system. For all practical purposes today, although the Constitution vests the warmaking power in the Congress, for all practices the warmaking power is vested in the President of the United States, as we citizens learned during the Korean conflict, and there is very little or nothing that our Court can do about it.

Our Court can do nothing about the great question of what the government does in the field of spending government money for the general welfare of the people of the United States. We don't determine the size of the federal government. We don't even determine the size of our own budget. Congress can decide not to pay us. There is an old statement by one of our great Justices, "We don't have the power of either the purse or the sword." It's true. I am very mindful of the fact, as a former Secretary of Labor, that there is nothing we can do that will cure our unemployment in the United States. Nothing at all. At one time the Court assumed the role of preventing the legislatures from dealing with that subject, but the Court has yielded that role, as I pointed out in the Kansas case, and that's up to the Congress, the White House, the state legislatures, state executives, private industry. All of these relate to that subject, and, indeed, the very character of the society we have, in its economic sphere and in its foreign sphere, is out of our hands in large measure. And so any notion that we live in a society where the judges are supreme is a foolish notion, it is foolish for the people to have and it is foolish for judges to have. Our role is a limited role.

But I don't want you to get the feeling in conclusion that, having said it's limited it is not important. It is terribly important. The great bulk of the work of our Court today, and this perhaps distinguishes it from the Court of any other period, is to enforce not the extent of government power but the limits of government power on the individual. And in a great sense I say that this goes back to very, very old doctrine. What our Court today is doing (and for which, by the way, it has received a considerable amount of criticism, from which we are not immune and should not be immune)—when we get cases from the states charging that individual rights under the Constitution have been violated in criminal proceedings, by the unlawful introduction of evidence, by the coercion of confessions, or by being denied a trial, or we get cases from the states about whether prayers should be read in the public schools or not, or cases in the states involving equality of rights—what our Court is doing is applying and asserting the fundamental nature of the Great Experiment which went into the making of the Constitution of the United States. That is that, under our constitutional system, government, which must be armed with extraordinary powers, nevertheless is limited in its impact upon the human personality; that the human being, the individual, can be protected against governmental interference, and that these rights, which are very often minority, unpopular rights, are to be safeguarded if we are to have a vital, functioning democracy.

Now, in a very peculiar way, this unique, interesting conception of government is being challenged very vigorously. Not only is it being challenged by the Communist powers—we always say that, and we are bound to say it by rote. That we understand. The fundamental conception of a Soviet regime, as of the Nazi regime, is that the welfare of the community is always to be preferred over the rights of the individual. That's a theory of government. We rejected that theory. What is interesting to me, and what we don't talk about too much, I think, and ought to talk about more, is that this theory of government is also being challenged by a lot of newly developing countries which have broken away from colonialism. One of the disturbing things to me is that these new countries, many of them, do not accept this principle, do not accept the principle that individual rights, basic individual rights, are to be safeguarded as a necessary condition for a healthy, functioning democracy in their own country. I traveled, when I was in the Cabinet, to many of these countries and talked about this with their leaders, and very often the reason assigned was that the countries were weak, they were ineffective, they needed to consolidate their strength before they could accord the political and individual rights of conscience that our Constitution is based on.

I would like to remind you as a matter of constitutional history that when the framers adopted this theory of government we were a weak, imperiled country. Now we have to be a little tolerant, because in our weakness we, too, took steps at the time which repudiated the constitutional provisions which we had just adopted. The Alien and Sedition Laws are a very disreputable memory. Our statutes would show that men who themselves framed great principles of rights, under pressure, abandoned these principles. Fortunately for us, not for long. Those laws stayed on the books only a few years, and then expired and, until fairly recent times, there were no attempts to revive some of the principles. Under pressures, we did in recent times attempt to revive some of them.

But the great, great bulk of our litigation now, outside of the normal litigation of construing statutes and so on, the great bulk of constitutional litigation before our Court now deals with these basic principles of freedom of conscience, of criminal procedure, of fairness, of due process, of equal protection under the laws—great, great principles.

Finally, it's an interesting thing that at this stage in our life, after having been devoted for many years to establishing and dedicating ourselves to the concept of freedom, of liberty, that we are wrestling with the very difficult problem which is not always essential in freedom, but which is very essential in a democratic society—and that is equality.

The great course of constitutional adjudication today seems to me no longer to be the constitutional adjudication dealing with the due process clause, but the constitutional adjudication dealing with the equal protection clause of the Constitution.

. . . Being on the Court is a gratifying, enlightening and sobering experience. While I said that judges lack power to do many things, make war and peace, we do have the great power to assert our national conscience, which is, in a sense, what we do. I also must say to you that, while I don't agree with Learned Hand when he said—you know he was very cynical, really, about the limited role of the judiciary—he said that there really isn't much that the judges can do to protect liberty. Being a new judge, I naturally disagree with that.

But I will say this. You become very conscious when you are on the Court that ultimately those great values which our Constitution established must be protected by the judges, because that's their sworn duty, even when it's not popular. But the basic, underlying guarantee has to be the national consensus. It's your great task, when you go to the bar, not only to represent your client but to assert, to educate, to lead the national consensus in support of the great values of the Constitution. That's the obligation you have, which the bar very often has not discharged, but I am sure under the hands of a great faculty you will know that that is a part of the great calling of the law.

Hastings College of the Law, San Francisco, Calif., September 24, 1963

New Frontiers for Lawyers and the Law

In his Inaugural Address, President Kennedy asked us to consider what we could do for our country—not what our country might do for us. That has proved a provocative question not only for editorial writers but for each citizen as well.

It is compelling especially to lawyers, who stand in many ways at the prow of their communities, seeking out the proper course.

It has been said that the President might have provided a bill of particulars —a "you do this and you do that" directive.

My conviction, as the appointee to a Cabinet post that embraces many critical economic and social questions, is that such a bill of particulars should not be necessary in a viable and democratic society. In our society, by its very definition, duty arises from the prodding of a free conscience.

I have told labor and management groups, for example, that they do not need a writ from Washington to begin improving their own relationship by voluntary methods. That would certainly be a constructive contribution to our country.

Currently, at the request of the President, I am engaged in discussions with a wide variety of groups—unions of different kinds, contractors, industrial firms and government officials—to improve the labor-management situation in our missile and space program.

I should not have thought it to be necessary, and I do not believe it to be necessary, to tell all of those concerned—labor and management and government officials and individual employees and workers in the missile program —what they can do for their country. At this point of history nothing less than maximum effort is called for. They should be going all out. We should have nonstop production in the missile program, on an economical and fair basis—with the public interest as the dominant interest.

I said that the Law Institute's past had given me a text for this address. You have for years, without directive from the Department of Justice or any other government source, been voluntarily engaged in a tremendous undertaking to restate significant areas of the law. You have made a genuine contribution to the development of an orderly system of law and to the attainment of justice through the legal process.

In making that salute I am led to the larger question of what the legal profession as a whole can do to further our national interest and advance our general welfare.

In making that inquiry I proceed from a basic assumption: the legal profession has for many years, through many generations, been doing much for its country. It has been an indispensable part of the administration of justice.

Perhaps my question should be, then: What *more* can you do? (Or, if a politician may reverse the traditional question put to him: What have you done for us lately?)

One of the traditionally notable contributions that the legal profession has been making to the country is the devotion of legal training and experience to public service.

Lawyers have always occupied a prominent place in government at every level. Now, in President Kennedy's administration, that tradition continues with six Cabinet officers who are members of the bar. There are, in addition, 30 important sub-Cabinet posts held by lawyers, such as the Under Secretary of Defense, the Under Secretary of Agriculture, the Under Secretary of the Treasury, the Under Secretary of State for Economic Affairs, and the Under Secretary of Labor. In the Congress, 63 senators and some 230 representatives are members of the bar. Through the broad range of government, of course, there are many, many more lawyers in public service.

When a lawyer undertakes public service—I might say to this sympathetic audience—he often makes a larger personal sacrifice than a businessman, for example. He is called at the peak of his career. Usually he has no equity investment, stock option, pension plan, or other form of security—such as lawyers devise for other people. And there is no such thing as taking a leave of absence from a client—not with other willing and able lawyers around.

It is a tribute to the many fine lawyers in public service that they are willing to do that. Most notable, perhaps, are the judges in public service. They come from the top ranks of their profession. They invariably accept a reduction in pay for their promotion in grade.

From all of this it is obvious that lawyers are fulfilling their obligations to their country to a great extent. What worries me is whether we who are embarked upon government service are being equipped by our training—both our professional training and our practice—to the demands to which we must respond. Consider the range of duties now being performed by lawyers in government: It is as broad as government itself.

One of the distinguished members of the bar is negotiating disarmament at Geneva. Another is arguing our cause at the UN. Another is overseeing the vast and complex problems in our agricultural economy. Another is dealing with the problems of our interior resources and still another with the gigantic postal system. Several are operating at the top levels of fiscal and economic policy.

In Congress our fellow lawyers are dealing with all the broad questions of public policy involved. The experience is being duplicated at the state and local levels in greater numbers.

This raises the question: Are American colleges and law schools, and the nature of the practice of American law, adequately equipping lawyers for the role they play in modern America?

In view of the nature of world problems today, I wonder. In the past we relied upon the curricula to provide a good foundation for understanding the world. Curricula have been greatly broadened over the years. But now, as Henry Adams predicted, history is accelerating—and the curricula of our law schools often fail to accelerate with it.

A lawyer in government service today, for example, would profit greatly from a command of one or more foreign languages. More often than not, he speaks and writes only English—and too often he doesn't do even that very effectively. He should know something of science, especially if he is called to work in the broad fields related to the formulation of nuclear policy. He certainly should know something about economics, in a world where economic considerations loom so large. He should have a knowledge of history and public administration—more traditional subjects.

Can we safely just rely on the practice of law itself to sharpen the intellect and make for the qualities needed for public service? Can we rely upon the fact that articulate reasoning and a sharpened mind, qualities associated with legal practice, adequately equip men to discharge public responsibility?

I raise these questions without answering them because they are obviously very much present in my own mind as I face my own responsibilities in government.

Perhaps lawyers, law deans, law professors and college administrators should measure the training we are providing in the light of the duties to which the graduates may someday be called.

The law profession has served as a provider of first-rate talent to our system of self-government. I feel we should now support our expectation of that upon a firmer guarantee that such men will be forthcoming in the difficult years ahead.

There is another area in which a greater effort might be made to increase the profession's contribution to our country. The family lawyer—like the family doctor and the family farmer—is being replaced in importance by the large and powerful economic interest. Private groups and organizations, composed of masses of people and bearing immense economic weight, dominate our scene. The big corporation and the big labor union are two of the more prominent ones. There may be a nostalgic desire on our part to return to the simple days of small enterprise and warmer human relationships, but bigness will remain. It will remain despite vigorous enforcement of laws.

It is of prime importance, therefore, that these interests—whose decision making has such a powerful effect upon our lives—be represented with independence and objectivity on the part of the lawyer who services them.

I sometimes feel that lawyers are increasingly departing from the ancient traditions of their profession. One of the traditions of the bar is that it is an independent bar, that it is not a servant of a client but services a client, that the men and women of the bar are independent, give counsel and advice independently. They are lawyers and not organization men.

I will say quite candidly to you here that the best thing the bar can do is return to the old tradition of independence, from which we are so tempted to depart by this contemporary and material society of ours.

My own experience, in private practice, labor-management relations and now government, has led me to the view that far too often lawyers representing great decision-making groups do not do so in keeping with the tradition of the bar. There are, of course, notable exceptions. Each of us would like to believe that he is one of those exceptions.

But let us be frank with ourselves. I think we would have to admit that the much-vaunted independence of the lawyer, under the pressures toward conformity and demonstration of status, is in great danger of joining some other vanished American virtues. That does not have to be so, and certainly should not be so. The great leaders of the bar up to now are the men who have acted with independence and objectivity.

It would be an important contribution to the profession and to the country if the legal profession measured up to its responsibilities in this area. Many of the abuses which affect our society would be corrected if lawyers were real counselors and not just craftsmen executing the will of the client.

There is something else that lawyers might do in response to the President's concept of serving the national interest. It, too, is a return to an ancient tradition. The lawyers of this country can reaffirm the traditional obligation to accept any case and represent any client, however unpopular his cause may be at the moment, however unpopular his client might be.

There have been times in our recent history when lawyers have failed to show the courage that is a part of the proud tradition of the bar. In Great

Britain it is still part of a lawyer's obligation, if he is paid his fee, to take any brief—whether that of a notorious criminal or of a social dissenter.

We might well consider the words spoken in 1953 by the Rt. Hon. Sir Hartley Shawcross, chairman of the General Council of the Bar:

I have recently heard it said, that certain members of the Bar in one of Her Majesty's Colonies refused to accept a brief to defend an African, accused of offences of a quasi-political nature against public order. The suggestion is that those barristers made excuses and declined to act, their true reason being that they thought that their popularity or reputation might be detrimentally affected by appearing for the defence in such a case. For the prosecution they might appear, but not for the defence.

If this report were true it would disclose a wholly deplorable departure from the great traditions of our law and one which, if substantiated, both the Attorney-General and the Bar Council, would have to deal with in the severest possible way.

Among laymen on both sides of politics there are some foolish and shortsighted enough to think that a barrister may and should pick and choose the cases in which he is prepared to appear.

It would be well if those people remembered how the present rule—that a barrister must accept a brief on behalf of any client who wishes to retain him to appear before any court in which he holds himself out to practise—was finally established. It arose in 1792 over the prosecution of Tom Paine for publishing the second part of his Rights of Man. The great advocate, Erskine, who accepted the retainer to defend Paine, and was deprived of his Office as Attorney-General to the Prince of Wales for doing so, said—and said truly—in a famous speech: "From the moment that any advocate can be permitted to say that he will or will not stand between the Crown and the subject arraigned in the Court where he daily sits to practise, from that moment the liberties of England are at an end."

In our own country, a lawyer representing, say, an accused spy or a most disreputable racketeer—is performing one of the vital functions of a free society. Yet with us all too frequently he must move to protect his public reputation, to make clear that he is serving without compensation, that he is a court appointee.

I think that is nonsense. He is doing his job. He should take his fee. I do not think it should be necessary for a bar association or a court to appoint lawyers to serve without compensation to represent political nonconformists, for example.

It is the duty of any lawyer, paid his proper fee, to represent people with whom he may greatly disagree personally. And it is the duty of the bar to make sure that the public understands that a lawyer is not to be identified with the views of his client. This, it seems to me, would be an aid to the orderly administration of justice in a free society.

There is the opportunity, too—and the obligation—to make the law a dynamic, not a static, force in the society.

We are clearest about the stabilizing influence of the law, about its proper—but not exclusive—function as a preserver of precedents and an instrument of predictability in the guiding of human affairs. But the law must be a flexible, living instrument. It is a balance wheel, not a brake.

My practice was in a field where the common law—or so it seemed to me—stopped developing, failed to keep pace with a growing industrial society. I often wondered why the genius which produced a law of property rights or of commercial instruments failed utterly to produce a law of job rights.

The common law developed rules of reasonable notice to protect a tenant from unconscionable ejection—but left a man working in a factory vulnerable, despite years of faithful labor, to dismissal at the end of any day or at any hour.

The ingenuity which went into the constructive development of the corporate fiction that permitted the combination of working dollars was directed against the development of combinations of workingmen. Had the common law kept pace with the society, the Norris-LaGuardia Act would never have been necessary.

Collective bargaining developed as a private lawmaking process because the public lawmaking process ignored a whole area of impact—the impact on human beings—of the industrial revolution. Almost overnight, and by the common consent of private collective bargaining, the parties worked out for themselves—in their security clauses—a concept of job rights which "the law" could, and should, have developed, just as it did the concept of property rights.

I wonder sometimes why it is that the law came to recognize the obsolescence of machines but not—in any like degree—of men. I do not mean this as special pleading. I only take the field I know best. Each of you would, in your areas, find no fewer instances where the law has concentrated too fixedly, too inflexibly, on things as they are—or were. We are all liberals in the fields we know best and conservatives where we are strangers.

We would find common ground in our sense of the difficulties the law has faced as its role has shifted to governing the relationships between groups rather than individuals, as the pluralistic forces have emerged in the society, and as we try to adjust to the international and supranational agencies which put the traditions of sovereignty to new tests.

I face today, in my own office, the realities and the implications of technological change, automation, and the sharpening competition of new producers around the world. I realize how important it is going to be that labor and management, and "the public" too, be willing to adjust themselves to new economic forces and facts. There will have to be some changes in old assumptions—and some of these are written or reflected in the laws. One of the factors in unemployment is the common-law conception of the nature of employment.

When we speak of ourselves as "guardians" of the law we probably speak too narrowly. For we are the builders of the law, too—and that work will never be done. Perhaps we respond to the President's challenge if, to paraphrase what he said, we ask less what the law can do for us and a little more what we can do for the law. The seeking of justice within the common-law concept and outside the drastic referrals to legislation which our society have been forced to make is also within the traditions of our law.

There is another thing that lawyers might ponder in light of the President's statement. It, too, represents a return to ancient legal tradition. And it can be described quite simply:

Defend the courts. We cannot be defenders of the law if we leave the courts defenseless from abuse and unwarranted attacks. Courts cannot with propriety defend themselves. Only the bar can do so. Defense of the courts as part of the traditions of the bar exists regardless of personal convictions.

The organized opposition to Franklin D. Roosevelt's proposal to change the personnel of the Supreme Court is well remembered. The organized bar was in the forefront of the defense of the Court then. But this same spirit of defense is not so visible—with notable exceptions—with regard to the 1954 Supreme Court decision declaring segregated schools unconstitutional. Whatever one's personal views, I do not believe that any lawyer can differ with the idea that court decisions must be complied with unless changed by the orderly process of the law itself. Lawyers and their associates should speak out in support of the law and compliance with and respect for both the law and its instrumentalities.

The then president of the American Bar Association, Charles Rhyne, demonstrated what a lawyer in the real tradition of the law does under circumstances when the courts need to be defended. He was joined by others—but there were far too many who remained silent.

I could give other examples of what I consider to be some proper responses to the President's challenge. All of them, however, would rest upon the basic concept of those I have given. The way to meet the nation's needs is to return to your own best traditions. Where we fall short as a profession— when we do—is by not maintaining our ancient and honorable traditions. For lawyers, it seems to me, the way to the new frontier is to return to the old frontier.

I believe that lawyers, and the legal profession, and organizations like this Institute, have made admirable contributions to American society. As I said at the beginning of this talk, in a government by law, not by man, individual freedom rests with your devotion to your calling. Now the time is at hand when we must seek out additional service and perform it in the name of freedom everywhere.

American Law Institute, Washington, D.C., May 19, 1961

The Center of the Storm

It is not my purpose in writing about the work of the Supreme Court of the United States to enter into debates about the Court's recent decisions or justify and defend them. The tradition long held and seldom departed from is that the Court's justices speak on current cases only by and through their decisions. This tradition I respect.

But it is also a part of that tradition for justices from time to time to write and speak about the Court as an institution, of its role in American life, and of the nature of its judicial process. And even the Olympian Yankee, Justice Holmes, did not regard it to be a departure from tradition to express anguish that the Court's opinions are misunderstood and its motives wrongfully impugned. Justice Holmes, in a speech delivered more than fifty years ago, said:

. . . We are very quiet there, but it is the quiet of a storm center, as we all know. Science has taught the world skepticism and has made it legitimate to put everything to the test of proof. Many beautiful and noble reverences are impaired, but in these days no one can complain if any institution, system, or belief is called on to justify its continuance in life. Of course we are not excepted and have not escaped. Doubts are expressed that go to our very being. Not only are we told that when Marshall pronounced an Act of Congress unconstitutional he usurped a power that the Constitution did not give, but we are told that we are the representatives of a class—a tool of the money power. I get letters, not always anonymous, intimating that we are corrupt.

Well, gentlemen, I admit that it makes my heart ache. It is very painful, when one spends all the energies of one's soul in trying to do good work, with no thought but that of solving a problem according to the rules by which one is bound, to know that many see sinister motives and would be glad of evidence that one was consciously bad. But we must take such things philosophically.

I hasten to add, as Justice Holmes undoubtedly would have, that our Court, along with every institution of democracy, is not immune to criticism of its actions. I agree with a *New York Times* editorial comment on this subject: "Unlimited public discussion is a primary safeguard of our democracy. . . . The decisions of the Supreme Court are written by men on paper, not by gods in letters of fire across the sky. Critics may distort them. But the Court will have to trust the good sense of the people, just as the people trust the good sense of the Court." I trust the good sense of the people to recognize that, although the Court is a proper subject of public comment and criticism, what should not be called into question is our allegiance as a nation and a people to government under law—for on this we have truly staked our all.

Because of our allegiance to the rule of law, it is of the utmost importance in appraising the role of the Supreme Court in vindicating this noble concept that we recognize what is myth and what is reality about the Court.

The very first myth which apparently must be laid to rest in every generation is that the Court has usurped the function of passing upon the constitutionality of state and federal laws and action. This myth, always revived during times of storm over the Court, has no solid basis in history. Chief Justice Marshall did not write on a clean slate in asserting in *Marbury* v. *Madison* the right and duty of the Court to declare void an act of Congress contravening the Constitution. His action was forecast in the debates in the Constitutional Convention and urged by proponents as one of the solid reasons for the Constitution's adoption. Professor Charles T. Black, Jr., in his excellent book *The People and the Court,* has summarized the historical evidence. It supports his conclusion that "It seems very clear that the preponderance of the evidence lies on the side of judicial review." And the very first Congress, composed of men whose memories of the making of the Constitution were fresh, enacted the Judiciary Act of 1789 which, from that date to this, has expressly authorized the Court to review the constitutionality of state legislation. This enactment was shortly followed by a succession of laws providing for ultimate review by the Court of judgments of the lower federal courts.

Thus the reality rather than the myth about the Court is that it exercises judicial review as a consequence of intent as well as tradition. Judicial review is not a usurped power but a part of the grand design to ensure the supremacy of the Constitution as law—supreme law to which all branches of government, executive, legislative and judicial, state and federal, are subject. This is what the Constitution clearly imports.

The next great myth is that, even though judicial review was intended and is sanctioned, it is, nevertheless, undemocratic and, therefore, to be regarded with alert suspicion and its exercise to be dimly viewed. The argument has an obvious, albeit superficial, appeal. The justices are appointed for life and not elected by the people for limited terms, as the President and Congress are. The latter, so the argument goes, being representative of the popular will, should have their way—otherwise democracy will be forsaken; a guardianship, however benevolent, negates popular government.

This reasoning, however, overlooks the first facts about our Constitution—that its source is the people and that, as Dean Roscoe Pound once said, it is meant to restrain "not individuals alone, but whole people." It is they who mandated that the individual be protected and safeguarded in his constitutional rights even against the popular will of the moment as voiced by the legislature or the executive. Our courts were entrusted with the responsibility of judicial review, in large part, to protect individuals and minorities in their fundamental rights against abridgment by both government and majorities.

It is not a denial, therefore, but rather a supreme manifestation of democracy that the fundamental rights of the least among us are protected from government by the Constitution and safeguarded by an independent judiciary. History teaches that democracy and an independent judiciary are one and inseparable. A country where judges are faithful to the popular will rather than to the rule of law will not be a democratic country worthy of the name.

Another myth is that the Court reaches out and determines troublesome cases that would be best avoided. It enters, so it has been said at times, into thickets of controversy. The reality is that the cases which the Court decides are pressed upon it. It does not seek out cases or invite their filing. Under our Constitution it issues no advisory opinions—it decides only actual cases and controversies. These must be genuine and current; otherwise jurisdiction will be summarily declined.

But what of cases seeking protection of political rights, should not the Court shun them? The answer to this is that most of the cases before the Court deal with public issues of the first moment in our society—issues like reapportionment—commonly called political. As de Tocqueville said, "scarcely any political question arises in the United States that is not resolved, sooner or later, into a judicial question."

Solicitor General Archibald Cox has accurately described the nature of the cases coming before the Court.

The central qualities of Supreme Court litigation arise . . . out of the peculiarly American principle of constitutional adjudication. The real contest is not so much between individuals and business corporations as between institutions and ways of life; and in reaching decisions this fact is consciously recognized. Throughout American history the prime examples have been the contests between state and federal authority and the definitions of the powers of the executive and legislative branches, but familiarity does not lessen the intensity of the contest, and new aspects are always arising.

Through constitutional adjudication we have developed the extraordinary but very useful habit of casting social, economic, philosophical and political questions in the form of actions at law and suits in equity and in this way important aspects of a large proportion of the most fundamental issues of our times ultimately go before the Supreme Court for judicial determination. They are the issues upon which the community, consciously or unconsciously, is most deeply divided. They arouse the deepest emotions. Their resolution—one way or the other—often writes our future history.

My colleague Justice Brennan accurately observed in *Baker* v. *Carr*, the germinal decision of the reapportionment cases, that "the mere fact that the suit seeks protection of a political right does not mean it presents a political question. Such an objection is little more than a play upon words." If a claim is justiciable, there is no escaping the responsibility of decision just because the constitutional right asserted is a political one.

Whatever the justification in another age or time for seeking out ways of avoiding decisions on the merits of a case, the temper of the modern world demands that judges, like men in all walks of public and private life, avoid escapism and squarely and frankly confront even the most controversial and troublesome justiciable problems.

And surely, it should be agreed by all—supporters or critics of the Court alike—that the least possible justification for the Court to avoid adjudicating a claim of constitutional right is that the Court may injure *itself* if it decides the case. Is this not another way of saying that the Court should avoid unpopular decisions? I have always conceived it to be the first duty of any judge worthy of the name and office to abjure popularity in decision making.

Lord Mansfield long ago stated the creed of any worthy judge:

I will not do that which my conscience tells me is wrong to gain the huzzahs of thousands, or the daily praise of all the papers which come from the press; I will not avoid doing what I think is right, though it should draw on me the whole artillery of libels, all that falsehood and malice can invent, or the credulity of a deluded populace can swallow. . . . Once for all let it be understood, that no endeavors of this kind will influence any man who at present sits here.

The Court should—the Court must—decide the cases and controversies properly coming before it, however difficult and controversial they may be, by doing what the justices are appointed and sworn to do: "Faithfully and impartially [to] discharge and perform all the duties" of their office and to "administer justice . . . according to the best of [their] . . . abilities and understanding agreeably to the Constitution and laws of the United States." Judicial cowardice is far more likely to be the undoing of the Court as an institution than the faithful exercise of judicial responsibility.

There is a myth that the Court is against states' rights, oblivious of the great interests of federalism—interests which not only reflect our history and traditions but which require constant and vigilant attention if we are to avoid overcentralism of our national government and if we are to preserve viable local government.

There was considerable substance to this myth during three decades early in this century when the Court, in the name of due process, invalidated social and economic legislation of the states as well as the nation. But, as our recent decisions demonstrate, the present Court does not strike down state or federal legislation because it deems laws of this type unwise or unsound. The nation and the states are free to experiment, and never have their interests in federalism been better safeguarded than they are now.

But it is asserted that the present Court intervenes far more frequently than in the past to protect individuals in their constitutional rights against state action. Particularly is this true, so the argument goes, in connection with criminal prosecutions. The Court, critics charge, is following a double standard— it denies the application of the due process clause to economic cases; it applies the clause energetically to cases involving impairment of personal liberties.

There is a simple answer to this charge. There is no evidence that the framers intended the 5th and 14th Amendments to deny to the nation and the states their right of economic experimentation. There is every evidence that they intended the Bill of Rights and the 14th Amendment to safeguard the fundamental personal rights and liberties of all persons against governmental impairment or denial.

There is a myth, very popular these days, that the Court is divided into "liberal" and "conservative" wings, or, as some would put it, into "activists" and those who practice "judicial restraint." Labels of this kind are convenient but not accurate. Members of the Court, applying general constitutional provisions, understandably differ on occasion as to their meaning and application. This is inevitable in the interpretation of a document that is both brief and general by a human institution composed of strong-minded and independent members charged with a grave and difficult responsibility. But the inappropriateness of these labels becomes apparent upon even the most perfunctory analysis.

A judge may believe that under the Constitution a court without a jury may not adjudge guilty a defendant charged with serious criminal contempt. Is he a liberal or a conservative? Is he an activist or a believer in judicial restraint? Or a judge may refuse to hold a litigant or newspaper in contempt for biting comment on the guilt or innocence of a criminal defendant. Is he an activist or a follower of judicial restraint? Is he a liberal or a conservative? May not the denial of a claim or constitutional right be more activist in its effects upon our constitutional structure than the allowance of the claim?

Examples could be multiplied, but inevitably the classification of the justices as liberal or conservative, or activist or believer in judicial restraint, will depend upon the outlook of or the criteria employed by the classifier.

Finally, the fact is that the Court is not as divided as is commonly assumed. Last year [1963] the Court, by denial of certiorari or decision on their merits, disposed of more than 2,500 cases. In the overwhelming majority of these cases the Court was unanimous in its orders. But more importantly the Court is united in a common dedication to constitutional principles and to the rule of law. The members of the Court may differ as to a particular case, but all members of the Court attempt to emulate Chief Justice Marshall in "never [seeking] to enlarge the judicial power beyond its proper bounds, nor [fearing] to carry it to the fullest extent that duty requires."

The justices of the Court pursue a common method and aim, simply but eloquently described by Justice Frankfurter:

What is essential in judging is . . . first and foremost, humility and an understanding of the range of the problems and one's own inadequacy in dealing with them; disinterestedness, allegiance to nothing except the search, amid tangled words, amid limited insights; loyalty and allegiance to nothing except the effort to find that path through precedent, through policy, through history, through one's own gifts of insight to the best judgment that a poor fallible creature can arrive at in the most difficult of all tasks, the adjudication between man and man, between man and state, through reason called law.

I could continue this recital of myths about our Court, but I shall conclude with one that emanates from those who seek to support rather than condemn the Court. It is the myth that the Court is infallible. A simple and correct answer to this myth is the oft-quoted bon mot of Justice Jackson: "We are not final because we are infallible; we are infallible because we are final."

The reality is that as a human institution the Court is bound to err. It is a tribute to its awareness of human frailty, and the extent to which the Court seeks to avoid mistakes, that so few really serious ones have been made in the Court's history. And, of course, it is only proper to note that reserved to the people is the right to change the course of the Court's opinions—right or wrong—through the process of constitutional amendment.

There are more sophisticated mythologists who would seek to preserve the illusion of infallibility by banning dissenting opinions. The Court, by their lights, would then speak with a single authoritative voice not to be gainsaid. Some courts in other lands function in this fashion, burying their differences in a single opinion and judgment. But I, for one, would not have it this way, for I profoundly believe that in the long run the Court benefits, and certainly the people do, by the free expression of dissenting views. They educate and sometimes eventually prevail, and they always demonstrate that our judicial air, like all of the air of American life, is, and, God willing, will remain, free.

So long as the Court sits, myths about it will exist. Myths are not necessarily all or entirely bad, as the literature of mythology proves. But since we must live in this world and not in a make-believe world, myths about the Court or any other human institution must yield to reality. Otherwise our society will be the victim of our fantasies rather than the servant of our purposes.

New York Times Magazine, November 8, 1964

FREE MEN AND FREE LABOR

Fifty Years

Today two obvious challenges confront our labor-management system. The first is external—the continuing pressure of an economic opponent, the Communist block, always striving to match and surpass us as the leading innovators, producers and consumers of the world.

This is a challenge that I believe we can meet and master as we have—in full stride. Our free system of enterprise and of democratic unionism consistently outproduces the Communist-controlled system of both enterprise and "so called" unions. The wealth of our factories and farms and mines and businesses will continue to stand second to none, as will the economic power generated by the skill and energy of our people who find their own incentives and seek their own rewards.

But the second challenge will, I believe, demand a refocusing of purpose and productive will on our part. It comes, happily, from our friends and it represents, at its heart, the triumph in the free world of the American concept of fair and earnest competition. We are no longer the vast Island of Have in a sea of Have-Nots. We are engaged, instead, by strong free economies, by rising productive might, and by determined competitors.

And even though the work and wage and living standards of our free competitors are rising toward the eventual levels of our own, we cannot at this time compete successfully without a re-examination of our own methods and goals. I consider this the basic challenge today to American labor and American business and to the institution of collective bargaining that has served us so well in the past.

I believe this challenge carries its own moral. We must work not less but more. We must work not only hard but well, increasing our productive capability as we increase our production.

There are no short cuts and no panaceas to relieve us of the necessity for finding our own security in abundance, not in a sharing of scarcity. The only lasting security for both labor and management is in dedicated work at fair wages, in more sales at fair prices, in products of dependable quality, in meeting the markets of the world on terms that guarantee an increasing share of the world's business.

The attainment of this already difficult goal is made more complex because we must strive for it during a period of rapidly advancing technology. The dilemma that results is that yielding to technological demand creates many problems, often severe, often of a personal nature, for the American labor force, while not yielding to technological demand is sacrificing our best opportunity to improve our competitive position.

This dilemma has led to the proposals for scarcity sharing, for sharing work and distributing available markets among major producers. This solution is apparent rather than real. Expansion rather than contraction is the solution to the problems of both labor and management. In an expanding economy we can advance technologically and protect human values. We must do both. In increased productivity, labor, industry and the public can all benefit and share.

We have—and I am confident always will have—rejected compulsion as the instrument for serving the national interest. Legal strictures and statutory regulation are poor servants of a free economy.

Our policy must be not to stifle but to stimulate collective bargaining to an awareness of the full context of interests within which it operates, and which it influences. We must bring home to the parties and to the American people that bargaining, while remaining free, must also be realistic. This, I believe, is still our best hope for the future.

This policy has thus far worked. It has not worked perfectly, of course, as no policy ever will. There should be no tampering with our free institutions, no deprivation of responsibility, no prerogative of labor and management denied or questioned, and no interference in the final judgment of the parties. But to enjoy this freedom the parties to collective bargaining must exercise responsibility. No one has the monopoly to define the public interest; everyone has the obligation to serve it.

I would summarize the past fifty years of labor-management relations in the United States by saying that, having done well, we must strive to do better; having achieved much, we must determine to achieve more; always mindful that our goal is not material but spiritual—to safeguard and advance the dignity of the individual, this is the high purpose for which the Labor Department was established. May it continue its great service in the interests of mankind and our beloved country.

Fiftieth Anniversary Celebration of the Department of Labor, Washington, D.C.,
March 4, 1963

Moral Standards in Labor and Industry

The moral climate of American industrial society in the post-Civil War period has been eloquently put by a distinguished student of American culture. Let me read you from Vernon Parrington's *Main Currents in American Thought:*

. . . individualism had become the inalienable right to pre-empt, to exploit, to squander. Gone were the old ideals along with the old restraints. The idealism of the forties, the romanticism of the fifties—all the heritage of Jeffersonianism and the French Enlightenment—were put thoughtlessly away, and with no social conscience, no concern for civilization, no need for the future of democracy it talked so much about, the Gilded Age threw itself into the business of money-getting. From the sober restraints of aristocracy, the old inhibitions of Puritanism, the niggardliness of an exacting domestic economy, it swung far back in reaction, and with the discovery of limitless opportunities for exploitation it allowed itself to get drunk. Figures of earth, they followed after their own dreams. Some were builders with grandiose plans in their pockets; others were wreckers with no plans at all. It was an anarchistic world of strong, capable men, selfish, unenlightened, amoral —an excellent example of what human nature will do with undisciplined freedom. In the Gilded Age freedom was the freedom of buccaneers preying on the argosies of Spain.

This does not reflect accurately the state of industrial morality today, primarily because of three interacting influences which I would describe as (1) the "welfare state," (2) the labor movement, and (3) industry's heightened sense of social responsibility generated in large part by (1) and (2) above.

The contribution that I can best make to this discussion lies, I think, in outlining the role of the *union* in modifying the "anarchistic world" which Parrington talks about.

I am not sure that I am peculiarly equipped to give a rigorous philosophical definition of moral standards. Rather, I would prefer to convey my sense of what the phrase "moral standards" means by associating it with other ideas.

The polar extreme of morality in industrial society is profit making or personal power accumulation no matter the consequences. And it doesn't make any difference who is making the profit or accumulating the power. Here I am talking about the brutal pursuit of power or money without regard to its consequences for human personality or dignity. This is the central problem of our times.

The major point that I should like to make in my remarks is this: the labor union in its very essence is an instrument of moral force because it seeks to abate the demoralizing impact of profit making and unrestricted power on the large masses of people. And at the same time the labor union seeks to conserve human values in industrial society.

This is, of course, the ideal. As a labor lawyer I would be less than candid with you if I did not suggest that there are bleak and dreary chapters in the development of labor unions in the United States and elsewhere. We have had our Communists, our racketeers, our egomaniacs. I submit, however, that by and large these are, as the biologist would put it, sports. They do not reflect the main trend. Indeed, they are deviations from the accepted moral standards of trade union behavior.

The great moral achievement of the labor union has been the unique vehicle it has constructed through collective bargaining to encourage the worker in the plant to speak his piece without fear of reprisal. I cannot begin to communicate to you fully the enormous sense of accomplishment that a bargaining committee experiences when it negotiates with management, even where it happens, as it does, that the committee doesn't get any more than a beneficent employer might give on his own.

In the din and turmoil of our times, however, we have ignored the peaceful revolution that collective bargaining has brought about in the plants, factories and mines of our country. It is a revolution with very significant moral overtones. And this is particularly true of the mass production industries. The introduction of unionism and of collective bargaining in the mass production industries has brought with it a vehicle and machinery through which the workers can participate in the employment decisions affecting them. As important as wanting more money for their labors has been the workers' search for some say in the conditions of work which affect them.

Before the union came the individual worker was caught in the morass of corporate bureaucracy which, believe me, can be deadly—even more deadly —than government bureaucracy. The worker who is shifted from one job to another, the worker who is laid off without explanation, the worker who is told to come in only to find that there is no job, the worker who feels he is being victimized by favoritism, before the union came all of these men and women had no place to turn to for relief or explanation. The growth of effective unionism in the mass production industries has made it possible for the individual worker to use normal machinery to give expression to his gripes and dissatisfactions—gripes and dissatisfactions, to be sure, not always justified but certainly deserving of an answer. Before the union came there was no answer. With the union the right to know, the right to an explanation, has become a matter of right and not a matter of executive dispensation.

I suggest to you that, viewed from any moral or ethical system, this is a substantial gain. What is more important for maintaining one's morale and personal integrity than the right to be protected from being pushed around?

I do not want to discount the importance of the economic gains. These economic gains, too, have significant moral implications. Let me explore some of them with you.

A recent tendency in collective bargaining demands has been pension funds. The union's interest in pension funds, it seems to me, illustrates the influence of human values in the union's calculations in collective bargaining. In effect, when the union asks for a pension fund from an employer, this is what it is saying: The fact that a worker is no longer able to produce as vigorously or as efficiently as he once did because of advancing years cannot justify the employer's abandonment of him. Left to his own devices, industrial history records that the employer, guided by the dictum of the balance sheet, did not acknowledge any responsibility for a worker who was incapacitated by old age. The union says there is a large measure of responsibility that the employer still has. The human consequences of an impoverished old age must be considered by the employer even though it may conceivably show a lower net return.

The union says further to the employer that he must apply to the older worker the same accounting principles which he applies to obsolescent machinery. Just as the employer sets up an obsolescence and depreciation account for equipment which has outlived its usefulness, so, argues the union, the employer must set up an obsolescence and depreciation account for the workers who have produced his goods.

There is much hope for the future to be found in the general acceptability of the pension demand in collective bargaining. There may be disagreement about the details of pension plans. There is no disagreement, as far as I know, on the appropriateness of pensions as a term in the collective bargaining agreement.

This idea that industry has a *continuing* responsibility to provide a decent livelihood for every worker who has rendered it useful service will be given a further test as we begin to press seriously for the guaranteed annual wage. Parenthetically I might add that the pension and guaranteed annual wage benefits through collective bargaining provide a working laboratory in the handling of economic problems by voluntary action between unions and management. We need not accept government intervention in the resolution of economic issues as inevitable. But at the same time I think we have to recognize history's lesson that, if we cannot determine these issues through the action of voluntary groups, government (of whatever stripe) will be pressured to move in.

Take another illustration, for which unions have frequently been criticized. The union's attempt to deal with the human consequences of technological change represents an effort to deal with the human problems of displacement. I recognize, of course, that in a few instances unions have strenuously opposed the introduction of laborsaving devices on the ground that it would create mass unemployment among its members. I think a union which simply says that it will not permit the use of laborsaving devices is not on tenable grounds, economically, strategically, or from the viewpoint of the public welfare.

At the same time, however, it seems to me that the union cannot and should not stand idly by while the skills of many of its members are made worthless by the introduction of technological changes. I do not know by what standard anybody can justify the position that the worker must carry the sole burden of technological change-overs. And what the union attempts to do is to lighten as much as is possible the burden on the individual worker by making provisions for dismissal compensation, for training, and for other steps which will prevent the worker affected from being thrown on a scrap heap.

Another example: the so-called fringe benefits, vacations with pay, paid holidays, etc. The organized labor movement has for a long time argued that there is something more to living than working. I am not sure that I can improve on the language of a group of trade unionists who said, more than a hundred years ago in connection with their fight for shorter hours:

All men have a just right, derived from their Creator, to have sufficient time in each day for the cultivation of their mind and for self-improvement.

Even in such a prosaic protection as seniority, which unions have now introduced widely in industry, there is evident the drive for the achievement of human goals that we are talking about here. Admittedly the seniority principle of "first in, last out" is not perfect. I suggest to you, however, that it is far preferable to the rule of favoritism and uncertainty with respect to layoffs and rehiring and promotions which prevailed before the introduction of the seniority system.

I do not want to intimate that the commitment of the labor union to these human values is of recent origin. A reading of the history of the labor movement in the more than 175 years of its existence reveals that this dedication to the conservation of human values has ever been the vital element in labor's development. The fight to make democracy a meaningful thing in our lives is inextricably intertwined with the classic battles of the labor movement for free public education and shorter hours, for social security, and for more of the humanitarian objectives which we believe are part of our democratic tradition. Here is how a group of workers, organized into the Philadelphia Working Men's party in 1830, put the role of free public education in society:

All history corroborates the melancholy fact, that in proportion as the mass of the people becomes ignorant, misrule and anarchy ensue—their liberties are sub-verted, and tyrannic ambition has never failed to take advantage of their helpless condition. . . . [Education] is the rock on which the temple of moral freedom and independence is founded; any other foundation than this will prove inadequate to the protection of our liberties, and our republican institutions. In order to support the superstructure, the foundation must be broad. Our government is republican; our education should be equally so.

Let us take a look at the people who work for labor unions. There is one thing about these men and women that I am certain about. There is a genuine sense of mission which motivates these people. For the vast majority the labor movement is more than a job. It represents to them a way of life, a fulfillment of ethical and moral goals. Without this sense of mission it would be impossible to withstand the terrific toll which a job with a union takes on family life and, indeed, on physical well-being. Working for a union is a backbreaking and heartbreaking job.

No organizing situation is so bleak, no employer can be so oppressive, that there will not be somewhere a small nucleus of faithfuls who will stick to the union in the face of great personal peril. This kind of response and this kind of devotion would not be possible if the union were simply a business enterprise. And, indeed, you see we talk about the labor *movement* and the word "movement" connotes ideals, goals and humanitarian purposes.

It is a source of some encouragement to observe that there are segments of industry which are absorbing the human values philosophy which the labor movement has had to organize to get accepted. For example, the "human relations" movement in industry.

I see mixed motivation in the increasing popularity of the use of "human relations" techniques by management, and indeed, the human relations techniques can be good or bad, depending on whether the motivations are good or bad. It is bad where the objective is to re-create company paternalism in order to displace the union in the loyalties of the workers. Not only is it bad, it won't work.

The other motivation—in my judgment, the good motivation—is a human relations program by management which recognizes and works with the union in making the plant a better place to work in.

The bigness of modern industry requires the unions to be big in order to survive. The challenge to the American labor movement is whether, in spite of bigness, it can retain the underlying moral fervor which has been its historical *élan vital.*

I think it *can* retain its moral undertone. I know of no operating organization as large as the typical union that concerns itself, even today, so intimately with the welfare of the individual and seeks to protect him from the forces in modern life that try to convert him into merely a unit of labor power. It seems to me that here we have in this basic function of the union the very essence of moral force.

This statement was prepared by Mr. Goldberg when he was counsel to the Congress of Industrial Organizations.

The Gathering Crisis: 1958-1959

Imagination and maturity in the labor-management area were the keynote of Sidney Hillman's success. Passionately devoted to his own people, he was, nevertheless, completely objective in recognizing the problems, the doubts, the fears, the needs of the people who sat across from him at the collective bargaining table. Even when their disagreements were white hot—as they were on many occasions—Hillman declined to castigate management in the stereotype of the devil. He was able to look compassionately on the needs both of the clothing industry and of the workers of the clothing shops. Because he had maturity, because he had imagination, he was able to step out of the normal narrow-gauge track of collective bargaining as it was practiced three or four decades ago, and to propose new methods and techniques for achieving industrial peace and mutual respect.

More than any other man, Hillman was responsible for the use of the impartial arbitrator to settle labor-management disputes on the basis of facts rather than through conflict. Today, when the concept of the referee, the umpire, the "impartial" is widely recognized, it is almost difficult to recall that this was a pioneering step which required courage for a young labor leader to propose.

Sidney Hillman made a profound contribution to the philosophy of labor-management relations by recognizing the interrelationship of the workers' welfare and of the union's welfare to the well-being of the entire industry. The record of his collective bargaining successes demonstrates that this was not a question of surrender by the union to management; rather, it was a recognition of mutuality of interest. This concept in itself was certainly not foreign to the philosophy of the American labor movement, which has been fortunately free of theoretical class-warfare ideology. Hillman's contribution was to pay more than lip service to the idea; to set up institutional forms and to mold the thinking of his associates and others in the labor movement, and of his and other managements, to this concept of interdependence.

It is more than thirty years since the Hillman approach to mature labor-management relations became established and accepted in the clothing industry. Let us look about the country today and appraise briefly how widespread its acceptance has been on the entire labor-management scene.

Superficially, the portents in this field are good. Labor unions are strong in membership and resources. They have weathered the recession without fundamental organizational weaknesses. Despite widespread unemployment and underemployment, they are negotiating new contracts which provide higher wages and improved benefits. They have taken effective steps to keep the house of labor clean and free of corruption. Big strikes are few; major setbacks even fewer. Spokesmen for both major political parties, when they are overseas and therefore not campaigning, boast of our free democratic trade unions. Even at home—and even when campaigning—both parties extol free collective bargaining, and only the most Neanderthal among them attack the concept of trade unionism. Each year the Bureau of Labor Statistics adds more collective bargaining agreements to its already bulging files.

All is wonderful—or is it?

I suggest that if we probe beneath the superficiality of statistics we will find that we are a long way from universal achievement of the type of labor-management relations symbolized by the Sidney Hillman tradition.

One large geographical area—the deep South—has eluded successful organization by unions in many industries. At a time when we like to consider that "all of industry is organized," the Southern textile industry functions by and large on a nonunion basis, as it has for many decades. Great sectors of the clothing and garment industries in the South are also nonunion. So too is much of the construction industry, and broad areas of the service trades in which various unions have jurisdiction. Even in organized industries the South has become increasingly a haven for runaway shops and factories. Union growth in the South is unmistakably, undeniably slow. It is an understatement to say that the state of labor-management relations in the South is by and large unsatisfactory and far from the Sidney Hillman ideal.

Or take the problem of the white-collar workers. Despite repeated assurances by various groups of union leadership that the white-collar workers "must be organized," little progress has been made. Meanwhile, the technological revolution in America is producing a constantly smaller number of "blue-collar" production workers in relation to an increasing proportion of technicians and subtechnicians, engineers and subengineers, management and administrative people of various kinds. In the steel industry, for instance, the proportion of production workers goes steadily down; while the number of men who watch dials or keep a constant eye on closed circuit television pictures of the industrial process mount steadily. The same is true of electrical manufacturing, rubbermaking and automobile production. Yet, with few exceptions, the unions have not found the key, the technique, the message with which to bring the increasingly large number of this type of industrial personnel into the labor movement. And, with few exceptions, managements have resisted the organization of these workers into unions.

But even more serious than this resistance to new organization with respect to white-collar workers is a hardening of attitudes in the organized areas. This intangible factor is, in my opinion as a firsthand observer of the labor-management scene, the most serious problem of all. After some twenty years of responsible collective bargaining in the major industries, we reasonably might have expected a measure of the same understanding and good will, of ability to see the problems of the other side, of mutuality of efforts to reach solutions satisfactory to both, achieved by Hillman and his management colleagues in the clothing industry. Yet that result has not come about.

I say this most regretfully, but I must record the facts as I see them. I thought it was coming about ten years ago when we seemed to be on the road toward achievement of mutual respect and understanding in our major industries. The Wilson-Reuther agreement at General Motors, the Murray-Fairless agreements in steel, and others that could be mentioned, all pointed to an era of maturity in labor-management relations. But in the recent past I see a hardening of attitudes and retrogression rather than progress in understanding. Management is tougher, unions are tougher, and the end product is not necessarily good for either side. Each feels it must take a firm stand in behalf of its principles; and, as that distinguished public servant, a former director of the Federal Mediation Service, Cyrus Ching, has remarked, "nothing so impedes labor-management peace as principles."

Throughout American industry there is a widespread movement to replace genuine acceptance of and cooperation with unions by a philosophy of labor-management relations keyed to keeping the unions at arm's length, of working with the union as little as possible, of seeking, wherever possible, to go around the union to its members rather than to deal with the union as a living institution. This philosophy treats unions as necessary evils rather than as constructive partners in achieving harmonious and productive labor-management relations.

I have pondered about the reasons for this polarization of viewpoint. I don't believe that it can be fairly attributed to an overreaching on the part of the American labor movement. I don't think that in measuring the relative bargaining power of American employers and American labor unions it can be said that the bargaining power of the unions is superior to that of the employers. The results of the economic bargains which have been made between American unions and American employers in the past two decades do not support the charge of overweening labor power. Surely it cannot be established by responsible economists that there has been an unjustly high distribution of wages to workers as against the distribution of profits to shareholders. Of course, I recognize that situations can exist where the comparative bargaining strengths of unions and employers are not in balance. There are weak unions and there are strong unions. There are situations in which a labor surplus exists, union loyalty is small, and the market is such that the employer can afford to forgo production for a period of time. There are also situations where the opposite is true. Economic injury can occur when too great bargaining power exists on either side. But I think it is one of the essentials of our free economic system that we do not interfere to redress every individual instance of economic disequilibrium so long as there is no general pattern of imbalance.

The real question is whether it can be said that on the whole labor exercises too great economic power vis-à-vis the employers. If I were compelled to make a general assessment of the relative bargaining strengths of American unions and American employers, I would unhesitatingly say that in looking at the total picture the greater strength is still on the side of the employers. But, whether I am right on this or not, it is certainly true that the American industrial scene is not one in which poor, downtrodden, profitless business enterprises have every last penny extracted from them by powerful labor unions. Wage and profit statistics certainly do not point to such a picture for the economy as a whole. Nor do they show such a condition in the particular industries in which the large unions, which are usually denounced as monopolies by labor critics, exist.

If this hardening of attitudes which I see is not due to economics, then what is its cause? Frankly, I am not sure that I know, but I know that it exists. Perhaps it is a by-product of our political scene. For however successful collective bargaining may appear on the surface in organized industries—and as is apparent I am questioning even this—politically, legislatively, philosophically, labor and management today stand apart, and the degree of polarization of viewpoints in these areas is far greater than in collective bargaining. If we were to believe the political and business spokesmen of industry, labor and its allies are determined to socialize America, which everyone knows is plainly nonsense. And, to be entirely fair, I have just read a speech from an outstanding and respected labor leader charging a great American corporation with seeking a Fascist America—a charge which, in my opinion, is equally nonsensical.

Perhaps this hardening of attitudes stems from the bifurcated philosophy behind the Taft-Hartley Act which speaks of encouraging both collective bargaining and individual bargaining—a complete contradiction of terms. Perhaps it arises from the fact that we have a new generation of business, and to a lesser extent of labor, leadership. The generation passing from the scene developed mutual understanding and sometimes even friendship from their common experiences in important governmental posts such as the War Production Board and the War Labor Board during the last war. The present generation on both sides are more inclined to be organization men, with all of the parochial characteristics of that breed.

Whatever the cause, I think you must agree with me that opportunities for conversation, for a sensible, realistic exchange of views between the leaders of labor and the business community are becoming fewer and fewer. And the stereotype images, indeed the caricatures, are taking the place of reality. When the two sides meet, as they do now more and more infrequently, they meet almost solely at the bargaining table. The bargaining table, of course, plays an indispensable and essential role in our labor-management scene. But it has never been known as a place where one could think out loud about basic problems: every word counts too much! Thus, while I do not know the cause of the growing estrangement taking place between labor and management, and therefore cannot suggest a cure, nevertheless, as I look at the American labor-management scene today I know that one of our most conspicuous lacks is an area where men of divergent viewpoints can meet and exchange ideas, rather than make debating points, and think realistically about our common future.

Take the question of old age as an example. We can "point with pride" to the success both of social security and of collective bargaining in providing pensions for retired workers. But the collective bargaining table has obvious limitations as a forum for providing an adequate contribution, by both management and labor, to the complex problem of geriatrics. If a union in the course of collective bargaining raises the question of developing a program for retired employees, the discussion is likely to revolve around the narrow point whether, in law, the union has a right, and the company the obligation, to bargain for workers already retired. But, putting the legal question aside, can there be any doubt that both industry and unions have an obligation toward employees and members who have devoted long years of their lives to their respective interests? I have the deep feeling, unsupported by evidence, that if we could discuss this problem frankly and mutually, outside the collective bargaining table, joint programs could be evolved which would have a beneficial impact both within and without the framework of collective bargaining.

Since, save for the collective bargaining conference, there is little joint exchange of opinion, where, then, do management and labor express their views? The answer is clear: almost everywhere except together!

The Business Advisory Council of the Department of Commerce, composed of our leading business men, migrates to Hot Springs, locks itself behind closed doors and unanimously assures itself that labor is ruining the country. The NAM and the U.S. Chamber of Commerce go respectively to New York and Washington for annual conventions, at which a host of participants are already convinced that the labor movement and liberal politicians are the root of all evil. If you have a doubt that we have gone backward and not forward in understanding, contrast the Chamber of Commerce under Eric Johnston's leadership with the Chamber under its present heads.

And the labor movement itself does essentially the same thing. We talk to ourselves in our conventions and in our Executive Council meetings, we adopt our maximum positions and we hurl these neatly mimeographed resolutions over the fence to the opposition, which picks apart the commas and semicolons and "answers" them.

There have been occasional efforts, of course, to bridge this gap. Back during the war some leaders in the CIO proposed an Industrial Council Plan. Many people in management jumped on it as a blueprint rather than an idea, and tore it to bits. Perhaps to industry it connoted a sort of codetermination. If so, I would say, let us forget about the name. American labor has not the slightest interest in codetermination. In fact, while it recognizes the right of our European colleagues to proceed by their own lights, American labor, judging from the European experience, has by and large come to the conclusion that it infinitely prefers to make its gains through collective bargaining rather than through any joint control of industry.

And while I am on this subject, may I also say that any notion from the name "Industry Councils" that any responsible American labor leader believes in taking over "management prerogatives" is equally unfounded, even though in recent months I have detected increasing evidence of this false supposition. American labor completely respects management's right and regards it to be not only the right, but the responsibility, of industry to manage its plants. Only out of well-managed, profitable enterprise can American labor expect to make the gains in wages, hours and working conditions which is desires. But even where the name Industry Council was not used, recent attempts to reach a rapprochement between labor and management have failed.

The NAM in 1955 invited George Meany to address its convention. When he accepted in all good faith, he was subjected, as he sat on the platform, to a barrage of critical oratory that certainly did not contribute to mutual understanding. Is it surprising that he replied in kind?

Perhaps a Sidney Hillman, existing in today's environment, would have long since found methods of erecting a bridge across the philosophic chasm which during recent years has tended to split labor and management in America. Speaking in the Hillman tradition, I think it is necessary that we search for honorable methods of bridging this gap.

My own thinking leads to a proposal for a Labor-Management Assembly, modeled after the United Nations Assembly, as an instrument for bringing together the leading figures in American industry and the leading figures in the American trade-union movement for a periodic examination and discussion of the issues which affect us all and in which we find so little common ground.

I propose that the Labor-Management Assembly be convened under the auspices of the government of the United States and that the Secretaries of Commerce and Labor act as co-chairmen. But I immediately add that this should not be a government-dominated organization any more than the ILO, on the international level, is a government-dominated institution, although government participates along with labor and management representatives in its functioning.

I view the role of government as providing prestige, of supplying facts, and of bringing together a secretariat for the conduct of the meeting. It is not even important, it seems to me, whether the Secretary of Labor and the Secretary of Commerce see eye to eye—normally they don't—on these problems.

To serve its proper purposes and to achieve any beneficial results, the Labor-Management Assembly must meet at regular periodic intervals and must receive top-level attendance and top-level thinking from both sides. It must be attended by the chairmen of the board and the presidents of representative big and small corporations. It must be attended by the presidents of trade unions. Both should be accompanied by adequate staffs. I would propose that the present membership of the Business Advisory Council, enlarged by representative small businessmen, constitute the industry representation. The General Board of the AFL-CIO, on which sits at least one representative from each affiliated union, large and small, would constitute labor representation—with the proviso that respectable unaffiliated unions should of course also be invited.

I would hope that the Labor-Management Assembly would not issue statements unless they are unanimously agreed upon, and unless the common denominator is higher than agreement that sin is bad and morality is good. Primarily, if the Labor-Management Assembly is to be successful, it must be a place to discuss and think about important issues in the labor-management area on a broader basis than is possible in collective bargaining, not to fight and bicker over the words of a contract or a resolution. If the discussions are to be profitable, they should be "off the record" except for agreed-upon statements, so that no one need be concerned that his remarks will be cited against him. Indeed, I visualize more and greater benefits from small discussion groups under the auspices of the Labor-Management Assembly than from general plenary sessions.

Finally, I would hope that at the periodic meetings ample opportunities would be provided, as at international assemblies, for social intercourse between individuals in the respective groups—something that has been increasingly lacking since the wartime agencies functioned and the importance of which cannot be overestimated. I believe that our top-level labor and management representatives must be drawn together for a period of as long as two or three weeks, once or twice a year, under circumstances in which they have no alternative but to talk; and when they are through talking they should talk some more.

And there is plenty to talk about. I have already mentioned the problem of retired workers. Another example of a problem we are all concerned about is inflation. Inflation, if one is to read the industrial press, is caused solely by rising wages. Inflation, if one is to read the labor press, is the end result of superprofits and administered price policies. Is either side right, or are they both wrong? If each is right, why is inflation a worldwide problem —in underdeveloped countries, in countries that are primarily agricultural, in countries that export, in countries that import more than they export, in countries with effective labor movements and in countries with quite passive, or nonexistent, labor movements? Is a little, a controlled, inflation better, as Sumner Slichter—a conservative economist—has suggested, than deflation? Whatever the answer, if there is an answer, the problem is rarely discussed by responsible leaders of labor and management sitting together.

And what about automation? How often do the top leaders of labor and management get together to discuss all of the implications of automation, except for the very limited treatment that can be given to this all-important subject by their representatives trying to hammer out a collective bargaining agreement before a strike deadline?

Even the whole issue underlying the "right to work" laws has never been adequately discussed except in a political setting. It is ironical that in this campaign just concluded, "right to work" laws are supported by many companies whose industrial relations directors would be fearful of the stability of their personnel relations if they did not have a union shop.

What about the problem of corruption in the labor-management field? We have reached a new low in labor-management understanding in the varying viewpoints on the legislation called for in this area. The business community's literature calls for sweeping and one-sided legislation—laws aimed directly at the problem of corruption among labor people, but only among labor people, not also business or middlemen.

It is no secret that many businessmen have gloated over Dave Beck and consciously or unconsciously cast him in their public speeches as a symbol of all labor leaders. Many labor leaders, I know, are happy about the revelations concerning Nathan Shefferman and the businesses represented by him, and label them as characteristic of all businessmen. Yet businessmen and labor men both know better because, as honest businessmen and honest labor leaders, they deal with each other, and they learn early that the vast majority of both groups are honest. Should not this be talked about frankly and candidly so that good sense, rather than delusion, may prevail in the legislative area?

Is it being too much of an egghead to hope that a Labor-Management Assembly, with the help of academicians and public figures, could discuss the implications of John Galbraith's thesis that we have reached the stage of "an affluent society" and must seek goals other than steadily increasing production of consumer goods? Have we gone too far in seeking ever-increasing output of our industrial products?

Are labor and management satisfied with our national defense program? Both are committed to maximum security against present and potential Communist aggression. Are we meeting this challenge?

What about our educational system? Support for education is a foundation stone of the labor movement, which from the outset regarded free education to be indispensable to human dignity and progress. Is it not equally indispensable to the continued growth and development of American industry? And are not both labor and management also jointly concerned with mental, as well as physical, health in industry—a subject which neither seems to have explored and which might have remained unexplored were it not for the pioneering work in this, as well as other psychological areas, of the outstanding Menninger Foundation? The list of subjects which would be discussed and are not now being discussed is endless.

Now, I believe I am a realist. I know that creating a forum such as I propose will not solve, and may even aggravate, the problem of reaching mutual understanding. I am aware that at a meeting such as this men will read prepared speeches, setting forth their maximum positions. The pressure of their own sides against concessions may dim the chance of fruitful discussion. But I am similarly aware of what the General Assembly of the United Nations, with even greater problems, has accomplished, as well as what it has not accomplished, in relaxing international tensions. Without expecting too much, and without even hoping for too much, I believe that a Labor-Management Assembly will be good for labor and management and the American public. For if we take no step, if we make no effort, the alternative is discouraging—the widening of the chasm, a hardening of attitudes, all leading to an eventual militant class consciousness—the absence of which has been one of the strengths of democratic America.

Whether or not this proposal of mine has any merit, it is highly important that objective observers of the labor-management scene, such as the faculty of the University of Wisconsin, as well as our business leaders and labor leaders and their staffs, soberly reflect upon the present lack of fully mature labor-management relations in America. Out of their reflection may come other and more constructive proposals than mine for dealing with this problem.

What is called for is a reaffirmation and development of the Hillman tradition of labor-management relations. What is called for is a greater recognition of mutuality of interest. Mind you, as Hillman well knew, mutual respect does not mean artificial unanimity of thought. Within the framework of mutual acceptance and mutual respect there is wide room for diversity of opinion. But can we not work, labor and management alike, to solve common problems through the development of a program which will promote the nation's economic health and will advance the growth of both business enterprise and labor?

The creation of such a program would be a definite sign of developing responsibility. Such a program, it seems to me, would harmonize the public interest with the interests of both business and labor; for it would tend to produce constructive solutions from which every American will benefit.

I believe that the heritage of Sidney Hillman is still very much alive. If my belief is correct, there is certainly in existence in both management and labor the vision and imagination capable of developing a program built upon the solid premise that what is good for America is good for those who own and manage and for those who belong to our free trade unions.

Sidney Hillman Address, University of Wisconsin, November 5, 1958

Trade Unions and the World Community

The American trade-union movement is facing a period of great challenge. I can foresee four major responsibilities that union organizations like the Industrial Union Department will be asked to assume. I would like to describe them briefly.

Our concern as a people—through most of our history—has been with securing individual right in our own nation. We have built free institutions to help attain that goal. We have developed our resources and used them to attain high material standards. We have enjoyed political freedom and personal protection. Our unions have played a great part in this adventure toward a better life.

But we have not arrived at a conclusion. We have not reached a destination. We have only come to that place from which the higher adventure begins—not as an isolated and singular people, but as a member of the world community.

We cannot long survive—and are not worthy to survive—as an island of affluence and smug contentment surrounded by rising currents of hunger, disease and privation.

For a century American technology has created immense new wealth. The American social genius has made that wealth available on a broad basis. The individual—not the king, or the ruler, or the despot, or the owner, or the lucky few alone—the individual and his family have prospered. This is as startling and inspiring a revolution in the economic order as was our revolution in the political order.

To the great masses of people in Asia and Africa and South America—

whose hands are on the oars of history—we must show that our tradition of change does not stop with a guarantee of political freedom but goes on. This free way of life gives promise to the world of vast economic freedom and well-being.

And what voice can speak better than that of our union movement?

The labor movement helped create this social order. It is a free institution dedicated to this way of life. It speaks the same language of justice and conscience that one hears throughout the wanting nations. This, I believe, is the first responsibility on the new frontier of trade unionism.

American unions have done a great deal to project the image of economic justice to other nations. In the years ahead they must do more.

The activities of organizations like the International Confederation of Free Trade Unions and the International Labor Organization deserve, and must have, the full and active support of our labor movement.

These organizations reach to the people. They reflect the aspirations of the people. And they can bring to working people throughout the world the message that economic well-being and personal freedom are complementary, each supporting the other.

I believe that our government must do more also.

We spend many millions of dollars describing the fruits of American liberty. But too often these are confused with the material by-products, the things of American life, the appliances and automobiles and television sets. Too often we focus on an American kitchen and not on the free labor that built it.

Good trade unionism is a showcase for democratic procedure. We should advertise more broadly this kind of institution, created by the people themselves, as a voice for themselves in the ordering of social and economic life.

The Industrial Union Department and those great unions represented by it have been active and effective campaigners in this international area. Now the responsibility enlarges.

The second major challenge on the labor movement's new frontier turns directly inward, as the first turned outward.

The greatest danger to freedom is an inert people. The greatest danger to any institution is loss of spirit in its people. And the greatest danger to trade unionism today is an apathetic membership.

This is not the fault of our good union leadership. It is, rather, characteristic of a society where self-indulgence and comfort are considered by many to be inherent rights. "Let George do it" can become a way of life. With the problems that we Americans face, both at home and abroad, that way of life is suicidal.

A union whose membership is not vitally interested, articulate, ready to dissent or defend, alert to its needs and demanding of its leadership is not a union at all. It is a captive of its own indifference. It is open prey to incompetent or self-serving men whose mere activity can elevate them through a dormant body.

I have always believed that the labor movement had a great function as a stimulator, an activator. It should question and prod and awaken and lead men to think. But its own membership must be fully awake first.

Today television seems to be a competitor of trade unionism. While the old frontier marshal is being a hero in the living room, the new frontier union member is being a lot less than responsible.

There are millions in the world today who would willingly sacrifice and suffer to enjoy the freedoms of speech and assembly, the right of self-government in the economic order. The union member who enjoys such freedom should take every opportunity to exercise that right.

Even union organizations like the Industrial Union Department, noted for its democratic operation and good participation, might take another look at what it can do to make its members more active. For the labor movement as a whole, a major effort to overcome membership apathy is a necessary starting point for growth.

It is necessary as well to the third challenge to trade unionism—to cooperate in bringing the benefits of good unionism to areas needing it most.

In the early history of union organizations in America—as your Industrial Union Department unions such as the UAW and Steelworkers and others can testify—a young union could rely on the aid and assistance of its older and established brothers in the movement as a whole. There was a sense of common mission and purpose.

There are many places in our economic life where the dark of the past still lingers. There are great industries and areas of the nation where workingmen and women have no effective representation, no common strength to better their conditions.

There are people working in those places, and they need the help of strong unions to get their own organizations started. This has nothing to do with jurisdiction, but it has everything to do with the role of unionism in making a fairer society for all.

There is good evidence that you have not been doing the organizing that should be done and that must be done if the American labor movement is to remain the force for good that it has been in the past.

I have with me some preliminary figures compiled by the Department of Labor that will be released in a few weeks.

They do not make encouraging reading.

Since 1958 membership in national and international unions has increased only by an estimated 36,000.

The percentage of union members in nonagricultural establishments has declined each year since 1958—from 33.7 per cent of all employees in that year, to 32.8 per cent in 1959, to 32.1 per cent in 1960.

Union membership in white-collar industries, the fastest growing occupations, is estimated at little over 2 million—only 8,000 over 1958.

Half of all union members are in New York, Pennsylvania, Illinois, Ohio, and California—at a time when the geography of American industry is shifting south and west.

If you are seeking a challenge, there it is in black and white.

Finally, the fourth major challenge I see ahead is a broader role of partnership between labor and management. The individual interest of the American business and the American union can no longer be served without reference to the national interest. Both must now move together within a framework of accepted public responsibility.

On the old frontier unions were intent on organizing and winning wage benefits. They were fighting for a rightful place. Now they must examine the responsibilities that rightful place entails.

There are improvements on the old bread-and-butter issues, certainly. But beyond those is a new dimension of action demanded by a modern economy. We must have a higher rate of economic growth. We must attain this higher rate of growth without causing severe hardships to working families.

Growth means higher productivity, and that means, for management, modernization, improvement, change. Couple this need for change on management's part with the role of a union as protecting the welfare of its members. I think both the basis and the need for creative partnership are clear.

The problems of job security, of a competitive posture in the world markets, cannot be solved by either management or labor unilaterally.

I am confident that if management will move halfway toward partnership, labor will join them. I am equally confident that if labor will move halfway, management will come over. If both start now, then America can start growing.

Over the years American unions have faced many new frontiers. There was hostility. There was sacrifice and struggle.

Now those frontiers seem old to us—a mark of success. And now there stretch new ones, a range of opportunity that rises across the world itself, that goes on from here to far beyond our shores.

They demand of us our best, our deepest conviction. And those called to the task go to meet it in the certainty that in performance is honor.

This is a fine hour to be an American.

Industrial Union Department, AFL-CIO, Washington, D.C., November 17, 1961

Labor Standards

I welcome this opportunity to talk about the rights and responsibilities of a trade-union member. I recognize that, as a result of recent disclosures, there is a widespread and genuine concern with the subject.

The vast majority of union officials endeavor honestly to safeguard the rights and forward the interests of their members and to discharge the duties of their office. Yet, the reputations of the vast majority and of the labor movement are imperiled by the dishonest, corrupt and unethical practices of the few who betray their trust.

Union members who fail to exercise and practice their responsibilities as union citizens likewise bear a high degree of accountability for abridgment of their rights.

Most of the time—but not all of it, by any means—they *do* enjoy their rights as members of democratic unions. Most of the time—but, unfortunately, not enough of the time—they *do* exercise and practice their responsibilities as union members.

To make a detailed survey of the degree to which rights are being honored and responsibilities fully met would, I fear, be a career in itself. I doubt that a perfect score would be found in any trade union—or, for that matter, in any human organization. Nevertheless, many union organizations have conscientiously striven to provide constitutional safeguards for members' rights and have gone to considerable effort to instill among their members that sense of responsibility which is essential to a truly democratic organization. There are other union organizations where this process seems —if I may be charitable—retarded; and the AFL-CIO Executive Council, at its meeting in Washington tomorrow, may be called upon to make some decisions on this very issue.

Let me point out before I go further that the problem is one that faces many groups in our society—not only the labor movement.

In greater or lesser degree it is faced by churches, fraternal organizations, alumni clubs, and, in a larger sense, in connection with the exercise of the franchise, by government itself.

I have recently read that a panel of personnel experts of the American Management Association seems concerned that management may have been too successful in demoting individuality—that is, a sense of rights and responsibilities—in the ranks of industry. Too much success along those lines leads to a form of yes-man regimentation and a loss of the individual's willingness to speak up with his ideas or his doubts.

So, I gather, labor is not in a boat by itself; rather, because of the work of Congressional committees and the AFL-CIO itself, labor happens merely to be in a highly publicized boat.

Union citizenship bears strong resemblances to United States citizenship, of which it is indeed a part. There are rights and duties; there are privileges and responsibilities. In both the broad community of citizenship and the more limited citizenship of the labor movement there are bright spots and areas of deficiency. In both fields there are constitutions and laws, as well as the uncertain factor of human personality.

In neither government nor the labor movement do I know of any cure-alls that will bring perfection quickly.

Secondly, I am fearful that the traditional American alibi, "Let's pass a law," by which we so often mean "Let George do it," will not bring a complete solution to our problem.

If there is no truly simple problem and certainly no simple solution, then let us look with humility at the problem and at some of the solutions that I can visualize:

What are the rights of a union member vis-à-vis his union? I assume everyone interested in the subject has his own list. This is mine:

1. The right to a democratic union.
2. The right to due process of law in union disciplinary proceedings.
3. The right to a clean, honest union.
4. The right to an effective union.
5. The right to a union free from discrimination because of race, creed or color.
6. The right to a responsible union—responsible not only to its members and employers but to the community and to the nation as well.

I think that the mere enumeration of these rights explains them. Some elaboration, however, is undoubtedly required.

The entire labor movement in the United States and in all free countries in the world is based upon the democratic tradition. Freedom and democracy are the essential attributes of our labor movement. Labor organizations lacking these attributes, like Hitler's labor front, Franco's syndicates, and Moscow's captive unions, are unions in name only.

Authoritarian control, whether from within the labor movement or imposed from without by government, is contrary to the spirit, the tradition and the principles which should always guide and govern labor unions which call themselves free and democratic.

The overwhelming majority of American unions both preach and practice the principles of democracy. It is necessary, however, to recognize that the record of union democracy, like the record of our nation's democracy, is not perfect. A few unions do not adequately provide for the basic elements of democratic practice. A few unions, while giving lip service to them, do not practice or implement these principles. In all too many instances the membership, by apathy and indifference, forfeit their rights of union citizenship.

Thus far I have spoken generally about union democracy. Perhaps I should describe what I regard to be its basic element. It is defined in the AFL-CIO Code on Union Democratic Processes as the right of full and equal participation by each member in the affairs and processes of union self-government. This includes the right (*a*) to vote periodically for his local and national officers either directly by referendum vote or through delegate bodies, (*b*) to honest elections, (*c*) to stand for and to hold office subject only to fair qualifications, uniformly imposed, and (*d*) to voice his views as to the method in which the union affairs should be conducted.

The AFL-CIO in its Ethical Practices Code dealing with union democracy correctly points out that, since each union has grown up in its own tradition and with its own background, forms and procedures for conducting union elections differ widely. For example, many unions elect their national officers by vote of delegate bodies. Other unions do so by referendum vote. Whichever method is used, the important thing is that the election should be free, fair and honest and that adequate internal safeguards should be provided to ensure the achievement of that objective.

While unions should be free to determine their own governmental structure and to regulate their own affairs, the AFL-CIO, in the code I have mentioned, has enumerated additional safeguards designed to ensure union democracy and to safeguard the democratic character of the labor movement. Thus the AFL-CIO has called upon all of its affiliates to hold regular conventions at stated intervals, which should not be more than four years, to open all their general conventions to the public, and to make available to the membership and to the public convention proceedings. In addition, the AFL-CIO has called for periodic membership meetings of all local unions with proper notice of time and place; for limited terms of office for all union officials, not to exceed four years; for sparing exercise of the establishment of trusteeships over subordinate bodies; and for compliance by union officers and executive boards with the provisions of the union's constitution and decisions of the union's conventions.

I am aware that there is much discussion in this area of the need for legislation to effectuate these principles for ensuring union democracy. I have more faith in the actions being taken by the AFL-CIO in this area. Moreover, the real and lasting corrective is not so much the establishment of new principles as the exercise of rights presently recognized and accorded. Just as eternal vigilance is the price of liberty, so is the constant exercise of the rights of union citizenship the price of union democracy.

The AFL-CIO code dealing with this subject reaffirms what every decent labor organization has always recognized, that each member of a union is entitled to the right of fair treatment in the application of union rules and law. It seems to me that the general principles applicable to union disciplinary procedures can be simply stated, as they are in the code. Such procedures should contain all the elements of fair play. No particular formality is required. Court procedures need not be used and, in my opinion, should not be encouraged. The essential requirements of due process, however—notice, hearing, and judgment on the basis of the evidence—should be observed. A method of appeal to a higher body should be provided to ensure that judgment at the local level is not the result of prejudice or bias. Here, again, most unions provide for these basic elements of due process. A few do not. And the misdoings of these few have understandably created concern in the public mind. Here, too, I would rest my faith with the actions being taken by the AFL-CIO to ensure uniform compliance. Moreover, court decisions have increasingly protected the rights of individuals to union due process and there is little that legislation could add.

Union members have the absolute right to expect and to exact absolute honesty in the conduct of their union affairs. They have a right, let me add, to expect more honesty and ethics than may commonly be found in the market place. Making quick profits may be part of the climate of the business community. It can never be tolerated as part of the concepts of the labor community. The trades union movement is a brotherhood to serve the general welfare of its members and the public. It is not a means for individuals to serve their own selfish purposes. By the adoption of the constitution of the AFL-CIO the American labor movement has clearly accepted the responsibility to protect the movement "from any and all corrupt influences."

The codes adopted by the AFL-CIO to implement this constitutional provision set high standards for unions and union officials. Thus conflicts of interest in the investment and business interests of union officials are prohibited. The standard used is virtually the same as applied to public servants. In the language of the code "no responsible trade-union official should have a personal financial interest which conflicts with the full performance of his fiduciary duties as a workers' representative." This does not mean that an official of a union may not own a few shares of a publicly listed security. We in America are not that class conscious. It does mean, however, that a union official should not have "a substantial business interest in any business enterprise with which his union bargains collectively or in any business enterprise which is in competition with any other business enterprise with which his union bargains collectively."

In the handling of union and health and welfare funds all unions and all union officials are enjoined by the AFL-CIO codes to administer such funds as a high trust for the benefit of the members and to rigorously adhere to the highest ethical standards. Strict record keeping and audits are enjoined; dual salaries prohibited; adequate information to the membership required. Here, again, the codes set an extremely high standard. To quote the language of the code, "with respect to accounting and financial controls and the expenditure of its funds for proprietary functions, the labor movement, it goes almost without saying, should follow the strictest rules applicable to all well-run institutions. With respect to the policies governing its financial and proprietary decisions, a higher obligation rests upon the trade-union movement: to conduct its affairs and to expend and invest its funds, not for profit, but for the benefit of its membership and the great purposes for which they have joined together in the fraternity of the labor movement."

The codes establish further and more self-evident requirements. Crooks and racketeers are barred from holding office in the labor movement. Here the test is not conviction but a practical one; "obviously a person commonly known to be a crook or racketeer should not enjoy immunity to prey upon the labor movement because he has somehow managed to escape conviction. In this area determinations must be made as a matter of common sense and with due regard to the rights of labor unions and the individuals involved."

Paper charters are prohibited. Affiliates are enjoined that a charter should never be used as a hunting license or granted to persons who are known to traffic in local union charters for illicit or improper purposes. Kickbacks, under-the-table payments, gifts or personal payments from an employer or business enterprise with which the official's union bargains are condemned. Finally, the entire labor movement is reminded by the codes that any departure from the most exacting ethical principles is harmful not only to the people directly affected but to our whole society.

I believe that the adoption of these codes by the AFL-CIO constitutes a most significant step in protecting the rights of union members to clean unions. I am fully aware that the mere adoption of these codes standing alone will not assure honesty and eliminate corruption. But the AFL-CIO has done far more than merely adopt high-sounding principles. Six unions, including the largest one in the Federation, have been charged and found guilty of violating the labor movement's own standards of ethical practices. One union has already been suspended from the Federation, two have been virtually placed under Federation trusteeship; and tomorrow the Federation's Executive Council will deal with the other three found subject to corrupt influences. It is not for me to predict what the Council will do, but I am entirely confident that the leadership of the Federation will, without fear or favor, and without regard to the size or strength of any of its affiliates, carry out the constitutional determination to keep the labor movement free from any taint of corruption.

The action which has been and will be taken perhaps will not satisfy those who seek absolute perfection. I would remind you that the Constitution of the AFL-CIO and its Ethical Practices Codes are a good deal younger than the Ten Commandments, with which mankind for several thousand years has had major enforcement problems. I trust that labor's friends will, therefore, be tolerant at least for a time—tolerant not of criminality but of the efforts of unions to overcome it.

The primary function of labor unions in a democracy pledged, as we are, to private enterprise is collective bargaining. A good contract is the fundamental object of every union. Each member has a right to efficient and effective representation at the bargaining table. He should also be able to expect that when his union meets with the employer it is armed with all the weapons and techniques of this important process. He has a right to expect that his officers know the facts, that professional and technical assistance is available to his officials, that legal, research, educational and public relations techniques have been utilized as fully as possible. In short, the union member has the right to expect that his leaders and collective bargaining representatives will leave no stone unturned in getting him the best possible agreement on wages, working hours, working conditions and security.

In reviewing the record I have found, for example, that far greater losses have resulted to the membership of unions by lack of expert help in the field of health and welfare funds than from corruption on the part of union officials. In this connection it is significant that one of the codes adopted by the AFL-CIO, in recognizing this, says:

As a fundamental part of any approach to the problem of policing health and welfare funds, affiliated unions, through education, publicity, and discussion programs, should seek to develop the widest possible degree of active and informed interest in all phases of these programs on the part of the membership at large. International unions should, wherever possible, have expert advice available for the negotiation, establishment and administration of health and welfare plans, and should provide training for union representatives in the techniques and standards of proper administration of welfare plans.

An important right which the union member should have every reason to expect is full protection, in his union and by his union, of the basic civil rights of American democracy.

Discrimination against minorities is one of the great and unresolved problems of America; yet in the postwar years we have made heartening and almost astonishing progress to overcome this obstacle to our democratic society, with its concept of full human rights for every citizen. It is a source of pride to me that so many unions have stood in the forefront of the fight for civil rights. The constitution of the AFL-CIO recognizes the right of all workers, without regard to race, creed, color or national origin, to share in the full benefits of trade unionism.

The day of the restrictive clause in union constitutions, fortunately, is close to twilight. Nevertheless, it would be unrealistic to think that, despite the progress which has been made, and the standards that, for the most part, compare most favorably with other community organizations, there is not room in many sections of the trade-union movement for the strengthening of basic civil rights of every member.

The union member has the right to expect that his union be a responsible one—responsible to him as a member, responsible to employers under its collective bargaining agreements, but more importantly, responsible to the community and to the nation at large.

With labor's growth and maturity, American unions have rapidly emerged from the status of a narrow pressure group into an area of broader interest in the general problems of the nation and the specific community. Labor leadership cannot afford to let a situation develop in which there is any difference in the mind of the public between desirable goals for the whole society and desirable goals for the labor movement. It is unfortunate that a few labor leaders have not yet come to realize the public service character of the union and its functions. It is fortunate that the leadership of the AFL-CIO and most of its affiliates do. It is for the best interests of unions and their members that they must now live in the goldfish bowl of national curiosity. The goldfish bowl is not a bad symbol for responsible organizations in the American democratic society. To maintain the good will of fair-minded employers, of public officials, and of the mass of plain ordinary citizens labor will constantly have to reaffirm that it has nothing to hide and much to proclaim. "What is good for America is good for labor" is an admirable and catchy slogan. But, glib as it sounds, it voices a fundamental truth that our labor movement should not forget.

I have thus far dealt with the rights of a trade-union member, but these rights cannot be achieved by a union membership that does not exercise its responsibilities, a union membership that sits back, bored or smug, and challenges its officialdom to pull economic and ethical rabbits out of the union hat.

The first responsibility of the union member is to participate in the affairs of his union. When union members regard their unions as slot machines which may pay back a quarter for each nickel invested, or as an insurance policy that can be obtained at little cost, then that union member is devaluating his union.

A certain recipe for corruption in the leadership is lethargy of the membership. As Monsignor George G. Higgins of the National Catholic Welfare Conference pointed out, in a recent speech to the last convention of the United Automobile Workers, union members tend to get the sort of leadership they deserve; but since luck has been on their side, they have often gotten better leadership than their degree of participation would suggest they deserve.

To those who would blame all the faults of the labor movement on its leaders, let me point to the increasingly effective campaigns being conducted by many union leaderships to get the members to come in decent numbers to union meetings. After all, nobody "forces" the union member to stay home watching television.

The union member has a second responsibility: to help set the broad ethical standards under which his union operates. A union is composed of individual members who create a "public opinion" of their own. Like politicians, the union leader is sensitive to his public. And he responds quickly to the straws in the wind.

The individual union member has a responsibility to make sure that the public opinion which he helps to mold does not provide a climate in which tolerance for making a fast buck is a major factor. He has, indeed, a responsibility to let his leaders know that the union's members expect—more than that, demand—that they will be honest servants of the organization and its membership.

Thirdly, the membership has a responsibility to adhere to our American concept of respect for minorities.

Let us be frank: Too many union members joined White Citizens Councils in the South. Too many union members took part in the disgraceful anti-Negro riots at Trumbull Park here in Chicago. Too many union members are not willing to accord to minorities the civil rights which they would want for themselves.

There is a responsibility on the part of union members to give full support to our broad national program of civil rights and to insist that their unions keep in step with the fair-minded sections of our national population.

Fourth, there is a responsibility on the members to be good citizens and to recognize fully the role of their union as a responsible volunteer organization in the national society. This, in my mind, embraces the concept I have already mentioned, that what is good for America is good for its trade unions. The union member has a responsibility to recognize that his union is not an island unto itself, but that it must, in the American way, work together with other sections of the community to make our country a better place in which to live and the world a better place for all mankind.

And, finally, the union member has the responsibility to be loyal to his union.

The right of an individual member to criticize the policies and personalities of his union officers—and he has this unquestioned right—does not in the language of the AFL-CIO code "include the right to undermine the union as an institution."

That means that each union member should support wholeheartedly and intelligently the union's collective bargaining goals arrived at by democratic processes. It means that he must be ready to support the services which the modern union requires in order that it can represent the member effectively at the collective bargaining table. It means that the union member has a responsibility to make the most of the democratic process within his own organization. It means that the duty of policing and enforcing ethical standards is shared by every union member as well as by his officials. It means recognition that the best safeguards against abuses of union rights lie in the hands of a vigilant, informed and active membership.

These are difficult days for labor in America. The enemies of labor will seek to use the present situation substantially to weaken it. The friends of labor will be called upon to safeguard labor from unwarranted restrictions and to support labor's own program to correct abuses. The public should remember that a democratic and strong labor movement is a bulwark to our free way of life.

Conference on Freedom and Responsibility in the Industrial Community, Northwestern University Law School, October 23, 1957

THE PEACEABLE SETTLEMENT OF DISPUTES

The Current Scene

This great center of industry and of labor [Chicago] has known both struggle and achievement, both tumult and peace in its industrial past. It is, therefore, a good place for me to speak plainly about the state of labor-management relations today.

I believe the key to those relations is the plain fact that our destiny as a free nation depends as never before on the achievement of a greater sense of national unity.

For the country that is the world's foremost industrial power, the building of a stronger and more durable industrial peace is clearly a precondition of national unity. Keeping and enlarging the industrial peace therefore stands at the very top of the list of American priorities. But in domestic affairs as in international affairs, we are not advocates of peace at any price. Industrial peace must come about by settlements reasonably negotiated and consistent with our national interests, goals and objectives.

These are facts which are eloquently evident to all of you, I know. I emphasize them here and now only because I am aware of your dedication to giving greater meaning—and greater effort—to these facts.

We have just closed a year that marked the greatest period of industrial peace in the United States since the end of World War II. The 3,300 work stoppages recorded in 1961 were the smallest number since the war. Mandays lost because of these strikes dropped from 19.1 million in the previous year to 16.5 million, a low mark for the postwar period. Total strike idleness amounted to 0.15 per cent of the estimated working time during the year, making 1961 the most peaceful year in recent history.

We are now beginning a year that holds both serious threats of industrial conflict and the promise of unparalleled progress toward amity and cooperation between labor and management. We must make good that promise. Though the difficulties to be met and overcome are large and real, I am increasingly hopeful that management and labor will meet this challenge fully and make constructive use of the great opportunity that it presents.

In making an assessment of where we stand and where we are going, it is important that we deal with facts.

The central fact is that the factors working for continued industrial peace are growing in number and gaining in weight.

One of the more significant facts is the change that already has occurred in the whole industrial climate in the past year.

We have come to a hopeful turning that seemed very far away indeed three years ago, when management and labor were moving toward one of their most devastating tests of economic strength in our history. The industrial storm clouds were many and ominous in November of 1958, when, as a private citizen, I was invited to give my views of the state of labor-management relations at that time.

It was necessary to report, in 1958, that a trend away from responsible and imaginative collective bargaining was setting in. There was a hardening of attitudes, particularly in the major organized areas; a retrogression rather than progress in understanding. Management was tougher, unions were tougher, and it did not appear that the end product necessarily would be good for either side.

The situation, as you know, became even more aggravated in 1959, when the cold war between management and labor erupted into conflict in the steel industry. All of us, I believe, learned a lesson from the 1959 steel strike, which ran on for 116 days and brought grave economic dislocations that were reflected in the 1960 recession.

On the one hand, the steel and other companies came to understand that, despite the loose talk one occasionally hears, American workers will stand by their trade unions and endure the most severe hardship to sustain them.

On the other hand, the steel and other unions came to a clearer realization that the best way to solve problems is not by the test of strength in a strike but through the collective bargaining process. Both sides in steel have found a useful new instrumentality for that purpose in the Human Relations Committees which were established in the aftermath of the 1959 strike.

For its part, the nation learned that a long strike of this character, preceded by an artificial build-up of inventories, is a matter of grave import to the entire economy.

It is a universally shared and obvious truth that we cannot this year afford a repetition of the 1959 steel strike. The President, speaking for all of the American people, has called upon the parties to take appropriate and early steps to avert this. I am confident that they will measure up to their plain responsibility to the nation to conclude an early and noninflationary settlement in the public interest.

Today the climate of industrial relations is much improved over 1959. The lessons learned from the steel strike were partially responsible. There were also other reasons.

Another factor contributing greatly to a broader approach to labor-management relations is that all of us are increasingly aware of the many challenges that come to us from abroad. Events daily impress upon us the immediate interrelation of domestic developments and foreign affairs. Both management and labor have become increasingly conscious that the state of their relations here at home have become an important factor in our posture in world affairs. Our isolation from the world economy ceased long ago, and that fact steadily becomes more apparent. Such issues as price stability, balance of payments, and international trade are directly involved with labor-management decisions at home affecting wages, workday standards and profit margins.

An unfortunate factor which also contributed to better relations between management and labor was the impact of the recession on both. The stern economic realities have made both management and labor more responsible and less belligerent. Neither has walked around with a chip on his shoulder during this period. It seems to me that we should be able to carry over into periods of prosperity the same restraints which are exercised during recessions.

There is in addition, of course, the fact of the new Administration which has made a significant contribution by taking affirmative steps to improve the climate of labor-management relations. The establishment of the President's Advisory Committee on Labor-Management Policy is a matter of major importance in American industrial life.

When this 21-man Committee was first set up many people were skeptical about its value and possible success. When one looks back at the history of other such committees such a concern is understandable.

While the results of this Committee have not been dramatic, I believe that the skepticism has abated. The fact that the Committee has continued to meet is a success in itself, especially when one remembers that most prior committees broke up before they even got started.

Certainly the first report of the Committee—on the subject of automation —is a heartening herald of its possible future activities. A group of sophisticates in the area of industrial relations such as yourselves will readily understand the importance of the Committee's work in opening the channels of communication between labor and management which were being increasingly closed in 1958.

The President's Committee was not established to pass resolutions. We do not intend that it should attempt to obtain or enforce a rigid and pale unanimity of opinion. Rather, the purpose of the Committee is to permit an interchange of views between labor and management and to articulate a consensus of these views.

As you know, the Committee is dealing with very large subjects. In addition to automation, it is now considering collective bargaining and industrial peace, economic growth and unemployment, our competitive position in world markets, and wage and price policies.

Besides the result of the work of the Committee itself, we are getting many welcome indirect dividends. Local committees are being established to bring labor and management together in continuing communication. This is a most welcome development.

In addition our Committee has had international implications. I read with great interest about the establishment in Great Britain of a similar committee—the National Economic Development Council. It was reported that one factor leading to the participation by the British Trade Union Congress on the Council was the participation by American labor on the President's Committee.

From its progress so far I would suggest, if I may, that no one need be surprised by the possible achievements of the President's Committee. This

Committee can contribute to labor-management relations in this country benefits not now even anticipated.

With today's improvement in the climate of labor-management relations come other and even greater challenges to American statesmanship in this field.

The goals before us are, I think, clear:

To prevent inflation and maintain price stability;

To increase productivity so that labor, management and the public can all rightfully share in the fruits of progress;

To remain competitive in world markets;

To achieve a rate of economic growth that will prove the means of meeting our domestic and international needs.

The attainment of these goals is clearly in the national interest. The implications for labor and management seem equally clear, especially in terms of the abandonment of restrictive policies that impair efficiency in the exercise of statesmanship in meeting the social consequences of change and in the formulation of wage and price policies. It remains to be seen whether these things can be done.

Our aim must be to attain these objectives without sacrificing the free operation of private bargaining. Under no circumstances can we afford to lose sight of the fact that collective bargaining is an integral element of all our freedoms, an institution essential to a free society.

It is an imperative to freedom that collective bargaining work in America, that it remain the center of economic decision and the agency to which employees, managers and the public can look with full expectation of justice and fairness. While we strive for this ideal, we must always be conscious that its pursuit involves not only this positive view—that it is a wonderful thing when freedom works—but also the opposite—that it is more than tragic when it does not.

In any free society the establishment of controls outside a time of national emergency is an admission of failure in self-government. We do not want that in this country, and we will not have that in this country, especially in the free economic life that has given to the American citizen the power to break history's long stranglehold of want and privation. I do not want to suggest that we have only these limited choices of self-control or outside control. The field between is both broad and wide. We are not an imitative society, parasitic on others' ideas. We are the great innovators and inventors of human history—builders of a good society and operators of a good economy. We can certainly now stand to the full height of that tradition and develop in our private relationships the ways and means to advance the public interest without sacrifice of freedom in any measure.

This is not a task which a single labor-management committee or a single company or union engaged in collective bargaining can manage unassisted. It is a task for many hands, and minds and spirits. We exist only as part of a team. Help must come from the whole labor and management community. We must find techniques that will enable us to understand the other's problems to a degree we have only rarely observed in the past.

A much larger understanding of the issues and the difficulties of solution is required of us all. For instance, labor organizations, in formulating their wage and price policies and other policies, must now look beyond the counsel of their tradition and out into the broad fields of modern economic realities, both at home and abroad. A union has existed for the benefit of its members, and still must do so, but the policies to achieve that end must include both long-range and the immediate welfare. It may be fine to save a job but it may not be so fine if the precedent of that action endangers many other jobs over a period of time.

If the nation as a whole is able to achieve the goals I have described, then union members and their organizations will also flourish because there will be more jobs and more opportunity. Blind resistance to change can have only one effect—stagnation.

Management, too, must also stop its blind resistance to change. The management community, for example, takes an almost automatic stand against proposals to improve the unemployment insurance system. The result is that proposals calling for measures to provide the same or even greater protection find their way to the bargaining table. When a question like this, I need not tell you, is on the bargaining agenda, it may well be decided not solely on its merits but on sheer bargaining power.

The management community takes an institutional stand of opposition to proposals to provide medical care for the aged through tested Social Security techniques. At least in part, that opposition is based on the cost factor, since Social Security is a tax. But eventually the demand for this kind of assistance—the same demand that underlies legislative proposals—will push this question into the bargaining area. The result may well be more expensive for management than an increase in the tax.

Resistance to change as a management attitude is becoming increasingly critical in the broad field of job security. The President correctly pointed out in a recent press conference that technological change and automation are the most vital domestic issues of the 1960's. The President's Advisory Committee, in its report on automation, made known its conviction that both private and public programs are needed. No one element of our society can resolve the complex problems involved in change and its impact upon lives. Even labor and management working as a team cannot do it. But a great cooperative effort of labor and management and government can find the ways to a solution.

I have said before, and I repeat now, that unions are very pragmatic organizations. The American people are a very pragmatic people. When they are troubled, or in need, or facing difficulty, they set about doing something. And I feel that if the men and women in our labor force today cannot get help from Springfield, or from Washington, they will look for it at the bargaining tables in Chicago and Detroit.

I do not mean to exclude the role of collective bargaining from these areas under any circumstances. There is always room, at any time, for supplemental collective bargaining improvements over the minimum standards provided by legislation. There is a definite role for both.

It is time that labor and management embark together for the new world of the economic future and leave behind the old hostilities and inadequate ideas and misconceptions that have so long delayed a needed mutual effort.

The President is convening in Washington, sometime in the late spring or early summer, a White House Conference on National Economic Issues at which leading management, labor and public representatives would confer with appropriate government officials regarding the major economic issues facing the country, and ways of promoting our economic progress.

This Conference will seek to facilitate understanding rather than seek agreement. It will not be the intention of this Conference to try to get resolutions adopted. Rather, we look toward constructive consultation by all members of our national community. This is one effort to find a mutual way so that free men will continue to direct their economic destiny.

The issues in labor-management affairs are far too complex, far too potent, and far too influential on the rest of society to be resolved on the old testing grounds of force and power. Yet many times the parties are unable to find an alternate ground without the aid and assistance of a third party. The mediation and arbitration process today must be used to a greater extent to avert the wasteful referral of disputes to mere clashes of power. This truth also calls for the greater exercise of government responsibility in the area of collective bargaining.

When I suggest that government should exercise greater responsibility in the collective bargaining area I do not mean by this that the government should impose or dictate terms of settlement. I do not mean that it is desirable to impose by law the decisions of a third party. I am sure that I share with you the conviction that compulsory arbitration is inimical to our traditions and system of free collective bargaining.

The government, rather, should improve its historic role of defining the national goal and of utilizing mediation to assist in keeping the peace and in making sure the peace is a sound and beneficial peace. In the past when government officials were called upon to assist in collective bargaining their only aim was to achieve a settlement.

Today, in the light of our nation's commitments both at home and abroad, government and private mediators must increasingly provide guidelines to the parties to ensure that the settlements reached are right settlements that are not only in the interest of the parties themselves but which also take into account the public interest.

The government must give better aid to collective bargaining through improved good office and mediation procedures but also through better and more precise economic data—which is provided before the fact not as a post-mortem inquest; so as to assist settlements, not simply analyze them.

And most important of all, the government must have the courage to assert the national interest as President Kennedy is doing so forthrightly. No one wants government intervention, but everyone expects the government to assert and define the national interest.

The continued growth of the American economy is a matter of inescapable concern and, directly thereby, of responsibility to whatever Administration is in office. If this responsibility is carried out with vigor and with insight, based on the desire that all the parties involved should benefit from the outcome, we are likely to attain a new consensus in the field of labor-management relations—a new consensus that will have the most profound and beneficent effect on American life and the national interests of the United States.

The Executives' Club, Chicago, Ill., February 23, 1962

Collective Bargaining and Industrial Peace

We in the Administration are totally committed to free collective bargaining as the major means of wage determination in our industrial democracy. We are deeply committed to private enterprise as the generator of our wealth and to collective bargaining as the source of its just distribution in industrial life.

We are against compulsory arbitration and correspondingly against government imposition of the terms of settlement, whether in small industries or large. We have not proposed and do not propose wage controls or price controls. We defend and will preserve the right of employees and employers to assert their economic force in collective bargaining situations. However, while recognizing the necessity for preserving these important aspects of free decision making, we seek, by all available means, to minimize economic conflicts in collective bargaining, since recourse to economic force should always be a final and, if at all possible, an avoidable result.

Wherever the national health and safety are involved, this Administration will act unhesitatingly to safeguard it with all the means Congress has provided, and if these are inadequate will unhesitatingly recommend to Congress additional means. But our total interest cannot begin or end with the statement or observation of such principles. More is involved.

We in the Administration are not disinterested, nor can we be, in the total result of collective bargaining in the country, and whether or not it leads or contributes to a sound or an inflationary economy. We are not disinterested, nor can we be, in whether particular bargaining in critical industries leads to industrial peace or economic war, in which the public interest may be severely injured before the parties themselves are.

We are not disinterested because these events in our economic life have a direct bearing upon our ability to meet the aggressive challenge of communism, to maintain our security forces in a state of readiness, to help new nations along their own path to freedom, to keep our dollar sound, to maintain our balance of payments, to respond to the competitive challenge of expanding world markets, to preserve and protect our standard of living here at home. The government's interest in the progress and stability of our economy is related directly to its obligations as leader of the free world and to promote the general welfare of our people.

Now, that is a broad context, but it is the context not only of collective bargaining but of the total of American life today.

National responsibilities of this character are clear to all during time of war. Private decision during total war has willingly submitted to controls, bending every individual effort to the success of the war effort and the survival of the country. Equally, in the days of total peace, such as the days when our private enterprise system was first fashioned behind the security of our oceans, the open and free play of an uninhibited economy was a total public policy. Today neither of these conditions exists. We have neither total war nor can anyone describe our condition as total peace. And our present circumstance will continue, I believe, for a long time.

The challenge of collective bargaining today is—in the face of national responsibilities as great as those involved in past total wars—to operate and function without controls and in a condition of freedom. The key to meeting this challenge is in the interrelationship of freedom and responsibility. To be free, collective bargaining must be responsible; so long as collective bargaining is responsible, it will always be free.

Free, of course, means free of controls, free to exercise the right of final decision making. It does not and cannot exclude government concern, interest, good offices procedures, mediation—all traditionally compatible with and helpful to freedom in this area.

Responsible means that collective bargaining must be responsive to the interests of the parties, the employers and the workers, but responsive also to the common interest, the national interest.

Rather than seeking to reduce the freedom which labor and management enjoy in collective bargaining, government policy today is striving to preserve that freedom in the only way it can be preserved, through the responsibility of the managers and the workers themselves so to conduct their business that all benefit and the national interest is safeguarded. This responsibility of labor and management, of course, extends beyond collective bargaining to policies of both in all areas.

And government, of course, must act responsibly too. Collective bargaining or other private decisions alone do not determine the total economic result. Government policies also enter, and of this our Administration is well aware. The government has a responsibility in collective bargaining, too, which it cannot avoid. For if the parties are to be asked to be responsive in collective bargaining because the national interest requires it, then the national interest must be defined.

Now, the government has no monopoly in defining the national interest in collective bargaining or for that matter in any other area. In our free democracy, the free press, free decision makers, citizens in all walks of life can all assert and be conscious of the national interest and have every right and duty to appraise it. But, while it has no monopoly on defining the national interest, a democratically elected government, under our Constitution, has a clear mandate and an inescapable responsibility also to define the national interest in all vital segments of American life, including collective bargaining. After all, the right of free speech extends to government, too.

Of necessity, in an area like collective bargaining, this can only be done in general terms. The Administration can say, as it has said, that we must have a stable price level if we are to be competitive, if we are to protect against the drain on gold, if we are to have a sound dollar, if we are to prevent the inroads in our standard of living that come with inflation, and if we are to meet our defense commitments and maintain our necessary aid payments abroad.

We can state the economic truth that, if wages and benefits negotiated in collective bargaining exceed the growth of productivity, someone pays the piper—profits and efficiency fall off, or prices rise, or demand is curtailed.

This is not new doctrine. President Eisenhower, in his Economic Report of 1960, said that "improvements in compensation rates must, on the average, remain within the limits of general productivity gains if reasonable stability of prices is to be achieved and maintained."

From the same Report, this conclusion: "In the last analysis, the only way to assure that, for the economy as a whole, maximum employment and maximum production also mean maximum purchasing power is to keep wage improvements within the range of productivity advance."

This same economic truth was stated in President Truman's Economic Reports. In 1947 he stated: "It is in the interest of steady expansion of the economy that, with the aid of collective bargaining, prices and wages be brought in line with general productivity trends." Again, in 1948, the Report asserted: "Rising wages and rising standards of living, based on increasing productivity and fair distribution of income, is the American way."

President Kennedy has made the same declaration in his 1962 Economic Report: "Ultimately, it is rising output per man-hour which must yield the ingredients of a rising standard of living. Growth in productivity makes it possible for real wages and real profits to rise side by side."

These statements of economic principle are not orders. They are laid before the common sense of every man who has to make a decision in this area as a simple truth it is in the public interest to observe. Since we are operating in a condition of freedom, bargainers are free to observe it or reject it. But if bargainers in total reject these principles, they must take their share of the responsibility for the impact upon the economy and the state of the nation.

I am not suggesting, nor has the Council of Economic Advisors suggested, that their principles or guidelines are an inflexible formula to be applied mechanically to every collective bargaining situation. In any given situation the result of collective bargaining will depend upon the circumstances. Rather the principles contained in the last Economic Report, and enunciated in every Economic Report, are intended as reminders of the economic realities and as aids to collective bargainers in discharging their responsibilities. The important thing, the thing that concerns all of the people and the obvious public interest, is that total bargaining come out right in the end, or as near right as it can.

I know the most popular thing that can be said to any business or labor audience, or to both meeting together, is: Let the government stay out of collective bargaining. To that I say that the government wants out, provided the parties discharge their responsibility to us all. The government can never stay out if the sum total of private decision making in collective bargaining impairs our national strength, health, safety, economy or ability to surive as a free nation.

I hope that our discussions during this Conference—all of us, labor and management, and the public, and the Administration each enjoying our respective right of free speech—will make a contribution to the national welfare. I am sure they will. We all, in the end, have only one interest at heart—that this great and mighty nation of ours continue in strength and vitality as the champion of human freedom.

White House Conference on National Economic Issues, Washington, D.C., May 21, 1962

The Uses of Arbitration

There was, in times now happily past, a judicial prejudice against arbitration, exemplified by the old common-law rule against the specific enforceability of agreements to arbitrate. The most quoted condemnation was that of Lord Campbell in *Scott* v. *Avery*,[1] who ascribed the traditional rule to the fact that the pay of judges depended mainly, or almost entirely, upon fees and that the judges were opposed, for that reason, to anything that would deprive them of jurisdiction, and hence of compensation. As Judge Hough said in 1915, "A more unworthy genesis cannot be imagined."[2]

On the other hand, supporters of the common-law rule have argued that this was not in fact the genesis of the rule and that the objection was not to the use of "these peaceable and domestic tribunals," but was simply a reluctance by the courts to hold parties to agreements which would have the effect of adjudicating their rights without protections provided in a court of law.

Whatever the original reason, modern courts recognize, as they should, that arbitration has the advantage, in the words of Mr. Justice Frankfurter, "of providing a speedier, more economic, and more effective enforcement of rights than can be had by the tortuous course of litigation." In a series of recent cases the Supreme Court of the United States has given firm endorsement to the enforcement of agreements to arbitrate labor disputes, deeming this required by specific provisions of federal labor statutes. In doing so the Court has recognized that, although labor arbitration has a resemblance to commercial arbitration, in the sense that both arise out of contract, nevertheless, there is a significant difference which basically distinguishes the two forms of arbitration. Labor arbitration, whether contract or grievance arbitration, fulfills one vital function: the substitute of the judgment of a third party for the use of economic force. It is not a substitute for litigation, which is the main characteristic of commercial arbitration. Labor arbitration is, rather, a device by which the parties agree to accept the judgment of a third party instead of fighting the issue out by industrial warfare—the strike

[1] 25 L.J. [N.S., Ex] 308, 313.
[2] *U.S. Asphalt Refining Co.* v. *Trinidad Lake Petroleum Co.*, 222 Fed. 1006, 1007.

or lockout. The American Arbitration Association has wisely recognized that labor arbitration is so different from commercial arbitration that different procedures and different standards must govern the two kinds of proceedings.

The important role that labor arbitration plays, as a substitute for economic force, is illustrated by its widespread use in the industrial relations field. A survey by the Bureau of National Affairs showed that 91 per cent of the collective bargaining agreements surveyed provided for arbitration of some kind and 89 per cent contained some variety of "no strike" clauses.

The savings to the parties—employers and employees—the savings to the nation and the public at large from the widespread use of labor arbitration, as a substitute for strikes and lockouts, is incalculable.

While commercial arbitrations, unlike labor arbitrations, are not generally a substitute for economic force, the economies resulting from the use of arbitration in commercial disputes are likewise substantial. And it must be remembered that here too the public—the consumer—is the ultimate beneficiary. It is he who in the long run must pay the expenses of prolonged litigation of commercial disputes, since these expenses are necessarily reflected in the prices at which goods and services are sold.

The strong support which voluntary arbitration is receiving from modern judges carries with it great responsibilities on the part of arbitrators and organizations like the American Arbitration Association which espouse the cause of voluntary arbitration. First and foremost it necessitates that the arbitrator be a highly dedicated man whose impartiality, integrity and honesty are beyond question. It goes without saying that he also must be competent for the particular arbitration he is called upon to resolve.

I have had more than thirty years of experience with both labor and commercial arbitrators and therefore can bear witness that they, by and large, are an honorable and dedicated class of men. They bring to their fine calling basically the same qualities which make a good judge: "humility and an understanding of the range of the problems . . . disinterestedness, allegiance to nothing except the search, amid tangled words, amid limited insights; loyalty and allegiance to nothing except the effort to find [the] path . . . through one's own gifts of insight to the best judgment that a poor fallible creature can arrive at in the most difficult of all tasks, the adjudication between man and man." In particular, I can testify that arbitrators have made an enormous contribution to good labor-management relations to the benefit of both employers and employees and to the larger cause of the public interest.

The American Arbitration Association, through its code of ethics and day-by-day supervision of the activities of arbitrators, plays an indispensable role in assuring that this first responsibility of arbitrators—impartiality, honesty, integrity and competence—is met.

The second responsibility of those who believe in arbitration is to make sure that arbitration continues to be "a speedier, more economic and more effective enforcement of rights than can be had by the tortuous course of litigation." I know that the American Arbitration Association shares my concern that labor arbitration in particular is becoming increasingly characterized by both delays and inordinate expense. Not every employer is a big employer; not every union is a big union. All workers, whether employed by a large or small employer or represented by a big or small union, suffer from inordinate delay in the resolution of their grievances. Employers, large and small, likewise are disadvantaged if grievances are permitted to fester unresolved for an undue period of time. And employers, in days when business survival requires cost consciousness, likewise legitimately have concern with untoward arbitration expenses. All who believe, as the American Arbitration Association does and as I do, in a system of voluntary arbitration, not imposed or run by government, must make this matter one of continuing concern and vigilant supervision.

There is a third responsibility for those who believe in the arbitral process. Voluntary arbitration must be voluntary in a real and genuine sense. There can be little concern that it is genuinely voluntary, when arbitration is agreed upon in collective bargaining, between unions and employers possessing an equality, more or less, of bargaining power. The same is true of commercial arbitrations between business concerns which enter into arbitration agreements knowingly and advisedly. The situation is far different, however, where an arbitration clause appears as "boiler plate" in an installment sales contract, a lease, or other document between a well-informed and well-advised party and another with limited choice and no adviser. I particularly note that the American Arbitration Association has taken steps to make sure that the locale of arbirations is one consciously agreed upon and not burdensome to either party. It is equally important, as I know the Association recognizes, that where there is an arbitration provision in a private agreement it is there knowingly, so as to be genuinely voluntary. The courts have understandable reluctance to hold parties to agreements which would have the effect of adjudicating their rights without protections provided in a court of law, where the important elements of voluntariness are, in fact, absent.

In the United States we can properly take pride that we probably lead all countries in acceptance and application of the principle of voluntary arbitration in commercial and labor disputes. There is one area of arbitration, not within the jurisdiction of the American Arbitration Association, where our nation lags rather than leads. I refer to the important field of arbitration of international disputes. It was not always so. From the beginnings of the Republic until fairly modern times the United States was a leading exponent of international arbitration. We initiated international conventions promoting such arbitration and we participated in several awards affecting our interests. Regretfully, however, as an aftermath of the struggle involving the League of Nations, the United States has lagged in its adherence to and support of arbitration of disputes between nations. Our accession to the International Court of Justice is subject to an unwarranted and unnecessary reservation. Our support of the Universal Declaration of Human Rights of the United Nations has not been characterized by that strong leadership which our commitment to its lofty ideals should entail. . . .

I trust that I will be excused my comment on this latter subject which is not, as I have already noted within the domain of the American Arbitration Association. I have done so because of my profound belief that the many precedents which have been established, with the great assistance of the American Arbitration Association, proving the value of voluntary arbitration in the domestic field are relevant in the international field as well. I have done so because I have profound faith in voluntary arbitration, both in the domestic area and in the sphere of international relations.

American Arbitration Association, New York, N.Y., March 17, 1965

II

THE JUDICIAL OPINIONS

I 🌿

The Fundamental Rights

POINTER V. TEXAS, 380 U.S. 400

[Early in the nineteenth century the Court held that the Bill of Rights applies only to the federal government. The states are denied the power to infringe liberties of the individual by the Fourteenth Amendment, which provides that no person shall be deprived of liberty without due process of law. The Court has long been divided over the extent to which the guarantees afforded the individual against the states by the Fourteenth Amendment are the same as the guarantees given by the Bill of Rights against action by the federal government.

[Justice Black in *Adamson* v. *California* expresses his view that all of the liberties protected by the Bill of Rights against Federal infringement are also protected by the Fourteenth Amendment against state infringement. He believes that the Fourteenth Amendment was intended to incorporate the entire Bill of Rights. Justice Harlan, on the other hand, believes that the Fourteenth Amendment protects only fundamental liberties and does not include all those mentioned in the Bill of Rights. Moreover, in his view, even when the same basic liberty is protected by both the Bill of Rights and the Fourteenth Amendment, the standards imposed upon the states by the Fourteenth Amendment may be less stringent than those imposed upon the federal government by the Bill of Rights. For example, although both the states and the federal government are prohibited from abridging freedom of speech, Justice Harlan believes that the states under the Fourteenth Amendment have greater power to censor material they believe obscene than does the federal government under the First Amendment.

[Justice Goldberg set out his view on this issue in *Pointer* v. *Texas*, a case in which the Court held that the Sixth Amendment's requirement that an accused be allowed to confront the witnesses against him is imposed upon the states by the Fourteenth Amendment. In this concurrence Justice Goldberg wrote that he does not believe that the Fourteenth Amendment incorporates the entire Bill of Rights. He believes that it protects fundamental rights from infringement by the states and therefore it incorporates those provisions of the Bill of Rights that protect fundamental rights from abridgment by the federal government. Moreover, in his view, once it has been determined that a particular guarantee of the Bill of Rights protects a fundamental right, the standards which it imposes upon the federal government and the standards imposed by the Fourteenth Amendment upon the states concerning the protection of that right are identical.]

I agree with the holding of the Court[1] that "the Sixth Amendment's right of an accused to confront the witnesses against him is . . . a fundamental right and is made obligatory on the states by the Fourteenth Amendment." *Ante*, at 403. I therefore join in the opinion and judgment of the Court. My Brother Harlan, while agreeing with the result reached by the Court, deplores the Court's reasoning as "another step in the onward march of the long-since discredited 'incorporation' doctrine," *Ante*, at 408. Since I was not on the Court when the incorporation issue was joined, see *Adamson* v. *California*, 332 U. S. 46, I deem it appropriate to set forth briefly my view on this subject.

I need not recapitulate the arguments for or against incorporation whether "total" or "selective." They have been set forth adequately elsewhere. My Brother Black's view of incorporation has never commanded a majority of the Court, though in *Adamson* it was assented to by four Justices. The Court in its decisions has followed a course whereby certain guarantees "have been taken over from the early articles of the Federal Bill of Rights and brought within the Fourteenth Amendment," *Palko* v. *Connecticut*, 302 U. S. 319, 326, by a process which might aptly be described as "a process of absorption." *Ibid.* See *Cohen* v. *Hurley*, 366 U. S. 117, 154 (dissenting opinion of Mr. Justice Brennan); Brennan, The Bill of Rights and the States, 36 N.Y.U.L. Rev. 761 (1961). Thus the Court has held that the Fourteenth Amendment guarantees against infringement by the states the liberties of the First Amendment, the Fourth Amendment, the Just Compensation Clause of the Fifth Amendment, the Fifth Amendment's privilege against self-incrimination, the Eighth Amendment's prohibition of cruel and unusual punishments, and the Sixth Amendment's guarantee of the assistance of counsel for an accused in a criminal prosecution.

With all deference to my Brother Harlan, I cannot agree that this process has "come into the sunlight in recent years." *Ante*, at 408. Rather, I believe that it has its origins at least as far back as *Twining* v. *New Jersey*, 211 U. S.

[1] April 5, 1965. Case No. 577. Mr. Justice Goldberg concurring.

78, 99, where the Court stated that "it is possible that some of the personal rights safeguarded by the first eight amendments against national action may also be safeguarded against state action, because a denial of them would be a denial of due process of law. *Chicago, Burlington & Quincy Railroad* v. *Chicago,* 166 U. S. 226." This passage and the authority cited make clear that what is protected by the Fourteenth Amendment are "rights," which apply in every case, not solely in those cases where it seems "fair" to a majority of the Court to afford the protection. Later cases reaffirm that the process of "absorption" is one of extending "rights." See *Ker* v. *California,* 374 U. S. 23; *Malloy* v. *Hogan,* 378 U.S. 1, and cases cited by Mr. Justice Brennan in his dissenting opinion in *Cohen* v. *Hurley, supra,* at 156. I agree with these decisions, as is apparent from my votes in *Gideon* v. *Wainwright,* 372 U. S. 335; *Malloy* v. *Hogan, supra,* and *Murphy* v. *Waterfront Comm'n,* 378 U. S. 52, and my concurring opinion in *New York Times Co.* v. *Sullivan,* 376 U. S. 254, 297, and I subscribe to the process by which fundamental guarantees of the Bill of Rights are absorbed by the Fourteenth Amendment and thereby applied to the states.

Furthermore, I do not agree with my Brother Harlan that once a provision of the Bill of Rights has been held applicable to the states by the Fourteenth Amendment, it does not apply to the states in full strength. Such a view would have the Fourteenth Amendment apply to the states "only a watered-down subjective version of the individual guarantees of the Bill of Rights." *Malloy* v. *Hogan, supra,* at 10-11. It would allow the states greater latitude than the federal government to abridge concededly fundamental liberties protected by the Constitution. While I quite agree with Mr. Justice Brandeis that "[i]t is one of the happy incidents of the federal system that a . . . state may . . . serve as a laboratory; and try novel social and economic experiments," *New State Ice Co.* v. *Liebmann,* 285 U. S. 262, 280, 311 (dissenting opinion), I do not believe that this includes the power to experiment with the fundamental liberties of citizens safeguarded by the Bill of Rights. My Brother Harlan's view would also require this Court to make the extremely subjective and excessively discretionary determination as to whether a practice, forbidden the federal government by a fundamental constitutional guarantee is, as viewed in the factual circumstances surrounding each individual case, sufficiently repugnant to the notion of due process as to be forbidden the states.

Finally, I do not see that my Brother Harlan's view would further any legitimate interests of federalism. It would require this Court to intervene in the state judicial process with considerable lack of predictability and with a consequent likelihood of considerable friction. This is well illustrated by the difficulties which were faced and were articulated by the state courts attempting to apply this Court's now discarded rule of *Betts* v. *Brady,* 316 U. S. 455.

See Green, the Bill of Rights, the Fourteenth Amendment and the Supreme Court, 46 Mich. L. Rev. 869, 897-898. These difficulties led the attorneys general of 22 states to urge that this Court overrule *Betts* v. *Brady* and to apply fully the Sixth Amendment's guarantee of right to counsel to the states through the Fourteenth Amendment. See *Gideon* v. *Wainwright, supra*, at 336. And, to deny to the states the power to impair a fundamental constitutional right is not to increase federal power, but, rather, to limit the power of both federal and state governments in favor of safeguarding the fundamental rights and liberties of the individual. In my view this promotes rather than undermines the basic policy of avoiding excess concentration of power in government, federal or state, which underlies our concepts of federalism.

I adhere to and support the process of absorption by means of which the Court holds that certain fundamental guarantees of the Bill of Rights are made obligatory on the states through the Fourteenth Amendment. Although, as this case illustrates, there are differences among members of the Court as to the theory by which the Fourteenth Amendment protects the fundamental liberties of individual citizens, it is noteworthy that there is a large area of agreement, both here and in other cases, that certain basic rights are fundamental—not to be denied the individual by either the state or federal governments under the Constitution. See, e. g., *Cantwell* v. *Connecticut*, 310 U. S. 296; *NAACP* v. *Alabama ex rel. Patterson*, 357 U. S. 449; *Gideon* v. *Wainwright, supra; New York Times Co.* v. *Sullivan, supra; Turner* v. *Louisiana*, 379 U.S. 466.

Griswold v. Connecticut, 381 U.S. 479

[Justice Goldberg's constitutional philosophy, discussed in *Pointer* v. *Texas*, is further elaborated in his concurring opinion in *Griswold*. In *Pointer* he wrote that the Fourteenth Amendment does not protect from infringement by the states all the liberties that are specifically mentioned in the Bill of Rights. In *Griswold* he adds that the Fourteenth Amendment protects some liberties that are not specifically mentioned in the Bill of Rights.

[The Court, in *Griswold*, held unconstitutional a Connecticut statute that prohibited all persons, married or unmarried, from using birth control devices. Justice Douglas, joined by the Chief Justice and Justices Clark, Brennan and Goldberg, delivered the opinion of the Court, which held that Connecticut's law unconstitutionally infringed the right of marital privacy. Justices Black and Stewart, in dissent, argued that the Constitution did not protect a right of marital privacy, for such a right was not specifically mentioned anywhere in that document. In his concurring opinion Justice Goldberg, joined by the Chief Justice and Justice Brennan, wrote that the Fourteenth Amendment's guarantee against the deprivation of liberty without due process of law does not protect only liberties specifically referred to elsewhere in the Constitution. Rather, it protects all fundamental personal liberties. And, that the Constitution's framers believed that fundamental personal liberties exist that are not specifically mentioned in the Bill of Rights is shown by the Ninth Amendment, which states that "The enumeration in the Constitution, of certain rights, shall not be construed to deny or disparage others retained by the people." Justice Goldberg agreed with the Court that the right of marital privacy is a fundamental personal right protected by the Fourteenth Amendment and that the state of Connecticut has not shown an interest in its birth control legislation sufficiently strong to justify constitutionally its serious infringement of the right of privacy in marriage.]

I agree with the Court[1] that Connecticut's birth control law unconstitutionally intrudes upon the right of marital privacy, and I join in its opinion and judgment. Although I have not accepted the view that " 'due process' as used in the Fourteenth Amendment incorporates all of the first eight Amendments," id., at 516 (see my concurring opinion in Pointer v. Texas, 380 U. S. 400, 410, and the dissenting opinion of Mr. Justice Brennan in Cohen v. Hurley, 366 U. S. 117, 154), I do agree that the concept of liberty protects those rights that are fundamental, and is not confined to the specific terms of the Bill of Rights. My conclusion that the concept of liberty is not so restricted and that it embraces the right of marital privacy though that right is not mentioned explicitly in the Constitution[2] is supported both by numerous decisions of this Court, referred to in the Court's opinion, and by the language and history of the Ninth Amendment. In reaching the conclusion that the right of marital privacy is protected, as being within the protected penumbra of specific guarantees of the Bill of Rights, the Court refers to the Ninth Amendment, ante, at 484. I add these words to emphasize the relevance of that Amendment to the Court's holding.

The Court stated many years ago that the Due Process Clause protects

[1] June 7, 1965. Case No. 496. Mr. Justice Goldberg, whom the Chief Justice and Mr. Justice Brennan join, concurring.

[2] My Brother Stewart dissents on the ground that he "can find no . . . general right of privacy in the Bill of Rights, in any other part of the Constitution, or in any case ever before decided by this Court." Post, at 530. He would require a more explicit guarantee than the one which the Court derives from several constitutional amendments. This Court, however, has never held that the Bill of Rights or the Fourteenth Amendment protects only those rights that the Constitution specifically mentions by name. See, e. g., Bolling v. Sharpe, 347 U.S. 497; Aptheker v. Secretary of State, 378, U.S. 500; Kent v. Dulles, 357 U.S. 116; Carrington v. Rash, 380, U.S. 89, 96; Schware v. Board of Bar Examiners, 353, U.S. 232; NAACP v. Alabama, 360 U.S. 240; Pierce v. Society of Sisters, 268, U.S. 510; Meyer v. Nebraska, 262, U.S. 390. To the contrary, this Court, for example, in Bolling v. Sharpe, supra, while recognizing that the Fifth Amendment does not contain the "explicit safeguard" of an equal protection clause, id., at 499, nevertheless derived an equal protection principle from that Amendment's Due Process Clause. And in Schware v. Board of Bar Examiners, supra, the Court held that the Fourteenth Amendment protects from arbitrary state action the right to pursue an occupation, such as the practice of law.

those liberties that are "so rooted in the traditions and conscience of our people as to be ranked as fundamental." *Snyder* v. *Massachusetts*, 291 U. S. 97, 105. In *Gitlow* v. *New York*, 268 U.S. 652, 666, the Court said:

> For present purposes we may and do assume that freedom of speech and of the press—which are protected by the First Amendment from abridgment by Congress—are among the *fundamental* personal rights and 'liberties' protected by the due process clause of the Fourteenth Amendment from impairment by the States. [Emphasis added.]

And, in *Meyer* v. *Nebraska*, 262 U. S. 390, 399, the Court, referring to the Fourteenth Amendment, stated:

> While this Court has not attempted to define with exactness the liberty thus guaranteed, the term has received much consideration and some of the included things have been definitely stated. Without doubt, it denotes not merely freedom from bodily restraint, but also [for example,] the right . . . to marry, establish a home and bring up children. . . .

This Court, in a series of decisions, has held that the Fourteenth Amendment absorbs and applies to the states those specifics of the first eight amendments which express fundamental personal rights.[3] The language and history of the Ninth Amendment reveal that the framers of the Constitution believed that there are additional fundamental rights, protected from governmental infringement, which exist alongside those fundamental rights specifically mentioned in the first eight constitutional amendments.

The Ninth Amendment reads, "The enumeration in the Constitution, of certain rights, shall not be construed to deny or disparage others retained by the people." The Amendment is almost entirely the work of James Madison. It was introduced in Congress by him and passed the House and Senate with little or no debate and virtually no change in language. It was proffered to quiet expressed fears that a bill of specifically enumerated rights[4] could not be sufficiently broad to cover all essential rights and that the specific mention of certain rights would be interpreted as a denial that others were protected.[5]

---

[3] See, e. g., *Chicago, B. & Q. R. Co.* v. *Chicago*, 166 U.S. 226; *Gitlow* v. *New York*, *supra*; *Cantwell* v. *Connecticut*, 310 U.S. 296; *Wolf* v. *Colorado*, 338 U.S. 25; *Robinson* v. *California*, 370 U.S. 660; *Gideon* v. *Wainwright*, 372 U.S. 335; *Malloy* v. *Hogan*, 378 U.S. 1; *Pointer* v. *Texas*, *supra*; *Griffin* v. *California*, 380 U.S. 609.

[4] Madison himself had previously pointed out the dangers of inaccuracy resulting from the fact that "no language is so copious as to supply words and phrases for every complex idea." *The Federalist*, No. 37 (Cooke ed. 1961), at 236.

[5] Alexander Hamilton was opposed to a bill of rights on the ground that it was unnecessary because the federal government was a government of delegated powers and it was not granted the power to intrude upon fundamental personal rights. *The Federalist*, No. 84 (Cooke ed. 1961), at 578–579. He also argued, "I go further, and affirm that bills of rights, in the sense and in the extent in which they are contended for, are not only unnecessary in the proposed constitution, but would even be dangerous. They would contain various exceptions to powers which are not granted; and on this very

In presenting the proposed Amendment, Madison said:

It has been objected also against a bill of rights, that, by enumerating particular exceptions to the grant of power, it would disparage those rights which were not placed in that enumeration; and it might follow by implication, that those rights which were not signaled out, were intended to be assigned into the hands of the general government, and were consequently insecure. This is one of the most plausible arguments I have ever heard urged against the admission of a bill of rights into this system; but, I conceive, that it may be guarded against. I have attempted it, as gentlemen may see by turning to the last clause of the fourth resolution [the Ninth Amendment]. I Annals of Congress 440 (Gales and Seaton ed. 1834).

While this Court has had little occasion to interpret the Ninth Amendment,[6] "it cannot be presumed that any clause in the constitution is intended to be without effect." *Marbury* v. *Madison*, 1 Cranch 137, 174. In interpreting the Constitution, "real effect should be given to all the words it uses." *Myers* v. *United States*, 272 U. S. 52, 151. The Ninth Amendment to the Constitution may be regarded by some as a recent discovery and may be forgotten by others, but since 1791 it has been a basic part of the Constitution which we are sworn to uphold. To hold that a right so basic and fundamental and so deep-rooted in our society as the right of privacy in marriage may be infringed because that right is not guaranteed in so many words by the first eight

---

account, would afford a colourable pretext to claim more than were granted. For why declare that things shall not be done which there is no power to do? Why for instance, should it be said, that the liberty of the press shall not be restrained, when no power is given by which restrictions may be imposed? I will not contend that such a provision would confer a regulating power, but it is evident that it would furnish, to men disposed to usurp, a plausible pretence for claiming that power." *Id.*, at 579.

The Ninth Amendment and the Tenth Amendment, which provides, "The powers not delegated to the United States by the Constitution, nor prohibited by it to the States, are reserved to the States respectively, or to the people," were apparently also designed in part to meet the above-quoted argument of Hamilton.

[6] This Amendment has been referred to as "The Forgotten Ninth Amendment," in a book with that title by Bennet B. Patterson (1955). Other commentary on the Ninth Amendment includes Redlich, "Are There Certain Rights . . . Retained by the People?" 37 N. Y. U. L. Rev. 787 (1962), and Kelsey, "The Ninth Amendment of the Federal Constitution," 11 Ind. L. J. 309 (1936). As far as I am aware, until today this Court has referred to the Ninth Amendment only in *United Public Workers* v. *Mitchell*, 330 U.S. 75, 94–95; *Tennessee Electric Power Co.* v. *TVA*, 306 U.S. 118, 143–144; and *Ashwander* v. *TVA*, 297 U.S. 288, 330–331. See also *Calder* v. *Bull*, 3 Dall. 386, 388; *Loan Assn.* v. *Topeka*, 20 Wall. 655, 662–663.

In *United Public Workers* v. *Mitchell*, *supra*, at 94–95, the Court stated: "We accept appellants' contention that the nature of political rights reserved to the people by the Ninth and Tenth Amendments [is] involved. The right claimed as inviolate may be stated as the right of a citizen to act as a party official or worker to further his own political views. Thus we have a measure of interference by the Hatch Act and the Rules with what otherwise would be the freedom of the civil servant under the First, Ninth and Tenth Amendments. And, if we look upon due process as a guarantee of freedom in those fields, there is a corresponding impairment of that right under the Fifth Amendment."

amendments to the Constitution is to ignore the Ninth Amendment and to give it no effect whatsoever. Moreover, a judicial construction that this fundamental right is not protected by the Constitution because it is not mentioned in explicit terms by one of the first eight amendments or elsewhere in the Constitution would violate the Ninth Amendment, which specifically states that "the enumeration in the Constitution, of certain rights, shall not be *construed* to deny or disparage others retained by the people." [Emphasis added.]

A dissenting opinion suggests that my interpretation of the Ninth Amendment somehow "broaden[s] the powers of this Court." *Post*, at 520. With all due respect, I believe that it misses the import of what I am saying. I do not take the position of my Brother Black in his dissent in *Adamson* v. *California*, 332 U.S. 46, 68, that the entire Bill of Rights is incorporated in the Fourteenth Amendment, and I do not mean to imply that the Ninth Amendment is applied against the states by the Fourteenth. Nor do I mean to state that the Ninth Amendment constitutes an independent source of rights protected from infringement by either the states or the federal government. Rather, the Ninth Amendment shows a belief of the Constitution's authors that fundamental rights exist that are not expressly enumerated in the first eight amendments and an intent that the list of rights included there not be deemed exhaustive. As any student of this Court's opinions knows, this Court has held, often unanimously, that the Fifth and Fourteenth Amendments protect certain fundamental personal liberties from abridgment by the federal government or the states. See, e.g., *Bolling* v. *Sharpe*, 347 U.S. 497; *Aptheker* v. *Secretary of State*, 378 U.S. 500; *Kent* v. *Dulles*, 357 U.S. 116; *Cantwell* v. *Connecticut*; 310 U.S. 296; NAACP v. *Alabama*, 357 U.S. 449; *Gideon* v. *Wainwright*, 372 U.S. 335; *New York Times Co.* v. *Sullivan*, 376 U.S. 254. The Ninth Amendment simply shows the intent of the Constitution's authors that other fundamental personal rights should not be denied such protection or disparaged in any other way simply because they are not specifically listed in the first eight constitutional amendments. I do not see how this broadens the authority of the Court; rather it serves to support what this Court has been doing in protecting fundamental rights.

Nor am I turning somersaults with history in arguing that the Ninth Amendment is relevant in a case dealing with a *state's* infringement of a fundamental right. While the Ninth Amendment—and indeed the entire Bill of Rights—originally concerned restrictions upon *federal* power, the subsequently enacted Fourteenth Amendment prohibits the states as well from abridging fundamental personal liberties. And the Ninth Amendment, in indicating that not all such liberties are specifically mentioned in the first eight amendments, is surely relevant in showing the existence of other fundamental personal rights, now protected from state, as well as federal, infringement. In sum, the Ninth Amendment simply lends strong support to the view that the "liberty" protected by the Fifth and Fourteenth Amendments from infringement by the federal government or the states is not restricted to rights specifically mentioned in the first eight amendments. Cf. *United Public Workers* v. *Mitchell*, 330 U.S. 75, 94-95.

In determining which rights are fundamental, judges are not left at large to decide cases in light of their personal and private notions. Rather, they must look to the "traditions and [collective] conscience of our people" to determine whether a principle is "so rooted [there] . . . as to be ranked as fundamental." *Snyder* v. *Massachusetts*, 291 U. S. 97, 105. The inquiry is whether a right involved "is of such a character that it cannot be denied without violating those 'fundamental principles of liberty and justice which lie at the base of all our civil and political institutions.' . . . ." *Powell* v. *Alabama*, 287 U. S. 45, 67. "Liberty" also "gains content from the emanations of . . . specific [constitutional] guarantees" and "from experience with the requirements of a free society." *Poe* v. *Ullman*, 367 U. S. 497, 517 (dissenting opinion of Mr. Justice Douglas).[7]

I agree fully with the Court that, applying these tests, the right of privacy is a fundamental personal right, "emanating from the totality of the constitutional scheme under which we live." *Id.*, at 521. Mr. Justice Brandeis, dissenting in *Olmstead* v. *United States*, 277 U. S. 438, 478, comprehensively summarized the principles underlying the Constitution's guarantees of privacy:

The protection guaranteed by the [Fourth and Fifth] Amendments is much broader in scope. The makers of our Constitution undertook to secure conditions favorable to the pursuit of happiness. They recognized the significance of man's spiritual nature, of his feelings and of his intellect. They knew that only a part of the pain, pleasure, and satisfactions of life are to be found in material things. They sought to protect Americans in their beliefs, their thoughts, their emotions and their sensations. They conferred, as against the Government, the right to be let alone—the most comprehensive of rights and the right most valued by civilized men.

[7] In light of the tests enunciated in these cases it cannot be said that a judge's responsibility to determine whether a right is basic and fundamental in this sense vests him with unrestricted personal discretion. In fact, a hesitancy to allow too broad a discretion was a substantial reason leading me to conclude in *Pointer* v. *Texas, supra,* at 413-414, that those rights absorbed by the Fourteenth Amendment and applied to the states because they are fundamental apply with equal force and to the same extent against both federal and state governments. In *Pointer* I said that the contrary view would require "this Court to make the extremely subjective and excessively discretionary determination as to whether a practice, forbidden the federal government by a fundamental constitutional guarantee is, as viewed in the factual circumstances surrounding each individual case, sufficiently repugnant to the notion of due process as to be forbidden the States." *Id.*, at 413.

The Connecticut statutes here involved deal with a particularly important and sensitive area of privacy—that of the marital relation and the marital home. This Court recognized in *Meyer* v. *Nebraska, supra,* that the right "to marry, establish a home and bring up children" was an essential part of the liberty guaranteed by the Fourteenth Amendment. 262 U. S., at 399. In *Pierce* v. *Society of Sisters,* 268 U. S. 510, the Court held unconstitutional an Oregon Act which forbade parents from sending their children to private schools because such an act "unreasonably interferes with the liberty of parents and guardians to direct the upbringing and education of children under their control." 268 U. S., at 534-535. As this Court said in *Prince* v. *Massachusetts,* 321 U. S. 158, at 166, the *Meyer* and *Pierce* decisions "have respected the private realm of family life which the state cannot enter."

I agree with Mr. Justice Harlan's statement in his dissenting opinion in *Poe* v. *Ullman,* 367 U. S. 497, 551-552: "Certainly the safeguarding of the home does not follow merely from the sanctity of property rights. The home derives its pre-eminence as the seat of family life. And the integrity of that life is something so fundamental that it has been found to draw to its protection the principles of more than one explicitly granted constitutional right. . . . Of this whole 'private realm of family life' it is difficult to imagine what is more private or more intimate than a husband and wife's marital relations."

The entire fabric of the Constitution and the purposes that clearly underlie its specific guarantees demonstrate that the rights to marital privacy and to marry and raise a family are of similar order and magnitude as the fundamental rights specifically protected.

Although the Constitution does not speak in so many words of the right of privacy in marriage, I cannot believe that it offers these fundamental rights no protection. The fact that no particular provision of the Constitution explicitly forbids the state from disrupting the traditional relation of the family—a relation as old and as fundamental as our entire civilization—surely does not show that the government was meant to have the power to do so. Rather, as the Ninth Amendment expressly recognizes, there are fundamental personal rights such as this one, which are protected from abridgment by the government though not specifically mentioned in the Constitution. . . .

In a long series of cases this Court has held that where fundamental personal liberties are involved, they may not be abridged by the states simply on a showing that a regulatory statute has some rational relationship to the effectuation of a proper state purpose. "Where there is a significant encroachment upon personal liberty, the state may prevail only upon showing a subordinating interest which is compelling," *Bates* v. *Little Rock,* 361 U.S. 516, 524. The law must be shown "necessary, and not merely rationally related, to the accomplishment of a permissible state policy." *McLaughlin* v. *Florida,* 379 U.S. 184, 196. See *Schneider* v. *Irvington,* 308 U.S. 147, 161.

Although the Connecticut birth control law obviously encroaches upon a fundamental personal liberty, the state does not show that the law serves any "subordinating state interest which is compelling" or that it is "necessary . . . to the accomplishment of a permissible state policy." The state, at most, argues that there is some rational relation between this statute and what is admittedly a legitimate subject of state concern—the discouraging of extra-marital relations. It says that preventing the use of birth control devices by married persons helps prevent the indulgence by some in such extramarital relations. The rationality of this justification is dubious, particularly in light of the admitted widespread availability to all persons in the state of Connecticut, unmarried as well as married, of birth control devices for the prevention of disease, as distinguished from the prevention of conception, see *Tileston* v. *Ullman*, 129 Conn. 84, 26 A. 2d 582. But, in any event, it is clear that the state interest in safeguarding marital fidelity can be served by a more discriminately tailored statute, which does not, like the present one, sweep unnecessarily broadly, reaching far beyond the evil sought to be dealt with and intruding upon the privacy of all married couples. See *Aptheker* v. *Secretary of State*, 378 U. S. 500, 514; *NAACP* v. *Alabama*, 377 U. S. 288, 307-308; *McLaughlin* v. *Florida, supra*, at 196. Here, as elsewhere, "precision of regulation must be the touchstone in an area so closely touching our most precious freedoms." *NAACP* v. *Button*, 371 U. S. 415, 438. The state of Connecticut does have statutes, the constitutionality of which is beyond doubt, which prohibit adultery and fornication. See Conn. Gen. Stat. §§ 53-218, 53-219 *et seq.* These statutes demonstrate that means for achieving the same basic purpose of protecting marital fidelity are available to Connecticut without the need to "invade the area of protected freedoms." *NAACP* v. *Alabama, supra*, at 307. See *McLaughlin* v. *Florida, supra*, at 196. . . .

In sum, I believe that the right of privacy in the marital relation is fundamental and basic—a personal right "retained by the people" within the meaning of the Ninth Amendment. Connecticut cannot constitutionally abridge this fundamental right, which is protected by the Fourteenth Amendment from infringement by the states. I agree with the Court that petitioners' convictions must therefore be reversed.

GIBSON v. FLORIDA LEGISLATIVE INVESTIGATING COMMITTEE
372 U.S. 539

[The Court has often found it difficult to reconcile the legitimate governmental interest in conducting legislative investigations with the rights of individuals and organizations to free speech and free association. Prior to *Gibson* the Court had held that a Congressional investigating committee may lawfully ask a witness about Communist party membership. The Court had also held,

however, that in the absence of a compelling state interest the NAACP could
not be forced to disclose its membership.

[In the *Gibson* case a committee of the Florida legislature, investigating
activities of Communists in various organizations operating in the state,
ordered the president of the Miami chapter of the NAACP to appear before
it with the chapter's membership records to tell the Committee whether certain persons whom it thought subversive were NAACP members. The president appeared before the committee and offered to answer questions from
memory but refused to produce the organization's records. He was convicted
of contempt.

[Justice Goldberg, joined by Justices Brennan, Black, Douglas, and the
Chief Justice, wrote the Court's opinion reversing the contempt conviction.
The Court held that the Committee could not inquire into NAACP membership without a showing of some connection between the NAACP and Communist activities, justifying this intrusion into the NAACP's affairs. Since no
such connection was shown, the Committee could not compel Gibson to
bring the NAACP's records with him when he appeared before it.]

. . . We are here[1] called upon once again to resolve a conflict between individual rights of free speech and association and governmental interest in
conducting legislative investigations. Prior decisions illumine the contending
principles.

This Court has repeatedly held that rights of association are within the
ambit of the constitutional protections afforded by the First and Fourteenth
Amendments. *NAACP* v. *Alabama*, 357 U. S. 449; *Bates* v. *Little Rock*, 361
U. S. 516; *Sheldon* v. *Tucker*, 364 U. S. 479; *NAACP* v. *Button*, 371 U. S.
415. The respondent Committee does not contend otherwise, nor could it,
for, as was said in *NAACP* v. *Alabama, supra,* "It is beyond debate that freedom to engage in association for the advancement of beliefs and ideas is an
inseparable aspect of the 'liberty' assured by the Due Process Clause of the
Fourteenth Amendment, which embraces freedom of speech." 357 U. S., at
460. And it is equally clear that the guarantee encompasses protection of
privacy of association in organizations such as that of which the petitioner is
president; indeed, in both the *Bates* and *Alabama* cases, *supra*, this Court held
NAACP membership lists of the very type here in question to be beyond the
states' power of discovery in the circumstances there presented.

The First and Fourteenth Amendment rights of free speech and free association are fundamental and highly prized, and "need breathing space to survive." *NAACP* v. *Button*, 371 U. S. 415, 433. "Freedoms such as these are
protected not only against heavy-handed frontal attack, but also from being

[1] March 25, 1963. Case No. 6. Mr. Justice Goldberg delivered the opinion of the Court.

stifled by more subtle governmental interference." *Bates* v. *Little Rock, supra,*
361 U. S., at 523. And, as declared in *NAACP* v. *Alabama, supra,* 357 U. S., at
462, "It is hardly a novel perception that compelled disclosure of affiliation
with groups engaged in advocacy may constitute [an] . . . effective . . .
restraint on freedom of association. . . . This Court has recognized the vital
relationship between freedom to associate and privacy in one's associations.
. . . Inviolability of privacy in group association may in many circumstances
be indispensable to perservation of freedom of association, particularly
where a group espouses dissident beliefs." So it is here.

At the same time, however, this Court's prior holdings demonstrate that
there can be no question that the state has power adequately to inform
itself—through legislative investigation, if it so desires—in order to act and
protect its legitimate and vital interests. As this Court said in considering the
propriety of the Congressional inquiry challenged in *Watkins* v. *United
States,* 354 U. S. 178: "The power . . . to conduct investigations is inherent
in the legislative process. That power is broad. It encompasses inquiries concerning the administration of existing laws as well as proposed or possibly
needed statutes. It includes surveys of defects in our social, economic or
political system for the purpose of enabling the Congress to remedy them."
354 U. S., at 187. And, more recently, it was declared that "The scope of the
power of inquiry, in short, is as penetrating and far-reaching as the potential
power to enact and appropriate under the Constitution." *Barenblatt* v. *United
States,* 360 U. S. 109, 111. It is no less obvious, however, that the legislative
power to investigate, broad as it may be, is not without limit. The fact that
the general scope of the inquiry is authorized and permissible does not compel
the conclusion that the investigatory body is free to inquire into or demand all
forms of information. Validation of the broad subject matter under investigation does not necessarily carry with it automatic and wholesale validation of
all individual questions, subpoenas and documentary demands. See, e. g., *Watkins* v. *United States, supra,* 354 U. S., at 197-199. See also *Barenblatt* v.
United States, supra 360 U. S., at 127-130. When, as in this case, the claim is
made that particular legislative inquiries and demands infringe substantially
upon First and Fourteenth Amendment associational rights of individuals, the
courts are called upon to, and must, determine the permissibility of the challenged actions, *Watkins* v. *United States, supra,* 354 U. S., at 198-199; "the
delicate and difficult task falls upon the courts to weigh the circumstances and
to appraise the substantiality of the reasons advanced in support of the regulation of the free enjoyment of the rights," *Schneider* v. *State,* 308 U. S. 147,
161. The interests here at stake are of significant magnitude, and neither their
resolution nor impact is limited to, or dependent upon, the particular parties
here involved. Freedom and viable government are both, for this purpose,

indivisible concepts; whatever affects the rights of the parties here affects all.

Significantly, the parties are in substantial agreement as to the proper test to be applied to reconcile the competing claims of government and individual and to determine the propriety of the Committee's demands. As declared by the respondent Committee in its brief to this Court, "Basically, this case hinges entirely on the question of whether the evidence before the Committee [was] . . . sufficient to show probable cause or nexus between the NAACP Miami branch and Communist activities." We understand this to mean—regardless of the label applied, be it "nexus," "foundation," or whatever—that it is an essential prerequisite to the validity of an investigation which intrudes into the area of constitutionally protected rights of speech, press, association and petition that the state convincingly show a substantial relation between the information sought and a subject of overriding and compelling state interest. Absent such a relation between the NAACP and conduct in which the state may have a compelling regulatory concern, the Committee has not "demonstrated so cogent an interest in obtaining and making public" the membership information sought to be obtained as to "justify the substantial abridgment of associational freedoms which such disclosure will effect." *Bates* v. *Little Rock, supra,* 361 U. S., at 524. "Where there is a significant encroachment upon personal liberty, the state may prevail only upon showing a subordinating interest which is compelling." *Ibid.*

Applying these principles to the facts of this case, the respondent Committee contends that the prior decisions of this Court in *Uphaus* v. *Wyman,* 360 U. S. 72; *Barenblatt* v. *United States,* 360 U. S. 109; *Wilkinson* v. *United States,* 365 U. S. 399; and *Braden* v. *United States,* 365 U. S. 431, compel a result here upholding the legislative right of inquiry. In *Barenblatt, Wilkinson,* and *Braden,* however, it was a refusal to answer a question or questions concerning the witness' *own* past or present membership *in the Communist party* which supported his conviction. It is apparent that the necessary preponderating governmental interest and, in fact, the very result in those cases was founded on the holding that the Communist party is not an ordinary or legitimate political party, as known in this country, and that, because of its particular nature, membership therein is *itself* a permissible subject of regulation and legislative scrutiny. Assuming the correctness of the premises on which those cases were decided, no further demonstration of compelling governmental interest was deemed necessary, since the direct object of the challenged questions there was discovery of membership in the Communist party, a matter held pertinent to a proper subject then under inquiry.

Here, however, it is not alleged Communists who are the witnesses before the Committee and it is not discovery of their membership in that party which is the object of the challenged inquiries. Rather, it is the NAACP itself which is the subject of the investigation, and it is its local president, the petitioner, who was called before the Committee and held in contempt because he refused to divulge the contents of its membership records. There is no suggestion that the Miami branch of the NAACP or the national organization with which it is affiliated was, or is, itself a subversive organization. Nor is there any indication that the activities or policies of the NAACP were either Communist dominated or influenced. In fact, this very record indicates that the association was and is against communism and has voluntarily taken steps to keep Communists from being members. Each year since 1950, the NAACP has adopted resolutions barring Communists from membership in the organization. Moreover, the petitioner testified that all prospective officers of the local organization are thoroughly investigated for Communist or subversive connections and, though subversive activities constitute grounds for termination of association membership, no such expulsions from the branch occurred during the five years preceding the investigation.

Thus, unlike the situation in *Barenblatt, Wilkinson* and *Braden, supra,* the Committee was not here seeking from the petitioner or the records of which he was custodian any information as to whether he, himself, or even other persons were members of the Communist party, Communist front or affiliated organizations, or other allegedly subversive groups; instead, the entire thrust of the demands on the petitioner was that he disclose whether other persons were members of the NAACP, itself a concededly legitimate and nonsubversive organization. Compelling such an organization, engaged in the exercise of First and Fourteenth Amendment rights, to disclose its membership presents, under our cases, a question wholly different from compelling the Communist party to disclose its own membership. Moreover, even to say, as in *Barenblatt, supra,* 360 U. S., at 129, that it is permissible to inquire into the subject of Communist infiltration of educational or other organizations does not mean that it is permissible to demand or require from such other groups disclosure of their membership by inquiry into their records when such disclosure will seriously inhibit or impair the exercise of constitutional rights and has not itself been demonstrated to bear a crucial relation to a proper governmental interest or to be essential to fulfillment of a proper governmental purpose. The prior holdings that governmental interest in controlling subversion and the particular character of the Communist party and its objectives outweigh the right of individual Communists to conceal party membership or affiliations by no means require the wholly different conclusion that other groups—concededly legitimate—automatically forfeit their rights to privacy of association simply because the general subject matter of the legislative inquiry is Communist subversion or infiltration. The fact that governmental interest was deemed compelling in *Barenblatt, Wilkinson,* and *Braden* and held to support the inquiries there made into membership in the Communist party does not resolve the issues here, where the challenged questions go to membership in an admittedly lawful organization. . . .

In the absence of directly determinative authority, we turn, then, to consideration of the facts now before us. Obviously, if the respondent were still seeking discovery of the entire membership list, we could readily dispose of this case on the authority of *Bates* v. *Little Rock*, and *NAACP* v. *Alabama*, *supra;* a like result would follow if it were merely attempting to do piecemeal what could not be done in a single step. Though there are indications that the respondent Committee intended to inquire broadly into the NAACP membership records, there is no need to base our decision today upon a prediction as to the course which the Committee might have pursued if initially unopposed by the petitioner. Instead, we rest our result on the fact that the record in this case is insufficient to show a substantial connection between the Miami branch of the NAACP and Communist *activities* which the respondent Committee itself concedes is an essential prerequisite to demonstrating the immediate, substantial and subordinating state interest necessary to sustain its right of inquiry into the membership lists of the association.

[After summarizing the evidence relied upon by the Committee the Court concluded:]

This summary of the evidence discloses the utter failure to demonstrate the existence of any substantial relationship between the NAACP and subversive or Communist activities. In essence, there is here merely indirect, less than unequivocal, and mostly hearsay testimony that in years past some 14 people who were asserted to be, or to have been, Communists or members of Communist front or "affiliated organizations" attended occasional meetings of the Miami branch of the NAACP "and/or" were members of that branch, which had a total membership of about 1,000.

On the other hand, there was no claim made at the hearings, or since, that the NAACP or its Miami branch was engaged in any subversive activities or that its legitimate activities have been dominated or influenced by Communists. Without any indication of present subversive infiltration in, or influence on, the Miami branch of the NAACP, and without any reasonable, demonstrated factual basis to believe that such infiltration or influence existed in the past, or was actively attempted or sought in the present—in short without any showing of a meaningful relationship between the NAACP, Miami branch, and subversives or subversive or other illegal activities—we are asked to find the compelling and subordinating state interest which must exist if essential freedoms are to be curtailed or inhibited. This we cannot do. The respondent Committee has laid no adequate foundation for its direct demands upon the officers and records of a wholly legitimate organization for disclosure of its membership; the Committee has neither demonstrated nor pointed out any threat to the state by virtue of the existence of the NAACP or the pursuit of its activities or the minimal associational ties of the 14 asserted Communists. The strong associational interest in maintaining the privacy of membership lists of groups engaged in the constitutionally protected free trade in ideas and beliefs may not be substantially infringed upon such a slender showing as here made by the respondent. While, of course, all legitimate organizations are the beneficiaries of these protections, they are all the more essential here, where the challenged privacy is that of persons espousing beliefs already unpopular with their neighbors and the deterrent and "chilling" effect on the free exercise of constitutionally enshrined rights of free speech, expression and association is consequently the more immediate and substantial. What we recently said in *NAACP* v. *Button, supra*, with respect to the state of Virginia is, as appears from the record, equally applicable here: "We cannot close our eyes to the fact that the militant Negro civil rights movement has engendered the intense resentment and opposition of the politically dominant white community." 371 U.S. at 435.

Of course, a legislative investigation—as any investigation—must proceed "step by step," *Barenblatt* v. *United States, supra*, 360 U. S., at 130, but step by step or in totality, an adequate foundation for inquiry must be laid before proceeding in such a manner as will substantially intrude upon and severely curtail or inhibit constitutionally protected activities or seriously interfere with similarly protected associational rights. No such foundation has been laid here. The respondent Committee has failed to demonstrate the compelling and subordinating governmental interest essential to support direct inquiry into the membership records of the NAACP.

Nothing we say here impairs or denies the existence of the underlying legislative right to investigate or legislate with respect to subversive activities by Communists or anyone else; our decision today deals only with the manner in which such power may be exercised and we hold simply that groups which themselves are neither engaged in subversive or other illegal or improper activities nor demonstrated to have any substantial connections with such activities are to be protected in their rights of free and private association. As declared in *Sweezy* v. *New Hampshire*, 354 U.S. 234, 245 (opinion of the Chief Justice), "It is particularly important that the exercise of the power of compulsory process be carefully circumscribed when the investigative process tends to impinge upon such highly sensitive areas as freedom of speech or press, freedom of political association, and freedom of communication of ideas."

To permit legislative inquiry to proceed on less than an adequate foundation would be to sanction unjustified and unwarranted intrusions into the very heart of the constitutional privilege to be secure in associations in legitimate organizations engaged in the exercise of First and Fourteenth Amendment rights; to impose a lesser standard than we here do would be inconsistent with the maintenance of those essential conditions basic to the preservation of our democracy.

New York Times Co. v. Sullivan, 376 U.S. 254
Abernathy v. Sullivan, 376 U.S. 254

[The *New York Times* published an advertisement entitled "Heed Their Rising Voices," which described difficulties encountered in Montgomery, Alabama, by Southern Negro students in their attempt to secure equal rights. Several statements in the advertisement were factually inaccurate. The city commissioner of Montgomery, charged with supervising the police, claimed that the advertisement implicitly referred to him and that because of its inaccuracies it was libelous. An Alabama jury found that the *Times* and those who had placed the advertisement had libeled the commissioner and awarded him $500,000.

[The Court, in an opinion by Mr. Justice Brennan, unanimously overturned the libel judgment, holding that Alabama's libel laws unconstitutionally abridged the defendants' rights of free speech. The Court held that criticism of the official actions of any government official is constitutionally protected from libel suits unless that criticism is made with actual knowledge that it is false or with reckless disregard of whether or not it is false. Justice Goldberg, joined by Justice Douglas, concurred, but believed that the Court was wrong to allow *any* libel action based upon criticism of the official action of government officers. In Justice Goldberg's view, if juries are left at all free to find that criticism of government is libelous, legitimate discussion of governmental conduct will be inhibited. He would therefore hold that the Constitution immunizes *all* speech concerning official activities of government officers from the threat of libel judgments.]

The Court today[1] announces a constitutional standard which prohibits "a public official from recovering damages for a defamatory falsehood relating to his official conduct unless he proves that the statement was made with 'actual malice'—that is, with knowledge that it was false or with reckless disregard of whether it was false or not." . . . The Court thus rules that the Constitution gives citizens and newspapers a "conditional privilege" immunizing nonmalicious misstatements of fact regarding the official conduct

---

[1] March 9, 1964. Cases Nos. 39 and 40. Mr. Justice Goldberg, with whom Mr. Justice Douglas joins, concurring in the result.

of a government officer. The impressive array of history and precedent marshaled by the Court, however, confirms my belief that the Constitution affords greater protection than that provided by the Court's standard to citizen and press in exercising the right of public criticism.

In my view, the First and Fourteenth Amendments to the Constitution afford to the citizen and to the press an absolute, unconditional privilege to criticize official conduct despite the harm which may flow from excesses and abuses. The prized American right "to speak one's mind," cf. *Bridges* v. *California*, 314 U. S. 252, 270, about public officials and affairs needs "breathing space to survive," *NAACP* v. *Button*, 371 U. S. 415, 433. The right should not depend upon a probing by the jury of the motivation of the citizen or press. The theory of our Constitution is that every citizen may speak his mind and every newspaper express its view on matters of public concern and may not be barred from speaking or publishing because those in control of government think that what is said or written is unwise, unfair, false or malicious. In a democratic society, one who assumes to act for the citizens in an executive, legislative or judicial capacity must expect that his official acts will be commented upon and criticized. Such criticism cannot, in my opinion, be muzzled or deterred by the courts at the instance of public officials under the label of libel.

It has been recognized that "prosecutions for libel on government have [no] place in the American system of jurisprudence." *City of Chicago* v. *Tribune Co.*, 307 Ill. 595, 601, 139 N. E. 86, 88. I fully agree. Government, however, is not an abstraction; it is made up of individuals—of governors responsible to the governed. In a democratic society, where men are free by ballots to remove those in power, any statement critical of governmental action is necessarily "of and concerning" the governors and any statement critical of the governors' official conduct is necessarily "of and concerning" the government. If the rule that libel on government has no place in our Constitution is to have real meaning, then libel on the official conduct of the governors likewise can have no place in our Constitution. . . .

It may be urged that deliberately and maliciously false statements have no conceivable value as free speech. That argument, however, is not responsive to the real issue presented by this case, which is whether that freedom of speech which all agree is constitutionally protected can be effectively safeguarded by a rule allowing the imposition of liability upon a jury's evaluation of the speaker's state of mind. If individual citizens may be held liable in damages for strong words, which a jury finds false and maliciously motivated, there can be little doubt that public debate and advocacy will be constrained. And if newspapers, publishing advertisements dealing with public issues, thereby risk liability, there can also be little doubt that the ability of minority groups to secure publication of their views on public affairs and to seek support for their causes will be greatly diminished. . . .

This is not to say that the Constitution protects defamatory statements directed against the private conduct of a public official or private citizen. Freedom of press and of speech ensure that government will respond to the will of the people and that changes may be obtained by peaceful means. Purely private defamation has little to do with the political ends of a self-governing society. The imposition of liability for private defamation does not abridge the freedom of public speech. This, of course, cannot be said "where public officials are concerned or where public matters are involved. . . . [O]ne main function of the First Amendment is to ensure ample opportunity for the people to determine and resolve public issues. Where public matters are involved, the doubts should be resolved in favor of freedom of expression rather than against it." Douglas, *The Right of the People* (1958), p. 41.

In many jurisdictions, legislators, judges and executive officers are clothed with absolute immunity against liability for defamatory words uttered in the discharge of their public duties. . . .

If the government official should be immune from libel actions so that his ardor to serve the public will not be dampened and "fearless, vigorous, and effective administration of policies of government" not be inhibited . . . then the citizen and the press should likewise be immune from libel actions for their criticism of official conduct. Their ardor as citizens will thus not be dampened and they will be free "to applaud or to criticize the way public employees do their jobs, from the least to the most important." If liability can attach to political criticism because it damages the reputation of a public official as a public official, then no critical citizen can safely utter anything but faint praise about the government or its officials. The vigorous criticism by press and citizen of the conduct of the government of the day by the officials of the day will soon yield to silence if officials in control of government agencies, instead of answering criticisms, can resort to friendly juries to forestall criticism of their official conduct.

The conclusion that the Constitution affords the citizen and the press an absolute privilege for criticism of official conduct does not leave the public official without defenses against unsubstantiated opinions or deliberate mis-statements. "Under our system of government, counter argument and education are the weapons available to expose those matters, not abridgment . . . of free speech. . . ." *Wood* v. *Georgia*, 370 U. S. 375, 389. The public official certainly has equal if not greater access than most private citizens to media of communication. In any event, despite the possibility that some excesses and abuses may go unremedied, we must recognize that "the people of this nation have ordained in the light of history, that, in spite of the probability of excesses and abuses, [certain] liberties are, in the long view, essential to enlightened opinion and right conduct on the part of the citizens of a democracy." *Cantwell v. Connecticut*, 310 U. S. 296, 310. As Mr. Justice Brandeis correctly observed, "sunlight is the most powerful of all disinfectants."

Cox v. Louisiana, 379 U.S. 536, 379 U.S. 559

[The *Cox* cases raise the problem of reconciling the right of free expression with the need of the state to regulate the time, manner and place of demonstrations. In Justice Goldberg's view regulations are permissible only if they are narrowly drawn to serve legitimate state interests and if they do not allow state officials to discriminate among demonstrations, allowing some but prohibiting others, on the basis of the type of idea which is being expressed.

[The Reverend Mr. Cox led a group of 2,000 Negro students protesting segregation and the arrest of other Negro students for participating in a "sit-in." The demonstrators marched through downtown Baton Rouge, Louisiana, in an orderly manner and stopped across the street from the courthouse where they sang songs, prayed, and listened to a speech. The city sheriff ordered the group to leave, and when they refused to do so, the police fired tear gas into the crowd. For his part in the demonstration Mr. Cox was convicted of violating three Louisiana laws, which prohibit breaching the peace, blocking a public sidewalk, and demonstrating near a courthouse.

[Justice Goldberg spoke for a unanimous Court in reversing Cox's conviction for breach of the peace. He wrote that the state cannot constitutionally punish as a breach of the peace the peaceful and orderly demonstration which Cox led. Moreover, Louisiana's statute, as interpreted by its courts, is far too broad and may be used to prohibit legitimate demonstrations that pose no threat to public order. Four other members of the Court joined Justice Goldberg in reversing as unconstitutional Cox's conviction for blocking the sidewalk. Although recognizing that governmental authorities have the duty and responsibility to keep their streets open and available for movement, the Court held that the statute here as applied and enforced by the local officials gave them too much discretion to discriminate among demonstrators on the basis of whether or not they liked the ideas being expressed. Justices Black and Clark concurred in the reversal on other grounds, and Justices Harlan and White dissented. Finally, Justice Goldberg wrote that the state statute prohibiting demonstrations near a courthouse was constitutional as a narrowly drawn, reasonable regulation of the place where demonstrations might be held. Moreover, it might constitutionally be applied to prohibit Cox and the Negro students from meeting across the street from the Baton Rouge courthouse. However, because city officials had given the students permission to assemble across the street from the courthouse, the Court held that to convict them for meeting there constituted a sort of entrapment that the Constitution forbids. Five members of the Court agreed that Cox's conviction must be reversed because of this entrapment; Justices Black, Clark, Harlan and White dissented, but the Court was unanimous in holding that the statute regulating the place of demonstration was constitutional as a narrowly drawn regulation protecting an important state interest. Excerpts from the opinion dealing with the regulation of speech and expression are printed here.]

Appellant was convicted[1] of violating a Louisiana "disturbing the peace" statute, which provides:

Whoever with intent to provoke a breach of the peace, or under circumstances such that a breach of the peace may be occasioned thereby . . . crowds or congregates with others . . . in or upon . . . a public street or public highway, or upon a public sidewalk, or any other public place or building . . . and who fails or refuses to disperse and move on, . . . when ordered so to do by any law enforcement officer of any municipality, or parish, in which such act or acts are committed, or by any law enforcement officer of the state of Louisiana, or any other authorized person . . . shall be guilty of disturbing the peace.—La. Rev. Stat. 14:103.1 (Cum. Supp. 1962).

It is clear to us that on the facts of this case, which are strikingly similar to those present in *Edwards* v. *South Carolina*, 372 U.S. 229, and *Fields* v. *South Carolina*, 375 U.S. 44, Louisiana infringed appellant's rights of free speech and free assembly by convicting him under this statute. . . .

The Louisiana courts have held that appellant's conduct constituted a breach of the peace under state law, and as in *Edwards*, "we may accept their decision as binding upon us to that extent," *Edwards* v. *South Carolina*, *supra*, at 235; but our independent examination of the record, which we are required to make,[2] shows no conduct which the state had a right to prohibit as a breach of the peace.

---

[1] January 18, 1965. Cases No. 24 and 49. Mr. Justice Goldberg delivered the opinion of the Court.

[2] Because a claim of constitutionally protected right is involved, it "remains our duty in a case such as this to make an independent examination of the whole record." *Edwards* v. *South Carolina*, 372 U.S. 229, 235; *Blackburn* v. *Alabama*, 361 U.S. 199, 205, n. 5; *Pennekamp* v. *Florida*, 328 U.S. 331, 335; *Fiske* v. *Kansas*, 274 U.S. 380, 385–386. In the area of First Amendment freedoms as well as areas involving other constitutionally protected rights, "we cannot avoid our responsibilities by permitting ourselves to be 'completely bound by state court determination of any issue essential to decision of a claim of federal right, else federal law could be frustrated by distorted fact finding.'" *Haynes* v. *Washington*, 373 U.S. 503, 515–516; *Stern* v. *New York*, 346 U.S. 156, 181.

Appellant led a group of young college students who wished "to protest segregation" and discrimination against Negroes and the arrest of 23 fellow students. They assembled peaceably at the state capitol building and marched to the courthouse where they sang, prayed and listened to a speech. A reading of the record reveals agreement on the part of the state's witnesses that Cox had the demonstration "very well controlled," and until the end of Cox's speech, the group was perfectly "orderly." Sheriff Clemens testified that the crowd's activities were not "objectionable" before that time. They became objectionable, according to the sheriff himself, when Cox, concluding his speech, urged the students to go downtown and sit in at lunch counters. The sheriff testified that the sole aspect of the program to which he objected was "the inflammatory manner in which he [Cox] addressed the crowd and told them to go on uptown, go to four places on the protest list, sit down and if they don't feed you, sit there for one hour." Yet this part of Cox's speech obviously did not deprive the demonstration of its protected character under the Constitution as free speech and assembly. See *Edwards* v. *South Carolina, supra; Cantwell* v. *Connecticut,* 310 U.S. 296; *Thornhill* v. *Alabama,* 310 U.S. 88; *Garner* v. *Louisiana,* 368 U.S. 157, 185 (concurring opinion of Mr. Justice Harlan).

The state argues, however, that, while the demonstrators started out to be orderly, the loud cheering and clapping by the students in response to the singing from the jail converted the peaceful assembly into a riotous one.[3] The record, however, does not support this assertion. . . . Our conclusion that the entire meeting from the beginning until its dispersal by tear gas was orderly[4] and not riotous is confirmed by a film of the events taken by a

[3] The cheering and shouting were described differently by different witnesses, but the most extravagant descriptions were the following: "a jumbled roar like people cheering at a football game," "loud cheering and spontaneous clapping and screaming and a great hullabaloo," "a great outburst," a cheer of "conquest . . . much wilder than a football game," "a loud reaction, not disorderly, loud," "a shout, a roar," and an emotional response "in jubilation and exhortation." Appellant agreed that some of the group "became emotional" and "tears flowed from young ladies' eyes."

[4] There is much testimony that the demonstrators were well controlled and basically orderly throughout. G. Dupre Litton, an attorney and witness for the state, testified, "I would say that it was an orderly demonstration. It was too large a group, in my opinion, to congregate at that place at that particular time, which is nothing but my opinion . . . but generally . . . it was orderly." Robert Durham, a news photographer for WRBZ, a state witness, testified that, although the demonstration was not "quiet and peaceful," it was basically "orderly." James Erwin, news director of WIBR, a witness for the state, testified as follows:
"Q. Was the demonstration generally orderly?
"A. Yes, Reverend Cox had it very well controlled."
On the other hand, there is some evidence to the contrary: Erwin also stated:
"Q. Was it orderly up to the point of throwing the tear gas?
"A. No, there was one minor outburst after he called for the sit-ins, and then a minor reaction, and then a loud reaction, not disorderly, loud . . . . A loud reaction when the singing occurred upstairs."

television news photographer, which was offered in evidence as a state exhibit. We have viewed the film, and it reveals that the students, though they undoubtedly cheered and clapped, were well-behaved throughout. The singing and cheering does not seem to us to differ significantly from the constitutionally protected activity of the demonstrators in *Edwards*,[5] who loudly sang "while stamping their feet and clapping their hands." *Edwards* v. *South Carolina, supra*, at 233.[6]

And James Dumigan, a police officer, thought that the demonstrators showed a certain disorder "by hollering loud, clapping their hands." But this latter evidence is surely not sufficient, particularly in face of the film, to lead us to conclude that the cheering was so disorderly as to be beyond that held constitutionally protected in *Edwards* v. *South Carolina, supra*.

[5] Moreover, there are not significantly more demonstrators here than in *Fields* v. *South Carolina, supra*, at 44, which involved more than 1,000 students.

[6] Witnesses who concluded that a breach of the peace was threatened or had occurred based their conclusions, not upon the shouting or cheering, but upon the fact that the group was demonstrating at all, upon Cox's suggestion that the group sit-in, or upon the reaction of the white onlookers across the street. Rush Biossat, a state witness, testified that while appellant "didn't say anything of a violent nature," there was "emotional upset," "a feeling of disturbance in the air," and "agitation"; he thought, however, that all this was caused by Cox's remarks about "black and white together." James Erwin, a state witness, and news director of WIBR, testified that there was "considerable stirring" and a "restiveness," but among the white group. He also stated that the reaction of the white group to Cox's speech "was electrifying." "You could hear grumbling from the small group of white people, some total of two hundred fifty, perhaps . . . and there was a definite feeling of ill will that had sprung up." He was afraid that "violence was about to erupt" but also thought that Cox had his group under control and did not want violence. G. L. Johnston, a police officer and a witness for the state, felt that the disorderly part of the demonstration was Cox's suggestion that the group sit-in. Vay Carpenter, and Mary O'Brien, legal secretaries and witnesses for the state, thought that the mood of the crowd changed at the time of Cox's speech and became "tense." They thought this was because of the sit-in suggestion. Chief Kling of the sheriff's office, testifying for the state, said that the situation became one "that was explosive and one that had gotten to the point where it had to be handled or it would have gotten out of hand"; however, he based his opinion upon "the mere presence of these people in downtown Baton Rouge in such great numbers." Police Captain Font also testified for the state that the situation was "explosive"; he based his opinion on, "how they came, such a large group like that, just coming out of nowhere, just coming, filling the streets, filling the sidewalks. We are prepared—we have traffic officers. We can handle traffic situations if we are advised that we are going to have a traffic situation, if the sidewalk is going to be blocked, if the street is going to be blocked, but we wasn't advised of it. They just came and blocked it." He added that he feared "bloodshed," but based this fear upon "when the sheriff requested them to move, they didn't move; when they cheered in a conquest type of tone, their displaying of the signs, the deliberate agitation that 25 people had been arrested the day before, and then they turned right around and just agitated the next day in the same prescribed manner." He also felt that the students displayed their signs in a way which was "agitating." Inspector Trigg testified for the state that "from their actions, I figured they were going to try to storm the courthouse and take over the jail and try to get the prisoners that they had come down here to protest." However, Trigg based his conclusions upon the students having marched down from the capitol and paraded in front of the courthouse; he thought they were "violent" because "they continued to march around this courthouse, and they continued to march down here and do things that disrupts our way of living down here." Sheriff Clemens testified that the assembly "became objectionable" at the time of Cox's speech. The

Finally, the state contends that the conviction should be sustained because of fear expressed by some of the state witnesses that "violence was about to erupt" because of the demonstration. It is virtually undisputed, however, that the students themselves were not violent and threatened no violence. The fear of violence seems to have been based upon the reaction of the group of white citizens looking on from across the street. One state witness testified that "he felt the situation was getting out of hand" as on the courthouse side of St. Louis Street "were small knots or groups of white citizens who were muttering words, who seemed a little bit agitated." A police officer stated that the reaction of the white crowd was not violent, but "was rumblings." Others felt the atmosphere became "tense" because of "mutterings," "grumbling," and "jeering" from the white group. There is no indication, however, that any member of the white group threatened violence. And, this small crowd estimated at between 100 and 300 was separated from the students by "seventy-five to eighty" armed policemen, including "every available shift of the City Police," the "Sheriff's Office in full compliment," and "additional help from the State Police," along with a "fire truck and the Fire Department." As Inspector Trigg testified, they could have handled the crowd.

This situation, like that in *Edwards*, is "a far cry from the situation in *Feiner v. New York*, 340 U.S. 315." See *Edwards v. South Carolina, supra*, at 236. Nor is there any evidence here of "fighting words." See *Chaplinsky v. New Hampshire*, 315 U.S. 568. Here again, as in *Edwards*, this evidence "showed no more than that the opinions which . . . [the students] were peaceably expressing were sufficiently opposed to the views of the majority of the community to attract a crowd and necessitate police protection." *Edwards v. South Carolina, supra*, at 237. Conceding this was so, the compelling answer . . . is that constitutional rights may not be denied simply because of hostility to their assertion or exercise." *Watson v. Memphis*, 373 U.S. 526, 535.

There is an additional reason why this conviction cannot be sustained. The statute at issue in this case, as authoritatively interpreted by the Louisiana Supreme Court, is unconstitutionally vague in its overly broad scope. The statutory crime consists of two elements: (1) congregating with others

---

sheriff objected to "the inflammatory manner in which he addressed that crowd and told them to go on up town, go to four places on the protest list, sit down and if they don't feed you, sit there for one hour. Prior to that though, out from under these coats, some signs of—picketing signs. I don't know what's coming out of there next. It could be anything under a coat. It became inflammatory, and when he gestured, go on up town and take charge of these places . . . of business. That is what they were trying to do is take charge of this courthouse."

A close reading of the record seems to reveal next to no evidence that anyone thought that the shouting and cheering was what constituted the threatened breach of the peace.

"with intent to provoke a breach of the peace, or under circumstances such that a breach of the peace may be occasioned," and (2) a refusal to move on after having been ordered to do so by a law-enforcement officer. While the second part of this offense is narrow and specific, the first element is not. The Louisiana Supreme Court in this case defined the term "breach of the peace" as "to agitate, to arouse from a state of repose, to molest, to interrupt, to hinder, to disquiet." 244 La., at 1105; 156 So. 2d, at 455. In *Edwards*, defendants had been convicted of a common-law crime similarly defined by the South Carolina Supreme Court. Both definitions would allow persons to be punished merely for peacefully expressing unpopular views. Yet, a "function of free speech under our system of government is to invite dispute. It may indeed best serve its high purpose when it induces a condition of unrest, creates dissatisfaction with conditions as they are, or even stirs people to anger. Speech is often provocative and challenging. It may strike at prejudice and preconceptions and have profound unsettling effects as it presses for acceptance of an idea. That is why freedom of speech . . . is . . . protected against censorship or punishment. . . . There is no room under our Constitution for a more restrictive view. For the alternative would lead to standardization of ideas either by legislatures, courts, or dominant political groups." *Terminiello* v. *Chicago*, 337 U.S. 1, 4-5. In *Terminiello* convictions were not allowed to stand because the trial judge charged that speech of the defendants could be punished as a breach of the peace " 'if it stirs the public to anger, invites dispute, brings about a condition of unrest, or creates a disturbance, or if it molests the inhabitants in the enjoyment of peace and quiet by arousing alarm.' " *Id.*, at 3. The Louisiana statute, as interpreted by the Louisiana court, is at least as likely to allow conviction for innocent speech as was the charge of the trial judge in *Terminiello*. Therefore, as in *Terminiello* and *Edwards*, the conviction under this statute must be reversed as the statute is unconstitutional in that it sweeps within its broad scope activities that are constitutionally protected free speech and assembly. Maintenance of the opportunity for free political discussion is a basic tenet of our constitutional democracy. As Chief Justice Hughes stated in *Stromberg* v. *California*, 283 U.S. 359, 369: "A statute which upon its face, and as authoritatively construed, is so vague and indefinite as to permit the punishment of the fair use of this opportunity is repugnant to the guaranty of liberty contained in the Fourteenth Amendment."

For all these reasons we hold that appellant's freedom of speech and assembly, secured to him by the First Amendment as applied to the States, by the Fourteenth Amendment, were denied by his conviction for disturbing the peace. The conviction on this charge cannot stand. . . .

We now turn to the issue of the validity of appellant's conviction for violating the Louisiana statute, La. Rev. Stat. 14:100.1 (Cum. Supp. 1962), which provides:

Obstructing Public Passages

. . . No person shall wilfully obstruct the free, convenient and normal use of any public sidewalk, street, highway, bridge, alley, road, or other passageway, or the entrance, corridor or passage of any public building, structure, water craft or ferry, by impeding, hindering, stifling, retarding or restraining traffic or passage thereon or therein.

Providing however nothing herein contained shall apply to a bona fide legitimate labor organization or to any of its legal activities such as picketing, lawful assembly or concerted activity in the interest of its members for the purpose of accomplishing or securing more favorable wage standards, hours of employment and working conditions.

Appellant was convicted under this statute, not for leading the march to the vicinity of the courthouse, which the Louisiana Supreme Court stated to have been "orderly," 244 La., at 1096, 156 So. 2d, at 451, but for leading the meeting on the sidewalk across the street from the courthouse. *Id.*, at 1094, 1106-1107, 156 So. 2d, at 451, 455. In upholding appellant's conviction under this statute, the Louisiana Supreme Court thus construed the statute so as to apply to public assemblies which do not have as their specific purpose the obstruction of traffic. There is no doubt from the record in this case that this far sidewalk was obstructed, and thus, as so construed, appellant violated the statute.

Appellant, however, contends that as so construed and applied in this case. the statute is an unconstitutional infringement on freedom of speech and assembly. This contention on the facts here presented raises an issue with which this Court has dealt in many decisions. That is, the right of a state or municipality to regulate the use of city streets and other facilities to assure the safety and convenience of the people in their use and the concomitant right of the people of free speech and assembly. See *Lovell* v. *Griffin*, 303 U.S. 444; *Hague* v. *CIO*, 307 U.S. 496; *Schneider* v. *State*, 308 U.S. 147; *Thornhill* v. *Alabama*, 310 U.S. 88; *Cantwell* v. *Connecticut*, 310 U.S. 296; *Cox* v. *New Hampshire*, 312 U.S. 569; *Largent* v. *Texas*, 318 U.S. 418; *Saia* v. *New York*, 334 U.S. 558; *Kovacs* v. *Cooper*, 336 U.S. 77; *Niemotko* v. *Maryland*, 340 U.S. 268; *Kunz* v. *New York*, 340 U.S. 290; *Poulos* v. *New Hampshire*, 345 U.S. 395.

From these decisions certain clear principles emerge. The rights of free speech and assembly, while fundamental in our democratic society, still do not mean that everyone with opinions or beliefs to express may address a group at any public place and at any time. The constitutional guarantee of liberty implies the existence of an organized society maintaining public order, without which liberty itself would be lost in the excesses of anarchy. The control of travel on the streets is a clear example of governmental responsibility to ensure this necessary order. A restriction in that relation, designed to promote the public convenience in the interest of all, and not susceptible to abuses of discriminatory application, cannot be disregarded by the attempted exercise of some civil right which, in other circumstances, would be entitled to protection. One would not be justified in ignoring the familiar red light because this was thought to be a means of social protest. Nor could one, contrary to traffic regulations, insist upon a street meeting in the middle of Times Square at the rush hour as a form of freedom of speech or assembly. Governmental authorities have the duty and responsibility to keep their streets open and available for movement. A group of demonstrators could not insist upon the right to cordon off a street, or entrance to a public or private building, and allow no one to pass who did not agree to listen to their exhortations. See *Lovell* v. *Griffin, supra*, at 451; *Cox* v. *New Hampshire, supra*, at 574; *Schneider* v. *State, supra*, at 160-161; *Cantwell* v. *Connecticut, supra*, at 306-307; *Giboney* v. *Empire Storage & Ice Co.*, 336 U.S. 490; *Poulos* v. *New Hampshire, supra*, at 405-408; see also, *Edwards* v. *South Carolina, supra*, at 236.

We emphatically reject the notion urged by appellant that the First and Fourteenth Amendments afford the same kind of freedom to those who would communicate ideas by conduct such as patrolling, marching, and picketing on streets and highways, as these amendments afford to those who communicate ideas by pure speech. See the discussion and cases cited in No. 49, *post*, at 563. We reaffirm the statement of the Court in *Giboney* v. *Empire Storage & Ice Co., supra*, at 502, that "it has never been deemed an abridgment of freedom of speech or press to make a course of conduct illegal merely because the conduct was in part initiated, evidenced, or carried out by means of language, either spoken, written, or printed."

We have no occasion in this case to consider the constitutionality of the uniform, consistent, and nondiscriminatory application of a statute forbidding all access to streets and other public facilities for parades and meetings.[7]

---

[7] It has been argued that, in the exercise of its regulatory power over streets and other public facilities, a state or municipality could reserve the streets completely for traffic and other facilities for rest and relaxation of the citizenry. See *Kovacs* v. *Cooper, supra*, at 98 (opinion of Mr. Justice Jackson); *Kunz* v. *New York, supra*, at 298 (Mr. Justice Jackson, dissenting). The contrary, however, has been indicated, at least to the point that some open area must be preserved for outdoor assemblies. See *Hague* v. *CIO, supra*, at 515-516 (opinion of Mr. Justice Roberts); *Kunz* v. *New York, supra*, at 293; *Niemotko* v. *Maryland, supra*, at 283 (Mr. Justice Frankfurter, concurring). See, generally, *Poulos* v. *New Hampshire, supra*, at 403; *Niemotko* v. *Maryland, supra*, at 272-273.

Although the statute here involved on its face precludes all street assemblies and parades,[8] it has not been so applied and enforced by the Baton Rouge authorities. City officials who testified for the state clearly indicated that certain meetings and parades are permitted in Baton Rouge, even though they have the effect of obstructing traffic, provided prior approval is obtained. This was confirmed in oral argument before this Court by counsel for the state. He stated that parades and meetings are permitted, based on "arrangements . . . made with officials." The statute itself provides no standards for the determination of local officials as to which assemblies to permit or which to prohibit. Nor are there any administrative regulations on this subject which have been called to our attention.[9] From all the evidence before us it appears that the authorities in Baton Rouge permit or prohibit parades or street meetings in their completely uncontrolled discretion.

The situation is thus the same as if the statute itself expressly provided that there could only be peaceful parades or demonstrations in the unbridled discretion of the local officials. The pervasive restraint on freedom of discussion by the practice of the authorities under the statute is not any less effective than a statute expressly permitting such selective enforcement. A long line of cases in this Court makes it clear that a state or municipality cannot "require all who wish to disseminate ideas to present them first to police authorities for their consideration and approval, with a discretion in the police to say some ideas may, while others may not, be . . . disseminate[d]. . . ." *Schneider* v. *State, supra,* at 164. See *Lovell* v. *Griffin, supra; Hague* v. *CIO, supra; Largent* v. *Texas, supra; Saia* v. *New York, supra; Niemotko* v. *Maryland, supra; Kunz* v. *New York, supra.*

This Court has recognized that the lodging of such broad discretion in a public official allows him to determine which expressions of view will be permitted and which will not. This thus sanctions a device for the suppres-

---

[8] With the express exception, of course, of labor picketing. This exception points up the fact that the statute reaches beyond mere traffic regulation to restrictions on expression.

[9] Although cited by neither party, research has disclosed the existence of a local ordinance of Baton Rouge, Baton Rouge City Code, Tit. 11, § 210 (1957), which prohibits "parades . . . along any street except in accordance with a permit issued by the chief of police." A similar ordinance was in existence in *Fields* v. *South Carolina, supra.* As in *Fields,* this ordinance is irrelevant to the conviction in this case as not only was appellant not charged with this violation but the existence of the ordinance was never referred to by the state in any of the courts involved in the case, including this one, and neither the Louisiana trial court nor the Supreme Court relied on the ordinance in sustaining appellant's convictions under the three statutes here involved. Moreover, since the ordinance apparently sets forth no standards for the determination of the chief of police as to which parades to permit or which to prohibit, obvious constitutional problems would arise if appellant had been convicted for parading in violation of it. See the discussion in text above; *Lovell* v. *Griffin, supra,* at 452–453; *Hague* v. *CIO, supra,* at 518; *Saia* v. *New York, supra,* at 559–560.

sion of the communication of ideas and permits the official to act as a censor. See *Saia* v. *New York, supra*, at 562. Also inherent in such a system allowing parades or meetings only with the prior permission of an official is the obvious danger to the right of a person or group not to be denied equal protection of the laws. See *Niemotko* v. *Maryland, supra*, at 272, 284; cf. *Yick Wo* v. *Hopkins*, 118 U. S. 356. It is clearly unconstitutional to enable a public official to determine which expressions of view will be permitted and which will not or to engage in invidious discrimination among persons or groups either by use of a statute providing a system of broad discretionary licensing power or, as in this case, the equivalent of such a system by selective enforcement of an extremely broad prohibitory statute.

It is, of course, undisputed that appropriate, limited discretion, under properly drawn statutes or ordinances, concerning the time, place, duration, or manner of use of the streets for public assemblies may be vested in administrative officials, provided that such limited discretion is "exercised with 'uniformity of method of treatment upon the facts of each application, free from improper or inappropriate considerations and from unfair discrimination' . . . [and with] a 'systematic, consistent and just order of treatment, with reference to the convenience of public use of the highways. . . .' " *Cox* v. *New Hampshire, supra*, at 576. See *Poulos* v. *New Hampshire, supra*.

But here it is clear that the practice in Baton Rouge allowing unfettered discretion in local officials in the regulation of the use of the streets for peaceful parades and meetings is an unwarranted abridgment of appellant's freedom of speech and assembly secured to him by the First Amendment, as applied to the states by the Fourteenth Amendment. It follows, therefore, that appellant's conviction for violating the statute as so applied and enforced must be reversed. . . .

Appellant [also] was convicted[1] of violating a Louisiana statute which provides:

Whoever, with the intent of interfering with, obstructing or impeding the administration of justice, or with the intent of influencing any judge, juror, witness, or court officer, in the discharge of his duty pickets or parades in or near a building housing a court of the State of Louisiana . . . shall be fined not more than five thousand dollars or imprisoned not more than one year, or both.—La. Rev. Stat. § 14:401 (Cum. Supp. 1962).

We shall first consider appellant's contention that this statute must be declared invalid on its face as an unjustified restriction upon freedoms guaranteed by the First and Fourteenth Amendments to the United States Constitution.

[1] January 18, 1965. Case No. 49.

This statute was passed by Louisiana in 1950 and was modeled after a bill pertaining to the federal judiciary, which Congress passed in 1950, 64 Stat. 1018, 18 U.S.C. § 1507 (1958 ed.). . . .

This statute, unlike the two previously considered, is a precise, narrowly drawn regulatory statute which proscribes certain specific behavior. Cf. *Edwards* v. *South Carolina*, 372 U.S. 229, 236. It prohibits a particular type of conduct, namely, picketing and parading, in a few specified locations, in or near courthouses.

There can be no question that a state has a legitimate interest in protecting its judicial system from the pressures which picketing near a courthouse might create. Since we are committed to a government of laws and not of men, it is of the utmost importance that the administration of justice be absolutely fair and orderly. This Court has recognized that the unhindered and untrammeled functioning of our courts is part of the very foundation of our constitutional democracy. See *Wood* v. *Georgia*, 370 U.S. 375, 383. The constitutional safeguards relating to the integrity of the criminal process attend every stage of a criminal proceeding, starting with arrest and culminating with a trial "in a courtroom presided over by a judge." *Rideau* v. *Louisiana*, 373 U.S. 723, 727. There can be no doubt that they embrace the fundamental conception of a fair trial, and that they exclude influence or domination by either a hostile or friendly mob. There is no room at any stage of judicial proceedings for such intervention; mob law is the very antithesis of due process. See *Frank* v. *Mangum*, 237 U.S. 309, 347 (Justice Holmes dissenting). A state may adopt safeguards necessary and appropriate to assure that the administration of justice at all stages is free from outside control and influence. A narrowly drawn statute such as the one under review is obviously a safeguard both necessary and appropriate to vindicate the state's interest in assuring justice under law.

Nor does such a statute infringe upon the constitutionally protected rights of free speech and free assembly. The conduct which is the subject of this statute—picketing and parading—is subject to regulation even though intertwined with expression and association. The examples are many of the application by this Court of the principle that certain forms of conduct mixed with speech may be regulated or prohibited. The most classic of these was pointed out long ago by Mr. Justice Holmes: "The most stringent protection of free speech would not protect a man in falsely shouting fire in a theatre and causing a panic." *Schenck* v. *United States*, 249 U.S. 47, 52. A man may be punished for encouraging the commission of a crime, *Fox* v. *Washington*, 236 U.S. 273, or for uttering "fighting words," *Chaplinsky* v. *New Hampshire*, 315 U.S. 568. This principle has been applied to picketing and parading in labor disputes. See *Hughes* v. *Superior Court*, 339 U.S. 460;

Giboney v. *Empire Storage & Ice Co.*, 336 U.S. 490; *Building Service Employees* v. *Gazzam*, 339 U.S. 532. But cf. *Thornhill* v. *Alabama*, 310 U.S. 88. These authorities make it clear, as the Court said in *Giboney*, that "it has never been deemed an abridgment of freedom of speech or press to make a course of conduct illegal merely because the conduct was in part initiated, evidenced or carried out by means of language, either spoken, written or printed." *Giboney* v. *Empire Storage & Ice Co.*, *supra*, at 502.

Bridges v. California, 314 U.S. 252, and *Pennekamp* v. *Florida*, 328 U.S. 331, do not hold to the contrary. Both these cases dealt with the power of a judge to sentence for contempt persons who published or caused to be published writings commenting on judicial proceedings. They involved newspaper editorials, an editorial cartoon, and a telegram sent by a labor leader to the Secretary of Labor. Here we deal not with the contempt power—a power which is "based on a common law concept of the most general and undefined nature." *Bridges* v. *California*, *supra*, at 260. Rather, we are reviewing a statute narrowly drawn to punish specific conduct that infringes a substantial state interest in protecting the judicial process. See *Cantwell* v. *Connecticut*, 310 U.S. 296, 307-308; *Giboney* v. *Empire Storage & Ice Co.*, *supra*. We are not concerned here with such a pure form of expression as newspaper comment or a telegram by a citizen to a public official. We deal in this case not with free speech alone, but with expression mixed with particular conduct. In *Giboney*, this Court expressly recognized this distinction when it said, "In holding this, we are mindful of the essential importance to our society of a vigilant protection of freedom of speech and press. *Bridges* v. *California*, 314 U.S. 252, 263. States cannot consistently with our Constitution abridge those freedoms to obviate slight inconveniences or annoyances. *Schneider* v. *State*, 308 U.S. 147, 162. But placards used as an essential and inseparable part of a grave offense against an important public law cannot immunize that unlawful conduct from state control." 336 U.S., at 501-502.

We hold that this statute on its face is a valid law dealing with conduct subject to regulation so as to vindicate important interests of society and that the fact that free speech is intermingled with such conduct does not bring with it constitutional protection. . . .

We now deal with the Louisiana statute as applied to the conduct in this case. The group of 2,000, led by appellant, paraded and demonstrated before the courthouse. Judges and court officers were in attendance to discharge their respective functions. It is undisputed that a major purpose of the demonstration was to protest what the demonstrators considered an "illegal" arrest of 23 students the previous day. While the arraignment or trial of the students had not been set for any day certain, they were charged with violation of the law, and the judges responsible for trying them and passing upon the legality of their arrest were then in the building.

It is, of course, true that most judges will be influenced only by what they see and hear in court. However, judges are human; and the legislature has the right to recognize the danger that some judges, jurors and other court officials will be consciously or unconsciously influenced by demonstrations in or near their courtrooms both prior to and at the time of the trial. A state may also properly protect the judicial process from being misjudged in the minds of the public. Suppose demonstrators paraded and picketed for weeks with signs asking that indictments be dismissed, and that a judge, completely uninfluenced by these demonstrations, dismissed the indictments. A state may protect against the possibility of a conclusion by the public under these circumstances, that the judge's action was in part a product of intimidation and did not flow only from the fair and orderly working of the judicial process. See S. Rep. No. 732, 81st Cong., 1st Sess. 4.

Appellant invokes the clear and present danger doctrine in support of his argument that the statute cannot constitutionally be applied to the conduct involved here. He says, relying upon *Pennekamp* and *Bridges,* that "no reason exists to apply a different standard to the case of a criminal penalty for a peaceful demonstration in front of a courthouse than the standard of clear and present danger applied in the contempt cases." . . . He defines the standard to be applied to both situations to be whether the expression of opinion presents a clear and present danger to the administration of justice.

We have already pointed out the important differences between the contempt cases and the present one, *supra*, at 563-564. Here we deal not with the contempt power but with a narrowly drafted statute and not with speech in its pristine form but with conduct of a totally different character. Even assuming the applicability of a general clear and present danger test, it is one thing to conclude that the mere publication of a newspaper editorial or a telegram to a secretary of labor, however critical of a court, presents no clear and present danger to the administration of justice and quite another thing to conclude that crowds, such as this, demonstrating before a courthouse may not be prohibited by a legislative determination based on experience that such conduct inherently threatens the judicial process. We therefore reject the clear and present danger argument of appellant.

[After determining that Cox's conviction must be set aside because of entrapment, the Court concluded:]

Nothing we have said here or in No. 24, *ante*, is to be interpreted as sanctioning riotous conduct in any form or demonstrations, however peaceful their conduct or commendable their motives, which conflict with properly drawn statutes and ordinances designed to promote law and order, protect the community against disorder, regulate traffic, safeguard legitimate interests in private and public property, or protect the administration of justice and other essential governmental functions.

Liberty can only be exercised in a system of law which safeguards order. We reaffirm the repeated holdings of this Court that our constitutional command of free speech and assembly is basic and fundamental and encompasses peaceful social protest, so important to the preservation of the freedoms treasured in a democratic society. We also reaffirm the repeated decisions of this Court that there is no place for violence in a democratic society dedicated to liberty under law, and that the right of peaceful protest does not mean that everyone with opinions or beliefs to express may do so at any time and at any place. There is a proper time and place for even the most peaceful protest and a plain duty and responsibility on the part of all citizens to obey all valid laws and regulations. There is an equally plain requirement for laws and regulations to be drawn so as to give citizens fair warning as to what is illegal; for regulation of conduct that involves freedom of speech and assembly not to be so broad in scope so as to stifle First Amendment freedoms, which "need breathing space to survive," *NAACP* v. *Button*, 371 U. S. 415, 433; for appropriate limitations on the discretion of public officials where speech and assembly are intertwined with regulated conduct; and for all such laws and regulations to be applied with an equal hand. We believe that all of these requirements can be met in an ordered society dedicated to liberty. We reaffirm our conviction that "[f]reedom and viable government are . . . indivisible concepts." *Gibson* v. *Florida Legislative Comm.*, 372 U. S. 539, 546.

The application of these principles requires us to reverse the judgment of the Supreme Court of Louisiana.

School District of Abington v. Schempp, 374 U.S. 203

[In Schempp the Court, with only Justice Stewart dissenting, held that reading passages from the Bible and reciting prayers in a public school at the beginning of each school day violated the constitutional prohibition against laws respecting the establishment of religion. Justice Goldberg, joined by Justice Harlan, in a concurring opinion expressed his belief that the First Amendment does not require the state's exclusive devotion to secular activities, but rather that there are numerous permissible and even required accommodations between church and state. Whether a particular accommodation is permissible or required is a delicate issue that must be determined in each case in light of the First Amendment's objectives. Justice Goldberg agreed with the Court that school prayers and Bible reading involve the state so

significantly and directly in religious affairs that they create devisive influences that the First Amendment was designed to preclude, and that, therefore, such practices do not represent a permissible accommodation between
church and state but rather are unconstitutional.]

As is apparent from the opinions filed today,[1] delineation of the constitutionally permissible relationship between religion and government is a most
difficult and sensitive task, calling for the careful exercise of both judicial and
public judgment and restraint. The considerations which lead the Court today
to interdict the clearly religious practices presented in these cases are to me
wholly compelling; I have no doubt as to the propriety of the decision and
therefore join the opinion and judgment of the Court. The singular sensitivity
and concern which surround both the legal and practical judgments involved
impel me, however, to add a few words in further explication, while at the
same time avoiding repetition of the carefully and ably framed examination
of history and authority by my brethren.

The First Amendment's guarantees, as applied to the states through the
Fourteenth Amendment, foreclose not only laws "respecting an establishment
of religion" but also those "prohibiting the free exercise thereof." These two
proscriptions are to be read together, and in light of the single end which they
are designed to serve. The basic purpose of the religion clause of the First
Amendment is to promote and assure the fullest possible scope of religious
liberty and tolerance for all and to nurture the conditions which secure the
best hope of attainment of that end.

The fullest realization of true religious liberty requires that government
neither engage in nor compel religious practices, that it effect no favoritism
among sects or between religion and nonreligion, and that it work deterrence
of no religious belief. But devotion even to these simply stated objectives
presents no easy course, for the unavoidable accommodations necessary to
achieve the maximum enjoyment of each and all of them are often difficult of
discernment. There is for me no simple and clear measure which by precise
application can readily and invariably demark the permissible from the
impermissible.

It is said, and I agree, that the attitude of government toward religion must
be one of neutrality. But untutored devotion to the concept of neutrality
can lead to invocation or approval of results which partake not simply of
that noninterference and noninvolvement with the religious which the
Constitution commands, but of a brooding and pervasive devotion to the
secular and a passive, or even active, hostility to the religious. Such results

[1] June 17, 1963. Cases Nos. 142 and 119. Mr. Justice Goldberg, with whom Mr. Justice
Harlan joins, concurring.

are not only not compelled by the Constitution, but, it seems to me, are prohibited by it.

Neither government nor this Court can or should ignore the significance of the fact that a vast portion of our people believe in and worship God and that many of our legal, political and personal values derive historically from religious teachings. Government must inevitably take cognizance of the existence of religion and, indeed, under certain circumstances the First Amendment may require that it do so. And it seems clear to me from the opinions in the present and past cases that the Court would recognize the propriety of providing military chaplains and of the teaching *about* religion, as distinguished from the teaching *of* religion, in the public schools. The examples could readily be multiplied, for both the required and the permissible accommodations between state and church frame the relation as one free of hostility or favor and productive of religious and political harmony, but without undue involvement of one in the concerns or practices of the other. To be sure, the judgment in each case is a delicate one, but it must be made if we are to do loyal service as judges to the ultimate First Amendment objective of religious liberty.

The practices here involved do not fall within any sensible or acceptable concept of compelled or permitted accommodation and involve the state so significantly and directly in the realm of the sectarian as to give rise to those very divisive influences and inhibitions of freedom which both religion clauses of the First Amendment preclude. The state has ordained and has utilized its facilities to engage in unmistakably religious exercises—the devotional reading and recitation of the Holy Bible—in a manner having substantial and significant import and impact. That it has selected, rather than written, a particular devotional liturgy seems to me without constitutional import. The pervasive religiosity and direct governmental involvement inhering in the prescription of prayer and Bible reading in the public schools, during and as part of the curricular day, involving young impressionable children whose school attendance is statutorily compelled, and utilizing the prestige, power and influence of school administration, staff and authority, cannot realistically be termed simply accommodation, and must fall within the interdiction of the First Amendment. I find nothing in the opinion of the Court which says more than this. And, of course, today's decision does not mean that all incidents of government which import of the religious are therefore and without more banned by the strictures of the Establishment Clause. As the Court declared only last term in *Engel* v. *Vitale*, 370 U.S. 421, 435, n. 21:

There is of course nothing in the decision reached here that is inconsistent with the fact that school children and others are officially encouraged to express love for our country by reciting historical documents such as the Declaration of Independence which contain references to the Deity or by singing officially espoused anthems which include the composer's professions of faith in a Supreme Being, or with the fact that there are many manifestations in our public life of belief in God. Such patriotic or ceremonial occasions bear no true resemblance to the unquestioned religious exercise that the state . . . has sponsored in this instance.

The First Amendment does not prohibit practices which by any realistic measure create none of the dangers which it is designed to prevent and which do not so directly or substantially involve the state in religious exercises or in the favoring of religion as to have meaningful and practical impact. It is of course true that great consequences can grow from small beginnings, but the measure of constitutional adjudication is the ability and willingness to distinguish between real threat and mere shadow.

APTHEKER V. SECRETARY OF STATE, 378 U.S. 500

[In Aptheker the Court was asked to decide whether a Congressional statute, which forbids members of Communist-action organizations to apply for passports, unconstitutionally abridged the right of Americans to travel. After the Subversive Activities Control Board determined that the Communist party was a Communist-action organization, the State Department revoked the passports of certain high party officials. Aptheker, one of these officials, contended that, although the revocation of his passport might be required by the statute, this requirement was unconstitutional. Justice Goldberg, writing for the Court, concluded that the statute imposed an unconstitutionally broad curtailment upon the right to travel, for it did not distinguish between knowing and unknowing members of the party, between active and inactive members, or between innocent and malevolent purposes for traveling abroad. He wrote that this sweeping ban imposed far too great a burden upon the fundamental liberty of the individual to travel, for it was not narrowly drawn to meet the evil at which it was aimed. The Court went on to hold that the statute could not be construed in a way to narrow its scope without violating the intent of Congress in passing it. Justice Goldberg was joined by the Chief Justice and Justices Douglas, Brennan and Stewart. Justice Black concurred in the result, and Justices Clark, Harlan and White dissented. Portions of the opinion dealing with the constitutionality of the statute on its face are reproduced here.]

Appellants[1] attack § 6, both on its face and as applied, as an unconstitutional deprivation of the liberty guaranteed in the Bill of Rights. The

[1] June 22, 1964. Case No. 461. Mr. Justice Goldberg delivered the opinion of the Court.

government, while conceding that the right to travel is protected by the Fifth Amendment, contends that the Due Process Clause does not prevent the reasonable regulation of liberty and that § 6 is a reasonable regulation because of its relation to the danger the world Communist movement presents for our national security. . . .

We hold, for the reasons stated below, that § 6 of the Control Act too broadly and indiscriminately restricts the right to travel and thereby abridges the liberty guaranteed by the Fifth Amendment. . . .

In 1958 in *Kent* v. *Dulles*, 357 U.S. 116, 127, this Court declared that the right to travel abroad is "an important aspect of the citizen's 'liberty'" guaranteed in the Due Process Clause of the Fifth Amendment. . . . The present case . . . is the first in which this Court has been called upon to consider the constitutionality of the restrictions which § 6 imposes on the right to travel.

The substantiality of the restrictions cannot be doubted. The denial of a passport, given existing domestic and foreign laws, is a severe restriction upon, and in effect a prohibition against, worldwide foreign travel. Present laws and regulations make it a crime for a United States citizen to travel outside the Western Hemisphere or to Cuba without a passport. By its plain import § 6 of the Control Act effectively prohibits travel anywhere in the world outside the Western Hemisphere by members of any "Communist organization"—including "Communist-action" and "Communist-front" organizations. The restrictive effect of the legislation cannot be gainsaid by emphasizing, as the government seems to do, that a member of a registering organization could recapture his freedom to travel by simply in good faith abandoning his membership in the organization. Since freedom of association is itself guaranteed in the First Amendment, restrictions imposed upon the right to travel cannot be dismissed by asserting that the right to travel could be fully exercised if the individual would first yield up his membership in a given association.

Although previous cases have not involved the constitutionality of statutory restrictions upon the right to travel abroad, there are well-established principles by which to test whether the restrictions here imposed are consistent with the liberty guaranteed in the Fifth Amendment. It is a familiar and basic principle, recently reaffirmed in *NAACP* v. *Alabama*. 377 U.S. 288, 307, that "a governmental purpose to control or prevent activities constitutionally subject to state regulation may not be achieved by means which sweep unnecessarily broadly and thereby invade the area of protected freedoms." See, e.g., *NAACP* v. *Button*, 371 U.S. 415, 438; *Louisiana ex rel. Gremillion* v. *NAACP*, 366 U.S. 293; *Shelton* v. *Tucker*, 364 U.S. 479, 488; *Schware* v. *Board of Bar Examiners*, 353 U.S. 232, 239; *Martin* v.

Struthers, 319 U.S. 141, 146-149; *Cantwell* v. *Connecticut*, 310 U.S. 296, 304-307; *Schneider* v. *State*, 308 U.S. 147, 161, 165. In applying this principle the Court in *NAACP* v. *Alabama, supra*, referred to the criteria enunciated in *Shelton* v. *Tucker, supra*, at 488:

[E]ven though the governmental purpose be legitimate and substantial, that purpose cannot be pursued by means that broadly stifle fundamental personal liberties when the end can be more narrowly achieved. The breadth of legislative abridgment must be viewed in the light of less drastic means for achieving the same basic purpose.

This principle requires that we consider the Congressional purpose underlying § 6 of the Control Act. The government emphasizes that the legislation in question flows, as the statute itself declares, from the Congressional desire to protect our national security. That Congress under the Constitution has power to safeguard our nation's security is obvious and unarguable. Cf. *Kennedy* v. *Mendoza-Martinez*, 372 U.S. 144, 159-160. As we said in *Mendoza-Martinez*, "while the Constitution protects against invasions of individual rights, it is not a suicide pact." *Id.*, at 160. At the same time the Constitution requires that the powers of government "must be so exercised as not, in attaining a permissible end, unduly to infringe" a constitutionally protected freedom. *Cantwell* v. *Connecticut, supra*, at 304.

Section 6 provides that any member of a Communist organization which has registered or has been ordered to register commits a crime if he attempts to use or obtain a United States passport. The section applies to members who act "with knowledge or notice" that the organization is under a final registration order. "Notice" is specifically defined in § 13 (k). That section provides that publication in the Federal Register of the fact of registration or of issuance of a final registration order "shall constitute notice to all members of such organization that such order has become final." Thus the terms of § 6 apply whether or not the member actually knows or believes that he is associated with what is deemed to be a "Communist-action" or a "Communist-front" organization. The section also applies whether or not one knows or believes that he is associated with an organization operating to further aims of the world Communist movement and "to establish a Communist totalitarian dictatorship in the countries throughout the world." 64 Stat. 987, 50 U.S.C. § 781 (1). The provision therefore sweeps within its prohibition both knowing and unknowing members. In related contexts this Court has had occasion to consider substantiality of the relationship between an individual and a group where, as here, the fact of membership in that group has been made the sole criterion for limiting the individual's freedom. In *Wieman* v. *Updegraff*, 344 U.S. 183, the Court held that the due process guarantee of the Constitution was violated when a state, in an attempt to bar disloyal individuals from its employ, excluded persons solely on the basis of organizational memberships without regard to their knowledge concerning the organizations to which they had belonged. The Court concluded that "Indiscriminate classification of innocent with knowing activity must fall as an assertion of arbitrary power." *Id.*, at 191.

Section 6 also renders irrelevant the member's degree of activity in the organization and his commitment to its purpose. These factors, like knowledge, would bear on the likelihood that travel by such a person would be attended by the type of activity which Congress sought to control. As the Court has elsewhere noted, "men in adhering to a political party or other organization notoriously do not subscribe unqualifiedly to all of its platforms or asserted principles." Cf. *Schneiderman* v. *United States,* 320 U.S. 118, 136. It was in this vein that the Court in *Schware* v. *Board of Bar Examiners,* 353 U.S., at 246, stated that even "assuming that some members of the Communist party . . . had illegal aims and engaged in illegal activities, it cannot automatically be inferred that all members shared their evil purposes or participated in their illegal conduct." Section 6, however, establishes an irrebuttable presumption that individuals who are members of the specified organizations will, if given passports, engage in activities inimical to the security of the United States.

In addition to the absence of criteria linking the bare fact of membership to the individual's knowledge, activity or commitment, § 6 also excludes other considerations which might more closely relate the denial of passports to the stated purpose of the legislation. The prohibition of § 6 applies regardless of the purposes for which an individual wishes to travel. Under the statute it is a crime for a notified member of a registered organization to apply for a passport to travel abroad to visit a sick relative, to receive medical treatment, or for any other wholly innocent purpose. In determining whether there has been an abridgment of the Fifth Amendment's guarantee of liberty, this Court must recognize the danger of punishing a member of a Communist organization "for his adherence to lawful and constitutionally protected purposes, because of other and unprotected purposes which he does not necessarily share." *Noto* v. *United States,* 367 U.S. 290, 299-300; *Scales* v. *United States,* 367 U.S. 203, 229-230. In addition it must be noted that § 6 applies to a member regardless of the security-sensitivity of the areas in which he wishes to travel. As a result, if a notified member of a registered organization were to apply for a passport to visit a relative in Ireland, or to read rare manuscripts in the Bodleian Library of Oxford University, the applicant would be guilty of a crime; whereas, if he were to travel to Canada or Latin America to carry on criminal activities directed against the United States, he could do so free from the prohibitive reach of § 6.

In determining the constitutionality of § 6, it is also important to consider that Congress has within its power "less drastic" means of achieving the Congressional objective of safeguarding our national security. *Shelton* v. *Tucker*, 364 U.S., at 488. The Federal Employee Loyalty Program, which was before this Court in *Joint Anti-Fascist Refugee Comm.* v. *McGrath*, 341 U.S. 123, provides an example. Under Executive Order No. 9835, membership in a Communist organization is not considered conclusive but only as one factor to be weighed in determining the loyalty of an applicant or employee. It is relevant to note that less than a month after the decision in *Kent* v. *Dulles, supra,* President Eisenhower sent a message to Congress stating that "Any limitations on the right to travel can only be tolerated in terms of overriding requirements of our national security, and must be subject to substantive and procedural guaranties." Message from the President —Issuance of Passports, H. Doc. No. 417, 85th Cong., 2d Sess.; 104 Cong. Rec. 13046. The legislation which the President proposed did not make membership in a Communist organization, without more, a disqualification for obtaining a passport. S. 4110, H.R., 13318, 85th Cong., 2d Sess. Irrespective of views as to the validity of this or other such proposals, they demonstrate the conviction of the executive branch that our national security can be adequately protected by means which, when compared with § 6, are more discriminately tailored to the constitutional liberties of individuals.

In our view the foregoing considerations compel the conclusion that § 6 of the Control Act is unconstitutional on its face. The section, judged by its plain import and by the substantive evil which Congress sought to control, sweeps too widely and too indiscriminately across the liberty guaranteed in the Fifth Amendment. The prohibition against travel is supported only by a tenuous relationship between the bare fact of organizational membership and the activity Congress sought to proscribe. The broad and enveloping prohibition indiscriminately excludes plainly relevant considerations such as the individual's knowledge, activity, commitment and purposes in and places for travel. The section therefore is patently not a regulation "narrowly drawn to prevent the supposed evil," cf. *Cantwell* v. *Connecticut*, 310 U.S., at 307, yet here, as elsewhere, precision must be the touchstone of legislation so affecting basic freedoms, *NAACP* v. *Button*, 371 U.S., at 438. . . .

Similarly, since freedom of travel is a constitutional liberty closely related to rights of free speech and association, we believe that appellants in this case should not be required to assume the burden of demonstrating that Congress could have written a statute which might constitutionally have prohibited their travel.[2]

---

[2] Nor in our opinion should the Secretary of State or other Government officers be exposed to the risk of criminal penalties for violating § 6 (b) by issuing a passport to a member of a registered Communist-action organization who is subsequently found by a court to be a person whose travel, contrary to the belief of the government officer, could constitutionally be prohibited.

Accordingly the judgment of the three-judge District Court is reversed and the cause remanded for proceedings in conformity with this opinion.

ZEMEL V. RUSK, 381 U.S. 1

[In recent years the State Department has issued regulations restricting the foreign travel of American citizens. Prior to 1957 the department refused to issue passports to persons thought subversive. Passports have also been made invalid for travel to certain parts of the world, such as Cuba. In *Kent v. Dulles* the Court held that the Congressional statute providing that "The Secretary of State may grant and issue passports . . . under such rules as the President shall designate and prescribe" did not authorize the State Department to withhold passports from Communists. In *Zemel* the Court was asked to decide if this same statute allowed the State Department to make passports invalid for travel to Cuba.

[The Court held that Congress had authorized the State Department to impose area restrictions upon passports and that such restrictions upon the right to travel were constitutional. Justices Black, Douglas, and Goldberg dissented. Justice Goldberg, here as in *Aptheker* expressed his view that the right to travel was an important liberty guaranteed by the Constitution. He agreed with the Court that Congress constitutionally could regulate that right and allow the imposition of area restrictions for legitimate reasons of foreign policy. He did not agree, however, that Congress ever had authorized the Executive to impose such restrictions. And, he wrote that in his view the Executive surely does not possess an inherent right so to curtail the right to travel without Congressional authority.]

Last year approximately 2,750,000 Americans traveled abroad.[1] More than 1,100,000 passports were issued or renewed, nearly 4,000 of which were obtained by journalists.[2] This phenomenal amount of travel not only demonstrates our curiosity about things foreign, and the increasing importance of, and indeed often necessity for, travel, but it also reflects the long history of freedom of movement which Americans have enjoyed. Since the founding of the Republic our government has encouraged such travel.[3] For example, in 1820, when John Quincy Adams issued a passport to one Luther Bradish he certified that Bradish was about to visit foreign countries "with the view of gratifying a commendable curiosity."[4] In 1962, however, when appellant

[1] May 3, 1965. Case No. 86. Mr. Justice Goldberg dissenting.
[2] U.S. Dept. of State, Summary of Passport Statistics, January, 1965.
[3] Very recently the President has requested citizens voluntarily and temporarily to limit their travel abroad because of balance of payments difficulties.
[4] See U.S. Dept. of State, The American Passport 10 (1898).

requested that his passport be validated so that he might travel to Cuba "to satisfy my curiosity about the state of affairs in Cuba and to make me a better informed citizen," his request was denied upon the basis of Department of State regulations, issued under the alleged authority of an executive order, restricting travel to Cuba.

Appellant attacks the limitation imposed upon the validity of his passport as beyond the inherent power of the Executive, unauthorized by Congress, and beyond the constitutional authority of either the Executive or Congress. I agree with the Court that Congress has the constitutional power to impose area restrictions on travel, consistent with constitutional guarantees, and I reject appellant's arguments to the contrary. With all deference, however, I do not agree with the Court's holding that Congress has exercised this power. Moreover, I do not believe that the Executive has inherent authority to impose area restrictions in time of peace. I would hold, under the principles established by prior decisions of this Court, that inasmuch as Congress has not authorized the Secretary to impose area restrictions, appellant was entitled to a passport valid for travel to Cuba. . . .

This Court has recognized that the right to travel abroad is "an important aspect of the citizen's 'liberty' " guaranteed by the Due Process Clause of the Fifth Amendment. *Kent* v. *Dulles*, 357 U.S. 116, 127. In *Aptheker* v. *Secretary of State*, 378 U.S. 500, 517, we reaffirmed that "freedom of travel is a constitutional liberty closely related to rights of free speech and association." As nations have become politically and commercially more dependent upon one another and foreign policy decisions have come to have greater impact upon the lives of our citizens, the right to travel has become correspondingly more important. Through travel, by private citizens as well as by journalists and government officials, information necessary to the making of informed decisions can be obtained. And, under our constitutional system, ultimate responsibility for the making of informed decisions rests in the hands of the people. As Professor Chafee has pointed out, "An American who has crossed the ocean is not obliged to form his opinions about our foreign policy merely from what he is told by officials of our government or by a few correspondents of American newspapers. Moreover, his views on domestic questions are enriched by seeing how foreigners are trying to solve similar problems. In many different ways direct contact with other countries contributes to sounder decisions at home." Chafee, *Three Human Rights in the Constitution of 1787*, 195-196 (1956).

The constitutional basis of the right to travel and its importance to decision making in our democratic society led this Court in *Kent* v. *Dulles*, *supra*, to conclude that "if that 'liberty' is to be regulated, it must be pursuant to the law-making functions of the Congress." 357 U.S., at 129. Implicit in this statement, and at the very core of the holding in *Kent v. Dulles,* is a rejection of the argument there advanced and also made here by the government that the Executive possesses an inherent power to prohibit or impede travel by restricting the issuance of passports. The Court in *Kent* expressly recognized that a passport is not only of great value, but also is necessary[5] to leave this country and to travel to most parts of the world. *Kent v. Dulles, supra,* at 121. The Court demonstrates in *Kent v. Dulles,* and I shall show in detail below, that there is no long-standing and consistent history of the exercise of an alleged inherent executive power to limit travel or restrict the validity of passports. In view of the constitutional basis of the right to travel, the legal and practical necessity for passports, and the absence of a long-standing executive practice of imposing area restrictions, I would rule here, as this Court did in *Kent v. Dulles,* that passport restrictions may be imposed only when Congress makes provision therefor "in explicit terms." *Kent v. Dulles, supra,* at 130, consistent with constitutional guarantees. Cf. *Youngstown Sheet & Tube Co.* v. *Sawyer,* 343 U.S. 579. I would hold expressly that the Executive has no inherent authority to impose area restrictions in time of peace. . . .

I cannot accept the Court's view that authority to impose area restrictions was granted to the Executive by Congress in the Passport Act of 1926, 44 Stat. 887, 22 U.S.C. § 211a, which provides, "The Secretary of State may grant and issue passports . . . under such rules as the President shall designate and prescribe for and on behalf of the United States, and no other person shall grant, issue, or verify such passports." I do not believe that the legislative history of this provision, or administrative practice prior to its most recent re-enactment in 1926, will support the Court's interpretation of the statute. Moreover, the nature of the problem presented by area restrictions makes it unlikely that authority to impose such restrictions was granted by Congress in the course of enacting such a broad general statute. In my view, as the history I shall relate establishes, this statute was designed solely to centralize authority to issue passports in the hands of the Secretary of State in order to overcome the abuses and chaos caused by the fact that prior to the passage of the statute numerous unauthorized persons issued passports and travel documents. . . .

The 1926 provision has its origin in the Act of August 18, 1856, 11 Stat.

---

[5] Except for the years 1918 to 1921 and since 1941 American law did not require a passport for travel abroad. Currently, however, § 215 (b) of the Immigration and Nationality Act of 1952, 66 Stat. 190, 8 U. S. C. § 1185 (b) makes it unlawful, after the proclamation of a national emergency "to depart from or enter, or attempt to depart from or enter, the United States . . . [without] a valid passport." The Court expresses no views nor do I upon the validity or proper interpretation of this provision, which is currently involved in other litigation not now before us.

52, 60-61. Prior to 1856 the issuance of passports was not regulated by law. Governors of states, local mayors, and even notaries public issued documents which served as passports. This produced confusion abroad. . . . As is noted in an official history of the State Department, "The lack of legal provision on the subject [of passports] led to gross abuses, and 'the impositions practiced upon the illiterate and unwary by the fabrication of worthless passports' (IX Op. Atty. Genl. 350) led finally to the passage of the Act of August 18, 1856." *The Department of State of the United States: Its History and Functions*, 178 (1893). This act provided that "the Secretary of State shall be authorized to grant and issue passports, and cause passports to be granted, issued, and verified in foreign countries by such diplomatic or consular officers of the United States, and under such rules as the President shall designate and prescribe for and on behalf of the United States, and no other person shall grant, issue, or verify any such passports." 11 Stat. 60. That act made it a crime for a person to issue a passport who was not authorized to do so. This provision was re-enacted on July 3, 1926, 44 Stat. 887, in substantially identical form. There is no indication in the legislative history either at the time the act was originally passed in 1856 or when it was re-enacted, that it was meant to serve any purpose other than that of centralizing the authority to issue passports in the hands of the Secretary of State so as to eliminate abuses in their issuance. Thus, in my view, the authority to make rules, granted by the statute to the Executive, extends only to the promulgation of rules designed to carry out this statutory purpose. . . .

The administrative practice of the State Department prior to 1926 does not support the Court's view that when Congress re-enacted the 1856 provision in 1926 it intended to grant the Executive authority to impose area restrictions. Prior to the First World War the State Department had never limited the validity of passports for travel to any particular area. In fact, limitations upon travel had been imposed only twice. During the War of 1812 Congress specifically provided by statute that persons could not cross enemy lines without a passport, and in 1861 at the beginning of the Civil War the Secretary of State ruled that passports would not be issued to persons whose loyalty was in doubt. These restrictions were imposed in time of war. The first, restricting the area of travel, evidently was thought to require a specific statutory enactment by Congress, and the second did not limit the area of travel but, rather, limited the persons to whom passports would be issued.[6] Until fifty years ago peacetime limitations upon the right

[6] See *Kent* v. *Dulles, supra,* at 128, where the Court implies that regulation of travel based upon disloyalty to the country during wartime presents quite a different question from such regulation in time of peace.

of a citizen to travel were virtually unknown, see Chafee, *op. cit. supra*, at 193; Jaffe, "The Right to Travel: The Passport Problem," 35 *Foreign Affairs* 17, and it was in this atmosphere that the Act of 1856 was passed and its re-enactment prior to 1926 took place.

The only area restrictions imposed between 1856 and 1926 arose out of the First World War. Although Americans were not required by law to carry passports in 1915, certain foreign countries insisted that Americans have them. American consulates and embassies abroad were therefore authorized to issue *emergency* passports after the outbreak of the war, and in 1915 the Secretary of State telegraphed American ambassadors and ministers in France, Germany, Great Britain, Italy, the Netherlands and Denmark, "Do not issue emergency passports for use in Belgium [then occupied by German armed forces] unless applicants obliged to go thither by special exigency or authority by Red Cross or Belgian Relief Commission." See 3 Hackworth, *Digest of International Law*, 525-526 (1942). After the United States entered World War I travel to areas of belligerency and to enemy countries was restricted. Passports were marked not valid for travel to these areas, and Congress provided by statute that passports were necessary in order to leave or enter the United States. The Congressional Act requiring passports for travel expired in 1921, and soon after the official end of the war passports were marked valid for travel to all countries. See 3 Hackworth, *supra*, at 527; Hearings before the Senate Committee on Foreign Relations, on Department of State Passport Policies, 85th Cong., 1st Sess., 64 (hereafter Senate Hearings). Thus in 1926 freedom of travel was as complete as prior to World War I. In this atmosphere Congress re-enacted, in virtually identical terms, the 1856 statute, the sole purpose of which, as I have already noted, was to centralize passport issuance. Congress in doing so did not indicate the slightest intent or desire to enlarge the authority of the Executive to regulate the issuance of passports. Surely travel restrictions imposed while the United States was at war and a single telegram instructing ministers to deny emergency passports for a brief time in 1915 for travel to a theatre of war, do not show that Congress, by re-enacting the 1856 Act in 1926, intended to authorize the Executive to impose area restrictions upon travel in peacetime whenever the Executive believed such restrictions might advance American foreign policy. The long tradition of freedom of movement, the fact that no passport area restrictions existed prior to World War I, the complete absence of any indication in the legislative history that Congress intended to delegate such sweeping authority to the Executive all point in precisely the opposite direction. . . .

The Court's interpretation of the 1926 Passport Act not only overlooks the legislative history of the act and departs from the letter and spirit of this Court's decisions in *Kent* v. *Dulles, supra,* and *Aptheker* v. *Secretary of State, supra,* but it also implies that Congress resolved, through a sweeping grant of authority, the many substantial problems involved in curtailing a citizen's right to travel because of considerations of national policy. People travel abroad for numerous reasons of varying importance. Some travel for pleasure, others for business, still others for education. Foreign correspondents and lecturers must equip themselves with firsthand information. Scientists and scholars gain considerably from interchanges with colleagues in other nations. See Chafee, *op. cit. supra,* at 195.

Just as there are different reasons for people wanting to travel, so there are different reasons advanced by the government for its need to impose area restrictions. These reasons vary. The government says restrictions are imposed sometimes because of political differences with countries, sometimes because of unsettled conditions, and sometimes, as in this case, as part of a program, undertaken together with other nations, to isolate a hostile foreign country such as Cuba because of its attempts to promote the subversion of democratic nations. See Senate Hearings, 63-69. The Department of State also has imposed different types of travel restrictions in different circumstances. All newsmen, for example, were prohibited from traveling to China, see Senate Hearings, 67, but they have been allowed to visit Cuba. See Public Notice 179 (Jan. 16, 1961) 26 Fed. Reg. 492; Press Release No. 24, issued by the Secretary of State, Jan. 16, 1961. In view of the different types of need for travel restrictions, the various reasons for traveling abroad, the importance and constitutional underpinnings of the right to travel and the right of a citizen and a free press to gather information about foreign countries, it cannot be presumed that Congress, without focusing upon the complex problems involved, resolved them by adopting a broad and sweeping statute which, in the Court's view, confers unlimited discretion upon the Executive, and which makes no distinctions reconciling the rights of the citizen to travel with the government's legitimate needs. I do not know how Congress would deal with this complex area were it to focus on the problems involved, or whether, for example, in light of our commitment to freedom of the press, Congress would consent under any circumstances to prohibiting newsmen from traveling to foreign countries. But, faced with a complete absence of legislative consideration of these complex issues, I would not presume that Congress, in 1926, issued a blanket authorization to the Executive to impose area restrictions and define their scope and duration, for the nature of the problem seems plainly to call for a more discriminately fashioned statute. . . .

In my view it is clear that Congress did not mean the 1926 Act to authorize the Executive to impose area restrictions in time of peace, and, with all deference, I disagree with the Court's holding that it did. I agree with the

Court that Congress may authorize the imposition of travel restrictions consistent with constitutional guarantees, but I find it plain and evident that Congress has never considered and resolved the problem. After consideration Congress might determine that broad general authority should be delegated to the Secretary of State or it might frame a narrowed statute. I believe that here, as in other areas, appropriate delegation is constitutionally permissible where some standard for the application of delegated power is provided. See, e.g., *Lichter* v. *United States*, 334 U.S. 742, 785. However, in light of my conclusion that the 1926 Act did not deal with area restrictions I do not find it necessary to consider the question of whether the language of the 1926 Act might constitute an unconstitutionally broad delegation of power.

In view of the different types of need for area restrictions asserted by the government, the various reasons for travel abroad, the importance and constitutional underpinnings of the right of citizens and a free press to gather information about foreign countries—considerations which Congress did not focus upon—I would not infer, as the Court does, that Congress resolved the complex problem of area restrictions, which necessarily involves reconciling the rights of the citizen to travel with the government's legitimate needs, by the re-enactment of a statute that history shows was designed to centralize authority to issue passports in the Secretary of State so as to prevent abuses arising from their issuance by unauthorized persons. Since I conclude that the Executive does not possess inherent power to impose area restrictions in peacetime, and that Congress has not considered the issue and granted such authority to the Executive, I would reverse the judgment of the district court.

KENNEDY V. MENDOZA-MARTINEZ, 372 U.S. 144
RUSK V. CORT, 372 U.S. 144

[One of the first opinions Justice Goldberg wrote for the Court involved the delicate duty of considering the constitutionality of Congressional statutes. The acts of Congress involved divested an American of his citizenship for "departing from or remaining outside of the jurisdiction of the United States in time of war or . . . national emergency for the purpose of evading and avoiding training and service" in the nation's armed forces. In this case two great principles were brought into conflict; the right of an American citizen to retain his cherished citizenship and the countervailing right of the nation to self-preservation and enforcement of sanctions against those who refuse to answer the call to defend and protect the country. While recognizing the problem of the reconciliation of these conflicting principles, Justice Goldberg, writing for the Court, found that it was unnecessary to resolve it in those terms, for the statute involved was held to be constitutionally invalid on a separate ground. The divestiture of citizenship occurred under the statute without prior court or administrative findings of guilt. Since this citizenship forfeiture was penal in character, such divestiture constituted governmental punishment without due process of law and without the rights guaranteed all those accused of crimes by the Fifth and Sixth Amendments, rights including notice, confrontation, compulsory process for obtaining witnesses, trial by jury, and assistance of counsel.

We are called upon in these two cases[1] to decide the grave and fundamental problem, common to both, of the constitutionality of acts of Congress which divest an American of his citizenship, for "departing from or remaining outside of the jurisdiction of the United States in time of war or . . . national emergency for the purpose of evading or avoiding training and service" in the nation's armed forces.

Since the validity of an act of Congress is involved, we begin our analysis mindful that the function we are now discharging is "the gravest and most delicate duty that this Court is called upon to perform." *Blodgett* v. *Holden*, 275 U.S. 142, 148 (separate opinion of Holmes, J.). This responsibility we here fulfill with all respect for the powers of Congress, but with recognition of the transcendent status of our Constitution.

We deal with the contending constitutional arguments in the context of certain basic and sometimes conflicting principles. Citizenship is a most precious right. It is expressly guaranteed by the Fourteenth Amendment to the Constitution, which speaks in the most positive terms. The Constitution is silent about the permissibility of involuntary forfeiture of citizenship rights. While it confirms citizenship rights, plainly there are imperative obligations of citizenship, performance of which Congress in the exercise of its powers may constitutionally exact. One of the most important of these is to serve the country in time of war and national emergency. The powers of Congress to require military service for the common defense are broad and far-reaching, for while the Constitution protects against invasions of individual rights, it is not a suicide pact. Similarly, Congress has broad power under the Necessary and Proper Clause to enact legislation for the regulation of foreign affairs. Latitude in this area is necessary to ensure effectuation of this indispensable function of government.

[1] Dec. 4, 1962. Cases No. 2 and 3. Mr. Justice Goldberg delivered the opinion of the Court.

These principles, stemming, on the one hand, from the precious nature of the constitutionally guaranteed rights of citizenship and, on the other, from the power of Congress and the related obligations of individual citizens, are urged upon us by the parties here. The government argues that [these acts of Congress] are valid as an exercise of Congress' power over foreign affairs, of its war power, and of the inherent sovereignty of the government. Appellees urge the provisions' invalidity as not within any of the powers asserted, and as imposing a cruel and unusual punishment.

We recognize at the outset that we are confronted here with an issue of the utmost import. Deprivation of citizenship—particularly American citizenship, which is "one of the most valuable rights in the world today," Report of the President's Commission on Immigration and Naturalization (1953), 235—has grave practical consequences. An expatriate who, like Cort, had no other nationality becomes a stateless person—a person who not only has no rights as an American citizen but no membership in any national entity whatsoever. "Such individuals as do not possess any nationality enjoy, in general, no protection whatever, and if they are aggrieved by a state they have no means of redress, since there is no state which is competent to take up their case. As far as the Law of Nations is concerned, there is, apart from restraints of morality or obligations expressly laid down by treaty . . . no restriction whatever to cause a state to abstain from maltreating to any extent such stateless individuals." 1 Oppenheim, International Law (8th ed., Lauterpacht, 1955); § 291, at 640. The calamity is "not the loss of specific rights, then, but the loss of a community willing and able to guarantee any rights, whatsoever." Arendt, *The Origins of Totalitarianism* (1951), p. 294. The stateless person may end up shunted from nation to nation, there being no one obligated or willing to receive him, or, as in Cort's case, may receive the dubious sanctuary of a Communist regime lacking the essential liberties precious to American citizenship. . . .

We have come to the conclusion that there is a basic question in the present cases, the answer to which obviates a choice here between the powers of Congress and the constitutional guarantee of citizenship. That issue is whether the statutes here, which automatically—without prior court or administrative proceedings—forfeit citizenship, are essentially penal in character, and consequently have deprived the appellees of their citizenship without due process of law and without according them the rights guaranteed by the Fifth and Sixth Amendments, including notice, confrontation, compulsory process for obtaining witnesses, trial by jury, and assistance of counsel. . . .

It is fundamental that the great powers of Congress to conduct war and to regulate the nation's foreign relations are subject to the constitutional requirements of due process. The imperative necessity for safeguarding these rights to procedural due process under the gravest of emergencies has existed throughout our constitutional history, for it is then, under the pressing exigencies of crisis, that there is the greatest temptation to dispense with fundamental constitutional guarantees which, it is feared, will inhibit governmental action. "The Constitution of the United States is a law for rulers and people, equally in war and in peace, and covers with the shield of its protection all classes of men, at all times, and under all circumstances." *Ex parte Milligan*, 2 Wall. 2, 120-121. The rights guaranteed by the Fifth and Sixth Amendments are "preserved to every one accused of crime who is not attached to the army, or navy, or militia in actual service." *Id.*, at 123. "If society is disturbed by civil commotion—if the passions of men are aroused and the restraints of law weakened, if not disregarded—these safeguards need, and should receive the watchful care of those intrusted with the guardianship of the Constitution and laws. In no other way can we transmit to posterity unimpaired the blessings of liberty, consecrated by the sacrifices of the Revolution." *Id.*, at 124.

We hold [these acts] invalid because in them Congress has plainly employed the sanction of deprivation of nationality as a punishment—for the offense of leaving or remaining outside the country to evade military service —without affording the procedural safeguards guaranteed by the Fifth and Sixth Amendments. Our forefathers "intended to safeguard the people of this country from punishment without trial by duly constituted courts. . . . And even the courts to which this important function was entrusted were commanded to stay their hands until and unless certain tested safeguards were observed. An accused in court must be tried by an impartial jury, has a right to be represented by counsel, [and] must be clearly informed of the charge against him." . . . *United States* v. *Lovett*, 328 U.S. 303, 317. See also *Chambers* v. *Florida*, 309 U.S. 227, 235-238.

As the government concedes . . . the statutes automatically strip an American of his citizenship, with concomitant deprivation "of all that makes life worth living," *Ng Fung Ho* v. *White*, 259 U.S. 276, 284-285, whenever a citizen departs from or remains outside the jurisdiction of this country for the purpose of evading his military obligations. Conviction for draft evasion . . . is not prerequisite to the operation of this sanction. Independently of prosecution, forfeiture of citizenship attaches when the statutory set of facts develops. It is argued that the availability after the fact of administrative and judicial proceedings . . . to contest the validity of the sanction meets the measure of due process. But the legislative history and judicial expression with respect to every Congressional enactment relating to the provisions in question dating back to 1865 establish that forfeiture of citizenship is a penalty for the act of leaving or staying outside the country to avoid the draft. This being so, the Fifth and Sixth Amendments mandate that this punishment cannot be imposed without a prior criminal trial and all its incidents, including indictment, notice, confrontation, jury trial, assistance of counsel, and compulsory process for obtaining witnesses. If the sanction these sections impose is punishment, and it plainly is, the procedural safeguards required as incidents of a criminal prosecution are lacking. We need go no further. . . .

It is argued that our holding today will have the unfortunate result of immunizing the draft evader who has left the United States from having to suffer any sanction against his conduct, since he must return to this country before he can be apprehended and tried for his crime. The compelling answer to this is that the Bill of Rights which we guard so jealously and the procedures it guarantees are not to be abrogated merely because a guilty man may escape prosecution or for any other expedient reason. Moreover, the truth is that even without being expatriated, the evader living abroad is not in a position to assert the vast majority of his component rights as an American citizen. If he wishes to assert those rights in any real sense he must return to this country, and by doing that he will subject himself to prosecution. In fact, while he is outside the country evading prosecution, the United States may, by proper refusal to exercise its largely discretionary power to afford him diplomatic protection, decline to invoke its sovereign power on his behalf. Since the substantial benefits of American citizenship only come into play upon return to face prosecution, the draft evader who wishes to exercise his citizenship rights will inevitably come home and pay his debt, which within constitutional limits Congress has the power to define. This is what Mendoza-Martinez did, what Cort says he is willing to do, and what others have done. Thus our holding today does not frustrate the effective handling of the problem of draft evaders who leave the United States.

We conclude, for the reasons stated, that [these acts] are punitive and as such cannot constitutionally stand, lacking as they do the procedural safeguards which the Constitution commands. We recognize that draft evasion, particularly in time of war, is a heinous offense and should and can be properly punished. Dating back to Magna Charta, however, it has been an abiding principle governing the lives of civilized men that "no freeman shall be taken or imprisoned or disseised or outlawed or exiled . . . without the judgment of his peers or by the law of the land." What we hold is only that, in keeping with this cherished tradition, punishment cannot be imposed "without due process of law." Any lesser holding would ignore the constitutional mandate upon which our essential liberties depend.

UNITED STATES v. BARNETT, 376 U.S. 681

[After a lengthy legal battle, in 1962, a United States Court of Appeals ordered the previously all-white University of Mississippi to admit James Meredith, a Negro. The Court of Appeals also specifically ordered the state officials not to interfere with Meredith's admission. Despite these orders, an extensive state campaign of resistance was entered into which required President Kennedy to order a force of United States marshals and a detachment of the armed forces to enforce the court's orders. Compliance with the orders was achieved only after mass rioting had broken out and casualties had resulted. The Court of Appeals then ordered the United States government to commence criminal contempt proceedings against Ross R. Barnett, Governor of Mississippi at the time, and Paul B. Johnson, then Lieutenant Governor. Barnett and Johnson demanded a jury trial on the issue of their contempt. The Court of Appeals was evenly divided on the point of whether or not they were entitled to a jury trial on this issue, and certified this question to the Supreme Court. Justice Clark wrote the opinion for the majority of the Court in which he concluded that Barnett and Johnson had no statutory right to a jury trial on this criminal contempt charge and that the Sixth Amendment's guarantee of a trial by jury in all criminal cases does not apply to cases of criminal contempt. Justice Goldberg, however, in a dissent in which the Chief Justice and Justice Douglas joined, concluded that Barnett and Johnson were statutorily entitled to a jury trial and, more importantly, were constitutionally entitled to a jury trial pursuant to the Sixth Amendment. Justice Goldberg concluded that history demonstrated that only petty criminal contempts are, like other petty criminal offenses, not included in the Sixth Amendment's guarantee to the accused of trial by jury. It seemed quite clear that the contempt alleged in this case was serious and not petty and thus Barnett and Johnson were entitled to a jury trial on the determination of their guilt. Justice Goldberg reached this conclusion despite the government's argument that convictions (for criminal contempt) could not be obtained if jury trials—with juries necessarily composed of local residents—were required. As he stated, if this is true, it "is the price we have chosen to pay for our cherished liberties." "The Constitution of the United States is a law for rulers and people, equally in war and in peace, and covers with the shield of its protection all classes of men, at all times, and under all circumstances." Although written as a dissent, it is interesting to note that Justice Goldberg's views seem to have been shared, at least in part, by some members of the majority. A footnote in the opinion of the Court states: "Some members of the Court [majority] are of the view that . . . punishment without a jury would be constitutionally limited to that penalty provided for petty offenses."]

The Court,[1] in denying defendants' constitutional claim to a jury trial, rests on the history of criminal contempts relied on in its past decisions. The most recent of those decisions is *Green v. United States*, 356 U.S. 165, which was decided by a closely divided Court. The Court said:

The principle that criminal contempts of Court are not required to be tried by a jury under Article III or the Sixth Amendment is firmly rooted in our traditions. *Id.*, at 187.

Against this historical background [of the power to punish criminal contempts summarily at the time of the Constitution], this Court has never deviated from the view that the constitutional guarantee of trial by jury for "crimes" and "criminal prosecutions" was not intended to reach to criminal contempts. *Id.*, at 186.

A review of the original sources convinces me, however, that the history relied on by the decisions of this Court does not justify the relatively recent practice of imposing *serious* punishment for criminal contempts without a trial by jury. My research, which is confirmed by the authorities cited in the Appendix to the opinion of the Court, suggests the following explanation as to why criminal contempts were generally tried without a jury at the time of the Constitution: the penalties then authorized and imposed for criminal contempts were generally minor; and the courts were authorized to impose minor criminal penalties without a trial by jury for a variety of trivial offenses including, but not limited to, criminal contempts. . . .

In 1821 this Court recognized that there were "known and acknowledged limits of fine and imprisonment" for criminal contempt. *Anderson v. Dunn*, 6 Wheat. 204, 228. What these limits were at about the time of the Constitution can best be derived from the contemporary statutory and case law.

When the Bill of Rights was ratified, at least five of the original thirteen states had specific statutory limitations on the punishment which could be imposed summarily for criminal contempts. The Connecticut statute permitting summary punishment for certain types of contempts contained a proviso "that no single minister of justice shall inflict any other punishment [for criminal contempt] than . . . putting them in the stocks, there to set not exceeding two hours; or imposing a fine, not exceeding *five dollars*." (Emphasis in original.) The Delaware statute permitted a contemner to "be

[1] April 6, 1964. Case No. 107. Mr. Justice Goldberg, whom the Chief Justice and Mr. Justice Douglas join, dissenting.

fined in any sum not exceeding Five Pounds"; it did not permit imprisonment for criminal contempt. The Maryland statute permitted the court to hold the contemner "in close custody until the said process, rule or order, shall be fully performed" (civil contempt), but it permitted no punishment "exceeding ten pounds current money." The New Hampshire provision permitted imprisonment for contempt not exceeding 10 days and a fine "not to exceed ten pounds." The South Carolina statute permitted a fine not exceeding 10 pounds for any contempt "by word or gesture," and a fine "at the discretion of the said court, for anyone who shall "strike or use any violence in the said courts"; it did not permit imprisonment.

Within a short time after the ratification of the Bill of Rights other states enacted statutes containing specific limitations on the punishments which could be imposed summarily for criminal contempts. These statutes, which appear to be codification of existing practices and court decisions rather than newly created legislative limitations, shed additional light on the practice at about the time of the Constitution.

The New Jersey statute permitted a contemner to be punished by a fine "not exceeding fifty dollars." The Kentucky statute specified that "no court or judge shall, for any contempt against such court or judge, pass judgment for, decree, order or inflict, or cause to be inflicted any fine exceeding the sum of 10 pounds, nor any imprisonment exceeding one day, *without the trial by jury to assess the quantity of such fine, and determine the duration of such imprisonment.*" The Pennsylvania statute permitted an unspecified fine and if the contemner "shall be unable to pay such fine, such person may be committed to prison by the court for any time not exceeding three months." The New York statute permitted a maximum fine of $250 and imprisonment for 30 days in summary proceedings for criminal contempts.[2]

The Alabama criminal contempt statute declared that

whereas, the trial by jury in all penal, as well as criminal cases, is both a safe and adequate mode of investigation and decision, and should only be suspended in cases of absolute necessity. *Be it enacted,* that no court shall, for any contempt against such court . . . inflict . . . any fine exceeding the sum of twenty dollars, nor any imprisonment exceeding twenty-four hours, without the trial by jury, to assess the amount of such fine, and determine the duration of such imprisonment.

The Virginia statute was quite detailed. It contained the following proviso:

That no court shall, without the intervention of a jury, for any such contempt of misbehavior in the presence of the court, or so near thereto as to obstruct or interrupt the administration of justice therein, impose any fine on any person or persons, exceeding fifty dollars, or commit him, her or them, for a longer period

----

[2] N.Y. Rev. Stats. (1829) 276, 278. More extensive punishment was permitted upon indictment and trial by jury.

than ten days: *And provided*, That in any case of aggravated contempt . . . the court may impannel a jury, without any indictment, information or pleadings, in a summary manner, to ascertain the amount of fine or term of imprisonment, proper to be inflicted for such offense, and may impose the fine or imprisonment ascertained by the jury in manner aforesaid.

The laws of other states similarly limited the maximum penalties which could be imposed summarily for criminal contempts.

The available evidence of the practice in criminal contempt cases also suggests that punishments were trivial. This practice was described by Chief Justice Kent in 1809 as follows: "There is no such thing as an abuse of this power in modern times. The case probably is not to be found. An alarm cannot be excited at its existence, in the extent now laid down. . . . The tendency of the times, is rather to induce the courts to relax, than increase in the severity of their ancient discipline, to exercise their power over contempts with extreme moderation." *In the case of John V. N. Yates*, 4 Johnson's Rep. (N.Y. 1809) 317, 375-376. And, in 1916, the Supreme Court of Iowa summarized a century and a quarter of practice in criminal contempt cases in the following terms:

The authorities may be searched in vain for any precedent, under our constitutional form of government, holding it to be in the power of a state to clothe its courts with authority to visit infamous punishment upon any person for contempt or in any proceeding whatever, other than the orderly process of trial. *Flannagan* v. *Jepson*, 177 Iowa 393, 400, 158 N.W. 641, 643-644.

This Court has recognized that

At the time of the adoption of the Constitution there were numerous offenses, commonly described as "petty," which were tried summarily without a jury, by justices of the peace in England, and by police magistrates or corresponding judicial officers in the Colonies, and punished by commitment to jail, a workhouse, or a house of correction.—*District of Columbia* v. *Clawans*, 300 U.S. 617, 624.

New Jersey statutes, for example, permitted trial by a judge for offenses such as "profanely swearing" (punishable by a fine of "one half of a dollar," four hours in the stocks, or four days in the "common gaol"); "excessive use of spirituous, vinous, or other strong liquor" (fine of one dollar, four hours in the stocks, or four days in "gaol");[3] and disorderly conduct (three months in the workhouse).[4] In New York trial by jury was not required for offenses such as unlicensed practice by a physician (fine of five pounds);[5] offering copper coins of known inferior quality or weight (fine of six pounds or five times the value of coins, whichever is less);[6] "drunkenness or swearing" (fine of three shillings or four hours in the stocks);[7] and false pretenses

---

[3] Elmer's Digest of N.J. Law (1838), Act of Mar. 16, 1798, §§ 8-11, pp. 588, 589.
[4] Paterson's Laws of N.J. (1800) 410. See also *id.*, at 329, 333.
[5] 4 Colonial Laws of N.Y. (1760) 455.
[6] 1787 Laws (N.Y.), c. 97.
[7] 1 Colonial Laws of N.Y. (1708) 617.

(imprisonment for six months).[8] Maryland statutes permitted trial by a judge for offenses such as refusal by the mother of a bastard child to "discover" the father (fine of 30 shillings),[9] and disorderly conduct (three months in the workhouse).[10] Virginia permitted summary punishment for offenses ranging from improper issuing of notes (fine of 25 shillings)[11] to disorderly conduct (20 lashes and three months' imprisonment).[12]

This history has led the Court to conclude that "the intent [of the framers] was to exclude from the constitutional requirement of a jury the trial of petty criminal offenses." *Schick* v. *United States*, 195 U. S. 65, 70. It has similarly led the Court to conclude that "except in that class or grade of offenses called petty offenses . . . the guarantee of an impartial jury to the accused in a criminal prosecution . . . secures to him the right to enjoy that mode of trial from the first moment, and in whatever court, he is put on trial for the offense charged," *Callan* v. *Wilson*, 127 U. S. 540, 557, and that "the severity of the penalty" must be considered in determining whether a violation of law, "in other respects trivial and not a crime at common law, must be deemed so serious as to be comparable with common law crimes, and thus to entitle the accused to the benefit of a jury trial prescribed by the Constitution." *District of Columbia* v. *Clawans*, 300 U. S. 617, 625. . . .

There has been a dramatic increase in recent years in the severity of the punishment imposed in the federal courts without trial by jury for criminal contempt. For example, in *Green* v. *United States, supra,* and *Collins* v. *United States*, 269 F. 2d 745, sentences of imprisonment for three years were imposed; in *Piemonte* v. *United States*, 367 U.S. 556, a sentence of imprisonment for 18 months was imposed; in *Brown* v. *United States*, 359 U. S. 41, a sentence of imprisonment for 15 months was imposed; in *Nilva* v. *United States*, 352 U. S. 385, a sentence of imprisonment for one year and one day was imposed; and in *Levine* v. *United States*, 362 U. S. 610, a sentence of imprisonment for one year was imposed. . . .

The available evidence seems to indicate that (*a*) at the time of the Constitution criminal contempts triable without a jury were generally punishable by trivial penalties, and that (*b*) at the time of the Constitution all types of "petty" offenses punishable by trivial penalties were generally triable without a jury. This history justifies the imposition without trial by jury of no more than trivial penalties for criminal contempts. The Court, in light of the history reviewed here and in the Appendix to the opinion of the Court, has failed sufficiently to take into account the possibility that one significant

[8] 1785 Laws (N.Y.), cc. 40, 47, 31.
[9] 1752 Md. Sess. Laws 5.
[10] 1785 Md. Sess. Laws, c. 15, § 15.
[11] Act of Oct. 1777, c. 24, § 2.
[12] 1785 Va. Stats. (Oct. Sess.), c. 1, § 8; c. 4, § 3; c. 59; 1787 Va. Stats. (Oct. Sess), c. 48, § 13.

reason why criminal contempts were tried without a jury at the time of the Constitution was because they were deemed a species of petty offense punishable by trivial penalties. Since criminal contempts, as they are now punished, can no longer be deemed a species of petty offense punishable by trivial penalties, defendants' constitutional claim to trial by jury should not be denied on the authority of the history of criminal contempt at the time of the Constitution nor on the authority of the past decisions of this Court which relied on that history. Their claim should be evaluated by analyzing the real nature of criminal contempts and applying the policy of the constitutional requirement of trial by jury in "all crimes" and "all criminal prosecutions." . . .

I wish to make it clear that I am not here concerned with, nor do I question, the power of the courts to compel compliance with their lawful orders by the imposition of conditional punishment—commonly referred to as civil contempt. In such cases it may be said that "the defendant carries the keys to freedom in his willingness to comply with the court's directive." Nor am I here concerned with the imposition of the trivial punishments traditionally deemed sufficient for maintaining order in the courtroom. . . . I am concerned solely with the imposition, without trial by jury, of fixed nontrivial punishments *after* compliance with the court's order has been secured.

Thus limited, criminal contempts are not essentially different from other "crimes" or "criminal prosecutions." In each case punishment is imposed for a past violation of a mandate of a coordinate organ of government: criminal contempt involves punishment for violation of an order of a court; "crime" involves punishment for violation of a statute enacted by a legislature. I can see no greater need for certain and prompt punishment of the former than of the latter.

It may be true that a judge can dispose of a charge of criminal contempt, or any other criminal charge, more expeditiously and more cheaply than a jury.

But such trifling economies as may result have not generally been thought sufficient reason for abandoning our great constitutional safeguards aimed at protecting freedom and other basic human rights of incalculable value. Cheap, easy convictions were not the primary concern of those who adopted the Constitution and the Bill of Rights. Every procedural safeguard they established purposely made it more difficult for the government to convict those it accused of crimes. On their scale of values justice occupied at least as high a position as economy.—*Green* v. *United States, supra,* at 216.

Nor are criminal contempts substantially different from other crimes when measured by the "tests traditionally applied to determine whether [a given sanction] is penal or regulatory in character." . . . *Kennedy* v. *Mendoza-*

Martinez, 372 U. S. 144, 168. In the *Mendoza-Martinez* case, the tests were enumerated in the following terms:

Whether the sanction involves an affirmative disability or restraint, whether it has historically been regarded as a punishment, whether it comes into play only on a finding of *scienter*, whether its operation will promote the traditional aims of punishment—retribution and deterrence—whether the behavior to which it applies is already a crime, whether an alternative purpose to which it may rationally be connected is assignable for it, and whether it appears excessive in relation to the alternative purpose assigned. *Id.,* at 168–169.

Criminal contempt, when punished by a nontrivial penalty, certainly "involves an affirmative disability or restraint" under any reasonable definition of these terms. The sanction imposed for criminal contempt has always been "regarded as a punishment" designed to deter future defiances of the court's authority and to vindicate its dignity. No "alternative purpose" has been suggested to justify its existence. *Scienter* is generally required to support a charge of criminal contempt. And the behavior to which a charge of criminal contempt applies is generally "already a crime."

In my view, therefore, there is no justification, either in the history or policy of criminal contempt or in the history or policy of the Constitution, for treating criminal contempt differently from other "crimes" or "criminal prosecutions." If a criminal contempt (or any other violation of law) is punishable only by a trivial penalty, then the Constitution does not require trial by jury. If a violation of law is punishable by a nontrivial penalty, then the Constitution does require trial by jury whether the violation is labeled criminal contempt or anything else. . . .

It remains only to apply this conclusion to the facts here. Although the certified question does not specify the severity of the punishment which could be imposed upon the defendants if the allegations against them are proved, it would defy reality to assume that the contempt with which they are charged is a "trivial" one punishable by a minor penalty. The Solicitor General of the United States described the nature of the contempt to this Court in oral argument in the following words:

The Governor and Lieutenant Governor of a state sought to array the whole panoply of the state against a final adjudication by the federal courts. The contempt with which they are charged was rioting, loss of life, and the need for federal troops to uphold the law of the land.

One judge in the Court of Appeals said: "Never before has such a charge been brought by or in a Court of Appeals . . . against either a state officer or a private citizen." The certified question indicates that "the acts charged as constituting the alleged disobedience were of a character as to constitute also a criminal offense," punishable by imprisonment for a year. 18 U. S. C. § 1509. Another judge in the Court of Appeals said that "Respondents are charged with what amounts to a crime." These indicia, taken together with the severity of the sanction imposed in the civil contempt case which grew out of the same conduct, compel the conclusion that the contempt here charged was not "trivial." It was extraordinarily serious, among the most serious in this nation's history. If Green's contempt—jumping bail—was punishable by imprisonment for three years, and if Piemonte's contempt— refusal to answer a question before a grand jury—was punishable by imprisonment for a year and a half, it would be wholly unrealistic for us to assume that under the standards of punishment sanctioned by this Court in the past the present contempt may be characterized as a petty offense punishable by no more than a trivial penalty. For these reasons, I would answer the certified question in the affirmative and remand the case to the district court so that the accused may be tried by a jury and receive at a trial all the safeguards which our Constitution affords a criminal defendant.

In sum, therefore, I conclude that defendants' trial should be by a jury. This would accord . . . with the fundamental policy of the Constitution, that contempts which are punishable as crimes must be tried by a jury.

I reject the government's "necessity" argument, that "the independence of the federal courts . . . would be seriously undermined if their orders could be nullified by an unsympathetic jury." That is but another way of putting the oft-rejected assertion against trial by jury, that some guilty men may be acquitted. This possibility, however, is the price we have chosen to pay for our cherished liberties. "The imperative necessity for safeguarding these rights . . . under the gravest of emergencies has existed throughout our constitutional history, for it is then, under the pressing exigencies of crisis, that there is the greatest temptation to dispense with fundamental constitutional guarantees which, it is feared, will inhibit governmental action." *Kennedy* v. *Mendoza-Martinez,* 372 U.S., at 165. "The Constitution of the United States is a law for rulers and people, equally in war and in peace, and covers with the shield of its protection all classes of men, at all times, and under all circumstances." *Ex parte Milligan,* 4 Wall. 2, 120-121.

Escobedo v. Illinois, 378 U.S. 478

[Danny Escobedo was arrested for the murder of his brother. He was brought to the police station and interrogated extensively while being denied permission to see his attorney who was at the police station in an attempt to see him. There was testimony by the police that during the intensive questioning, Escobedo, a 22-year-old of Mexican extraction with no record of previous experience with the police, "was handcuffed" in a standing position and that he "was nervous, he had circles under his eyes and he was upset" and was "agitated" because "he had not slept well in over a week." At no time during this interrogation was Escobedo warned that what he said might be used against him and that he had a constitutional right to remain silent. He finally made several incriminating statements which were taken down by an assistant state's attorney. These incriminating statements were used, over his objections, against Escobedo at trial. Just a month prior to the decision in the *Escobedo* case, the Court had decided the case of *Massiah* v. *United States*, 377 U.S. 201, in which it had been held that incriminating statements made by an accused could not be used against him at trial where, after he had been indicted and released on bail, government agents elicited the statements from him in the absence of his attorney. Justice Goldberg, writing for the Court, relied upon *Massiah* in concluding that under all the circumstances of this case Escobedo was denied his constitutional right to the assistance of counsel when the police refused to permit him to consult with his counsel during the interrogation and thus his incriminating statements could not be used against him at trial. Justices Clark, Harlan, Stewart and White dissented.]

The critical question in this case[1] is whether, under the circumstances, the refusal by the police to honor petitioner's request to consult with his lawyer during the course of an interrogation constitutes a denial of "the assistance of counsel" in violation of the Sixth Amendment to the Constitution as "made obligatory upon the states by the Fourteenth Amendment," *Gideon* v. *Wainwright*, 372 U.S. 335, 342, and thereby renders inadmissible in a state criminal trial any incriminating statement elicited by the police during the interrogation. . . .

In *Massiah* v. *United States*, 377 U.S. 201, this Court observed that "a Constitution which guarantees a defendant the aid of counsel at . . . trial could surely vouchsafe no less to an indicted defendant under interrogation by the police in a completely extrajudicial proceeding. Anything less . . . might deny a defendant 'effective representation by counsel at the only stage when legal aid and advice would help him.' " *Id.*, at 204, quoting Justice Douglas, concurring in *Spano* v. *United States*, 360 U.S. 315, 326.

The interrogation here was conducted before petitioner was formally indicted. But in the context of this case, that fact should make no difference. When petitioner requested, and was denied, an opportunity to consult with

[1] June 22, 1964. Case No. 615. Mr. Justice Goldberg delivered the opinion of the Court.

his lawyer, the investigation had ceased to be a general investigation of "an unsolved crime." *Spano* v. *New York*, 360 U.S. 315, 327 (Justice Stewart concurring). Petitioner had become the accused, and the purpose of the interrogation was to "get him" to confess his guilt despite his constitutional right not to do so. At the time of his arrest and throughout the course of the interrogation, the police told petitioner that they had convincing evidence that he had fired the fatal shots. Without informing him of his absolute right to remain silent in the face of this accusation, the police urged him to make a statement. As this Court observed many years ago:

It cannot be doubted that, placed in the position in which the accused was when the statement was made to him that the other suspected person had charged him with a crime, the result was to produce upon his mind that fear that if he remained silent it would be considered an admission of guilt, and therefore render certain his being committed for trial as the guilty person, and it cannot be conceived that the converse impression would not also have naturally arisen, that by denying there was hope of removing the suspicion from himself. *Bram* v. *United States*, 168 U.S. 532, 562.

Petitioner, a layman, was undoubtedly unaware that under Illinois law an admission of "mere" complicity in the murder plot was legally as damaging as an admission of firing of the fatal shots. *Escobedo* v. *Illinois*, 28 Ill. 2d 41, 190 N.E. 2d 825. The "guiding hand of counsel" was essential to advise petitioner of his rights in this delicate situation. *Powell* v. *Alabama*, 287 U.S. 45, 69. This was the "stage when legal aid and advice" were most critical to petitioner. *Massiah* v. *United States, supra,* at 204. It was a stage surely as critical as was the arraignment in *Hamilton* v. *Alabama*, 368 U.S. 52, and the preliminary hearing in *White* v. *Maryland*, 373 U.S. 59. What happened at this interrogation could certainly "affect the whole trial," *Hamilton* v. *Alabama, supra,* at 54, since rights "may be as irretrievably lost, if not then and there asserted, as they are when an accused represented by counsel waives a right for strategic purposes." *Ibid*. It would exalt form over substance to make the right to counsel, under these circumstances, depend on whether at the time of the interrogation the authorities had secured a formal indictment. Petitioner had, for all practical purposes, already been charged with murder.

The New York Court of Appeals, whose decisions this Court cited with approval in *Massiah*, 377 U.S. 201, at 205, has recently recognized that, under circumstances such as those here, no meaningful distinction can be drawn between interrogation of an accused before and after formal indictment. In *People* v. *Donovan*, 13 N.Y. 2d 148, 193 N.E. 2d 628, that court, in an opinion by Judge Fuld, held that a "confession taken from a defendant, during a period of detention [prior to indictment], after his attorney had requested and been denied access to him" could not be used against him in a criminal trial. *Id.,* at 151, 193 N.E. 2d, at 629. The court observed that it "would be highly incongruous if our system of justice permitted the district attorney, the lawyer representing the state, to extract a confession from the accused while his own lawyer, seeking to speak with him, was kept from him by the police." *Id.*, at 152, 193 N.E. 2d, at 629.

In *Gideon* v. *Wainwright*, 372 U.S. 335, we held that every person accused of a crime, whether state or federal, is entitled to a lawyer at trial. The rule sought by the state here, however, would make the trial no more than an appeal from the interrogation; and the "right to use counsel at the formal trial [would be] a very hollow thing [if], for all practical purposes, the conviction is already assured by pretrial examination." *In re Groban*, 352 U.S. 330, 344 (Justice Black dissenting). "One can imagine a cynical prose-cutor saying: 'Let them have the most illustrious counsel, now. They can't escape the noose. There is nothing that counsel can do for them at the trial.' " *Ex parte Sullivan*, 107 F. Supp. 514, 517-518.

It is argued that if the right to counsel is afforded prior to indictment, the number of confessions obtained by the police will diminish significantly, because most confessions are obtained during the period between arrest and indictment, and "any lawyer worth his salt will tell the suspect in no un-certain terms to make no statement to police under any circumstances." *Watts* v. *Indiana*, 338 U.S. 49, 59 (Justice Jackson concurring in part and dissenting in part). This argument, of course, cuts two ways. The fact that many confessions are obtained during this period points up its critical nature as a "stage when legal aid and advice" are surely needed. *Massiah* v. *United States, supra,* at 204; *Hamilton* v. *Alabama, supra; White* v. *Maryland, supra.* The right to counsel would indeed be hollow if it began at a period when few confessions were obtained. There is necessarily a direct relationship between the importance of a stage to the police in their quest for a confession and the criticalness of that stage to the accused in his need for legal advice. Our Constitution, unlike some others, strikes the balance in favor of the right of the accused to be advised by his lawyer of his privilege against self-incrimination.

We have learned the lesson of history, ancient and modern, that a system of criminal law enforcement which comes to depend on the "confession" will, in the long run, be less reliable and more subject to abuses than a system which depends on extrinsic evidence independently secured through skillful investigation. . . .

This Court also has recognized that "history amply shows that confessions have often been extorted to save law-enforcement officials the trouble and effort of obtaining valid and independent evidence." *Haynes* v. *Washington,* 373 U.S. 503, 519.

We have also learned the companion lesson of history that no system of criminal justice can, or should, survive if it comes to depend for its continued effectiveness on the citizens' abdication through unawareness of their constitutional rights. No system worth preserving should have to *fear* that, if an accused is permitted to consult with a lawyer, he will become aware of, and exercise, these rights. If the exercise of constitutional rights will thwart the effectiveness of a system of law enforcement, then there is something very wrong with that system.

We hold, therefore, that where, as here, the investigation is no longer a general inquiry into an unsolved crime but has begun to focus on a particular suspect, the suspect has been taken into police custody, the police carry out a process of interrogations that lends itself to eliciting incriminating statements, the suspect has requested and been denied an opportunity to consult with his lawyer, and the police have not effectively warned him of his absolute constitutional right to remain silent, the accused has been denied "the assistance of counsel" in violation of the Sixth Amendment to the Constitution as "made obligatory upon the states by the Fourteenth Amendment," *Gideon* v. *Wainwright*, 372 U.S., at 342, and that no statement elicited by the police during the interrogation may be used against him at a criminal trial. . . .

Nothing we have said today affects the powers of the police to investigate "an unsolved crime," *Spano* v. *New York*, 360 U.S. 315, 327 (Justice Stewart concurring), by gathering information from witnesses and by other "proper investigative efforts." *Haynes* v. *Washington*, 373 U.S. 503, 519. We hold only that when the process shifts from investigatory to accusatory—when its focus is on the accused and its purpose is to elicit a confession—our adversary system begins to operate, and, under the circumstances here, the accused must be permitted to consult with his lawyer.

AGUILAR V. TEXAS, 378 U.S. 108

[The Supreme Court has held that it is unconstitutional for state courts to admit in evidence in criminal convictions evidence seized by government officials in violation of the Fourth Amendment, which provides: "The right of the people to be secure in their persons, houses, papers and effects, against unreasonable searches and seizures, shall not be violated, and no warrants shall issue, but upon probable cause, supported by oath or affirmation, and particularly describing the place to be searched, and the persons or things to be seized." In this and the following two cases Justice Goldberg was faced with the problem of determining whether a warrant issued for a search or arrest was based on probable cause as the Constitution requires. In *Aguilar*, the application for a warrant merely stated that the police had "received reliable information from a credible person and do believe" that narcotics were kept at a certain place in violation of the law. Writing for the Court, Justice Goldberg recognized that it is the purpose of the Fourth Amendment to encourage police to get a warrant from a magistrate. Courts will therefore sustain a magistrate's determination of probable cause when there is a substantial basis for the magistrate to conclude that probable cause existed. This was not true in this case, however, as all the magistrate had before him was the mere statement that an unidentified informant had concluded that a crime had been committed. The constitutional standard of probable cause here required that the magistrate have been informed of some of the underlying circumstances from which the informant concluded that the narcotics were where he said they were and some of the underlying circumstances from which the police concluded that the unnamed informant was reliable.]

Two Houston police officers[1] applied to a local justice of the peace for a warrant to search for narcotics in petitioner's home. In support of their application, the officers submitted an affidavit which, in relevant part, recited that:

"Affiants have received reliable information from a credible person and do believe that heroin, marijuana, barbiturates, and other narcotics and narcotic paraphernalia are being kept at the above described premises for the purpose of sale and use contrary to the provisions of the law."

The search warrant was issued.

In executing the warrant, the local police, along with federal officers, announced at petitioner's door that they were police with a warrant. Upon hearing a commotion within the house, the officers forced their way into the house and seized petitioner in the act of attempting to dispose of a packet of narcotics.

At his trial in the state court, petitioner, through his attorney, objected to the introduction of evidence obtained as a result of the execution of the warrant. The objections were overruled and the evidence admitted. Petitioner was convicted of illegal possession of heroin and sentenced to serve 20 years in the state penitentiary. . . .

An evaluation of the constitutionality of a search warrant should begin with the rule that "the informed and deliberate determinations of magistrates empowered to issue warrants . . . are to be preferred over the hurried action of officers . . . who may happen to make arrests." *United States* v. *Lefkowitz*, 285 U. S. 452-464. The reasons for this rule go to the foundations of the

[1] June 15, 1964. Case No. 548. Mr. Justice Goldberg delivered the opinion of the Court.

Fourth Amendment. A contrary rule "that evidence sufficient to support a magistrate's disinterested determination to issue a search warrant will justify the officers in making a search without a warrant would reduce the Amendment to a nullity and leave the people's homes secure only in the discretion of police officers." *Johnson* v. *United States*, 333 U. S. 10, 14. Under such a rule "resort to [warrants] would ultimately be discouraged." *Jones* v. *United States*, 362 U.S. 257, 270. Thus, when a search is based upon a magistrate's, rather than a police officer's, determination of probable cause, the reviewing courts will accept evidence of a less "judicially competent or persuasive character than would have justified an officer in acting on his own without a warrant," *ibid.*, and will sustain the judicial determination so long as "there was substantial basis for [the magistrate] to conclude that the narcotics were probably present." *Id.*, at 271.

Although the reviewing court will pay substantial deference to judicial determinations of probable cause, the court must still insist that the magistrate perform his "neutral and detached" function and not serve merely as a rubber stamp for the police.

In *Nathanson* v. *United States*, 290 U. S. 41, a warrant was issued upon the sworn allegation that the affiant "has cause to suspect and does believe" that certain merchandise was in a specified location. *Id.*, at 44. The Court, noting that the affidavit "went upon a mere affirmation of suspicion and belief *without any statement of adequate supporting facts,*" *id.*, at 46 (emphasis added), announced the following rule:

> "Under the Fourth Amendment, an officer may not properly issue a warrant to search a private dwelling unless he can find probable cause therefor from *facts or circumstances* presented to him under oath or affirmation. Mere affirmance of belief or suspicion is not enough." *Id.*, at 47. [Emphasis added.]

The Court, in *Giordenello* v. *United States*, 357 U. S. 480, applied this rule to an affidavit similar to that relied upon here. Affiant, in that case, swore that petitioner "did receive, conceal, etc., narcotic drugs . . . with knowledge of unlawful importation." *Id.*, at 481.

The vice in the present affidavit is at least as great as in *Nathanson* and *Giordenello*. Here the "mere conclusion" that petitioner possessed narcotics was not even that of the affiant himself; it was that of an unidentified informant. The affidavit here not only "contains no affirmative allegation that the affiant spoke with personal knowledge of the matters contained therein," it does not even contain an "affirmative allegation" that the affiant's unidentified source "spoke with personal knowledge." For all that appears, the source here merely suspected, believed or concluded that there were narcotics in petitioner's possession. The magistrate here certainly could not "judge for himself the persuasiveness of the facts relied on . . . to show probable cause."

He necessarily accepted "without question" the informant's "suspicion," "belief" or "mere conclusion."

Although an affidavit may be based on hearsay information and need not reflect the direct personal observations of the affiant, *Jones* v. *United States*, 362 U. S. 257, the magistrate must be informed of some of the underlying circumstances from which the informant concluded that the narcotics were where he claimed they were, and some of the underlying circumstances from which the officer concluded that the informant, whose identity need not be disclosed, see *Rugendorf* v. *United States*, 376 U. S. 528, was "credible" or his information "reliable." Otherwise, "the inferences from the facts which lead to the complaint" will be drawn not "by a neutral and detached magistrate," as the Constitution requires, but instead by a police officer "engaged in the often competitive enterprise of ferreting out crime" . . . . or, as in this case, by an unidentified informant.

UNITED STATES v. VENTRESCA, 380 U.S. 102

[The essence of the affidavit on which a search warrant was issued in this case is set forth in the opinion. Writing for the Court, Justice Goldberg here concluded that the warrant did meet the requirements of *Aguilar* as it set forth some of the underlying circumstances so as to enable a disinterested magistrate to make an independent judgment that probable cause existed. It was only by an overtechnical reading that the lower court had held that this affidavit was not sufficient under *Aguilar*. Justice Goldberg rejected such a reading, stating that since the Fourth Amendment's commands, like all constitutional requirements, are practical and not abstract, affidavits for search warrants must be tested by courts and magistrates in a common-sense and realistic fashion.]

Respondent Ventresca was convicted[1] in the United States District Court for Massachusetts for possessing and operating an illegal distillery. The conviction was reversed by the Court of Appeals (one judge dissenting) on the ground that the affidavit for a search warrant pursuant to which the still was found was insufficient to establish probable cause.

The affidavit upon which the warrant was issued was made and submitted to a United States commissioner on August 31, 1961, by Walter Mazaka, an investigator for the Alcohol and Tobacco Division of the Internal Revenue Service. He stated that he had reason to believe that an illegal distillery was in operation in respondent Ventresca's house at 148½

[1] March 1, 1965. Case No. 28. Mr. Justice Goldberg delivered the opinion of the Court.

Coburn Avenue in Worcester, Massachusetts. The grounds for this belief were set forth in detail in the affidavit, prefaced with the following statement:

Based upon observations made by me, and based upon information received officially from other investigators attached to the Alcohol and Tobacco Tax Division assigned to this investigation, and reports orally made to me describing the results of their observations and investigation, this request for the issuance of a search warrant is made.

The affidavit then described seven different occasions between July 28 and August 30, 1961, when a Pontiac car was driven into the yard to the rear of Ventresca's house. On four occasions the car carried loads of sugar in 60-pound bags; it made two trips loaded with empty tin cans; and once it was merely observed as being heavily laden. Garry, the car's owner, and Incardone, a passenger, were seen on several occasions loading the car at Ventresca's house and later unloading apparently full five-gallon cans at Garry's house late in the evening. On August 28, after a delivery of empty tin cans to Ventresca's house, Garry and Incardone were observed carrying from the house cans which appeared to be filled and placing them in the trunk of Garry's car. The affidavit went on to state that at about 4 A.M. on August 18, and at about 4 A.M. on August 30, "investigators" smelled the odor of fermenting mash as they walked along the sidewalk in front of Ventresca's house. On August 18 they heard, "at or about the same time . . . certain metallic noises." On August 30, the day before the warrant was applied for, they heard (as they smelled the mash) "sounds similar to that of a motor or a pump coming from the direction of" Ventresca's house. The affidavit concluded: "The foregoing information is based upon personal knowledge and information which has been obtained from investigators of the Alcohol and Tobacco Tax Division, Internal Revenue Service, who have been assigned to this investigation."

The District Court upheld the validity of the warrant on a motion to suppress. The divided Court of Appeals held the warrant insufficient because it read the affidavit as not specifically stating in so many words that the information it contained was based upon the personal knowledge of Mazaka or other reliable investigators. The Court of Appeals reasoned that all of the information recited in the affidavit might conceivably have been obtained by investigators other than Mazaka, and it could not be certain that the information of these other investigators was not in turn based upon hearsay received from unreliable informants rather than their own personal observations. For this reason the court found that probable cause had not been established. We granted certiorari to consider the standards by which a reviewing court should approach the interpretation of affidavits supporting warrants which have been duly issued by examining magistrates. 377 U.S. 989. For the reasons stated below, we reverse the judgment of the Court of Appeals. . . .

While a warrant may issue only upon a finding of "probable cause," this Court has long held that "the term 'probable cause' means less than evidence which would justify condemnation," *Locke* v. *United States*, 7 Cranch 339, 348, and that a finding of "probable cause" may rest upon evidence which is not legally competent in a criminal trial. *Draper* v. *United States*, 358 U. S. 307, 311. As the Court stated in *Brinegar* v. *United States*, 338 U. S. 160, 173, "There is a large difference between the two things to be proved [guilt and probable cause], as well as between the tribunals which determine them, and therefore a like difference in the *quanta* and modes of proof required to establish them." Thus hearsay may be the basis for issuance of the warrant "so long as there . . . is a substantial basis for crediting the hearsay." *Jones* v. *United States, supra*, at 272. And, in *Aguilar* we recognized that "an affidavit may be based on hearsay information and need not reflect the direct personal observations of the affiant," so long as the magistrate is "informed of some of the underlying circumstances" supporting the affiant's conclusions and his belief that any informant involved "whose identity need not be disclosed . . . was 'credible' or his information 'reliable.'" *Aguilar* v. *Texas, supra*, at 114.

These decisions reflect the recognition that the Fourth Amendment's commands, like all constitutional requirements, are practical and not abstract. If the teachings of the Court's cases are to be followed and the constitutional policy served, affidavits for search warrants, such as the one involved here, must be tested and interpreted by magistrates and courts in a common-sense and realistic fashion. They are normally drafted by nonlawyers in the midst and haste of a criminal investigation. Technical requirements of elaborate specificity once exacted under common law pleadings have no proper place in this area. A grudging or negative attitude by reviewing courts toward warrants will tend to discourage police officers from submitting their evidence to a judicial officer before acting.

This is not to say that probable cause can be made out by affidavits which are purely conclusory, stating only the affiant's or an informer's belief that probable cause exists without detailing any of the "underlying circumstances" upon which that belief is based. See *Aguilar* v. *Texas, supra*. Recital of some of the underlying circumstances in the affidavit is essential if the magistrate is to perform his detached function and not serve merely as a rubber stamp for the police. However, where these circumstances are detailed, where reason for crediting the source of the information is given, and when a magistrate has found probable cause, the courts should not invalidate the warrant by interpreting the affidavit in a hypertechnical, rather than a common-sense, manner. Although in a particular case it may not be easy to determine when an affidavit demonstrates the existence of probable cause, the resolution of doubtful or marginal cases in this area should be largely determined by the preference to be accorded to warrants. . . . *Jones* v. *United States, supra,* at 270.

This Court is alert to invalidate unconstitutional searches and seizures whether with or without a warrant. See *Aguilar* v. *Texas, supra; Stanford* v. *Texas,* 379 U. S. 476; *Preston* v. *United States,* 376 U. S. 364; *Beck* v. *Ohio,* 379 U. S. 89. By doing so, it vindicates individual liberties and strengthens the administration of justice by promoting respect for law and order. This Court is equally concerned to uphold the actions of law-enforcement officers consistently following the proper constitutional course. This is no less important to the administration of justice than the invalidation of convictions because of disregard of individual rights or official overreaching. In our view the officers in this case did what the Constitution requires. They obtained a warrant from a judicial officer "upon probable cause, supported by oath or affirmation and particularly describing the place to be searched and the . . . things to be seized." It is vital that having done so their actions should be sustained under a system of justice responsive both to the needs of individual liberty and to the rights of the community.

Jaben v. United States, 381 U.S. 214

[In this case Justice Goldberg again applied the principles as to sufficiency of affidavits for warrants which he set forth in *Aguilar* and *Ventresca.* Although not a search and seizure case, in the view of the majority of the Court it was relevant to the decision to determine whether the affidavit filed in this case met the standards of probable cause required by the Fourth Amendment. The case involved a conviction for income tax fraud and the affidavit, on which a magistrate issued a summons for an accused to appear at a hearing, was sworn to by a special agent of the Internal Revenue Service. The affidavit recited the fact that the agent had conducted an investigation of Mr. Jaben's tax liability for a certain year "by examining the said taxpayer's tax returns for the year 1956 and other years; by identifying and interviewing third parties with whom the taxpayer did business; by consulting public and private records reflecting the said taxpayer's income; and by interviewing third persons having knowledge of the said taxpayer's financial condition." Based on this investigation, and without any further statement of the basis of the conclusion, the agent stated his conclusion that Mr. Jaben reported some $23,000 less in income for 1956 than he had actually earned in that year. On this aspect of the case, six members of the Court concluded that the affidavit was sufficient to allow the magistrate to make an independent determination of probable cause as required by *Aguilar* and *Ventresca*. Justice Goldberg dissented from this point in an opinion in which the Chief Justice and Justice Douglas joined. In his view, if the Court meant that the same standard of probable cause applied in this case concerning the issuance of a summons as in *Aguilar* and *Ventresca* concerning arrest and search warrants, then the Court was wrong in holding that the affidavit was here sufficient to meet the *Aguilar-Ventresca* test.]

I agree with the Court[1] that the purpose of the tolling provision in the statute of limitations before us, as evidenced by its language and its legislative history, is to avoid penalizing the government when a criminal defendant cannot be indicted merely because no grand jury is sitting at the time the limitation period expires. In keeping with this purpose, the government ought to be allowed to present a case prepared before the expiration of the limitation period to the grand jury when it next convenes, but it ought not to be allowed to take advantage of a nine-month extension to prepare a case which was not ready for submission before the end of the statutory period. I believe that the Court, therefore, is quite correct in rejecting the government's argument that the filing of any complaint which meets the formal requirements of Rule 3 of the Federal Rules of Criminal Procedure is sufficient to toll the statute of limitations. The government's argument would, in effect, allow it an additional nine months in every case. Rather, the view that I would accept as correct is that the only complaint that tolls the statute is one that begins effectively the criminal process prescribed by the Federal Rules.

I further agree with the Court that a complaint has effectively begun the criminal process only when all of the preindictment steps detailed in Rules 3, 4, and 5 have been taken. Only when it has been determined in the preliminary hearing required by Rule 5 that probable cause exists "to believe that an offense has been committed and that the defendant has committed it" can we say with any assurance that the complaint was not filed merely to extend the limitation period, but that it was a complaint which does what a complaint normally does, namely, starts the criminal procedure in motion. A speedy determination by a disinterested magistrate—the United States commissioner—that probable cause exists also provides assurance that the government in fact had a case ready for presentation to the grand jury before the limitation period expired. Thus I join the Court's opinion in so far

[1] May 17, 1965. Case No. 347. Mr. Justice Goldberg, with whom The Chief Justice and Mr. Justice Douglas join, concurring in part and dissenting in part.

as it holds that only those complaints toll the statute of limitations which also start the criminal machinery in motion by leading to a preliminary hearing in compliance with Rules 3, 4, and 5. . . .

The facts of this case lead me to conclude, however, that the procedure outlined in Rule 5 was not followed, for a preliminary hearing was not scheduled within a reasonable time as the rule requires. A person who is arrested must be taken before a commissioner immediately and informed of his rights, and a preliminary examination to determine whether probable cause exists to believe that an offense has been committed and that he committed it must be held at that time or promptly thereafter. See *Mallory* v. *United States*, 354 U. S. 449, 454. This preliminary examination must be held promptly because it normally determines whether holding a defendant in custody pending action by the grand jury is warranted. Even when a defendant is not actually in custody but is free on bond a speedy hearing is still necessary, for he should not be required to maintain bond unless it has been determined by a disinterested commissioner that probable cause exists. While normally when a summons is issued, rather than an arrest warrant, the period of time within which a preliminary examination must be held may be longer than when a defendant has been arrested, for he is not in custody nor need he post bond, in the special circumstances present here involving a statutory period of repose, it is important that the preliminary hearing be held with expedition similar to that necessary when the defendant is in custody or free on bond. A prompt preliminary hearing in this type of case serves as a check to prevent the government from beginning a prosecution when the case was not ready for submission to the grand jury before the limitation period expires. I should think that, in view of this purpose, it would be sound practice, consistent with the statutory policy of repose, to hold the preliminary hearing and secure a magistrate's determination of probable cause before the statutory period expires. Only then can it be certain that the government had evidence showing probable cause at hand before the end of the limitation period. And, in an exceptional case, such as the one before us, where the complaint is filed so late that the hearing cannot be held within the limitation period, surely, in order to serve the statutory purpose, the hearing must be held with the same promptness as when a defendant is in custody or on bond, even though a summons, rather than an arrest warrant, was issued.

In this case the complaint was filed the day before the limitation period expired. In accordance with the government's wishes, the summons was made returnable 30 days later, and, at the government's subsequent request, the hearing date was postponed an additional week. In my view, to schedule a hearing to be held 36 days after the limitation period expires, when that hearing normally should have been held before the end of the statutory time for prosecution, is not to schedule it within the "reasonable time" which the Court itself says is required. Nor can it be said under the circumstances here present that the petitioner waived the right to have the probable cause determination made promptly. Whatever the burden on a defendant may be under other circumstances to move to accelerate a date fixed by a Commissioner upon an *ex parte* application of the government, it would be unjust to apply any waiver concept here. Until the holding today there was no authoritative construction that the statute, read in conjunction with the Federal Criminal Rules, entitles the charged defendant to a hearing after issuance of a summons. There is no basis, therefore, for concluding that petitioner, by being silent under these circumstances, knowingly and consciously waived his right to a speedy hearing and determination of whether probable cause existed.

I would conclude that a preliminary hearing, which was to determine whether probable cause existed, was not held within a "reasonable time" as Rule 5 requires, and that since the government did not fulfill all the requirements of this rule, the complaint did not serve to institute the proper preindictment criminal procedure. It therefore, in my view, was not the type of complaint that tolls the statute of limitations under Internal Revenue Code § 6531, and petitioner's prosecution should be barred. . . .

While it is not necessary, under my view of this case, to determine whether the complaint showed probable cause, since the Court reaches that issue, I believe it appropriate to express my disagreement with its conclusion. If the Court means that the standards of probable cause required for the issuance of a summons directing the defendant to appear for a preliminary hearing is the same as the standard required for issuance of a search warrant or an arrest warrant, which will place the defendant under immediate physical restraint, the complaint before us fails to demonstrate probable cause, for it clearly fails to meet the standards laid down in *Giordenello* v. *United States*, 357 U. S. 480, and *Aguilar* v. *Texas*, 378 U. S. 108.

This Court in *Giordenello* held that a finding of "probable cause" must be made by a "neutral and detached" magistrate who "assess[es] *independently* the probability that . . . [an accused] committed the crime charged." *Giordenello* v. *United States*, *supra*, at 486-487. (Emphasis added.) The Court also stated:

The purpose of a complaint . . . is to enable the appropriate magistrate . . . to determine whether the "probable cause" required to support a warrant exists. The commissioner must judge for himself the persuasiveness of the facts relied on by a complaining officer to show probable cause. He should not accept without question the complainant's mere conclusion that the person whose arrest is sought has committed a crime.—*Id.*, at 486.

In order to make an independent determination that probable cause exists, the magistrate must be presented with more than the fact that the affiant or his sources are reliable and the affiant's conclusion that the accused is believed to have committed a crime. As we stated in *Aguilar* v. *Texas, supra,* at 114, the magistrate or commissioner must also "be informed of some of the underlying circumstances" supporting the affiant's belief that the accused has committed a crime. This statement was recently reaffirmed in *United States* v. *Ventresca,* 380 U.S. 102, 108. To allow a magistrate to find probable cause when a reliable affiant does no more than swear, as the agent did here, that his investigations led him to conclude that petitioner understated his income, is to remove the function of making an independent determination of probable cause from the hands of the magistrate and to place it in the hands of the agent.

The affidavit presented by the revenue agent in this case does no more than list the agent's *sources* of information—examination of public and private records and interviews with third persons—and concludes that the petitioner understated his income. Without the slightest indication of what the agent's examinations and interviews revealed, it is impossible for a "neutral and detached magistrate" to determine for himself whether probable cause existed. The agent need not set out *all* the information obtained, but, as we held in *Aguilar, some* of the underlying facts must be indicated.

I cannot accept the Court's view that the nature of the offense charged in this case excuses the government from setting out *any* of the facts underlying the conclusion that the petitioner understated his income. Surely, defendants in criminal tax cases—whether based upon a net worth theory or otherwise—are as entitled to a magistrate's independent determination of "probable cause" as any other defendant. Furthermore, I do not believe it impossible, or even very difficult, for the government to give some indication of the type of information obtained through its perusal of petitioner's books and its interviews with third persons. But I do believe that it is impossible for a magistrate or commissioner to determine whether probable cause exists without some indication of the facts which led the affiant to his conclusion.

It is as true of the complaint before us as of the affidavit in *Giordenello* that "it is difficult to understand how the commissioner could be expected to assess independently the probability that petitioner committed the crime charged." 357 U. S., at 486-487. In my view, *Giordenello* and *Aguilar* require that the complaint not only state the ultimate conclusion that petitioner understated his income and set out the *sources* of information leading to that conclusion, but that it also set out some of the underlying facts upon which that conclusion is based. Since none of the underlying facts are set out in the complaint before us, I conclude that the probable cause standard of *Giordenello* and *Aguilar* is not met. For all the reasons stated, I would reverse the judgment of the Court of Appeals.

RUDOLPH v. ALABAMA, 375 U.S. 889

[Justice Goldberg held closely to previous decisions of the Supreme Court that recognize that constitutions "are not ephemeral enactments, designed to meet passing occasions. They are, to use the words of Chief Justice Marshall, 'designed to approach immortality as nearly as human institutions can approach it.' The future is their care and provision for events of good and bad tendencies of which no prophecy can be made. In the application of a constitution, therefore, our contemplation cannot be only of what has been but of what may be." *Weems* v. *United States*, 217 U.S. 349, 373 (1910). The Court has also long recognized, as a particularization of the rule that the Constitution must be interpreted as a living document, that the Eighth Amendment's proscription of "cruel and unusual punishment" (a proscription made applicable to the states by the Fourteenth Amendment) is not a static concept. As the Court stated in 1885, "What punishments shall be considered as infamous may be affected by the changes of public opinion from one age to another. In former times, being put in the stocks was not considered as necessarily infamous. . . . But at the present day [it] might be thought an infamous punishment." *Ex Parte Wilson*, 114 U.S. 417, 427-428. Faithful to this philosophy, Justice Goldberg, joined by Justices Douglas and Brennan, dissented from the Court's refusal to hear a case and consider the question of whether the Constitution today permits the imposition of the death penalty on a convicted rapist who has neither taken nor endangered human life. It should be noted that in this dissent, while considering this issue to be worthy of argument and consideration, Justice Goldberg does not pass upon it.]

I would grant certiorari in this case[1] . . . to consider whether the Eighth and Fourteenth Amendments to the United States Constitution permit the imposition of the death penalty on a convicted rapist who has neither taken nor endangered human life.

The following questions, *inter alia*, seem relevant and worthy of argument and consideration:

(1) In light of the trend both in this country and throughout the world

---

[1] October 21, 1963. Case No. 308 Misc. Mr. Justice Goldberg, with whom Mr. Justice Douglas and Mr. Justice Brennan join, dissenting.

against punishing rape by death,[2] does the imposition of the death penalty by those states which retain it for rape violate "evolving standards of decency that mark the progress of [our] maturing society"[3] or "standards of decency more or less universally accepted"?[4]

(2) Is the taking of human life to protect a value other than human life consistent with the constitutional proscription against "punishments which by their excessive . . . severity are greatly disproportioned to the offenses charged"?[5]

(3) Can the permissible aims of punishment (e.g., deterrence, isolation, rehabilitation)[6] be achieved as effectively by punishing rape less severely

---

[2] The United Nations recently conducted a survey on the laws, regulations and practices relating to capital punishment throughout the world. In addition to the United States, 65 countries and territories responded. All but five—Nationalist China, Northern Rhodesia, Nyasaland, Republic of South Africa, and the United States—reported that their laws no longer permit the imposition of the death penalty for rape.

The following of the United States reported that their laws no longer permit the imposition of the death penalty for rape: Alaska, Arizona, California, Colorado, Connecticut, Delaware, Hawaii, Idaho, Illinois, Indiana, Iowa, Kansas, Maine, Massachusetts, Michigan, Minnesota, Montana, Nebraska, New Hampshire, New Jersey, New Mexico, New York, North Dakota, Ohio, Oregon, Pennsylvania, South Dakota, Tennessee, Utah, Vermont, Washington, Wisconsin and Wyoming. The laws of the remaining states permit the imposition of the death penalty for rape, but some states do not, in fact, impose it. United Nations, *Capital Punishment* (prepared by Mr. Marc Ancel, Justice of the French Supreme Court) (N.Y., 1962) pp. 38, 71-75. See, Resolution 934 (xxxv), adopted by the United Nations Economic and Social Council (April 9, 1963).

[3] *Trop* v. *Dulles*, 356 U.S. 86, 101 (opinion of Warren, C. J., joined by Justices Black, Douglas, and Whittaker).

[4] *Francis* v. *Resweber*, 329 U.S. 459, 469 (Frankfurter, J., concurring). See *Weems* v. *United States*, 217 U.S. 349, 373:

"Legislation, both statutory and constitutional, is enacted, it is true, from an experience of evils, but its general language should not, therefore, be necessarily confined to the form that evil had theretofore taken. Time works changes, brings into existence new conditions and purposes. Therefore a principle to be vital must be capable of wider application than the mischief which gave it birth. This is peculiarly true of constitutions. They are not ephemeral enactments, designed to meet passing occasions. They are, to use the words of Chief Justice Marshall, 'designed to approach immortality as nearly as human institutions can approach it.' The future is their care and provision for events of good and bad tendencies of which no prophecy can be made. In the application of a constitution, therefore, our contemplation cannot be only of what has been but of what may be. Under any other rule a constitution would indeed be as easy of application as it would be deficient in efficacy and power. Its general principles would have little value and be converted by precedent into impotent and lifeless formulas. Rights declared in words might be lost in reality."

Also see *Ex parte Wilson*, 114 U.S. 417, 427-428:

"What punishments shall be considered as infamous may be affected by the changes of public opinion from one age to another. In former times, being put in the stocks was not considered as necessarily infamous. . . . But at the present day [it] might be thought an infamous punishment."

[5] *Weems* v. *United States*, 217 U.S. 349, 371, quoting from the dissenting opinion of Field, J., in *O'Neil* v. *Vermont*, 144 U.S. 323, 339-340. Cf. *Lambert* v. *California*, 355 U.S. 225, 231 (dissenting opinion of Frankfurter, J.).

[6] See, e. g., *Williams* v. *New York*, 337 U.S. 241; *Trop* v. *Dulles*, 356 U.S. 86, 111 (concurring opinion of Brennan, J.); *Blyew* v. *United States*, 13, Wall. 581, 600.

than by death (e.g., by life imprisonment);[7] if so, does the imposition of the death penalty for rape constitute "unnecessary cruelty"?[8]

GOLDWATER V. FCC, 379 U.S. 893

[Near the end of the 1964 presidential campaign, President Johnson appeared on national television to speak about various developments in foreign affairs. His opponent, Barry Goldwater, sought equal television time pursuant to the statute set forth in the following opinion. The FCC concluded that the President's speech was not within the statute. Senator Goldwater sought review of that decision in the Supreme Court. The Court denied review but Justice Goldberg, with Justice Black joining, dissented.]

I would grant certiorari and the application of the petitioner to set the case[1] for oral argument on Thursday, October 29, 1964.

In my view the question raised by the petition is substantial and warrants argument, which, in view of the imminence of the election, should be set for Thursday, if petitioner is to be given any practical relief before next Tuesday's election.

Section 315 (a) of the Federal Communications Act of 1934, as amended, 47 U.S.C. § 315 (a), (1958 ed., Supp. V), is as follows:

If any licensee shall permit any person who is a legally qualified candidate for any public office to use a broadcasting station, he shall afford equal opportunities to all other such candidates for that office in the use of such broadcasting station: Provided, that such licensee shall have no power of censorship over the material broadcast under the provisions of this section. No obligation is imposed upon any licensee to allow the use of its station by any such candidate. Appearance by a legally qualified candidate on any—
  (1) bona fide newscast,
  (2) bona fide news interview,

---

[7] The United Nations Report on Capital Punishment noted: "In Canada, rape ceased to be punishable with death in 1954: it is reported that there were 37 convictions for rape in 1950, 44 in 1953 and only 27 in 1954, the year of abolition; from 1957 to 1959 a steady decrease in convictions was noted (from 56 to 44), while in the same period the population of Canada increased by 27 per cent." United Nations, Capital Punishment, supra, note 1, at 54–55.
Such statistics must of course be regarded with caution. See, e. g., Royal Commission Report on Capital Punishment (1953), p. 24; Hart, "Murder and Its Punishment," 52 Nw. U.L. Rev. 433, 457 (1957); Allen, "Review," 10 Stan. L. Rev. 595, 600 (1958). In Canada, for example, the death sentence was rarely imposed for rape even prior to its formal abolition in 1954. In 1961 there was a slight increase in the number of convictions for rape. See United Nations, Capital Punishment, supra, note 1, at 55.
[8] Weems v. United States, 217 U.S. 349, 370. See Robinson v. California, 370 U.S. 660, 677 (concurring opinion of Douglas, J.).
[1] October 28, 1964. Case No. 636. Mr. Justice Goldberg, with whom Mr. Justice Black joins, dissenting from the denial of certiorari and application for expedited consideration.

(3) bona fide news documentary (if the appearance of the candidate is incidental to the presentation of the subject or subjects covered by the news documentary), or

(4) on-the-spot coverage of bona fide news events (including but not limited to political conventions and activities incidental thereto),

shall not be deemed to be use of a broadcasting station within the meaning of this subsection. Nothing in the foregoing sentence shall be construed as relieving broadcasters, in connection with the presentation of newscasts, news interviews, news documentaries, and on-the-spot coverage of news events, from the obligation imposed upon them under this chapter to operate in the public interest and to afford reasonable opportunity for the discussion of conflicting views on issues of public importance.

The statute on its face plainly requires that a licensee who permits any legally qualified candidate for any public office to use its broadcast facilities afford equal opportunities to all other qualified candidates. No exemption is made for a legally qualified candidate who is the incumbent President of the United States. The express exceptions to the broad scope of the statute for bona fide broadcasts, news interviews, news documentaries, and on-the-spot coverage of bona fide news events do not appear to apply to the address made by the President on Sunday, October 18, 1964, which does not seem to fit into any of these categories.

The Federal Communications Commission's own interpretations of the statute have not been wholly consistent. The Commission has ruled that a spot announcement wherein President Eisenhower, then a candidate for re-election, appeared appealing for a Community Fund Drive constituted a use requiring equal time to all other candidates. *Columbia Broadcasting System*, 14 Pike and Fischer Radio Reg. 524 (1956). The Commission, in a divided decision, held, in 1956, that the Democratic candidate for President, the Honorable Adlai E. Stevenson, was not entitled to equal time resulting from use of the network facilities by the Republican candidate, President Eisenhower, to report on the Suez crisis. *Columbia Broadcasting System*, 14 Pike and Fischer, Radio Reg. 720 (1956). Finally, the Commission has recently held that the full broadcasting of a presidential news conference would be subject to the equal time requirement. *Columbia Broadcasting System*, F.C.C. 64-887, 56865 (Sept. 30, 1964). These varied holdings of the Commission, and the express language of the act, confirm my view of the substantiality of the question and the need for immediate argument and speedy decision of this case.

The importance of the question is, I believe, plainly apparent. The statute reflects a deep Congressional conviction and policy that in our democratic society all qualified candidates should be given equally free access to broadcasting facilities, regardless of office or financial means, if any candidate is granted free time. This Court, in the recent past, has recognized the importance of making broadcasting facilities "available to candidates for office without discrimination." *Farmers Educational & Cooperative Union* v. *WDAY, Inc.*, 360 U.S. 525, 529. Perhaps on argument, considerations may be advanced which would cast more light on what now appears to me to be a clear and unequivocal expression of Congressional intent. But, since the Court has denied the petition and the application for expedited argument, I am impelled to record this dissent.

2

The Negro Revolution

Watson v. Memphis, 373 U.S. 526

[In 1960 a suit was brought to desegregate immediately the municipal parks and other city-owned or -operated recreational facilities in Memphis, Tennessee. The District Court denied the relief sought and ordered the city to submit, within six months, a plan providing for desegregation of the relevant facilities. An appeal was taken from this order and in May, 1963, Justice Goldberg, writing for a unanimous Court, held that the facilities should be desegregated immediately. In fact, the plan that was finally submitted by the city did not provide for complete desegregation until 1971. In the opinion Justice Goldberg made clear that the 1955 decision in *Brown* that required desegregation of public educational facilities "with all deliberate speed" never contemplated indefinite delay in elimination of racial barriers in schools, let alone other public facilities not involving the same physical problems or comparable conditions.]

The issue in this case,[1] simply stated, is whether the city of Memphis may further delay in meeting fully its constitutional obligation under the Fourteenth Amendment to desegregate its public parks and other municipal recreational facilities.

The petitioners, adult Negro residents of Memphis, commenced this action against the city in May, 1960, in the United States District Court for the Western District of Tennessee, seeking declaratory and injunctive relief directing immediate desegregation of municipal parks and other city-owned or -operated recreational facilities from which Negroes were then still excluded. The city denied neither the fact that the majority of the relevant facilities were operated on a segregated basis nor its duty under the Four-

[1] May 27, 1963. Case No. 424. Mr. Justice Goldberg delivered the opinion of the Court.

teenth Amendment to terminate its policy of conditioning use of such facilities on race. Instead, it pointed to the partial desegregation already effected and attempted to justify its further delay in conforming fully and at once to constitutional mandates by urging the need and wisdom of proceeding slowly and gradually in its desegregation efforts.

The District Court denied the relief sought by the petitioners and ordered the city to submit, within six months, a plan providing additional time for desegregation of the relevant facilities. The Court of Appeals for the Sixth Circuit affirmed. 303 F. 2d 863. We granted certiorari, 371 U. S. 909, to consider the important question presented and the applicability here of the principles enunciated by this Court in the second *Brown* decision, *Brown* v. *Board of Education*, 349 U. S. 294, upon which the courts below relied in further delaying complete vindication of the petitioners' constitutional rights.

We find the second *Brown* decision to be inapplicable here and accordingly reverse the judgment below.

It is important at the outset to note the chronological context in which the city makes its claim to entitlement to additional time within which to work out complete elimination of racial barriers to use of the public facilities here involved. It is now more than nine years since this Court held in the first *Brown* decision, *Brown* v. *Board of Education*, 347 U.S. 483, that racial segregation in state public schools violates the Equal Protection Clause of the Fourteenth Amendment. And it was almost eight years ago—in 1955, the year after the decision on the merits in *Brown*—that the constitutional proscription of state-enforced racial segregation was found to apply to public recreational facilities. See *Dawson* v. *Mayor and City Council of Baltimore*, 220 F. 2d 386, aff'd, 350 U.S. 877; see also *Muir* v. *Louisville Park Theatrical Assn.*, 347 U.S. 971.

Thus, the applicability here of the factors and reasoning relied on in framing the 1955 decree in the second *Brown* decision, *supra*, which contemplated the possible need of some limited delay in effecting total desegregation of public schools, must be considered not only in the context of factual similarities, if any, between that case and this one, but also in light of the significant fact that the governing constitutional principles no longer bear the imprint of newly enunciated doctrine. In considering the appropriateness of the equitable decree entered below inviting a plan calling for an even longer delay in effecting desegregation, we cannot ignore the passage of a substantial period of time since the original declaration of the manifest unconstitutionality of racial practices such as are here challenged, the repeated and numerous decisions giving notice of such illegality, and the many intervening opportunities heretofore available to attain the equality of treatment which the Fourteenth Amendment commands the states to achieve. These factors must inevitably and substantially temper the present import of such broad policy considerations as may have underlain, even in part, the form of decree ultimately framed in the *Brown* case. Given the extended time which has elapsed, it is far from clear that the mandate of the second *Brown* decision requiring that desegregation proceed with "all deliberate speed" would today be fully satisfied by types of plans or programs for desegregation of public educational facilities which eight years ago might have been deemed sufficient. *Brown* never contemplated that the concept of "deliberate speed" would countenance indefinite delay in elimination of racial barriers in schools, let alone other public facilities not involving the same physical problems or comparable conditions. . . .

When, in 1954, in the first *Brown* decision, this Court declared the constitutional impermissibility of racial segregation in public schools, it did not immediately frame a decree, but instead invited and heard further argument on the question of relief. In its subsequent opinion, the Court noted that "full implementation of these [applicable] constitutional principles may require solution of varied and local school problems" and indicated an appropriate scope for the application of equitable principles consistent with both public and private need and for "exercise of [the] . . . traditional attributes of equity power." 349 U. S., at 299-300. The District Courts to which the cases there under consideration were remanded were invested with a discretion appropriate to ultimate fashioning of detailed relief consonant with properly cognizable local conditions. This did not mean, however, that the discretion was even then unfettered or exercisable without restraint. Basic to the remand was the concept that desegregation must proceed with "all deliberate speed," and the problems which might be considered and which might justify a decree requiring something less than immediate and total desegregation was severely delimited. Hostility to the constitutional precepts underlying the original decision was expressly and firmly pretermitted as such an operative factor. *Id.*, at 300.

The nature of the ultimate resolution effected in the second *Brown* decision largely reflected no more than a recognition of the unusual and particular problems inhering in desegregating large numbers of schools throughout the country. The careful specification of factors relevant to a determination whether any delay in complying fully and completely with the constitutional mandate would be warranted demonstrated a concern that delay not be conditioned upon insufficient reasons or, in any event, tolerated unless it imperatively and compellingly appeared unavoidable.

This case presents no obvious occasion for the application of *Brown*. We are not here confronted with attempted desegregation of a local school system with any or all of the perhaps uniquely attendant problems, administrative and other, specified in the second *Brown* decision as proper considerations in weighing the need for further delay in vindicating the Fourteenth Amendment rights of petitioners. Desegregation of parks and other recreational facilities does not present the same kinds of cognizable difficulties inhering, in elimination of racial classification in schools, at which attendance is compulsory, the adequacy of teachers and facilities crucial, and questions of geographic assignment often of major significance.

Most importantly, of course, it must be recognized that even the delay countenanced by *Brown* was a necessary, albeit significant, adaptation of the usual principle that any deprivation of constitutional rights calls for prompt rectification. The rights here asserted are, like all such rights, *present* rights; they are not merely hopes to some *future* enjoyment of some formalistic constitutional promise. The basic guarantees of our Constitution are warrants for the here and now and, unless there is an overwhelmingly compelling reason, they are to be promptly fulfilled. The second *Brown* decision is but a narrowly drawn, and carefully limited, qualification upon usual precepts of constitutional adjudication and is not to be unnecessarily expanded in application.

Solely because of their race, the petitioners here have been refused the use of city-owned or -operated parks and other recreational facilities which the Constitution mandates be open to their enjoyment on equal terms with white persons. The city has effected, continues to effect, and claims the right or need to prolong patently unconstitutional racial discriminations violative of now long-declared and well-established individual rights. The claims of the city to further delay in affording the petitioners that to which they are clearly and unquestionably entitled cannot be upheld except upon the most convincing and impressive demonstration by the city that such delay is manifestly compelled by constitutionally cognizable circumstances warranting the exercise of an appropriate equitable discretion by a court. In short, the city must sustain an extremely heavy burden of proof.

Examination of the facts of this case in light of the foregoing discussion discloses with singular clarity that this burden has not been sustained; indeed, it is patent from the record that the principles enunciated in the second *Brown* decision have absolutely no application here.

The findings of the District Court disclose an unmistakable and pervasive pattern of local segregation, which, in fact, the city makes no attempt to deny, but merely to justify as necessary for the time being. Memphis owns 131 parks, all of which are operated by the Memphis Park Commission. Of these, only 25 were at the time of trial open to use without regard to race; 58 were restricted to use by whites and 25 to use by Negroes; the remaining 23 parks were undeveloped raw land. Subject to exceptions, neighborhood parks were generally segregated according to the racial character of the area in which located. The City Park Commission also operates a number of additional recreational facilities, by far the largest share of which were found to be racially segregated. Though a zoo, an art gallery and certain boating and other facilities are now desegregated, about two thirds (40) of the 61 city-owned playgrounds were at the time of trial reserved for whites only, and the remainder were set aside for Negro use. Thirty of the 56 playgrounds and other facilities operated by the municipal Park Commission on property owned by churches, private groups, or the School Board were set aside for the exclusive use of whites, while 26 were reserved for Negroes. All 12 of the municipal community centers were segregated, eight being available only to whites and four to Negroes. Only two of the seven city golf courses were open to Negroes; play on the remaining five was limited to whites. While several of these properties have been desegregated since the filing of suit, the general pattern of racial segregation in such public recreational facilities persists.

The city asserted in the court below, and states here, that its good faith in attempting to comply with the requirements of the Constitution is not in issue, and contends that gradual desegregation on a facility-by-facility basis is necessary to prevent interracial disturbances, violence, riots, and community confusion and turmoil. The compelling answer to this contention is that constitutional rights may not be denied simply because of hostility to their assertion or exercise. See *Wright* v. *State of Georgia, ante,* p. 284; *Brown* v. *Board of Education,* 349 U.S. 294, 300. Cf. *Taylor* v. *Louisiana,* 370 U.S. 154. As declared in *Cooper* v. *Aaron,* 358 U.S. 1, 16, "law and order are not . . . to be preserved by depriving the Negro children of their constitutional rights." This is really no more than an application of a principle enunciated much earlier in *Buchanan* v. *Warley,* 245 U.S. 60, a case dealing with a somewhat different form of state-ordained segregation—enforced separation of Negroes and whites by neighborhood. A unanimous Court, in striking down the officially imposed pattern of racial segregation there in question, declared almost a half century ago:

It is urged that this proposed segregation will promote the public peace by preventing race conflicts. Desirable as this is, and important as is the preservation of the public peace, this aim cannot be accomplished by laws or ordinances which deny rights created or protected by the Federal Constitution. 245 U.S., at 81.

Beyond this, however, neither the asserted fears of violence and tumult nor the asserted inability to preserve the peace were demonstrated at trial to be anything more than personal speculations or vague disquietudes of city officials. There is no indication that there had been any violence or meaningful disturbances when other recreational facilities had been desegregated. In fact, the only evidence in the record was that such prior transitions had been peaceful. The chairman of the Memphis Park Commission indicated that the city had "been singularly blessed by the absence of turmoil up to this time on this race question"; notwithstanding the prior desegregation of numerous recreational facilities, the same witness could point as evidence of the unrest or turmoil which would assertedly occur upon complete desegregation of such facilities only to a number of anonymous letters and phone calls which he had received. The Memphis chief of police mentioned without further description some "troubles" at the time bus service was desegregated and referred to threatened violence in connection with a "sit-in" demonstration at a local store, but, beyond making general predictions, gave no concrete indication of any inability of authorities to maintain the peace. The only violence referred to at any park or recreational facility occurred in segregated parks and was not the product of attempts at desegregation. Moreover, there was no factual evidence to support the bare testimonial speculations that authorities would be unable to cope successfully with any problems which in fact might arise or to meet the need for additional protection should the occasion demand.

The existing and commendable good will between the races in Memphis, to which both the District Court and some of the witnesses at trial made express and emphatic reference as in some inexplicable fashion supporting the need for further delay, can best be preserved and extended by the observance and protection, not the denial, of the basic constitutional rights here asserted. The best guarantee of civil peace is adherence to, and respect for, the law.

The other justifications for delay urged by the city or relied upon by the courts below are no more substantial, either legally or practically. It was, for example, asserted that immediate desegregation of playgrounds and parks would deprive a number of children—both Negro and white—of recreational facilities; this contention was apparently based on the premise that a number of such facilities would have to be closed because of the inadequacy of the "present" park budget to provide additional "supervision" assumed to be necessary to operate unsegregated playgrounds. As already noted, however, there is no warrant in this record for assuming that such added supervision would, in fact, be required, much less that police and recreation personnel would be unavailable to meet such needs if they should arise. More significantly, however, it is obvious that vindication of conceded constitutional rights cannot be made dependent upon any theory that it is less expensive to deny than to afford them. We will not assume that the citizens of Memphis accept the questionable premise implicit in this argument or that either the resources of the city are inadequate, or its government unresponsive, to the needs of all of its citizens.

In support of its judgment, the District Court also pointed out that the recreational facilities available for Negroes were roughly proportional to their number and therefore presumably adequate to meet their needs. While the record does not clearly support this, no more need be said than that, even if true, it reflects an impermissible obeisance to the now thoroughly discredited doctrine of "separate but equal." The sufficiency of Negro facilities is beside the point; it is the segregation by race that is unconstitutional.

Finally, the District Court deferred ruling as to the propriety of ordering elimination of racial barriers at one facility, an art museum, pending initiation of, and decision in, a state court action to construe a racially restrictive covenant contained in the deed of the property to the city. Of course, the outcome of the state suit is irrelevant to whether the city may constitutionally enforce the segregation, regardless of the effect which desegregation may have on its title. Cf. *Pennsylvania* v. *Board of Trusts*, 353 U.S. 230. In any event, there is no reason to believe that the restrictive provision will be invoked. The museum has already been opened to Negroes one day a week without complaint.

Since the city has completely failed to demonstrate any compelling or convincing reason requiring further delay in implementing the constitutional proscription of segregation of publicly owned or operated recreational facilities, there is no cause whatsoever to depart from the generally operative and here clearly controlling principle that constitutional rights are to be promptly vindicated. The continued denial to petitioners of the use of city facilities solely because of their race is without warrant. Under the facts in this case, the District Court's undoubted discretion in the fashioning and timing of equitable relief was not called into play; rather, affirmative judicial action was required to vindicate plain and present constitutional rights. Today, no less than fifty years ago, the solution to the problems growing out of race relations "cannot be promoted by depriving citizens of their constitutional rights and privileges." *Buchanan* v. *Warley*, *supra*, 245 U.S., at 80-81.

WRIGHT V. ROCKEFELLER, 376 U.S. 52

[This suit was brought by Manhattan voters alleging that the Manhattan Congressional district boundaries had been gerrymandered on racial lines in violation of the Fourteenth and Fifteenth Amendments so as to concentrate Negro and Puerto Rican voters in one district and exclude them from the others. The Court, with Justice Black writing the opinion, affirmed the dismissal of the suit on the ground that it accepted the District Court's finding that it had not been shown that the challenged part of the New York statute was the product of a state contrivance to segregate on the basis of race or place of origin. Justice Goldberg, with Justice Douglas joining, dissented. In his view the statutory scheme on its face clearly indicated the irregular district lines had been drawn on racial considerations, and thus it was the burden of the state to come forward with evidence that this was not so. As the state had not done so, Justice Goldberg was compelled to conclude that racial segregation was a criterion in—or a purpose of—the districting scheme, and that the scheme was, therefore, unconstitutional.]

The question for decision in this case[1] is whether appellants have sustained their burden of proving that the boundaries of the Seventeenth and Eighteenth Congressional Districts of New York were purposefully drawn on racial lines. The Court resolves this question against appellants by accepting "the District Court's finding that appellants have not shown that the challenged part of the New York Act was not the product of a state contrivance to segregate on the basis of race or place of origin."

My difficulty with this conclusion is that the record does not support the Court's treatment of the District Court's finding. The District Court was a three-judge court and the three judges did not agree upon and, as a court, made no express findings of fact. Instead there were three separate and differing opinions. Judge Moore implied that racially segregated voting districts are constitutional absent a showing of serious underrepresentation or other specific harm to the individual complainants. 211 F. Supp. 460, 467-468. He also suggested that segregated voting districts could be constitutionally justified because they may enable persons of the same race or place of origin "to obtain representation in legislative bodies which otherwise would be denied to them." *Id.*, at 467. Finally, Judge Moore intimated that factually segregated voting districts would be unconstitutional only where the legislature was "motivated or influenced" to create such districts. *Ibid.* To establish this motivation or influence complainants must introduce proof, and in this case no such proof was tendered by the appellants who, therefore, failed to make a case "upon the facts and the law." *Id.*, at 468.

Judge Moore did not in my view apply the proper constitutional standard. The Constitution, I strongly believe, proscribes state-sanctioned racial segregation in legislative districting as well as in voting and in public schools and facilities. E.g., *Brown* v. *Board of Education*, 347 U.S. 483; *Gomillion* v.

---

[1] February 17, 1964. Case No. 96. Mr. Justice Goldberg, with whom Mr. Justice Douglas joins, dissenting.

Lightfoot, 364 U.S. 339; *Johnson* v. *Virginia,* 373 U.S. 61; *Watson* v. *City of Memphis,* 373 U.S. 526; *Goss* v. *Board of Education,* 373 U.S. 683; *Anderson* v. *Martin,* 375 U.S. 399. Certainly in these areas the Fourteenth Amendment "nullifies sophisticated as well as simple-minded modes of discrimination." Cf. *Lane* v. *Wilson,* 307 U.S. 268, 275. This Court has declared state-sanctioned segregation invalid on the ground that, under the Constitution, distinctions by law between citizens because of their race, ancestry, color or religion "are by their very nature odious to a free people whose institutions are founded upon the doctrine of equality." *Hirabayashi* v. *United States,* 320 U.S. 81, 100. Given this settled principle that state-sanctioned racial segregation is unconstitutional *per se*, a showing of serious underrepresentation or other specific harm to individual complainants is irrelevant. I understand the Court's decisions since *Brown* v. *Board of Education, supra,* to hold that harm to the nation as a whole and to whites and Negroes alike inheres in segregation. The Fourteenth Amendment commands equality, and racial segregation by law is inequality. Judge Moore, therefore, did not apply the proper constitutional standard.

Furthermore, as I shall point out, Judge Moore also erred in holding that in any event appellants' proof was insufficient to establish a prima facie case of unconstitutional racial districting.

Judge Feinberg disagreed both with Judge Moore's implication that segregated voting districts are constitutional absent serious underrepresentation and with the view that segregated districts could be constitutionally justified by alleged advantages to persons of a particular race or place of origin. Judge Feinberg stated that the "constitutional vice would be use by the legislature of an impermissible standard, and the harm to plaintiffs that need be shown is only that such a standard was used." 211 F. Supp., at 468. He then frankly acknowledged that:

> The case is a closer one for me than the opinion of Judge Moore would indicate it is for him. Plaintiffs did introduce evidence which might justify an inference that racial considerations motivated the 1961 reapportionment of congressional districts in Manhattan. However, other inferences . . . are equally or more justifiable. Plaintiffs have a difficult burden to meet in attacking the constitutionality of this state statue.—*Id.,* at 469.

Judge Feinberg, on this reasoning, cast his vote for Judge Moore's result on the ground that appellants failed to sustain the "difficult burden" of attacking the constitutionality of this statute: Even where such racially segregated districting results and complainants' evidence "might justify an inference that racial considerations motivated" the districting, still complainants fail to sustain their burden unless they also disprove every other permissible or reasonable purpose which the legislature might have had in mind.

Judge Murphy, in his dissent, agreed with Judge Feinberg as to the applicable constitutional standard. But, on Judge Murphy's view of the record, the appellants carried their burden of proving that "the legislation was solely concerned with segregating white, and colored and Puerto Rican voters by fencing colored and Puerto Rican citizens out of the 17th district and into a district of their own (the 18th)"; that the legislation had effected "obvious segregation"; and that the statute constituted a "subtle exclusion" of Negroes from the Seventeenth and a "jamming in of colored and Puerto Ricans into the 18th or the kind of segregation that appeals to the inter-venors." *Id.*, at 473-475. Accordingly, Judge Murphy thought appellants had met their burden of proving segregation and, in the absence of any proof by the state or by intervenors, were entitled to a judgment declaring the statute unconstitutional under the Equal Protection Clause of the Fourteenth Amendment.

In light of these conflicting opinions and analyses, this case cannot be fairly decided on the ground stated in the opinion of the Court, viz., that "[w]e accept the District Court's finding." *Ante*, at 58. Which finding and under what constitutional standard—Judge Moore's, Judge Feinberg's or Judge Murphy's? Judges Moore and Feinberg, who comprised the majority below, differed both with regard to the constitutional standard and, as I read the opinions, with regard to the proof. It should not be forgotten that the conclusions of the District Court—both as to law and fact—have not been reviewed by an intermediate appellate tribunal. Instead the case has come directly to this Court from a three-judge district court and presents a record containing variant and inconsistent legal and factual conclusions. Even where a three-judge district court has made a unanimous finding of fact, this Court has given that finding less deference where, as here, it depends on evidence that is largely documentary and particularly where, as here, "the crucial issues involve mixed questions of law and fact." *United States* v. *United States Gypsum Co.*, 333 U.S. 364, 396. In my view, we cannot, in light of the record in this case, rest our decision on the "finding" of the District Court without abdicating our responsibility for principled constitutional adjudication. . . .

On the basis of the evidence, I agree with Judge Murphy's conclusion "that the only available inference from the . . . uncontradicted figure picture establishes *per se* a *prima facie* case of a legislative intent to draw Congres-sional district lines in the 17th and 18th Districts on the basis of race and national origin." *Id.*, at 472-473. At least, however, appellants' proof made it appear probable that a racial criterion shaped the 1961 reapportionment and that an inference of reliance on such an impermissible criterion was more reasonable than an inference that other factors alone had been used. In my view, then, this justifiable inference was sufficient to raise a rebuttable presumption of unconstitutionality and, without shifting the ultimate burden of proof, to place on the state the burden of going forward and introducing rebuttal evidence. See, Note, 72 Yale L. J. 1041, 1056-1061. It might be that the appellees and intervenors could have offered proof to counteract the inference of racial districting, but they chose not to do so. They might, for example, have attempted to prove that the lines were drawn in an attempt to equalize the population of districts or to follow neighborhood lines. The simple answer is that appellees made no attempt whatever to rebut the inference that race was a criterion in—or racial segregation a purpose of—the districting.

The question therefore recurs: What more need appellants have proved? Judge Moore apparently would have required them to introduce proof that the legislature's actual motive was to create racially segregated voting districts. Appellants, however, by their evidence established a pattern of segregation not adequately explained on a geometric, geographic, equalization, party-compromise, neighborhood or other basis. To require a showing of racial motivation in the legislature would place an impossible burden on complainants. For example, in this case the redistricting bill was recommended and submitted to the legislature on November 9, 1961, passed on November 10, 1961, and signed by the Governor on that date. No public hearings were had on the bill and no statements by the bill's managers or published debates were available. Under these circumstances, appellants' evidence, showing the factual pattern of segregation outlined by . . . Judge Murphy, was sufficient to establish a prima facie case of unconstitutional racial districting. Once this had been done, appellees should have introduced evidence negating the inference that racial segregation was a purpose of the districting. In the absence of such proof by the state, I am compelled to conclude that racial segregation was a criterion in—or a purpose of—the districting of New York's Seventeenth and Eighteenth Congressional Districts. I, therefore, respectfully dissent.

Bell v. Maryland, 378 U.S. 226

[This case arose out of the trespass convictions of Negroes who refused to remain seated peacefully in a restaurant after having been refused service on the grounds that the restaurant does not serve Negroes. The Court, with Justice Brennan writing the opinion, sent the case back to the Maryland courts for reconsideration in light of the fact that, since these convictions, Maryland had passed a statute making it a violation of the law for a restaurant such as this to refuse to serve persons because of their race. Justice Black, joined by Justices Harlan and White, dissented on the grounds that the state statute could have no application to these convictions that had occurred prior to its passage. More importantly, he stated his view that the Equal Protection Clause of the Fourteenth Amendment did not apply to what he considered to be private discrimination by the restaurant owner not involving action by the state. Justice Goldberg, joined by the Chief Justice, agreed with the Court that the case should go back to the State Court in light of the new statute. He wrote, however, to express his disagreement with Justice Black, for he believed that the Equal Protection Clause protects the right of all citizens to equal treatment in public accommodations. On this point Justice Goldberg was joined by Justice Douglas as well as the Chief Justice. Excerpts from Justice Goldberg's opinion on this point follow.]

The Declaration of Independence states[1] the American creed: "We hold these truths to be self-evident, that all men are created equal, that they are endowed by their Creator with certain unalienable Rights, that among these are Life, Liberty and the pursuit of Happiness." This ideal was not fully achieved with the adoption of our Constitution because of the hard and tragic reality of Negro slavery. The Constitution of the new nation, while heralding liberty, in effect declared all men to be free and equal—except black men who were to be neither free nor equal. This inconsistency reflected a fundamental departure from the American creed, a departure which it took a tragic civil war to set right. With the adoption, however, of the Thirteenth, Fourteenth, and Fifteenth Amendments to the Constitution, freedom and equality were guaranteed expressly to all regardless "of race, color, or previous condition of servitude." *United States* v. *Reese*, 92 U.S. 214, 218.

In light of this American commitment to equality and the history of that commitment, these amendments must be read not as "legislative codes which are subject to continuous revision with the changing course of events, but as the revelation of the great purposes which were intended to be achieved by the Constitution as a continuing instrument of government." *United States* v. *Classic*, 313 U.S. 299, 316. The cases following the 1896 decision in *Plessy* v. *Ferguson*, 163 U.S. 537, too often tended to negate this great purpose. In 1954 in *Brown* v. *Board of Education*, 347 U.S. 483, this Court unanimously concluded that the Fourteenth Amendment commands equality and that racial segregation by law is inequality. Since *Brown* the Court has consistently applied this constitutional standard to give real meaning to the Equal Protection Clause "as the revelation" of an enduring constitutional purpose.

[1] June 22, 1964. Case No. 12. Mr. Justice Goldberg, with whom the Chief Justice joins, and with whom Mr. Justice Douglas joins as to Parts II–V, concurring.

The dissent argues that the Constitution permits American citizens to be denied access to places of public accommodation solely because of their race or color. Such a view does not do justice to a constitution which is color blind and to the Court's decision in *Brown* v. *Board of Education*, which affirmed the right of all Americans to public equality. We cannot blind ourselves to the consequences of a constitutional interpretation which would permit citizens to be turned away by all the restaurants, or by the only restaurant, in town. The denial of the constitutional right of Negroes to access to places of public accommodation would perpetuate a caste system in the United States.

The Thirteenth, Fourteenth, and Fifteenth Amendments do not permit Negroes to be considered as second-class citizens in any aspect of our public life. Under our Constitution distinctions sanctioned by law between citizens because of race, ancestry, color or religion "are by their very nature odious to a free people whose institutions are founded upon the doctrine of equality." *Hirabayashi* v. *United States*, 320 U.S. 81, 100. We make no racial distinctions between citizens in exacting from them the discharge of public responsibilities: The heaviest duties of citizenship—military service, taxation, obedience to laws—are imposed evenhandedly upon black and white. States may and do impose the burdens of state citizenship upon Negroes and the states in many ways benefit from the equal imposition of the duties of federal citizenship. Our fundamental law which ensures such an equality of public burdens, in my view, similarly ensures an equality of public benefits. This Court has repeatedly recognized and applied this fundamental principle to many aspects of community life.

Of course our constitutional duty is "to construe, not to rewrite or amend, the Constitution." Our sworn duty to construe the Constitution requires, however, that we read it to effectuate the intent and purposes of the framers. We must, therefore, consider the history and circumstances indicating what the Civil War Amendments were in fact designed to achieve.

In 1873, in one of the earliest cases interpreting the Thirteenth and Fourteenth Amendments, this Court observed:

No one can fail to be impressed with the one pervading purpose found in . . . all [these amendments], lying at the foundation of each, and without which none of them would have been even suggested; we mean the freedom of the slave race, the security and firm establishment of that freedom, and the protection of the newly-made freeman and citizen from the oppressions of those who had formerly exercised unlimited dominion over him. . . . *Slaughter-House Cases,* 16 Wall. 36, 71.

A few years later, in 1880, the Court had occasion to observe that these amendments were written and adopted "to raise the colored race from that condition of inferiority and servitude in which most of them had previously stood, into perfect equality of civil rights with all other persons within the jurisdiction of the States." *Ex parte Virginia*, 100 U.S. 339, 344-345. In that same term, the Court in *Strauder* v. *West Virginia*, 100 U.S. 303, 307, stated that the recently adopted Fourteenth Amendment must "be construed liberally, to carry out the purposes of its framers." Such opinions immediately following the adoption of the amendments clearly reflect the contemporary understanding that they were "to secure to the colored race, thereby invested with the rights, privileges, and responsibilities of citizenship, the enjoyment of all the civil rights that, under the law, are enjoyed by white persons. . . ." *Neal* v. *Delaware*, 103 U.S. 370, 386.

The historical evidence amply supports the conclusion of the government, stated by the Solicitor General in this Court, that

it is an inescapable inference that Congress, in recommending the Fourteenth Amendment, expected to remove the disabilities barring Negroes from the public conveyances and places of public accommodation with which they were familiar, and thus to assure Negroes an equal right to enjoy these aspects of the public life of the community.

The subject of segregation in public conveyances and accommodations was quite familiar to the framers of the Fourteenth Amendment. Moreover, it appears that the contemporary understanding of the general public was that freedom from discrimination in places of public accommodation was part of the Fourteenth Amendment's promise of equal protection. . . .

The Fourteenth Amendment was in part designed to provide a firm constitutional basis for the Civil Rights Act of 1866, 14 Stat. 27, and to place that legislation beyond the power of Congressional repeal. The origins of subsequently proposed amendments and legislation lay in the 1866 bill and in a companion measure, the Freedmen's Bureau bill. The latter was addressed to states "wherein, in consequence of any state or local law . . . customs, or prejudice, any of the civil rights or immunities belonging to white persons, including the right . . . to have full and equal benefit of all laws and proceedings for the security of person and estate, are refused or denied to Negroes." Cong. Globe, 39th Cong., 1st Sess., 318. A review of the relevant Congressional debates reveals that the concept of civil rights which lay at the heart both of the contemporary legislative proposals and of the Fourteenth Amendment encompassed the right to equal treatment in public places—a right explicitly recognized to be a "civil" rather than a "social" right. It was repeatedly emphasized "that colored persons shall enjoy the same civil rights as white persons," that the colored man should have the right "to go where he pleases," that he should have "practical freedom," and that he should share "the rights and guarantees of the good old common law."

In the debates that culminated in the acceptance of the Fourteenth Amendment, the theme of granting "civil," as distinguished from "social," rights constantly recurred. Although it was commonly recognized that in some areas the civil-social distinction was misty, the critical fact is that it was generally understood that "civil rights" certainly included the right of access to places of public accommodation, for these were most clearly places and areas of life where the relations of men were traditionally regulated by governments. . . .

An 1873 decision of the Supreme Court of Iowa clearly reflects the contemporary understanding of the meaning of the Civil Rights Act of 1866. In *Coger* v. *The North West. Union Packet Co.*, 37 Iowa 145, a colored woman sought damages for assault and battery occurring when the officers of a Mississippi River steamboat ordered that she be removed from a dining table in accordance with a practice of segregation in the main dining room on the boat. In giving judgment for the plaintiff, the Iowa Supreme Court quoted the Civil Rights Act of 1866 and concluded that

Under this statute, equality in right is secured to the Negro. The language is comprehensive and includes the right to property and all rights growing out of contracts. It includes within its broad terms every right arising in the affairs of life. The right of the passenger under the contract of transportation with the carrier is included therein. The colored man is guaranteed equality and the equal protection of the laws with his white neighbor. These are the rights secured to him as a citizen of the United States, without regard to his color, and constitute his privileges, which are secured by [the Fourteenth Amendment]. *Id.,* at 156.

The Court then went on to reject the contention that the rights asserted were "social, and . . . not, therefore, secured by the constitution and statutes, either of the State or of the United States." *Id.,* at 157.

Underlying the Congressional discussions, and at the heart of the Fourteenth Amendment's guarantee of equal protection, was the assumption that the state by statute or by "the good old common law" was obligated to guarantee all citizens access to places of public accommodation. This obligation was firmly rooted in ancient Anglo-American tradition. In his work on bailments, Judge Story spoke of this tradition:

An innkeeper is bound . . . to take in all travelers and wayfaring persons, and to entertain them, if he can accommodate them, for a reasonable compensation; and he must guard their goods with proper diligence. . . . If an innkeeper improperly refuses to receive or provide for a guest, he is liable to be indicted therefor.—Story, *Commentaries on the Law of Bailments* (Schouler, 9th ed., 1878) § 476.

The first and most general obligation on [carriers of passengers] is to carry passengers whenever they offer themselves, and are ready to pay for their transportation. This results from their setting themselves up, like innkeepers, and common carriers of goods, for a common public employment on hire. They are no more at liberty to refuse a passenger, if they have sufficient room and accommodations, than an innkeeper is to refuse suitable room and accommodations to a guest.—*Id.*, at §§ 590, 591.

It was in this vein that the Supreme Court of Mississippi spoke when in 1873 it applied the equal accommodations provisions of the state's civil rights bill to a Negro refused admission to a theater:

Among those customs which we call the common law, that have come down to us from the remote past, are rules which have a special application to those who sustain a *quasi* public relation to the community. The wayfarer and the traveler had a right to demand food and lodging from the innkeeper; the common carrier was bound to accept all passengers and goods offered for transportation, according to his means. So, too, all who applied for admission to the public shows and amusements, were entitled to admission, and in each instance, for a refusal, an action on the case lay, unless sufficient reason were shown. The statute deals with subjects which have always been under legal control.—*Donnell* v. *State*, 48 Miss., 661, 680-681.

In a similar manner, Senator Sumner, discussing the Civil Rights Act of 1875, referred to and quoted from Holingshed, Story, Kent and Parsons on the common-law duties of innkeepers and common carriers to treat all alike. Cong. Globe, 42d Cong., 2d Sess. 382-383. With regard to "theaters and places of public amusement," the Senator observed that:

Theaters and other places of public amusement, licensed by law, are kindred to inns or public conveyances, though less noticed by jurisprudence. But, like their prototypes, they undertake to provide for the public under sanction of law. They are public institutions, regulated if not created by law, enjoying privileges, and in consideration thereof, assuming duties not unlike those of the inn and the public conveyance. From essential reason, the rule should be the same with all. As the inn cannot close its doors, or the public conveyance refuse a seat to any paying traveler, decent in condition, so must it be with the theater and other places of public amusement. Here are institutions whose peculiar object is the "pursuit of happiness," which has been placed among the equal rights of all. *Id.*, at 383.

The first sentence of § 1 of the Fourteenth Amendment, the spirit of which pervades all the Civil War Amendments, was obviously designed to overrule *Dred Scott* v. *Sanford*, 19 How. 393, and to ensure that the constitutional concept of citizenship with all attendant rights and privileges would henceforth embrace Negroes. It follows that Negroes as citizens necessarily became entitled to share the right, customarily possessed by other citizens, of access to public accommodations. The history of the affirmative obligations existing at common law serves partly to explain the negative—"deny to any person"—language of the Fourteenth Amendment. For it was assumed that under state law, when the Negro's disability as a citizen was removed, he would be assured the same public civil rights that the law had guaranteed white persons. . . . Evidence such as this demonstrates that Mr.. Justice Harlan, dissenting in the *Civil Rights Cases*, 109 U.S. 1, 26, was surely correct when he observed:

But what was secured to colored citizens of the United States—as between their respective states—by the national grant to them of state citizenship? With what rights, privileges or immunities did this grant invest them? There is one, if there be no other—exemption from race discrimination in respect of any civil rights belonging to the citizens of the white race in the same state. That surely is their constitutional privilege when within the jurisdiction of other states. And such must be their constitutional rights, in their own state, unless the recent amendments be splendid baubles, thrown out to delude those who deserved fair and generous treatment at the hands of the nation. Citizenship in this country necessarily imports at least equality of civil rights among citizens of every race in the same state. It is fundamental in American citizenship that, in respect of such rights, there shall be no discrimination by the state, or its officers, or by individuals or corporations exercising public functions or authority, against any citizen because of his race or previous condition of servitude.—*Id.*, at 48.

The framers of the Fourteenth Amendment, reacting against the Black Codes, made certain that the states could not frustrate the guaranteed equality by enacting discriminatory legislation or by sanctioning discriminatory treatment. At no time in the consideration of the Amendment was it suggested that the states could achieve the same prohibited result by withdrawing the traditional right of access to public places. In granting Negroes citizenship and the equal protection of the laws, it was never thought that the states could permit the proprietors of inns and public places to restrict their general invitation to the public and to citizens in order to exclude the Negro public and Negro citizens. The Fourteenth Amendment was therefore cast in terms under which judicial power would come into play where the state withdrew or otherwise denied the guaranteed protection "from legal discriminations, implying inferiority in civil society, lessening the security of [the Negroes'] enjoyment of the rights which others enjoy." *Strauder* v. *West Virginia*, 100 U.S., at 308.

Thus a fundamental assumption of the Fourteenth Amendment was that the states would continue, as they had for ages, to enforce the right of citizens freely to enter public places. This assumption concerning the affirmative duty attaching to places of public accommodation was so rooted in the experience of the white citizenry that law and custom blended together indistinguishably.

The Civil Rights Act of 1875, enacted seven years after the Fourteenth Amendment, specifically provided that all citizens must have "the full and equal enjoyment of the accommodations, advantages, facilities, and privileges of inns, public conveyances on land or water, theaters, and other places of public amusement." 18 Stat. 335. The constitutionality of this federal legislation was reviewed by this Court in 1883 in the *Civil Rights Cases*, 109 U.S. 3. The dissent in the present case purports to follow the "state action" concept articulated in that early decision. There the Court had declared that under the Fourteenth Amendment:

It is state action of a particular character that is prohibited. Individual invasion of individual rights is not the subject-matter of the amendment. It has a deeper and broader scope. It nullifies and makes void all state legislation, *and state action, of every kind,* which impairs the privileges and immunities of the citizens of the United States, or which injures them in life, liberty or property without due process of law, or which denies to any of them the equal protection of the laws.— 109 U.S., at 11. [Emphasis added.]

Mr. Justice Bradley, writing for the Court over the strong dissent of Mr. Justice Harlan, held that a proprietor's racially motivated denial of equal access to a public accommodation did not, without more, involve state action. It is of central importance to the case at bar that the Court's decision was expressly predicated:

on the assumption that a right to enjoy equal accommodation and privileges in all inns, public conveyances, and places of public amusement, is one of the essential rights of the citizen which no state can abridge or interfere with.—*Id.,* at 19.

The Court added that:

Innkeepers and public carriers, by the laws of all the states, so far as we are aware, are bound, to the extent of their facilities, to furnish proper accommodation to all unobjectionable persons who in good faith apply for them.—*Id.,* at 25.

This assumption, whatever its validity at the time of the 1883 decision, has proved to be unfounded. Although reconstruction ended in 1877, six years before the *Civil Rights Cases,* there was little immediate action in the South to establish segregation, in law or in fact, in places of public accommodation. This benevolent, or perhaps passive, attitude endured about a decade and then in the late 1880's states began to enact laws mandating unequal treatment in public places. Finally, three quarters of a century later, after this Court declared such legislative action invalid, some states began to utilize and make available their common law to sanction similar discriminatory treatment.

A state applying its statutory or common law to deny rather than protect the right of access to public accommodations has clearly made the assumption of the opinion in the *Civil Rights Cases* inapplicable and has, as the author of that opinion would himself have recognized, denied the constitutionally intended equal protection. Indeed, in light of the assumption so explicitly stated in the *Civil Rights Cases*, it is significant that Mr. Justice Bradley, who spoke for the Court, had earlier in correspondence with Circuit Judge Woods expressed the view that the Fourteenth Amendment "not only prohibits the making or enforcing of laws which shall abridge the privileges of the citizen; but prohibits the states from denying to all persons within its jurisdiction the equal protection of the laws." In taking this position, which is consistent with his opinion and the assumption in the *Civil Rights Cases*, he concluded that: "Denying includes inaction as well as action. And denying the equal protection of the laws includes the omission to protect, as well as the omission to pass laws for protection." These views are fully consonant with this Court's recognition that state conduct which might be described as "inaction" can nevertheless constitute responsible "state action" within the meaning of the Fourteenth Amendment. See, e.g., *Marsh* v. *Alabama*, 326 U.S. 501; *Shelley* v. *Kraemer*, 334 U.S. 1; *Terry* v. *Adams*, 345 U.S. 461; *Barrows* v. *Jackson*, 346 U.S. 249.

In spite of this, the dissent intimates that its view best comports with the needs of law and order. Thus it is said: "It would betray our whole plan for a tranquil and orderly society to say that a citizen, because of his personal prejudices, habits, attitudes, or beliefs, is cast outside the law's protection and cannot call for the aid of officers sworn to uphold the law and preserve the peace." This statement, to which all will readily agree, slides over the critical question: Whose conduct is entitled to the "law's protection"? Of course every member of this Court agrees that law and order must prevail; the question is whether the weight and protective strength of law and order will be cast in favor of the claims of the proprietors or in favor of the claims of petitioners. In my view the Fourteenth Amendment resolved this issue in favor of the right of petitioners to public accommodations and it follows that in the exercise of that constitutionally granted right they are entitled to the "law's protection." Today, as long ago, "the very essence of civil liberty certainly consists in the right of every individual to claim the protection of the laws." *Marbury* v. *Madison*, 1 Cranch 137, 163.

My Brother Douglas convincingly demonstrates that the dissent has constructed a straw man by suggesting that this case involves "a property owner's right to choose his social or business associates." *Post*, at 343. The restaurant involved in this case is concededly open to a large segment of the public. Restaurants such as this daily open their doors to millions of Americans. These establishments provide a public service as necessary today as the inns and carriers of Blackstone's time. It should be recognized that the claim asserted by the Negro petitioners concerns such public establishments and does not infringe upon the rights of property owners or personal associational interests.

Petitioners frankly state that the "extension of constitutional guarantees to the authentically private choices of man is wholly unacceptable, and any constitutional theory leading to that result would have reduced itself to absurdity." Indeed, the constitutional protection extended to privacy and private association assures against the imposition of social equality. As noted before, the Congress that enacted the Fourteenth Amendment was particularly conscious that the "civil" rights of man should be distinguished from his "social" rights. Prejudice and bigotry in any form are regrettable, but it is the constitutional right of every person to close his home or club to any person or to choose his social intimates and business partners solely on the basis of personal prejudices including race. These and other rights pertaining to privacy and private association are themselves constitutionally protected liberties.

We deal here, however, with a claim of equal access to public accommodations. This is not a claim which significantly impinges upon personal associational interests; nor is it a claim infringing upon the control of private property not dedicated to public use. A judicial ruling on this claim inevitably involves the liberties and freedoms both of the restaurant proprietor and of the Negro citizen. The dissent would hold in effect that the restaurant proprietor's interest in choosing customers on the basis of race is to be preferred to the Negro's right to equal treatment by a business serving the public. The history and purposes of the Fourteenth Amendment indicate, however, that the Amendment resolves this apparent conflict of liberties in favor of the Negro's right to equal public accommodations. As the Court said in *Marsh* v. *Alabama*, 326 U.S. 501, 506: "The more an owner, for his advantage, opens up his property for use by the public in general, the more do his rights become circumscribed by the statutory and constitutional rights of those who use it." The broad acceptance of the public in this and in other restaurants clearly demonstrates that the proprietor's interest in private or unrestricted association is slight. The relationship between the modern innkeeper or restaurateur and the customer is relatively impersonal and evanescent. This is highlighted by cases such as *Barr* v. *City of Columbia*, *ante*, at 146, *Bouie* v. *City of Columbia*, *post*, at 347, and *Robinson* v. *Florida*, *ante*, at 153, in which Negroes are invited into all departments of the store but nonetheless ordered, in the name of private association or property rights, not to purchase and eat food, as other customers do, on the premises. As the history of the common law and, indeed, of our own times graphically illustrates, the interests of proprietors of places of public accommodation have always been adapted to the citizen's felt need for public accommodations, a need which is basic and deep rooted. This history and the purposes of the Fourteenth Amendment compel the conclusion that the right to be served in places of public accommodation regardless of color cannot constitutionally be subordinated to the proprietor's interest in discriminatorily refusing service.

Of course, although the present case involves the right to service in a restaurant, the fundamental principles of the Fourteenth Amendment apply with equal force to other places of public accommodation and amusement. Claims so important as those presented here cannot be dismissed by asserting that the Fourteenth Amendment, while clearly addressed to inns and public conveyances, did not contemplate lunch counters and soda fountains. Institutions such as these serve essentially the same needs in modern life as did the innkeeper and the carrier at common law. It was to guard against narrow conceptions that Chief Justice Marshall admonished the Court never to forget "that it is *a constitution* we are expounding . . . . a constitution intended to endure for ages to come, and, consequently, to be adapted to the various *crises* of human affairs." *McCulloch* v. *Maryland*, 4 Wheat. 316, 407, 415. Today, as throughout the history of the Court, we should remember that "in determining whether a provision of the Constitution applies to a new subject matter, it is of little significance that it is one with which the framers were not familiar. For in setting up an enduring framework of government they undertook to carry out for the indefinite future and in all the vicissitudes of the changing affairs of men, those fundamental purposes which the instrument itself discloses." *United States* v. *Classic*, 313 U.S. 299, 316.

In my view the historical evidence demonstrates that the traditional rights of access to places of public accommodation were quite familiar to congressmen and to the general public who naturally assumed that the Fourteenth Amendment extended these traditional rights to Negroes. But even if the historical evidence were not as convincing as I believe it to be, the logic of *Brown* v. *Board of Education*, 347 U.S. 483, based as it was on the fundamental principle of constitutional interpretation proclaimed by Chief Justice Marshall, requires that petitioners' claim be sustained.

In *Brown*, after stating that the available history was "inconclusive" on the specific issue of segregated public schools, the Court went on to say:

In approaching this problem, we cannot turn the clock back to 1868 when the Amendment was adopted, or even to 1896 when *Plessy* v. *Ferguson* was written. We must consider public education in the light of its full development and its present place in American life throughout the nation. Only in this way can it be determined if segregation in public schools deprives these plaintiffs of the equal protection of the laws.—347 U.S., at 492-493.

The dissent makes no effort to assess the status of places of public accommodation "in the light of" their "full development and . . . present place" in the life of American citizens. In failing to adhere to that approach the dissent ignores a pervasive principle of constitutional adjudication and departs from the ultimate logic of *Brown*. As Mr. Justice Holmes so aptly said:

When we are dealing with words that also are a constituent act, like the Constitution of the United States, we must realize that they have called into life a being the development of which could not have been foreseen completely by the most gifted of its begetters. It was enough for them to realize or to hope that they had created an organism; it has taken a century and has cost their successors much sweat and blood to prove that they created a nation. The case before us must be considered in the light of our whole experience and not merely in that of what was said a hundred years ago.—*Missouri* v. *Holland*, 252 U.S. 416, 433.

The constitutional right of all Americans to be treated as equal members of the community with respect to public accommodations is a civil right granted by the people in the Constitution—a right which "is too important in our free society to be stripped of judicial protection." Cf. *Wesberry* v. *Sanders*, 376 U.S. 1, 7; *Baker* v. *Carr*, 369 U.S. 186. This is not to suggest that Congress lacks authority under § 5 of the Fourteenth Amendment, or under the Commerce Clause, Art. I, § 8, to implement the rights protected by § 1 of the Fourteenth Amendment. In the give-and-take of the legislative process, Congress can fashion a law drawing the guidelines necessary and appropriate to facilitate practical administration and to distinguish between genuinely public and private accommodations. In contrast, we can pass only on justiciable issues coming here on a case-to-case basis.

It is, and should be, more true today than it was over a century ago that "the great advantage of the Americans is that . . . they [are] born equal" and that in the eyes of the law they "are all of the same estate." The first Chief Justice of the United States, John Jay, spoke of the "free air" of American life. The great purpose of the Fourteenth Amendment is to keep it free and equal. Under the Constitution no American can, or should, be denied rights fundamental to freedom and citizenship.

Heart of Atlanta Motel v. United States, 379 U.S. 241
Katzenbach v. McClung, 379 U.S. 294

[While the Court was involved in the constitutional debate about equality in access to public accommodations represented in the *Bell* case, Congress passed the Civil Rights Act of 1964, which provides: "All persons shall be entitled to the full and equal enjoyment of the goods, services, facilities, privileges, advantages, and accommodation, as defined in this section . . . without discrimination or segregation on the ground of race, color, religion, or national origin." There are then listed four classes of business establishments, each of which "serves the public" and "is a place of public accommodation" within the meaning of the preceding sentence "if its operations affect [interstate] commerce, or if discrimination or segregation by it is supported by state action." In these cases a unanimous Supreme Court upheld the act as a valid exercise of Congressional power to regulate interstate commerce. Justice Goldberg added a short concurring opinion to emphasize the fact that in the act Congress was primarily concerned with the vindication of human dignity and not mere economics. In his view this is reinforced by the fact that the legislative history shows that Congress rested the act not only on its commerce power but on its power to legislate in implementation of the Equal Protection Clause of the Fourteenth Amendment.]

I join in the opinions and judgments of the Court,[1] since I agree "that the action of the Congress in the adoption of the Act as applied here . . . is within the power granted it by the Commerce Clause of the Constitution, as interpreted by this Court for 140 years," *ante*, at 261.

The primary purpose of the Civil Rights Act of 1964, however, as the Court recognizes, and as I would underscore, is the vindication of human dignity and not mere economics. The Senate Commerce Committee made this quite clear:

The primary purpose of . . . [the Civil Rights Act], then, is to solve this problem, the deprivation of personal dignity that surely accompanies denials of equal access to public establishments. Discrimination is not simply dollars and cents, hamburgers and movies; it is the humiliation, frustration, and embarrassment that a person must surely feel when he is told that he is unacceptable as a member of the public because of his race or color. It is equally the inability to explain to a child that regardless of education, civility, courtesy, and morality he will be denied the right to enjoy equal treatment, even though he be a citizen of the United States and may well be called upon to lay down his life to assure this nation continues.—S. Rep. No. 872, 88th Cong., 2d Sess., 16.

Moreover, that this is the primary purpose of the act is emphasized by the fact that while § 201 (c) speaks only in terms of establishments which "affect commerce," it is clear that Congress based this section not only on its power under the Commerce Clause but also on § 5 of the Fourteenth Amendment. The cases cited in the Court's opinions are conclusive that Congress could exercise its powers under the Commerce Clause to accomplish this purpose. As § § 201 (b) and (c) are undoubtedly a valid exercise of

[1] December 14, 1964. Cases Nos. 515 and 543. Mr. Justice Goldberg concurring.

the Commerce Clause power for the reasons stated in the opinion of the Court, the Court considers that it is unnecessary to consider whether it is additionally supportable by Congress's exertion of its power under § 5 of the Fourteenth Amendment.

In my concurring opinion in *Bell* v. *Maryland*, 378 U.S. 226, 317, however, I expressed my conviction that § 1 of the Fourteenth Amendment guarantees to all Americans the constitutional right "to be treated as equal members of the community with respect to public accommodations," and that "Congress [has] authority under § 5 of the Fourteenth Amendment, or under the Commerce Clause, Art. I, § 8, to implement the rights protected by § 1 of the Fourteenth Amendment. In the give-and-take of the legislative process, Congress can fashion a law drawing the guidelines necessary and appropriate to facilitate practical administration and to distinguish between genuinely public and private accommodations." The challenged act is just such a law and, in my view, Congress clearly had authority both under § 5 of the Fourteenth Amendment and the Commerce Clause to enact the Civil Rights Act of 1964.

Swain v. Alabama, 380 U.S. 202

[Robert Swain, a 19-year-old Negro, was convicted by an all-white jury in Talladega County, Alabama, of raping a 17-year-old white girl, and he was sentenced to death. He argued before the courts of Alabama and before the Supreme Court that his conviction must be set aside because Negroes were unconstitutionally excluded from the jury that tried and sentenced him. Although Negroes served on the jury panel from which the final jury was selected, no Negro had ever served on a jury in the history of Talladega County. Swain argued that in every case the prosecuting attorney systematically challenged and removed every Negro from the jury panel. Such a procedure was proper under Alabama law, which allows each attorney peremptory challenges to disqualify a certain number of jury panelists from serving on the jury without giving any reason for the disqualification.

[The Court affirmed Swain's conviction on the ground that he had not sufficiently demonstrated that the state was systematically excluding Negroes from juries. Justice Goldberg, joined by the Chief Justice and Justice Douglas, dissented vigorously, pointing to the long-standing rule that the exclusion of Negroes from juries was unconstitutional and that, once a defendant showed that Negroes did not serve on juries although qualified Negroes lived in the community, he made out a prima facie case of unconstitutional exclusion, and shifted the burden of proof to the state to show that it did not discriminate in jury selection.

[Justice Goldberg argued that Swain had clearly made out a prima facie case of unconstitutional jury exclusion, for no Negro had ever served on a Talladega County jury despite the large number of qualified Negroes living in the area. He believed that the "prima facie" case rule was being weakened and that the Court's opinion might allow widespread exclusion of Negroes from juries.]

In 1880 this Court,[1] in *Strauder* v. *West Virginia,* 100 U.S. 303, one of the first cases applying the Fourteenth Amendment to racial discrimination, held that under the Equal Protection Clause, a State cannot systematically exclude persons from juries solely because of their race or color. Since *Strauder* and until today this Court has consistently applied this constitutional principle. . . .

The reasons underlying the Court's decisions in these cases were well expressed in *Strauder:*

The very idea of a jury is a body of men composed of the peers or equals of the person whose rights it is selected or summoned to determine; that is, of his neighbors, fellows, associates, persons having the same legal status in society as that which he holds. Blackstone, in his Commentaries, says, "The right of trial by jury, or the country, is a trial by the peers of every Englishman, and is the grand bulwark of his liberties, and is secured to him by the Great Charter." It is also guarded by statutory enactments intended to make impossible what Mr. Bentham called "packing juries." It is well known that prejudices often exist against particular classes in the community, which sway the judgment of jurors, and which, therefore, operate in some cases to deny to persons of those classes the full enjoyment of that protection which others enjoy.—100 U.S., at 308-309.

Moreover,

the very fact that colored people are singled out and expressly denied by a statute all right to participate in the administration of the law, as jurors, because of their color, though they are citizens, and may be in other respects fully qualified, is practically a brand upon them, affixed by the law, an assertion of their inferiority, and a stimulant to that race prejudice which is an impediment to securing to individuals of the race that equal justice which the law aims to secure to all others.—100 U.S., at 308.

The principles and reasoning upon which this long line of decisions rests are sound. The need for their reaffirmation is present. The United States Commission on Civil Rights in its 1961 Report, Justice, 103, after exhaustive study of the practice of discrimination in jury selection, concluded that "the practice of racial exclusion from juries persists today even though it has long stood indicted as a serious violation of the Fourteenth Amendment." It is

[1] March 8, 1965. Case No. 64. Mr. Justice Goldberg, with whom the Chief Justice and Mr. Justice Douglas join, dissenting.

unthinkable, therefore, that the principles of *Strauder* and the cases following should be in any way weakened or undermined at this late date particularly when this Court has made it clear in other areas, where the course of decision has not been so uniform, that the States may not discriminate on the basis of race. Compare *Plessy* v. *Ferguson*, 163 U.S. 537, with *Brown* v. *Board of Education*, 347 U.S. 483; compare *Pace* v. *Alabama*, 106 U.S. 583, with *McLaughlin* v. *Florida*, 379 U.S. 184.

Regrettably, however, the Court today, while referring with approval to *Strauder* and the cases which have followed, seriously impairs their authority and creates additional barriers to the elimination of jury discrimination practices which have operated in many communities to nullify the command of the Equal Protection Clause. This is evident from an analysis of the Court's holding as applied to the facts which are virtually undisputed.

Petitioner, a 19-year-old Negro, was indicted in Talladega County for the rape of a 17-year-old white girl, found guilty, and sentenced to death by an all-white jury. The petitioner established by competent evidence and without contradiction that not only was there no Negro on the jury that convicted and sentenced him, but also that no Negro within the memory of persons now living has ever served on any petit jury in any civil or criminal case tried in Talladega County, Alabama. Yet, of the group designated by Alabama as generally eligible for jury service in that county, 74% (12,125) were white and 26% (4,281) were Negro.

Under well-established principles this evidence clearly makes out "a *prima facie* case of the denial of the equal protection which the Constitution guarantees." *Norris* v. *Alabama, supra,* at 591. The case here is at least as strong as that in *Norris* where

proof that Negroes constituted a substantial segment of the population of the jurisdiction, that some Negroes were qualified to serve as jurors, and that none had been called for jury service over an extended period of time, was held to constitute prima facie proof of the systematic exclusion of Negroes from jury service. This holding, sometimes called the "rule of exclusion," has been applied in other cases, and it is available in supplying proof of discrimination against any delineated class.—*Hernandez* v. *Texas, supra,* at 480.

It is clear that, unless the state here can "justify such an exclusion as having been brought about for some reason other than racial discrimination," *Patton* v. *Mississippi, supra,* at 466, this conviction "cannot stand." *Id.,* at 469. *Norris* v. *Alabama, supra,* at 596-598; *Arnold* v. *North Carolina, supra,* at 774. "Long continued omission of Negroes from jury service establishes a prima facie case of systematic discrimination. The burden of proof is then upon the state to refute it." *Harper* v. *Mississippi,* 251 Miss. 699, 707, 171 So. 2d 129, 132-133.

However, the Court affirms petitioner's conviction on the ground that petitioner has "failed to carry" his burden of proof. The Court holds this because it believes the record is silent as to whether the state participated in this total exclusion of all Negroes in previous cases. . . .

I cannot agree that the record is silent as to the state's involvement in the total exclusion of Negroes from jury service in Talladega County. [Instances of state participation are set out.]

Furthermore, the state concededly is responsible for the selection of the jury venire. As the Court recognizes, *ante*, at 205, the evidence showed that, while Negroes represent 26% of the population generally available to be called for jury service in Talladega County, Negroes constituted a lesser proportion, generally estimated from 10% to 15%, of the average venire. . . .

Finally, it is clear that Negroes were removed from the venire and excluded from service by the prosecutor's use of the peremptory challenge system in this case and that they have never served on the jury in any case in the history of the county. On these facts, and the inferences reasonably drawn from them, it seems clear that petitioner has affirmatively proved a pattern of racial discrimination in which the state is significantly involved, cf. *Burton* v. *Wilmington Parking Authority*, 365 U.S. 715, 722; *Lombard* v. *Louisiana*, 373 U.S. 267; *Peterson* v. *Greenville*, 373 U.S. 244, or for which the state is responsible, cf. *Terry* v. *Adams*, 345 U.S. 461, 473. As this Court held in *Strauder*, systematic exclusion of Negroes from jury service constitutes a brand of inferiority affixed upon them and state involvement in affixing such a brand is forbidden by the Fourteenth Amendment.

There is, however, a more fundamental defect in the Court's holding. Even if the Court were correct that the record is silent as to state involvement in previous cases in which Negroes have been systematically excluded from jury service, nevertheless, it is undisputed that no Negro has ever served on any petit jury in the history of Talladega County. Under *Norris, Patton* and the other cases discussed above, it is clear that petitioner by proving this made out a prima facie case of unlawful jury exclusion. The burden of proof then shifted to the state to prove, if it could, that this exclusion was brought about for some reason other than racial discrimination in which the state participates. . . .

Despite the fact that the petitioner therefore has made out what is, under the settled decisions of this Court, a prima facie case of jury exclusion which the state has not rebutted, the Court today affirms petitioner's conviction because, according to the Court, petitioner has "failed to carry" his burden of proof. The Court concedes that if this case involved exclusion of Negroes from jury panels, under *Norris* and *Patton* a prima facie case of unconstitutional jury exclusion would be made out. However, the Court argues that because this case involves exclusion from the jury itself and not from the jury venire, the burden of proof on a defendant should be greater. This distinction is novel to say the least.

The Court's jury decisions, read together, have never distinguished between exclusions from the jury panel and exclusion from the jury itself. Indeed, no such distinction can be drawn. The very point of all these cases is to prevent that deliberate and systematic discrimination against Negroes or any other racial group that would prevent them, not merely from being placed upon the panel, but from serving on the jury. . . .

The rule of exclusion . . . is a highly pragmatic one. It is designed to operate in jury cases so that once the defendant has made a showing of total exclusion, the burden on going forward with the evidence is placed upon the state, the party in the better position to develop the facts as to how the exclusion came about. The defendant is a party to one proceeding only, and his access to relevant evidence is obviously limited. The state is a party to all criminal cases and has greater access to the evidence, if any, which would tend to negative the state's involvement in discriminatory jury selection. The burden of proof rule developed in *Norris*, *Patton*, and other cases, which until today the Court has uniformly applied, is a simple and workable one designed to affectuate the Constitution's command. This is demonstrated by our past cases, as well as state cases. Because the same factors—availability of evidence, simplicity, and workability—exist whether exclusion from the jury panel or exclusion from the jury itself is involved, to apply the prima facie rule of *Norris* and *Patton* to this case is neither "blind" nor "wooden," but is realistic and sensible. . . .

Finally, the Court's reasoning on this point completely overlooks the fact that the total exclusion of Negroes from juries in Talladega County results from the interlocking of an inadequate venire selection system, for which the state concededly is responsible, and the use of peremptory challenges. All of these factors confirm my view that no good reason exists to fashion a new rule of burden of proof, which will make it more difficult to put an end to discriminatory selection of juries on racial grounds and will thereby impair the constitutional promise of "Equal Protection of the Laws," made effective by *Strauder* and the cases which follow it. By undermining the doctrine of the prima facie case while paying lip service to *Strauder* the Court today allies itself with those "that keep the word of promise to our ear and break it to our hope."

The Court departs from the long-established burden of proof rule in this area and imposes substantial additional burdens upon Negro defendants such as petitioner, because of its view of the importance of retaining inviolate the right of the state to use peremptory challenges. I believe, however, that the preference granted by the Court to the state's use of the peremptory challenge is both unwarranted and unnecessary.

To begin with, the peremptory challenge has long been recognized primarily as a device to protect *defendants*. As stated by Blackstone in a passage quoted with approval by this Court:

[I]n criminal cases, or at least in capital ones, there is, *in favorem vitae,* allowed to the prisoner an arbitrary and capricious species of challenge to a certain number of jurors, without showing any cause at all; which is called a *peremptory* challenge: a provision full of that tenderness and humanity to prisoners, for which our English laws are justly famous. This is grounded on two reasons:

1. As every one must be sensible, what sudden impressions and unaccountable prejudices we are apt to conceive upon the bare looks and gestures of another; and how necessary it is that a prisoner (when put to defend his life) should have a good opinion of his jury, the want of which might totally disconcert him; the law wills not that he should be tried by any one man against whom he has conceived a prejudice even without being able to assign a reason for such his dislike.

2. Because, upon challenges for cause shown, if the reason assigned proves insufficient to set aside the juror, perhaps the bare questioning his indifference may sometimes provoke a resentment; to prevent all ill consequences from which, the prisoner is still at liberty, if he pleases, peremptorily to set him aside.— 4 Bl. Comm. 353. Quoted with approval in *Lewis* v. *United States,* 146 U.S. 370, 376; see also *United States* v. *Marchant,* 12 Wheat. 480, 482.

Indeed in England, as the Court points out, *ante,* at 212-213, although the Crown at early common law had an unlimited number of peremptory challenges, as early as 1305 that right was taken away, and since that time in England peremptories may be exercised only by the defendant. Orfield, *Criminal Procedure from Arrest to Appeal* 355 (1947). Harris, *Criminal Law* 433 (20th ed. 1960). It appears that in modern times peremptories are rarely used in England, even by defendants. *Ibid.*

While peremptory challenges are commonly used in this country both by the prosecution and the defense, we have long recognized that the right to challenge peremptorily is not a fundamental right, constitutionally guaranteed, even as applied to a defendant, much less to the state. *Stilson* v. *United States,* 250 U.S. 583. This Court has sanctioned numerous incursions upon the right to challenge peremptorily. Defendants may be tried together even though the exercise by one of his right to challenge peremptorily may deprive his codefendant of a juror he desires or may require that codefendant to use his challenges in a way other than he wishes. *United States* v. *Marchant, supra.* A defendant may be required to exercise his challenges prior to the state, so that some may be wasted on jurors whom the state would have challenged. *Pointer* v. *United States,* 151 U.S. 396. Congress may regulate the number of peremptory challenges available to defendants by statute and may require codefendants to be treated as a single defendant so that each has only a small portion of the number of peremptories he would have, if tried separately. *Stilson* v. *United States, supra.* In *Stilson* this Court stated, "There is nothing in the Constitution of the United States which requires the Congress to grant peremptory challenges to defendants in criminal cases; trial by an impartial jury is all that is secured." 250 U.S., at 586. The Fourteenth Amendment would impose no greater obligation upon the states. Today this Court reverses *Stilson's* maxim, in effect holding that "There is nothing in the Constitution of the United States which requires the state to grant trial by an impartial jury so long as the inviolability of the peremptory challenge is secured."

Were it necessary to make an absolute choice between the right of a defendant to have a jury chosen in conformity with the requirements of the Fourteenth Amendment and the right to challenge peremptorily, the Constitution compels a choice of the former. *Marbury* v. *Madison,* 1 Cranch 137, settled beyond doubt that when a constitutional claim is opposed by a non-constitutional one, the former must prevail. But no such choice is compelled in this situation. The holding called for by this case is that where, as here, a Negro defendant proves that Negroes constitute a substantial segment of the population, that Negroes are qualified to serve as jurors, and that none or only a token number has served on juries over an extended period of time, a prima facie case of the exclusion of Negroes from juries is then made out; that the state, under our settled decisions, is then called upon to show that such exclusion has been brought about "for some reason other than racial discrimination," *Patton* v. *Mississippi, supra,* at 466; and that the state wholly fails to meet the prima facie case of systematic and purposeful racial discrimination by showing that it has been accomplished by ·the use of a peremptory challenge system unless the state also shows that it is not involved in the misuse of such a system to prevent all Negroes from ever sitting on any jury. Such a holding would not interfere with the rights of *defendants* to use peremptories, nor the right of the state to use peremptories as they normally and traditionally have been used.

It would not mean, as the Court's prior decisions, to which I would adhere, make clear, that Negroes are entitled to proportionate representation on a jury. *Cassell* v. *Texas, supra,* at 286-287 (opinion of Mr. Justice Reed). Nor would it mean that where systematic exclusion of Negroes from jury service has not been shown, that a prosecutor's motives are subject to question or judicial inquiry when he excludes Negroes or any other group from sitting on a jury in a particular case. Only where systematic exclusion has been shown would the state be called upon to justify its use of peremptories or to negative the state's involvement in discriminatory jury selection.

This holding would mean, however, that a conviction cannot stand where, as here, a Negro defendant, by showing widespread systematic exclusion, makes out a prima facie case of unconstitutional discrimination which the state does not rebut. Drawing the line in this fashion, in my view, achieves a practical accommodation of the constitutional right and the operation of the peremptory challenge system without doing violence to either.

I deplore the Court's departure from its holdings in *Strauder* and *Norris*. By affirming petitioner's conviction on this clear record of jury exclusion because of race, the Court condones the highly discriminatory procedures used in Talledaga County under which Negroes never have served on any petit jury in that county. By adding to the present heavy burden of proof required of defendants in these cases, the Court creates additional barriers to the elimination of practices which have operated in many communities throughout the nation to nullify the command of the Equal Protection Clause in this important area of the administration of justice. See 1961 United States Commission on Civil Rights Report, Justice, 81-103.

I would be faithful to the teachings of this Court in its prior jury exclusion cases and the view, repeatedly expressed by this Court, that distinctions between citizens solely because of their race, religion, or ancestry are odious to the Fourteenth Amendment. I would reaffirm and apply here what this Court said in *Smith* v. *Texas, supra*, at 130:

It is part of the established tradition in the use of juries as instruments of public justice that the jury be a body truly representative of the community. For racial discrimination to result in the exclusion from jury service of otherwise qualified groups not only violates our Constitution and the laws enacted under it but is at war with our basic concepts of a democratic society and a representative government. . . . The fact that the written words of a state's laws hold out a promise that no such discrimination will be practiced is not enough. The Fourteenth Amendment requires that equal protection to all must be given—not merely promised.

Applying these principles, I would reverse. This, of course, would "not mean that a guilty defendant must go free." *Patton* v. *Mississippi, supra*, at 469; see *Hill* v. *Texas, supra*, at 406. For, as the Court pointed out in *Patton* v. *Mississippi, supra*, at 469, the state, if it so desired, could retry petitioner by a jury "selected as the Constitution commands."

3 ᖈᖆᖇ
Labor and the Law

LABOR BOARD v. METROPOLITAN INSURANCE CO., 380 U.S. 438

[A noteworthy recent development in the law has been the growth of administrative agencies as initial fact-finding and law-developing units. Justice Goldberg has adhered to the established doctrine that courts should give great deference to administrative agency determinations in their areas of expertise. However, this deference is conditioned on the agency's setting forth with clarity its basis of decision and there being substantial evidence on the record as a whole to support the agency decision. In this and the following case, Justice Goldberg has applied these standards to determinations of the National Labor Relations Board.]

On petition[1] of Insurance Workers' International Union, AFL-CIO, and over the protest of respondent, Metropolitan Life Insurance Company, as to the appropriateness of the bargaining unit, the National Labor Relations Board, in a proceeding under § 9 (c) of the National Labor Relations Act, certified the union as the bargaining representative of all debit insurance agents, including all canvassing regular and office account agents, at respondent's district office in Woonsocket, Rhode Island. The Court of Appeals for the First Circuit refused to enforce the order on the grounds that in light of the "Board's failure to articulate specific reasons for its unit determination," 327 F. 2d 906, 909, the Board's apparently inconsistent determinations of appropriate units of respondents' employees in other cities or regions, its failure to discuss in these cases what weight, if any, it gives to the factor of the extent of union organization, and the fact that in these cases the Board consistently certified the unit requested by the union, the Court of Appeals could "only conclude . . . that the . . . Board . . . has indeed . . . [regarded] the extent of the union organization as controlling in violation of § 9 (c) (5) of the Act." 327 F. 2d, at 911.

[1] April 5, 1965. Case No. 98. Mr. Justice Goldberg delivered the opinion of the Court.

Section 9 (b) of the National Labor Relations Act, 49 Stat. 453, as amended, 29 U.S.C. § 159 (b) (1958 ed.) provides:

The Board shall decide in each case whether, in order to assure the employees the fullest freedom in exercising the rights guaranteed by this subchapter, the unit appropriate for the purposes of collective bargaining shall be the employer unit, craft unit, plant unit, or subdivision thereof.

This broad delegation of authority was limited in 1947 by the enactment of § 9 (c) (5) of the Act, 61 Stat. 143, 29 U.S.C. § 159 (c) (5), which provides that "in determining whether a unit is appropriate for the purposes specified in subsection (b) of this section the extent to which the employees have organized shall not be controlling."

Although it is clear that in passing this amendment Congress intended to overrule Board decisions where the unit determined could only be supported on the basis of the extent of organization, both the language and legislative history of § 9 (c) (5) demonstrate that the provision was not intended to prohibit the Board from considering the extent of organization as one factor, though not the controlling factor, in its unit determination.

The Court of Appeals here properly recognized this effect of § 9 (c) (5), but held, in light of the unarticulated bases of decision, and what appeared to it to be inconsistent determinations approving units requested by the union, that the only conclusion that it could reach was that the Board has made the extent of organization the controlling factor, in violation of the congressional mandate. We agree with the Court of Appeals that the enforcing court should not overlook or ignore an evasion of the § 9 (c) (5) command. We further agree that in determining whether or not there has been such an evasion, the results in other recent decisions of the Board are relevant. We cannot, however, agree that the only possible conclusion here is that the Board has violated § 9 (c) (5).

On the other hand, due to the Board's lack of articulated reasons for the decisions in and distinctions among these cases, the Board's action here cannot be properly reviewed. When the Board so exercises the discretion given to it by Congress, it must "disclose the basis of its order" and "give clear indication that it has exercised the discretion with which Congress has empowered it." Although Board counsel in his brief and argument before this Court has rationalized the different unit determinations in the variant factual situations of these cases on criteria other than a controlling effect being given to the extent of organization, the integrity of the administrative process requires that "courts may not accept appellate counsel's *post hoc* rationalizations for agency action." For reviewing courts to substitute counsel's rationale or their discretion for that of the Board is incompatible with the orderly function of the process of judicial review. Such action would not vindicate but would deprecate the administrative process, for it would "propel the court into the domain which Congress has set aside exclusively for the administrative agency." . . .

Accordingly, the judgment of the Court of Appeals is vacated and the case remanded to that court with instructions to remand it to the Board for further proceedings consistent with this opinion.

AMERICAN SHIPBUILDING CO. v. LABOR BOARD, 380 U.S. 300

[Whether or not an employer may lock out his employees solely to put economic pressure upon them has long been an important, unsettled issue of labor law. Prior to *Shipbuilding* the National Labor Relations Board had held that an employer may lock out his employees when a strike is threatened and to allow the union to control the strike would subject the employer and his customers to unusual economic injury. The Board had also held (with one minor exception) that, absent such special circumstances, an employer's lockout is an unfair labor practice.

[The employer company in *Shipbuilding* operated shipyards on the Great Lakes. Immediately after the expiration of its collective bargaining agreements during the slack season it locked out its employees, for it feared that otherwise they would strike during the busy winter season when a strike might seriously damage the employer and his customers whose ships would be in the yards. The Labor Board held that the employer's fear of a strike was unreasonable and that the lockout therefore was illegal. The Court, while accepting the Board's determination that the employer's fear of a strike was unreasonable, reversed the Board, for it held that after a bargaining impasse is reached an employer may lock out his employees for the sole purpose of bringing economic pressure to bear in support of his bargaining position. In other words, the Court held that, after a bargaining impasse, unless the employer is acting in order to discourage unionization, he may lock out his employees.

[Justice Goldberg, joined by the Chief Justice, concurred in the result, but believed that the Court was wrong to lay down a sweeping rule legalizing almost all economically motivated lockouts. He would have reversed the Board because its finding that the employer's fear of a strike was unreasonable was without any support in the record. In his view, since the facts revealed by the record clearly show that the employer was faced with a substantial strike threat, the lockout was legitimate under prior Board rules. While normally he would defer to findings of an administrative body, he would not accept a finding that was made without record support. Moreover, Justice Goldberg pointed out that lockouts arise in many different factual contexts, and the legitimate conflicting interests of the employer and the union vary considerably from one type of situation to another. There is no simple formula that readily demarks the permissible from the impermissible in this complex area of labor relations, and the Court should not in this case attempt to formulate one flat rule that covers numerous types of lockout situations.]

I concur in the Court's conclusion[1] that the employer's lockout in this case was not a violation of either § 8 (a) (1) or § 8 (a) (3) of the National Labor Relations Act, 49 Stat. 453, as amended, 29 U.S.C. §§ 158 (a) (1) and (3), and I therefore join in the judgment reversing the Court of Appeals. I reach this result not for the Court's reasons but because, from the plain facts revealed by the record, it is crystal clear that the employer's lockout here was justifiable. The very facts recited by the Court in its opinion show that this employer locked out his employees in the face of a threatened strike under circumstances where, had the choice of timing been left solely to the unions, the employer and his customers would have been subject to economic injury over and beyond the loss of business normally incident to a strike upon the termination of the collective bargaining agreement. A lockout under these circumstances has been recognized by the Board itself to be justifiable and not a violation of the labor statutes.

The trial examiner for the Labor Board found that the employer reasonably and "honestly believed that a strike might take place immediately, or when a vessel was docked, or that bargaining would be delayed until closer to the winter months when Respondent would be more vulnerable," and that the company "by its actions, therefore, did not violate . . . the Act." The Board did not dispute the trial examiner's finding that the employer *in fact* believed that a strike was threatened. Nor did it deny that if the employer reasonably believed that "there was a real strike threat," the lockout would be justified. The Board, however, rejected the ultimate finding of the trial examiner because it disagreed with his conclusion that the employer "had *reasonable grounds* to fear a strike." The Court of Appeals in a single sentence sustained the Board's holding on this point concluding, without detailed analysis, "that the Board's finding that respondent had no reasonable basis for fearing a strike is not without the requisite record support." In my view the Board's conclusion that the employer's admitted fear of a strike was unreasonable is not only without the requisite record support but is at complete variance with "the actualities of industrial relations," *Labor Board*

[1] March 29, 1965. Case No. 255. Mr. Justice Goldberg, with whom the Chief Justice joins, concurring in the result.

v. *Steelworkers*, 357 U.S. 357, 364, which the Board is to take into account in effectuating the national labor policy.

We do not deal with a case in which the facts are disputed and the Board has resolved testimonial controversies. The facts here are undisputed, and a review of them demonstrates that the employer's fear of a strike at a time strategically selected by the unions to cause him maximum damage and to give the unions the maximum economic advantage was totally reasonable.

The employer company is primarily engaged in repairing ships and operates four shipyards on the Great Lakes at Buffalo, New York; Lorain and Toledo, Ohio, and South Chicago, Illinois. As the Court points out, the employer's business is highly seasonal, concentrated in the winter months when the Great Lakes are frozen over and shipping is impossible. Speed is of the utmost importance in this business, for the shipping season is short and the tie-up of a ship for several weeks during the season or a delay in a ship's re-entry into service in the spring produces a severe economic impact. A work stoppage while a ship is in the yards can have serious economic consequences both for the employer and for his customers. Customers are justifiably wary of entrusting their ships to the yards at a time when a collective bargaining dispute is unresolved. For this reason the expiration date of a contract in situations such as this is a vital issue in collective bargaining. The employer seeks an expiration date during the slack season; the union seeks an expiration date during the busy season. In this case, as a result of past bargaining, the employer's contract expired on August 1, rather than during the busy season.

From 1952 until 1961, when the negotiations now under consideration began, the employer had negotiated five times with the eight unions here involved, and he had experienced exactly one strike per negotiation. The strikes in 1952, 1953, 1955, and 1956 lasted about three weeks each, and the 1958 strike continued for ten weeks. In 1955 employees had engaged in a slowdown before the agreement expired and thereby caught an $8,000,000 ship in the yard, the use of which was lost to the customer for four weeks during his busiest season. In February, 1961, at the height of the busy season, wildcat work stoppages occurred in Chicago and Buffalo.

Shortly before May, 1961, the unions notified the employer that they wished to modify the contract due to expire on August 1. At the first bargaining meeting on June 6, 1961, the employer spokesman maintained that competitive conditions prevented any increase in wages or benefits. The unions took an opposite view and asked for a substantial increase in pension and other benefits. The parties met on numerous occasions throughout June and July. As the negotiations progressed, the employer receded from his original position and offered improved wages and benefits; the unions receded from some of their demands, but a meeting of the minds was not reached. On July 20 and subsequently, with the August 1 expiration date approaching, the unions proposed a six-month extension of the current contract. This would have given the unions an expiration date at a time most advantageous to them; the employer rejected this proposal on the grounds that the contract would then expire on February 1, 1962, the very height of his busy season, and that no customer would risk its ships by putting them in the company's yards knowing that the labor contract was about to expire. On July 28 the union's negotiator informed the employer that the union members had voted "overwhelmingly to take a strike if necessary." On July 31 the employer make a new and increased offer on wages and benefits, asked that his proposals be submitted to the employees for a vote and offered to extend the contract for the limited period sufficient to enable this vote to be taken. The unions in turn asked that the labor agreement be extended indefinitely until a new agreement was reached. The employer refused to agree to an indefinite extension of his present contract on the ground that he could then be struck at any time of the unions' choosing.[2]

Although the contract expired on August 1, the unions did not call a strike on that date but continued to work on a day-to-day basis and submitted the employer's revised offer to a vote of the membership. On August 8 the unions informed the employer that his proposals had been "overwhelmingly" rejected by the employees. On August 9 the employer made a new package offer on many issues. The union negotiators rejected this new offer, refused to take it to the employees for a vote, and made no counteroffer. Negotiations were broken off without any definite plans for further meetings between the parties. Future meetings were left to the call of a federal mediator.

Faced with the situation of an expired contract and the unions free to strike at any time, in particular at a time of their own choosing during the busy season, or whenever the yard was filled with ships, the employer decided to shut down the Chicago yard completely and lay off all but two employees at Toledo. Notices were issued to employees at Chicago, Toledo, and to some in Buffalo, which stated, "Because of the labor dispute which has been unresolved since August 1, 1961, you are laid off until further notice." Negotiations were resumed after this lockout and continued until agreement was reached on October 27. The laid-off employees were then recalled to work. Since then the parties have engaged in other negotiations and have agreed upon contracts without either strike or lockout.

On this record the trial examiner held that the employer reasonably

---

[2] See note 4, *infra*.

feared that the unions would strike when the time was ripe. He found that
the employer reasonably believed that:

The unions' strategy was:

Keep working at Lorain, keep the nonproductive men on the payroll as long
as possible at the other yards until one of two things occurred: (a) A ship
owner would send a ship into one of the yards, and then by striking, the respondent would be forced to his knees in effecting a labor settlement satisfactory
to the union, and if this didn't occur, then, (b) continue to bargain, into the
winter months, and then execute an agreement effective in November, December,
January, or February, and in this way, when the agreement was reopened,
respondent would be sure to have ships in its docks, and a strike at such time
would bring the respondent to his knees in effecting an agreement.

Accordingly the trial examiner held that no unfair labor practice was committed. This holding followed settled Board doctrine that "lockouts are permissible to safeguard against unusual operational problems or hazards or
economic loss where there is reasonable ground for believing that a strike
[is] . . . threatened or imminent."

The Board overturned the trial examiner's ultimate holding, reaching
what, on this record, is a totally unsupportable conclusion—that the employer's fear of a strike was unreasonable. The Board rested its conclusion
upon the grounds that "the unions made every effort to convey to the Respondent their intention not to strike; and they also gave assurances that if a
strike were called, any work brought into respondent's yard before the
strike would be completed. The unions further offered to extend the existing contract [which contained a no-strike provision] for 6 months, or
indefinitely, until contract terms were reached." Upon analysis it is clear
that none of these grounds will support the Board's conclusion that the
employer had no reasonable basis to fear a strike.

The Board's finding that "the unions made every effort to convey to the
respondents their intention not to strike" is based upon statements made by
union negotiators during the course of the negotiations. The chief negotiator
for the unions testified that on the first day of negotiations, "I stated that
it was my understanding that in the past there seemed to have been a strike
at every—during every negotiation since World War II from information
I had received, and it was our sincere hope that we could negotiate this
agreement—go through those negotiations and negotiate a new agreement
without any strife, that personally I always had a strong dislike to strike
and that I thought if two parties sincerely desired to reach an agreement, one
could be reached without strike. The company . . . stated that the company
concurred in those thoughts, that they too disliked strikes, and it was their

hope, also, that an agreement could be reached amicably." The negotiators for the unions expressed this same sentiment on several other occasions during the negotiations.

These statements, which one would normally expect a union agent to make during the course of negotiations as a hopeful augury of their outcome rather than as a binding agreement not to strike, scarcely vitiate the reasonableness of the employer's fear of a strike in light of the long history of past strikes by the same unions. Further, they cannot be deemed to render the employer's fear of a strike unreasonable after the negotiations had reached an impasse, particularly in view of the fact that a strike vote had been taken by the unions' membership, and the membership rather than the union representatives had final authority to determine whether a strike would take place.

The fact that the assistant business managers of Local 85 and Local 374 of the Boilermakers Union "gave assurances that if a strike were called, any work brought into respondents' yard before the strike would be completed"[3] likewise cannot be deemed to offset the unions' threat of a strike and its consequences. These men were officials of locals in only one of the eight separate unions involved. At most they could give assurances as to a few of the men at two of the company's four yards. And even had all of the unions joined in these statements, which was not the case, the employer had been subject to wildcat strikes at a time when the unions were bound by a no-strike clause in their contract. Therefore, without impugning the good faith of these union agents, it surely was not unreasonable for the employer, notwithstanding this assurance, to fear that his employees might not complete work on ships when they were not bound by a no-strike clause.

The Board also relies on the fact that the unions offered a six-month extension of the present contract. As I have already pointed out, this would have caused the contract to expire during the employer's busiest season. The employer had a perfect right to reject this stratagem. Had he agreed, the unions would have achieved one of their important objectives without the necessity for striking. By the same token it is clear that the unions would have agreed not to strike had the employer accepted their proposals for increases in wages and benefits. Surely the employer had every right to reject these proposals, and his rejection of them would not show that he was unreasonable in fearing a strike based upon his failure to accede to the unions' demands.

Finally, the offer of an indefinite extension of the contract is an equally unsupportable basis for the Board's conclusion. An indefinite extension presumably would mean under traditional contract theory that the unions

[3] There is some evidence in the record that one other local business agent gave a similar assurance.

could strike at any time or after giving brief notice.[4] Surely the employer would be reasonable in fearing that such an arrangement would peculiarly place the timing of the strike in the unions' hands.

The sum of all this is that the record does not supply even a scintilla of, let alone any substantial evidence, to support the conclusion of the Board that the employer's fear of a strike was unreasonable, but, rather, this conclusion appears irrational. . . . I would therefore hold on this record that the employer's lockout was completely justified.

The fact that the Board held on the undisputed facts that the employer's fear of a strike was unreasonable and that the Court of Appeals has affirmed the Board does not preclude us from reviewing this determination. See *Public Service Comm.* v. *United States*, 356 U.S. 421. The standard to be applied by the Court of Appeals was whether the Board's finding was supported by substantial evidence when the record is viewed as a whole. *Universal Camera Corp.* v. *Labor Board*, 340 U.S. 474. . . . "The Board's findings are entitled to respect; but they must nonetheless be set aside when the record before a court of appeals clearly precludes the Board's decision from being justified by a fair estimate of the worth of the testimony of witnesses or its informed judgment on matters within its special competence or both." *Universal Camera Corp.* v. *Labor Board, supra*, at 490. Indeed, the Board here set aside the report of its trial examiner, and in *Universal Camera* this Court recognized "that evidence supporting a conclusion may be less substantial when an impartial, experienced examiner who has observed the witnesses and lived with the case has drawn conclusions different from the Board than when he has reached the same conclusion." 340 U.S., at 496. The Court of Appeals in my view in its summary affirmance on this issue grossly misapplied the standards laid down by *Universal Camera*. This case is properly before us on a substantial legal question, which necessarily involves a review of the entire record. In making such a review, although we give proper weight to what the first reviewing court decides, we cannot ignore our duty to apply the statutory standard that the Board's findings must be supported by substantial evidence. Since the Board's holding was not so supported, but, on the contrary, as the plain facts of the record reveal, was irrational, I would reverse the Court of Appeals on this ground.

My view of this case would make it unnecessary to deal with the broad question of whether an employer may lock out his employees solely to bring economic pressure to bear in support of his bargaining position. The question of which types of lockout are compatible with the labor statute is a complex one as this decision . . . illustrate[s]. . . . This Court has said that the

[4] See 1 Williston, *Contracts*, §§ 38, 39 (3d ed. 1957); cf. *Pacific Coast Association of Pulp & Paper Manufacturers*, 120 N. L. R. B. 990, 993.

problem of the legality of certain types of strike activity must be "revealed by unfolding variant situations" and requires "an evolutionary process for its rational response, not a quick, definitive formula as a comprehensive answer." *Electrical Workers* v. *Labor Board*, 366 U.S. 667, 674. . . . The same is true of lockouts.

The types of situation in which an employer might seek to lock out his employees differ considerably one from the other. This case presents the situation of an employer with a long history of union recognition and collective bargaining, confronted with a history of past strikes, who locks out only after considerable good-faith negotiation involving agreement and compromise on numerous issues, after a bargaining impasse has been reached, more than a week after the prior contract has expired, and when faced with the threat of a strike at a time when he and the property of his customers can suffer unusual harm. Other cases in which the Board has held a lockout illegal have presented far different situations. For example, in *Quaker State Oil Refining Corp.*, an employer locked out his employees the day after his contract with the union expired although no impasse had been reached in the bargaining still in progress, no strike had been threatened by the unions, which had never called a sudden strike during the thirteen years they had bargained with the employer, and the unions had offered to resubmit the employer's proposals to his employees for a vote. See also *Utah Plumbing and Heating Contractors Assn.*, 126 N.L.R.B. 973. These decisions of the Labor Board properly take into account, in determining the legality of lockouts under the labor statutes, such factors as the length, character, and history of the collective bargaining relation between the union and the employer, as well as whether a bargaining impasse has been reached. Indeed, the Court itself seems to recognize that there is a difference between locking out before a bargaining impasse has been reached and locking out after collective bargaining has been exhausted, for it limits its holding to lockouts in the latter type of situation without deciding the question of the legality of locking out before bargaining is exhausted. Since the examples of different lockout situations could be multiplied, the logic of the Court's limitation of its holding should lead it to recognize that the problem of lockouts requires "an evolutionary process," not "a quick, definitive formula," for its answer.

The Court should be chary of sweeping generalizations in this complex area. When we deal with the lockout and the strike we are dealing with weapons of industrial warfare. While the parties generally have their choice of economic weapons, see *Labor Board* v. *Insurance Agents*, 361 U.S. 477, this choice with respect to both the strike and the lockout, is not unrestricted. While we have recognized "the deference paid the strike weapon by the federal labor laws," *Labor Board* v. *Erie Resistor, supra*, at 235, not all forms of economically motivated strikes are protected nor even permissible under the labor statutes or the prior decisions of this Court. Moreover, a lockout prompted by an antiunion motive is plainly illegal under the National Labor Relations Act, though no similar restrictions as to motive operate to limit the legality of a strike. See *Labor Board* v. *Somerset Shoe Co.*, 11 F. 2d 681; *Labor Board* v. *Stremel*, 141 F. 2d 317; *Labor Board* v. *Somerset Classics, Inc.*, 193 F. 2d 613. The varieties of restriction imposed upon strikes and lockouts reflect the complexities presented by variant factual situations. . . .

The . . . cases show that the tests as to whether an employer's conduct violates § 8 (a) (1) or violate § 8 (a) (3) without a showing of antiunion motive come down to substantially the same thing: whether the legitimate economic interests of the employer justify his interference with the rights of his employees—a test involving "the balancing of the conflicting legitimate interests." *Labor Board* v. *Truck Drivers Union, supra*, at 96. As the prior decisions of this Court have held, "the function of striking . . . [such a] balance. . . . often a difficult and delicate responsibility. . . . Congress committed primarily to the National Labor Relations Board, subject to limited judicial review." *Ibid*.

This, of course, does not mean that reviewing courts are to abdicate their function of determining whether, giving due deference to the Board, the Board has struck the balance consistently with the language and policy of the Act. . . . Nor does it mean that reviewing courts are to rubber-stamp decisions of the Board where the application of principles in a particular case is irrational or not supported by substantial evidence on the record as a whole. Applying these principles to the factual situation here presented, I would accept the Board's carefully limited rule, fashioned by the Board after weighing the "conflicting legitimate interests" of employers and unions, that a lockout does not violate the Act where used to "safeguard against unusual operational problems or hazards or economic loss where there is reasonable ground for believing that a strike [is] . . . threatened or imminent." *Quaker State Oil Refining Corp., supra*, at 337. This rule is consistent with the policies of the Act and based upon the actualities of industrial relations. I would, however, reject the determination of the Board refusing to apply this rule to this case, for the undisputed facts revealed by the record bring this case clearly within the rule.

In view of the necessity for, and the desirability of, weighing the legitimate conflicting interests in variant lockout situations, there is not and cannot be any simple formula which readily demarks the permissible from the impermissible lockout. This being so, I would not reach out in this case to announce principles which are determinative of the legality of all economically motivated lockouts whether before or after a bargaining impasse has been reached. In my view both the Court and the Board, in reaching their opposite conclusions, have inadvisably and unnecessarily done so here. Rather, I would confine our decision to the simple holding, supported both by the record and the actualities of industrial relations, that the employer's fear of a strike was reasonable, and therefore, under the settled decisions of the Board, which I would approve, the lockout of his employees was justified.

United Mine Workers v. Pennington, 381 U.S. 657
Amalgamated Meat Cutters v. Jewel Tea Co., 381 U.S. 676

[The opinion of the Court in *Pennington* and that of Justice White, joined by Justice Brennan and the Chief Justice, in *Jewel Tea* significantly extend the application of the antitrust laws to the collective bargaining activities of unions and employers. In *Pennington* a small mine operator sued the United Mine Workers for treble damages under the Sherman Act alleging that the union had agreed with large mineowners to seek a high wage rate from the entire mining industry, knowing that some operators could not afford to pay such a rate and would be forced out of business. This agreement, it was claimed, constituted a restraint of trade forbidden by the antitrust laws, which, under these circumstances, apply to unions as well as employers. While the Court unanimously set aside the judgment for the employer on technical grounds and remanded the case for a new trial, six members of the Court also held that the employer's complaint stated a valid cause of action against the union under the antitrust laws. The Court held that the antitrust laws apply when a union and an employer agree to try to obtain a particular wage scale from other employers. Justice Goldberg, joined by Justice Harlan and Justice Stewart, dissented vigorously from this aspect of the Court's opinion. Justice Goldberg argued that the antitrust laws are completely inapplicable to bargaining activity concerning wages, hours and working conditions—mandatory subjects of collective bargaining. To hold otherwise would fly in the face of a Congressional intent—clearly set out in labor and antitrust statutes—to eliminate court interference in the economics of collective bargaining.

[In *Jewel Tea* a large supermarket operator claimed that an agreement with a union that butchers not work at night violated the antitrust laws. Six members of the Court held that the antitrust laws did not apply to such an agreement. Justice White, joined by Justice Brennan and the Chief Justice, wrote that this case differs from *Pennington* because the market operator did not claim that the union, having made an agreement with one group of employers, agreed to seek similar terms from another group of employers. Since they also felt that the trial court reasonably found that, under the circumstances of the case, an agreement as to when butchers would work was directly related to wages, hours, and working conditions, they believed that the antitrust laws were not applicable. Justice Goldberg, joined by Justice Harlan and Justice Stewart, agreed with the result for reasons similar to those stated concerning *Pennington*. Justice Black, Justice Douglas and Justice Clark dissented, believing that the antitrust laws should apply to the *Jewel Tea* agreement.]

Stripped of all the pejorative adjectives and reduced to their essential facts, both *Pennington* and *Jewel Tea*[1] represent refusals by judges to give full effect to Congressional action designed to prohibit judicial intervention via the antitrust route in legitimate collective bargaining. The history of these cases furnishes fresh evidence of the observation that in this area, necessarily involving a determination of "what public policy in regard to the industrial struggle demands," *Duplex Co.* v. *Deering*, 254 U.S. 479, 485 (dissenting opinion of Mr. Justice Brandeis), "courts have neither the aptitude nor the criteria for reaching sound decisions." Cox, "Labor and Antitrust Laws—A Preliminary Analysis," 104 U. Pa. L. Rev. 252, 269-270 (1955); see Winter, Collective Bargaining and Competition: "The Application of Antitrust Standards to Union Activities," 73 Yale L. J. 14 (1963).

Pennington presents a case of a union negotiating with the employers in the industry for wages, fringe benefits, and working conditions. Despite allegations of conspiracy, which connotes clandestine activities, it is no secret that the United Mine Workers, acting to further what it considers to be the best interests of its members, espouses a philosophy of achieving uniform high wages, fringe benefits, and good working conditions. As the *quid pro quo* for this, the Union is willing to accept the burdens and consequences of automation. Further, it acts upon the view that the existence of marginal operators who cannot afford these high wages, fringe benefits, and good working conditions does not serve the best interests of the working miner but, on the contrary, depresses wage standards and perpetuates undesirable conditions. This has been the articulated policy of the Union since 1933. . . . The Mine Workers has openly stated its preference, if need be, for a reduced working force in the industry, with those employed working at high wages, rather than for greater total employment at lesser wage rates. . . . Consistent with this view, the Union welcomes automation, insisting only that the workers participate in its benefits.

Jewel Tea presents another and different aspect of collective bargaining

---

[1] June 7, 1965. Cases Nos. 48 and 240. Mr. Justice Goldberg, with whom Mr. Justice Harlan and Mr. Justice Stewart join, dissenting from the opinion but concurring in the reversal in No. 48 and concurring in the judgment of the Court in No. 240.

philosophy. The Chicago Local of the Amalgamated Meat Cutters bargains
for its members with small, independent service butchers as well as large
automated self-service chains. It seeks from both a uniform policy that no
fresh meat be sold after 6 p.m. This union policy . . . has a long history dating
back to 1919 and has grown out of the union's struggle to reduce the long,
arduous hours worked by butchers, which in 1919 were 81 hours per week.
It took a long strike to achieve the first limitation on hours in 1920, and it has
required hard extensive collective bargaining since then to maintain the
policy and further reduce the number of hours worked. While it is claimed
by Jewel Tea, a large operator of automated self-service markets, that it can
operate beyond the set hours without increasing the work of butchers or
having others do butcher's work—a claim rejected by the trial court and the
majority of this Court—it is conceded, on this record, that the small,
independent service operators cannot do so. Therefore to the extent that the
union's uniform policy limiting hours of selling fresh meat has the effect of
aiding one group of employers at the expense of another, here the union
policy, unlike that in *Pennington*, aids the small employers at the expense of
the large.

Although evidencing these converse economic effects, both *Pennington*
and *Jewel Tea*, as the Court in *Pennington* and my Brother White's opinion
in *Jewel Tea* acknowledge, involve conventional collective bargaining on
wages, hours, and working conditions—mandatory subjects of bargaining
under the National Labor Relations Act. . . . Yet the Mine Workers' activity
in *Pennington* was held subject to an antitrust action by two lower courts.
This decision was based upon a jury determination that the union's economic
philosophy is undesirable, and it resulted in an award against the union of
treble damages of $270,000 and $55,000 extra for respondent's attorneys' fees.
In *Jewel Tea*, the union has also been subjected to an antitrust suit in which
a court of appeals, with its own notions as to what butchers are legitimately
interested in, would subject the union to a treble damage judgment in an as
yet undetermined amount.

Regretfully these cases, both in the lower courts and in expressions in the
various opinions filed today in this Court, as I shall demonstrate, constitute a
throwback to past days when courts allowed antitrust actions against unions
and employers engaged in conventional collective bargaining, "because a
judge considered" the union or employer conduct in question to be
"socially or economically" objectionable. *Duplex Co.* v. *Deering, supra*, at
485 (dissenting opinion of Mr. Justice Brandeis). It is necessary to recall that
history to place the cases before us in proper prospective. [The history is
then reviewed.]

In my view, this history shows a consistent Congressional purpose to limit
severely judicial intervention in collective bargaining under cover of the

wide umbrella of the antitrust laws, and, rather, to deal with what Congress deemed to be specific abuses on the part of labor unions by specific proscriptions in the labor statutes. I believe that the Court should respect this history of Congressional purpose and should reaffirm the Court's holdings in *Apex* and *Hutcheson* which, unlike earlier decisions, gave effect to, rather than frustrated, the Congressional design. The sound approach of *Hutcheson* is that the labor exemption from the antitrust laws derives from a synthesis of all pertinent Congressional legislation—the nature of the Sherman Act itself, §§ 6 and 20 of the Clayton Act, the Norris-LaGuardia Act, the Fair Labor Standards Act,[2] the Walsh-Healy[3] and Davis-Bacon[4] Acts, and the Wagner Act with its Taft-Hartley and Landrum-Griffin amendments. This last statute, in particular, provides that both employers and unions must bargain over "wages, hours, and other terms and conditions of employment." 29 U.S.C. §§ 158 (a) (5), (b) (3), (d) (1958 ed.). Following the sound analysis of *Hutcheson*, the Court should hold that, in order to effectuate Congressional intent, collective bargaining activity concerning mandatory subjects of bargaining under the Labor Act is not subject to the antitrust laws.[5] This rule flows directly from *Hutcheson* holding that a union acting as a union, in the interests of its members, and not acting to fix prices or allocate markets in aid of an employer conspiracy to accomplish these objects, with only indirect union benefits, is not subject to challenge under the antitrust laws. To hold that mandatory collective bargaining is completely protected would effectuate the Congressional policies of encouraging free collective bargaining, subject only to specific restrictions contained in the labor laws, and of limiting judicial intervention in labor matters via the antitrust route—an intervention which necessarily under the Sherman Act places on judges and juries the determination of "what public policy in regard to the industrial struggle demands." *Duplex* v. *Deering, supra,* at 485 (dissenting opinion of Mr. Justice Brandeis). See Winter, "Collective Bargaining and Competition: The Application of Antitrust Standards to Union Activities," 73 Yale L.J. 14 (1963).

Section 6 of the Clayton Act made it clear half a century ago that it is not national policy to force workers to compete in the "sale" of their labor as if it were a commodity or article of commerce. The policy was confirmed and extended in the subsequent Norris-LaGuardia Act. Other federal legislation establishing minimum wages and maximum hours takes labor standards out of competition. The Fair Labor Standards Act, 52 Stat. 1060, as amended, 29

[2] 52 Stat. 1060, as amended, 29 U.S.C. §§ 201–219 (1958 ed.).
[3] 49 Stat. 2036, as amended, 41 U.S.C. §§ 35–45 (1958 ed.).
[4] 46 Stat. 1494, as amended, 40 U.S.C. § 276 a (1958 ed).
[5] Although I agree with my Brother White in *Jewel Tea* that the doctrine of primary jurisdiction does not apply here, decisions of the Labor Board as to what constitutes a subject of mandatory bargaining are, of course, very significant in determination of the applicability of the labor exemption.

U.S.C. §§ 201-219 (1958 ed.), clearly states that the existence of "labor conditions" insufficient for a "minimum standard of living . . . constitutes an unfair method of competition in commerce." 29 U.S.C. § 202 (a). Moreover, this Court has recognized that in the Walsh-Healy Act, 49 Stat. 2036, as amended, 41 U.S.C. § 35-45 (1958 ed.), Congress brought to bear the "leverage of the government's immense purchasing power to raise labor standards" by eliminating substandard producers from eligibility for public contracts. *Endicott-Johnson Corp.* v. *Perkins*, 317 U.S. 501, 507. See also Davis-Bacon Act, 46 Stat. 1494, 40 U.S.C. § 276a (1958 ed.). The National Labor Relations Act itself clearly expresses one of its purposes to be "the stabilization of competitive wage rates and working conditions within and between industries." 29 U.S.C. § 151. In short, business competition based on wage competition is not national policy and "the mere fact of such restrictions on competition does not . . . bring the parties . . . within the condemnation of the Sherman Act." *Apex Hosiery Co.* v. *Leader, supra,* at 503.

The National Labor Relations Act also declares it to be the policy of the United States to promote the establishment of wages, hours, and other terms and conditions of employment by free collective bargaining between employers and unions. The act further provides that both employers and unions must bargain about such mandatory subjects of bargaining. This national scheme would be virtually destroyed by the imposition of Sherman Act criminal and civil penalties upon employers and unions engaged in such collective bargaining. To tell the parties that they must bargain about a point but may be subject to antitrust penalties if they reach an agreement is to stultify the Congressional scheme.

Moreover, mandatory subjects of bargaining are issues as to which union strikes may not be enjoined by either federal or state courts.[6] To say that the union can strike over such issues but that both it and the employer are subject to possible antitrust penalties for making collective bargaining agreements concerning them is to assert that Congress intended to permit the parties to collective bargaining to wage industrial warfare but to prohibit them from peacefully settling their disputes. This would not only be irrational but would fly in the face of the clear Congressional intent of promoting "the peaceful settlement of industrial disputes by subjecting labor-

---

[6] See, e. g., *Weber* v. *Anheuser-Busch, Inc.,* 348 U.S. 468; *Garner* v. *Teamsters Union,* 346 U.S. 485, 490-491. Although *Allen-Bradley* held that the Clayton and Norris-LaGuardia Acts precluded federal courts from enjoining activities concerned with even some nonmandatory subjects of bargaining, Congress has since provided that union insistence on bargaining over nonmandatory subjects as an unfair labor practice, cf. *Labor Board* v. *Wooster Division of Borg-Warner Corp.,* 356 U.S. 342, and thus the Labor Board can order the union to cease and desist from such assistance, as well as from auxiliary conduct like strikes designed to effectuate it; see *Local 164, Brotherhood of Painters* v. *Labor Board,* 110 U.S. App. D.C. 294, 293 F. 2d 133.

management controversies to the mediatory influence of negotiation." *Fibreboard Paper Prods. Corp.* v. *Labor Board,* 379 U.S. 203, 211.

Congress has also recognized that some labor organizations seek, as in *Pennington,* through industry-wide bargaining, to eliminate differences in labor standards among employers. This was common knowledge in 1935 when the Wagner Act was enacted. The aims and practices of unions engaging in industry-wide bargaining were well known in 1947 at the time of the Taft-Hartley revision. Then and on subsequent occasions Congress refused to enact bills to restrict or prohibit industry-wide bargaining. See, e.g., H. R. 3020, 80th Cong., 1st Sess., §§ 2 (16), 9 (f) (1), 12, 3 (A), 12 (4), H. R. Rep. No. 245, 80th Cong., 1st Sess., 24, 73; note 8, *supra,* and citations contained therein; H.R. 8449, 82d Cong., 2d Sess. Nor can it be seriously argued that multi-employer bargaining, as in *Jewel Tea,* introduces an illegal element or is otherwise opposed to the national labor policy. Indeed, this Court, to implement Congressional policy sanctioning multi-employer bargaining, permitted employers to resort, under certain circumstances, to lockouts to protect the integrity of the multi-employer bargaining unit. See *Labor Board* v. *Truck Drivers Union, No. 449,* 353 U.S. 87; *Labor Board* v. *Brown,* 380 U.S. 278.[7] The wisdom of permitting industry-wide and multi-employer bargaining is for Congress to decide, unless this Court is to return to the discredited approach of the majority in *Duplex* and substitute its notion for that of Congress as to how unions and employers should conduct their collective bargaining.

The Court in *Pennington* today ignores this history of the discredited judicial attempt to apply the antitrust laws to legitimate collective bargaining activity, and it flouts the clearly expressed Congressional intent that, since "the labor of a human being is not a commodity or article of commerce,"[8] the antitrust laws do not proscribe, and the national labor policy affirmatively promotes, the "elimination of price competition based on differences in labor standards," *Apex Hosiery Co.* v. *Leader, supra,* at 503. While pur-

[7] Today, between 80 and 100 per cent of the workers under union agreement are covered by multi-employer contracts in such important industries as men's and women's clothing, coal mining, building construction, hotels, longshoring, maritime, trucking, and warehousing. Between 60 and 80 per cent of unionized workers are under multi-employer pacts in baking, book and job printing, canning and preserving, textile dyeing and finishing, glass and glassware, malt liquor, pottery and retail trades. See Lloyd G. Reynolds, *Labor Economics and Labor Relations* (3d ed. 1959), p. 170. Furthermore, in some other major industries relatively uniform terms of employment are obtained through the negotiation of a contract with one leading employer and the subsequent acceptance of that contract's key provisions, with only minor modifications by the other employers in the industry. See N. W. Chamberlain, *Collective Bargaining* (1951), pp. 259–263.

[8] Section 6 of the Clayton Act.

porting to recognize the indisputable fact that the elimination of employer competition based on substandard labor conditions is a proper labor union objective endorsed by our national labor policy and that, therefore, "a union may make wage agreements with a multi-employer bargaining unit and may in the pursuance of its own interests seek to obtain the same terms from other employers," *Pennington, ante*, at 665, the Court holds that "a union forfeits its exemption from the antitrust laws when it is clearly shown that it has agreed with one set of employers to impose a certain wage scale on other bargaining units." *Ibid*.

This rule seems to me clearly contrary to the Congressional purpose manifested by the labor statutes, and it will severely restrict free collective bargaining. Since collective bargaining inevitably involves and requires discussion of the impact of the wage agreement reached with a particular employer or group of employers upon competing employers, the effect of the Court's decision will be to bar a basic element of collective bargaining from the conference room. If a union and employer are prevented from discussing and agreeing upon issues which are, in the great majority of cases, at the central core of bargaining, unilateral force will inevitably be substituted for rational discussion and agreement. Plainly and simply, the Court would subject both unions and employers to antitrust sanctions, criminal as well as civil, if in collective bargaining they concluded a wage agreement and, as part of the agreement, the union has undertaken to use its best efforts to have this wage accepted by other employers in the industry. Indeed, the decision today even goes beyond this. Under settled antitrust principles which are accepted by the Court as appropriate and applicable, which were the basis for jury instructions in *Pennington*, and which will govern it upon remand, there need not be direct evidence of an express agreement. Rather the existence of such an agreement, express or implied, may be inferred from the conduct of the parties. . . . Or, as my Brother Douglas, concurring in *Pennington*, would have it, conduct of the parties could be prima facie evidence of an illegal agreement. . . .

As the facts of *Pennington* illustrate, the jury is therefore at large to infer such an agreement from "clear" evidence that a union's philosophy that high wages and mechanization are desirable has been accepted by a group of employers and that the union has attempted to achieve like acceptance from other employers. For, as I have pointed out, stripped of all adjectives, this is what *Pennington* presents. Yet the Court today holds "the alleged agreement between UMW and the large operators to secure uniform labor standards throughout the industry, if proved, was not exempt from the antitrust laws." *Ante*, at 669.

The rational thing for an employer to do, when faced with union demands he thinks he cannot meet, is to explain why, in economic terms, he believes that he cannot agree to the union requests. Indeed, the Labor Act's compulsion to bargain in good faith requires that he meaningfully address himself to the union's requests. See *Labor Board* v. *Truitt Mfg. Co.*, 351 U.S. 149. A recurring and most understandable reason given by employers for their resistance to union demands is that competitive factors prevent them from accepting the union's proposed terms. Under the Court's holding today, however, such a statement by an employer may start both the employer and the union on the road to antitrust sanctions, criminal and civil. For a jury may well interpret such discussion and subsequent union action as showing an implicit or secret agreement to impose uniform standards on other employers. Nor does the Court's requirement that there be "direct or indirect evidence of the conspiracy"—whatever those undefined terms in the opinion may mean—provide any substantial safeguard for uninhibited collective bargaining discussions. In *Pennington* itself, the trial court instructed the jury that a union's unilateral actions did not subject it to antitrust sanctions, and yet the jury readily inferred a "conspiracy" from the "direct or indirect evidence" of the union's publicly stated policy in favor of high wages and mechanization, its collective bargaining agreement with a group of employers establishing high wages, and its attempts to obtain similar high wages from other employers.

Furthermore, in order to determine whether, under the Court's standard, a union is acting unilaterally or pursuant to an agreement with employers, judges and juries will inevitably be drawn to try to determine the purpose and motive of union and employer collective bargaining activities. The history I have set out, however, makes clear that Congress intended to foreclose judges and juries from roaming at large in the area of collective bargaining, under cover of the antitrust laws, by inquiry into the purpose and motive of the employer and union bargaining on mandatory subjects. Such roaming at large, experience shows, leads to a substitution of judicial for Congressional judgment as to how collective bargaining should operate.

. . . Congress in the Norris-LaGuardia Act and other labor statutes, as this Court recognized in *Apex* and *Hutcheson*, determined that judicial notions of the social and economic desirability of union action should not govern antitrust liability in the area of collective bargaining. . . .

The history I have set out makes clear that Congress intended to foreclose judges and juries from making essentially economic judgments in antitrust actions by determining whether unions or employers had good or bad motives for their agreements on subjects of mandatory bargaining. Moreover, an attempted inquiry into the motives of employers or unions for entering into collective bargaining agreements on subjects of mandatory bargaining is totally artificial. It is precisely in this area of wages, hours, and other working conditions that Congress has recognized that unions have a substantial, direct, and basic interest of their own to advance.

As I have discussed, the Court's test is not essentially different from the discredited purpose-motive approach. Only rarely will there be direct evidence of an express agreement between a union and an employer to impose a particular wage scale on other employers. In most cases, as was true of *Pennington*, the trial court will instruct the jury that such an illegal agreement may be inferred from the conduct—"indirect evidence"—of the union and employers. To allow a court or a jury to infer an illegal agreement from collective bargaining conduct inevitably requires courts and juries to analyze the terms of collective bargaining agreements and the purposes and motives of unions and employers in agreeing upon them. Moreover, the evidence most often available to sustain antitrust liability under the Court's theory would show, as it did in *Pennington*, simply that the motives of the union and employer coincide—the union seeking high wages and protection from low-wage, nonunion competition and the employer who pays high wages seeking protection from competitors who pay lower wages. When there is this coincidence of motive, does the illegality of the "conspiracy" turn on whether the union pursued its goal of a uniform wage policy through strikes and not negotiation? As I read the Court's opinion, this is precisely what the result turns on and thus unions are forced, in order to show that they have not illegally "agreed" with employers, to pursue their aims through strikes and not negotiations. Yet it is clear that such a result was precisely what the National Labor Relations Act was designed to prevent. The only alternative to resolution of collective bargaining issues by force available to the parties under the Court's holding is the encouragement of fraud and deceit. An employer will be forced to take a public stand against a union's wage demands, even if he is willing to accept them, lest a too ready acceptance be used by a jury to infer an agreement between the union and employer that the same wages will be sought from other employers. Yet, I have always thought that in collective bargaining, even more than in other areas of contractual agreement, the objective is open covenants openly arrived at.

Furthermore, I do not understand how an inquiry can be formulated in terms of whether the union action is unilateral or is a consequence of a "conspiracy" with employers independently of the economic terms of the collective bargaining agreement. The agreement must be admitted into evidence and the Court holds that its economic consequences are relevant. In the end, one way or another, the entire panoply of economic fact becomes involved, and judges and juries under the Court's view would then be allowed to speculate about why a union bargained for increased compensation, or any other labor standard within the scope of mandatory bargaining. It is precisely this type of speculation that Congress has rejected.

The plain fact is that it makes no sense to turn antitrust liability of employers and unions concerning subjects of mandatory bargaining on whether the union acted "unilaterally" or in "agreement" with employers. A union can never achieve substantial benefits for its members through unilateral action; I should have thought that the unsuccessful history of the Industrial Workers of the World, which eschewed collective bargaining and espoused a philosophy of winning benefits by unilateral action, proved this beyond question. See Dulles, *Labor in America*, pp. 208-223 (1949); Chaplin, *Wobbly* (1948). Furthermore, I cannot believe that Congress, by adopting the antitrust laws, put its stamp of approval on this discredited IWW philosophy of industrial relations; rather, in the Clayton Act and the labor statutes, Congress has repudiated such a philosophy. Our national labor policy is designed to encourage the peaceful settlement of industrial disputes through the negotiation of agreements between employers and unions. Unions cannot, as the history of the IWW shows, successfully retain employee benefits by unilateral action; nor can employers be assured of continuous operation without contractual safeguards. The history of labor relations in this country shows, as Congress has recognized, that progress and stability for both employers and employees can be achieved only through collective bargaining agreements involving mutual rights and responsibilities.

This history also shows that labor contracts establishing more or less standardized wages, hours, and other terms and conditions of employment in a given industry or market area are often secured either through bargaining with multi-employer associations or through bargaining with market leaders that sets a "pattern" for agreements on labor standards with other employers. These are two similar systems used to achieve the identical result of fostering labor peace through the negotiation of uniform labor standards in an industry. Yet the Court makes antitrust liability for both unions and employers turn on which of these two systems is used. It states that uniform wage agreements may be made with multi-employer units but an agreement cannot be made to affect employers outside the formal bargaining unit. I do not believe that the Court understands the effect of its ruling in terms of the practical realities of the automobile, steel, rubber, shipbuilding, and numerous other industries which follow the policy of pattern collective bargaining. See Chamberlain, *Collective Bargaining* 259-263 (1951) note 7, *supra*. I also do not understand why antitrust liability should turn on the form of unit determination rather than the substance of the collective bargaining impact on the industry.

Finally, it seems clear that the essential error at the core of the Court's reasoning is that it ignores the express command of Congress that "the labor of a human being is not a commodity or article of commerce,"[9] and therefore that the antitrust laws do not prohibit the "elimination of price competition based on differences in labor standards." *Apex Hosiery Co.* v. *Leader, supra,* at 503. This is made clear by a simple question that the Court does not face. Where there is an "agreement" to seek uniform wages in an industry, in what item is competition restrained? The answer to this question can only be that competition is restrained in employee wage standards. That is, the union has agreed to restrain the free competitive market for labor by refusing to provide labor to other employers below the uniform rate. Under such an analysis it would seem to follow that the existence of a union itself constitutes a restraint of trade, for the object of a union is to band together the individual workers in an effort, by common action, to obtain better wages and working conditions—i.e., to obtain a higher price for their labor. The very purpose and effect of a labor union is to limit the power of an employer to use competition among workingmen to drive down wage rates and enforce substandard conditions of employment. If competition between workingmen to see who will work for the lowest wage is the ideal, all labor unions should be eliminated. Indeed the Court itself apparently realizes that its holding that the antitrust laws are violated when a labor union agrees with employers not to compete on wages is premised on the belief that labor is a commodity and that this premise leads to the logical conclusion that unions themselves restrain trade in this commodity. This is the only reason I can imagine for the Court's felt need, in 1965, to assert that "the antitrust laws do not bar the existence and operation of labor unions *as such.*" *Pennington, ante,* at 661. (Emphasis added.)

As I have already discussed, however, if one thing is clear, it is that Congress has repudiated the view that labor is a commodity and thus there should be competition to see who can supply it at the cheapest price. . . . The kind of competition which is suppressed by employer-union agreement on uniform wages can only be competition between unions to see which union will agree to supply labor at a lower rate, or competition between employers in the sale of their products based on differences in labor costs. Neither type of "suppression," I submit, can be supported as a restraint of trade condemned by the antitrust laws. No one, I think, believes that Congress intended that there be an economic system under which unions would compete with each other to supply labor at the lowest possible cost. It is equally clear that Congress did not intend that competition among manufacturers should be carried on, not on the basis of their relative efficiency or ability to produce what the consumer demands, but on their

[9] Section 6 of the Clayton Act.

ability to operate at substandard wage rates. One of the important social advantages of competition mandated by the antitrust laws is that it rewards the most efficient producer and thus ensures the optimum use of our economic resources. This result, as Congress recognized, is not achieved by creating a situation in which manufacturers compete on the basis of who pays the lowest wages. As this Court stated in *Apex Hosiery Co.* v. *Leader, supra,* at 503-504, the "elimination of price competition based on differences in labor standards is the objective of any national labor organization. But this effect on competition has not been considered to be the kind of curtailment of price competition prohibited by the Sherman Act."

The assumption running through the Court's opinion in *Pennington*, as well as the opinion of my Brother Douglas, is that giving full scope to the Congressional exemption of labor unions from the antitrust laws will operate to the advantage of large employers and big unions to the prejudice of small employers. Although I cannot see how that should affect the result reached on the basis of Congressional intent even if the assumption were true, see *Hunt* v. *Crumbach*, 325 U.S. 821, 825, n. 1, I feel compelled to note that this assumption is not accurate and is belied by the actualities of industrial relations. Experience in this area shows that frequently unions first organize the small and weak employers. These small employers are understandably afraid that unless other, larger employers are also organized, effective competition will be impossible. They will thus often seek to have the union attempt to organize and bargain for similar labor standards with their larger competitors so that the requirement to pay high union wages will not force the small businessmen to close down their enterprises.

The Court's holding in *Pennington* today flies in the face of *Apex* and *Hutcheson* and restrains collective bargaining in the same way as did the holding of the majority in *Duplex*—a holding which Congress has expressly repudiated in favor of Mr. Justice Brandeis' dissenting views. It represents contemporary manifestations of the reluctance of judges to give full effect to Congressional purpose in this area and the substitution of judges' views for those of Congress as to how free collective bargaining should operate.[10]

[10] The Court in *Pennington* states that it "cannot conclude that the national labor policy provides any support" for agreements whereby unions undertake to attempt to obtain uniform terms from other employers in the industry. *Pennington, ante,* at 667. In making this statement the Court ignores clear Congressional expressions in §§ 6 and 20 of the Clayton Act, the Norris-LaGuardia Act, the Fair Labor Standards Act, the Walsh-Healy Public Contracts Act, the Davis-Bacon Act, and the express purpose of the National Labor Relations Act. See generally, pp. 709-713, *supra.* Moreover, the Court's reliance on three old Labor Board cases for its conclusions is clearly misplaced. These cases hold, at most, as the Court itself recognizes, that an employer may not refuse to recognize a union chosen by his employees or refuse to sign any contract until such time as the union has successfully organized the employer's competitors. Such situations, of course, are completely different from the situation in which an employer with

Moreover, while these cases involve suits against unions, we should not overlook the fact that if unions are held liable under the antitrust laws for collective bargaining activities concerning mandatory subjects, then the employer parties to this mandatory collective bargaining would also be subject to antitrust penalties, criminal and civil. It would seem the height of unfairness so to penalize employers for the discharge of their statutory duty to bargain on wages, hours, and other terms and conditions of employment, which duty, this Court has held, requires the employer to enter into a signed contract with the union embodying the collective bargaining terms agreed upon.

My view that Congress intended that collective bargaining activity on mandatory subjects of bargaining under the Labor Act not be subject to the antitrust laws does not mean that I believe that Congress intended that activity involving all nonmandatory subjects of bargaining be similarly exempt. That direct and overriding interests of unions in such subjects as wages, hours, and other working conditions, which Congress has recognized in making them subjects of mandatory bargaining, is clearly lacking where the subject of the agreement is price fixing and market allocation. Moreover, such activities are at the core of the type of anticompetitive commercial restraint at which the antitrust laws are directed.

Nor does my view mean that where a union operates as a businessman, exercising a proprietory or ownership function, that it is beyond the reach of the antitrust laws merely because it is a union. On the contrary, the labor exemption is inapplicable where the union acts not as a union but as an entrepreneur. . . . Therefore, if a union is found by sufficient evidence and under proper instructions to have participated as a proprietor in actions violative of the antitrust laws, it is no more shielded from antitrust sanctions than any other business participant. . . .

Finally, my conclusion that unions and employers are exempt from the operations of the antitrust laws for activities involving subjects of mandatory bargaining is based solely on Congressional statutes which I believe clearly grant such an exemption and not on any views past or present as to the economic desirability of such an exemption. Whether it is wise or sound public policy for this exemption to continue to exist in its present form, or at all, or whether the exemption gives too much power to labor organizations, is solely for Congress to determine. The problem of the application of

---

established collective bargaining relations voluntarily agrees with the union that the union will attempt to have other employers accept similar or uniform terms. They also are completely different from the situation in which an employer signs a collective bargaining agreement the terms of which contain a "most favored nation" clause, or labor standards on a sliding scale adjusted to the average or some other prevailing wage standard.

the antitrust laws to collective bargaining is but another aspect of the question of whether it is sound public policy to recognize or to limit the "right of industrial combatants to push their struggle to the limits of the justification of self-interest." *Duplex Co.* v. *Deering, supra,* at 488 (dissenting opinion of Mr. Justice Brandeis).

On this issue I am in agreement with the Court in *Hunt* v. *Crumboch, supra,* at 825, n. 1: "That which Congress has recognized as lawful, this Court has no constitutional power to declare unlawful, by arguing that Congress has accorded too much power to labor organizations."

For the reasons expressed above, I dissent from the opinion of the Court but concur in the reversal of the Court of Appeals in *Pennington* and concur in the judgment of the Court in *Jewel Tea.*

Index

ABOUT THE AUTHOR

Few persons in American history have been called to government service in as many and different capacities as Arthur J. Goldberg. In a period of five years, from 1961 to 1965, he was appointed Secretary of State, Associate Justice of the Supreme Court, and Ambassador to the United Nations. His book *The Defenses of Freedom* reflects these multiple concerns.

Mr. Goldberg was born in 1908 in the slums of Chicago, the son of Russian immigrant peddlers. After graduating from Crane Junior College, a city college, he received his B.S.L. and the degree of Doctor of Jurisprudence summa cum laude from Northwestern University, and practiced law in Chicago and Washington. During World War II he served as Chief of the Labor Division in the European theater with the Office of Strategic Services, and after the war he was General Counsel for the CIO and the United Steelworkers of America. He played an essential role in the merger of the AFL and the CIO, and served as Special Counsel for the AFL-CIO. In 1961 he was appointed Secretary of Labor, and in 1962 Associate Justice of the Supreme Court. In 1965 he became Ambassador to the United Nations. He is the author of *AFL-CIO: Labor United* and a contributor to various periodicals and journals of opinion.

About the Editor

Daniel Patrick Moynihan was an Assistant Secretary of Labor under Presidents Kennedy and Johnson. He is the author, with Nathan Glazer, of *Beyond the Melting Pot*, and the newly appointed director of the Joint Center for Urban Studies of the Massachusetts Institute of Technology and Harvard University. He will be one of the founding members of the Kennedy Institute of Government. He continues as Vice Chairman of the President's Commission on Pennsylvania Avenue, one of the many enterprises that originated in the Department of Labor during Arthur Goldberg's tenure.

Format by Ronald Farber
Set in Linotype Janson
Composed, printed and bound by The Haddon Craftsmen, Inc.
HARPER & ROW, PUBLISHERS, INCORPORATED